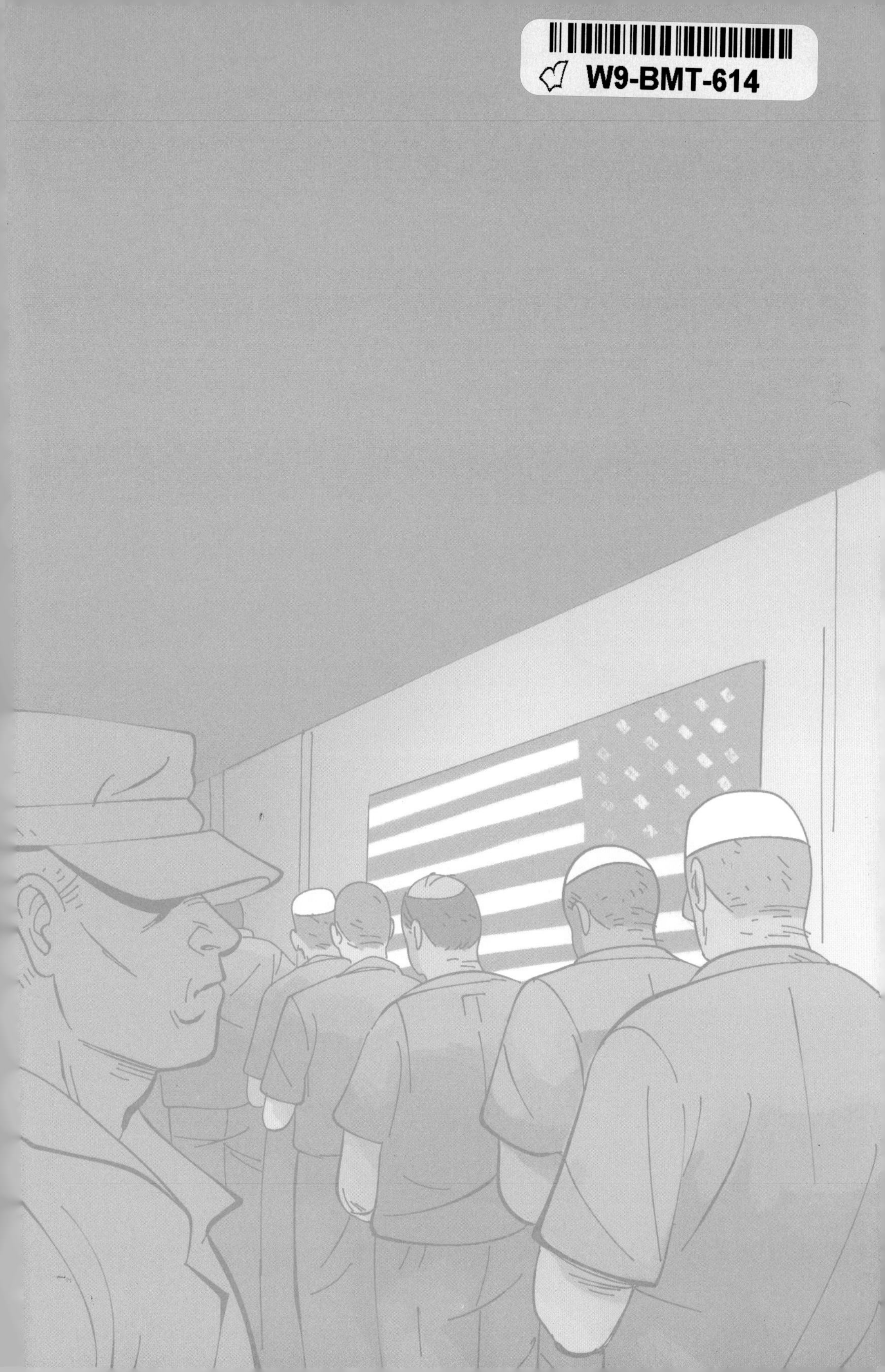

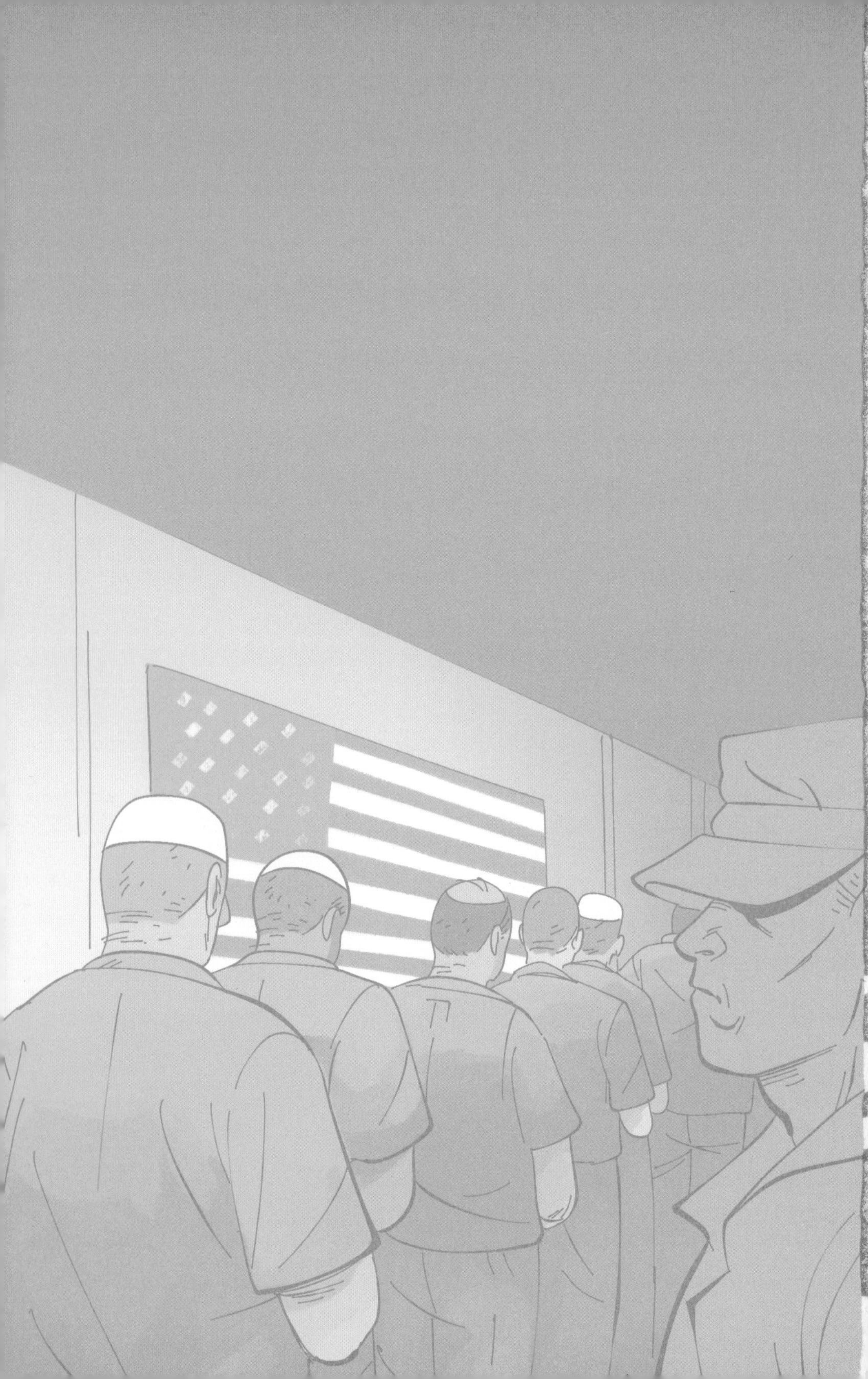

Guantanamo Voices

TRUE ACCOUNTS FROM THE WORLD'S MOST INFAMOUS PRISON

EDITED BY SARAH MIRK
INTRODUCTION BY OMAR EL AKKAD
ILLUSTRATED BY GERARDO ALBA, KASIA BABIS, ALEX
BEGUEZ, TRACY CHAHWAN, NOMI KANE, OMAR KHOURI,
KANE LYNCH, MAKI NARO, HAZEL NEWLEVANT, JEREMY
NGUYEN, CHELSEA SAUNDERS, ABU ZUBAYDAH

ABRAMS COMICARTS
NEW YORK

THIS BOOK IS DEDICATED TO TWO VETERANS: CHRIS ARENDT, WHO STARTED ME ON THIS JOURNEY, AND LAURA SANDOW, WHO KEPT ME ON IT. THANK YOU FOR HAVING THE COURAGE TO FACE THE DARK STUFF.

Editor: Charlotte Greenbaum
Designer: Megan Kelchner
Managing Editor: Annalea Manalili
Production Manager: Alison Gervais

Cataloging-in-Publication Data has been applied for and may be obtained from the Library of Congress.

ISBN 978-1-4197-4690-1
eISBN 978-1-64700-120-9

Illustrations by: Nomi Kane (ix–xv); Hazel Newlevant (1–17, 168–78); Gerardo Alba (18–41); Alex Beguez (42–63); Omar Khouri (64–85); Maki Naro (86–101); Jeremy Nguyen (102–15); Kane Lynch (116–29); Tracy Chahwan (130–43); Kasia Babis (144–55); Chelsea Saunders (156–67); Abu Zubaydah (180–81)

Printed and bound in China
10 9 8 7 6 5 4 3 2 1

Abrams ComicArts books are available at special discounts when purchased in quantity for premiums and promotions as well as fundraising or educational use. Special editions can also be created to specification. For details, contact specialsales@abramsbooks.com or the address below.

ABRAMS The Art of Books
195 Broadway, New York, NY 10007
abramsbooks.com

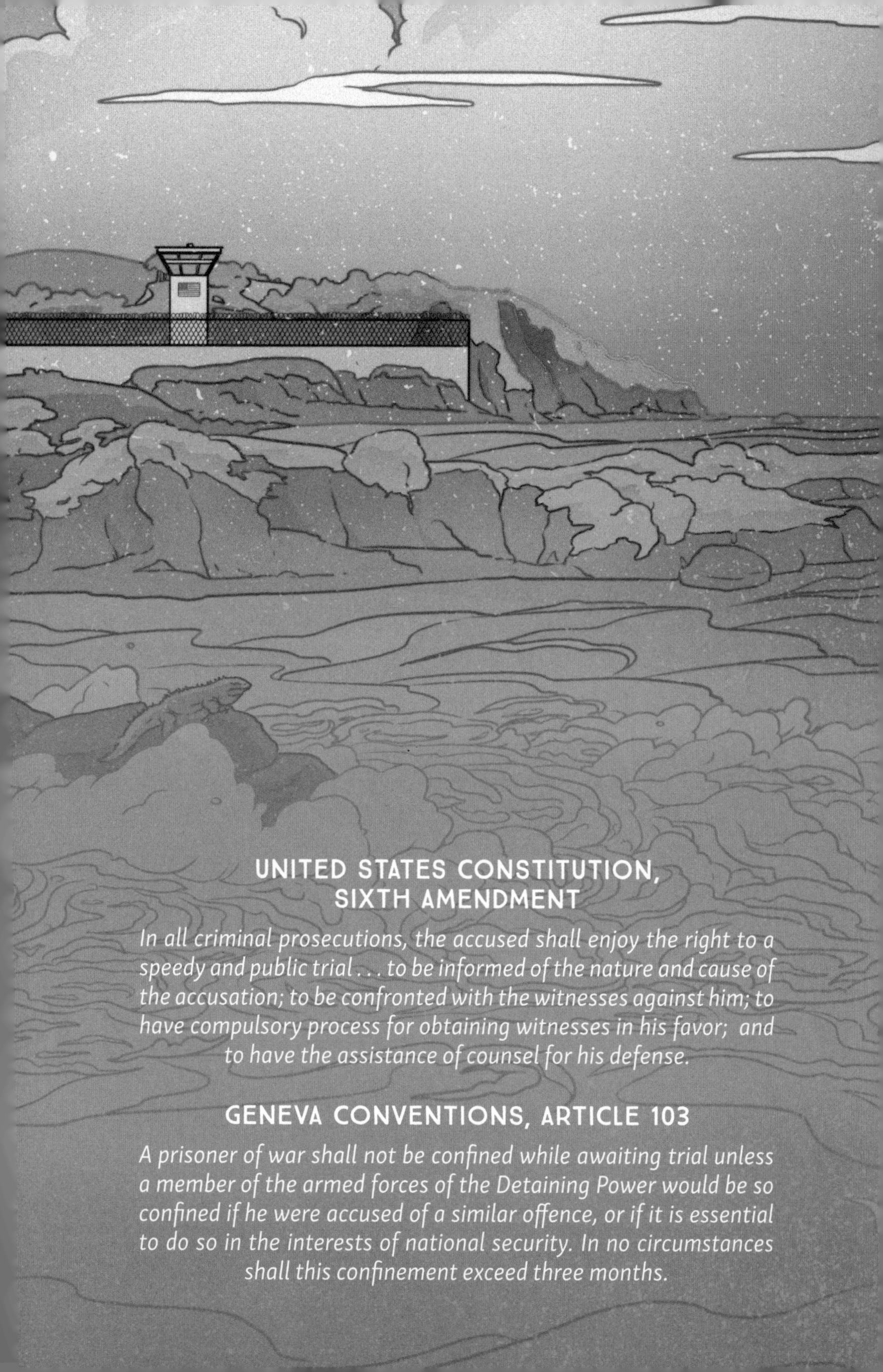

UNITED STATES CONSTITUTION, SIXTH AMENDMENT

In all criminal prosecutions, the accused shall enjoy the right to a speedy and public trial . . . to be informed of the nature and cause of the accusation; to be confronted with the witnesses against him; to have compulsory process for obtaining witnesses in his favor; and to have the assistance of counsel for his defense.

GENEVA CONVENTIONS, ARTICLE 103

A prisoner of war shall not be confined while awaiting trial unless a member of the armed forces of the Detaining Power would be so confined if he were accused of a similar offence, or if it is essential to do so in the interests of national security. In no circumstances shall this confinement exceed three months.

CONTENTS

A NOTE ON LANGUAGE

IS GUANTÁNAMO A PRISON?

The language we use to describe our world shapes our perception and understanding. And the language used to describe Guantánamo is hotly contested. The U.S. government describes the facility as a "detention camp" or a "detention facility" and the inhabitants as "detainees." Human rights advocates often call Guantánamo a "concentration camp." Journalists make all kinds of choices in describing Guantánamo (GITMO), from adopting the government's terminology to calling it an "offshore prison" or a "prison fortress."

My goals with my language choices in this book are to accurately describe reality and to use words that everyone can understand. The word "detainee" does not have the cultural weight of the word "prisoner"—I've been detained many times (by a TSA guard searching my bag, by transit police checking my ticket, or by an overly long work meeting), but I have never been a prisoner. I think the government's intentional choice of tepid, bureaucratic language to describe Guantánamo downplays the years people have spent and continue to spend in custody. In this book, I made the choice to describe Guantánamo as a "prison" and the men confined there as "prisoners." I made this choice after consulting the *Merriam-Webster Dictionary* definitions of prison and prisoner:

> **Prison:** *a state of confinement or captivity*
> **Prisoner:** *a person deprived of liberty and kept under involuntary restraint, confinement, or custody*

IS THIS ALL REAL?

I've worked to make this graphic narrative a nonfiction accounting of real life. The chapters in this book are all based on original interviews I did, as well as interviews conducted by Columbia University's Rule of Law project, and journalistic books about Guantánamo. Whenever possible, the illustrations in this book are based on photo and video references. However, because it's impossible to document what happened in every scene described in this book and the military does not allow media to photograph prisoners and many prison operations at Guantánamo, the artists have used their creativity to fill in the gaps.

INTRODUCTION

There's a place in Guantánamo Bay called Glass Beach. Likely the beach got its name from the pieces of shattered bottles that wash up on its shore. The sea scrubs the glass smooth, and so pretty are the little squares of red and green and brown that one of the officer's wives used to collect and make jewelry out of them.

I remember she came by the media office once to show them to us. This was in 2008; I was working as a journalist at the time and had been sent by my newspaper to cover the pre-trial hearings of Omar Khadr, a Canadian who'd been captured in Afghanistan at the age of fifteen and shipped to Guantánamo, where he would spend the next eight years of his life. We sat in the media office, a gaggle of maybe half a dozen reporters, leafing through documents describing the brutal interrogations this boy had been put through, the stress positions and sleep deprivation to which he'd been subjected. And all the while, nearby, the officer's wife showed off her homemade jewelry, the little squares of glass shimmering under the white fluorescents.

Of all the things I remember about the Guantánamo Bay detention camps, what has always struck me the most is the extent to which almost everyone I talked to there—from the camp guards to the base commander, from the prosecutors to the officers' spouses—had learned to cultivate a talent for dissociation, a talent for instantaneous forgetting. The same soldiers who escorted us on tours of the prisoners' isolation cells in the morning would escort us to beachside barbecues in the afternoon. The same military public relations officers who made sure to explain to us at length how respectfully the detainees were treated and how tactics such as waterboarding had only been used against the worst-of-the-worst detainees would come with us to the base's souvenir shop to buy T-shirts that read, "Guantánamo Bay—the Wetter, the Better."

Reporting from Guantánamo Bay, I often felt as though the entire enterprise had been preemptively confined to the past, its myriad cruelties and indignities and illegalities buried in euphemism and secrecy and spin such as to render them impossible to talk about with any degree of honesty.

Babies born on January 11, 2002—the day the first prisoners were blindfolded and flown to the makeshift kennels of Camp X-Ray in Guantánamo Bay—have now entered adulthood. An entire generation has come of age in the shadow of perpetual war against an ever-shifting enemy—at times a terror group, at times a country, at times an ideology. And the site of so many of the grotesque practices that have come to define that war—waterboarding, sleep deprivation, stress positions, indefinite detention—will seem to them, as to most Americans, an abstraction, a nowhere place in the middle of the Caribbean Sea that they will likely never visit or have to think about.

But the legacy of the Guantánamo camps—that moment a nation, caught up in the frenzy of revenge and immediacy of war, decided to set aside its laws and norms and principles—does not belong to the past. More than almost any other focal point in the War on Terror, the detention camps and the ideological bloodthirstiness that created them have come to influence so many of this country's darkest impulses ever since. One cannot look at the internment facilities currently housing refugee children along the southern border and not see a blueprint drawn up eighteen years earlier along the southeast Cuban shore. One cannot assess the new normal of extrajudicial drone killings, ordered by the president without oversight, and not see an echo of the made-up legal system designed specifically for Guantánamo detainees—an ad-hoc solution intended to skirt all the existing rules, to produce the desired results at any cost.

In this book are the stories of people whose lives were forever changed by what happened and continues to happen in Guantánamo Bay. Some were swept up during the early years of the war on terror, quickly found to pose no threat, and yet held in cages for more than a decade anyway, their freedom sacrificed at the altar of political and ideological necessity. Others willingly aided the implementation of the system, only to realize too late the grotesque injustice at its heart. And yet others tried to tell the world what was happening in these camps and had their livelihoods and their freedom taken away for their effort. But all of them, in one way or another, experienced firsthand the single most telling chapter of 21st-century American militarism, a chapter most of this country has spent the past decade trying to forget.

We think of war, first and foremost, as an outbreak of mass physical violence, a theater in which we tear one another to shreds with bullets and bombs. And this is of course the defining layer of wartime, but beneath it, supporting the physical violence, are other layers, each one a different kind of violence—a linguistic violence, a bureaucratic violence, a violence of apathy, and, always the concluding chapter, a violence of forgetting.

If Afghanistan and Iraq mark the epicenters of America's post-9/11 outbreak of physical violence, the detention camps at Guantánamo Bay mark the epicenter of every other kind of violence.

Anyone who spends any time observing the GITMO detention camp, and the bureaucratic regime that controls it, must quickly become fluent in the language of euphemism. There are no "prisoners" in Guantánamo Bay—every time I used the word while at the base, a nearby officer would correct me. There are only "detainees." The word "prisoner" implies a prison sentence, a well-defined thing; a detainee you can hold without charge forever. There are certainly no prisoners of war in Guantánamo Bay, only unlawful enemy combatants—a category dreamed up by the George W. Bush administration to effectively ignore all the established norms regarding the treatment of fighters captured during wartime.

Of these terms, the one I found most jarring was used to refer to the often brutal interrogations of captured enemies, the sessions of what the military famously refers to as "enhanced interrogation." But in reality, the interrogations themselves were never called interrogations. Whenever a prisoner was to be dragged into a small room to be subjected to this brutality in an effort to extract information, the soldiers would refer to it as a "reservation": As in, "The prisoner has an upcoming reservation." The entire system was constructed this way, dressed up in a costume of benign, antiseptic terminology.

I have no doubt that everyone responsible for the Guantánamo Bay prison camps—from the politicians who authorized their creation to the lawyers who penned opinions justifying them to the soldiers who carried out the day-to-day cruelty—will never face any real consequences for their actions. To indict the people who did this is to indict the country that allowed it to happen. Instead the man who wrote the memos providing legal cover for torture at the camps is today a law professor at Berkley. The president who oversaw the creation of the camps is today a respected elder statesman, appearing on daytime TV shows and peddling portraits of the soldiers he sent to be maimed in an illegal war. There is no reckoning, no conciliation, no acknowledgment. Many of the remaining prisoners in Guantánamo will likely grow old and die there, and unless there's another terror attack and a new president decides to begin shipping new prisoners there, the detention camps will slowly fade out of collective memory.

And this is perhaps the most insidious aspect of Guantánamo Bay's legacy— just how easy it is to forget. Even though the camps still house prisoners, the entire place feels like something from a prior epoch, a piece of ancient history, buried now beneath the daily scandals and calamities that have come to define the present moment in American politics.

The stories in this book are, first and foremost, an antidote to forgetting. Taken together, they represent not only a wide-ranging account of how Guantánamo Bay detention camps functioned, but also the impulses—the communal hatred, fear, and cowardice—that allowed such a place to exist.

Unless we confront these impulses, they will resurface and give rise to new nightmares—nightmares whose victims and perpetrators we will be forced, once more, to begin instantaneously forgetting.

Omar El Akkad was born in Cairo, Egypt, and grew up in the Middle East before moving to Canada. In a ten-year career as a reporter, he covered stories across the planet—from the war in Afghanistan to the military trials in Guantánamo Bay, the Arab Spring revolutions in the Middle East, and the protests in Ferguson, Missouri. Omar is a recipient of the National Newspaper Award for investigative reporting for his coverage of the "Toronto 18" terrorism arrests. He has also won the Edward Goff Penny Memorial Prize for Young Canadian Journalists, and has been nominated for several National Magazine Awards. He is a graduate of Queen's University and the author of the novel *American War*.

After September 11, 2001, the U.S. government dropped millions of these paper flyers over Afghanistan, offering cash payments to people who turned in members of al-Qaeda and the Taliban.

Get wealth and power beyond your dreams.
Help the Anti-Taliban Forces rid Afghanistan of
murderers and terrorists.*

You can receive millions of dollars for helping the
Anti-Taliban force catch Al-Qaeda and Taliban murderers.
This is enough money to take care of your family, your
village, your tribe for the rest of your life.
Pay for livestock and doctors and school books and
housing for all your people.*

*Translated from Arabic

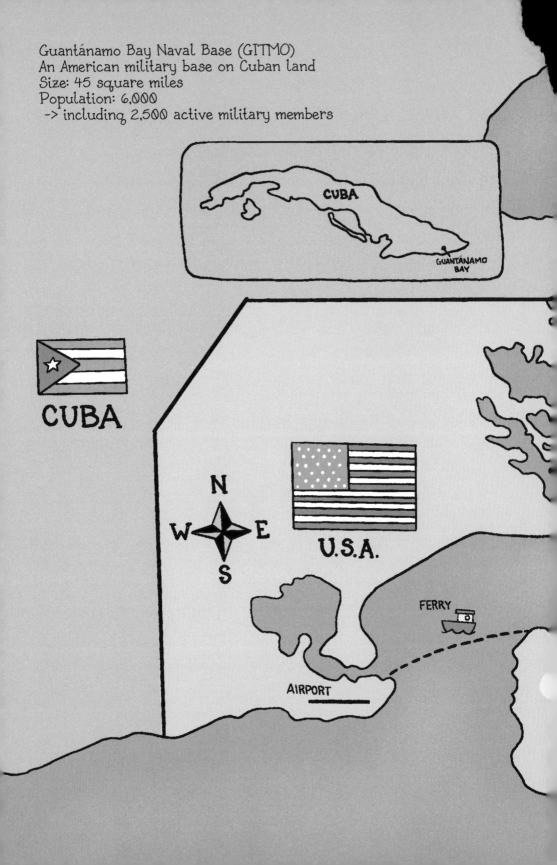

Guantánamo Bay Naval Base (GITMO)
An American military base on Cuban land
Size: 45 square miles
Population: 6,000
 -> including 2,500 active military members

CUBA

GUANTÁNAMO
BAY

CUBA

N
W   E
S

U.S.A.

FERRY

AIRPORT

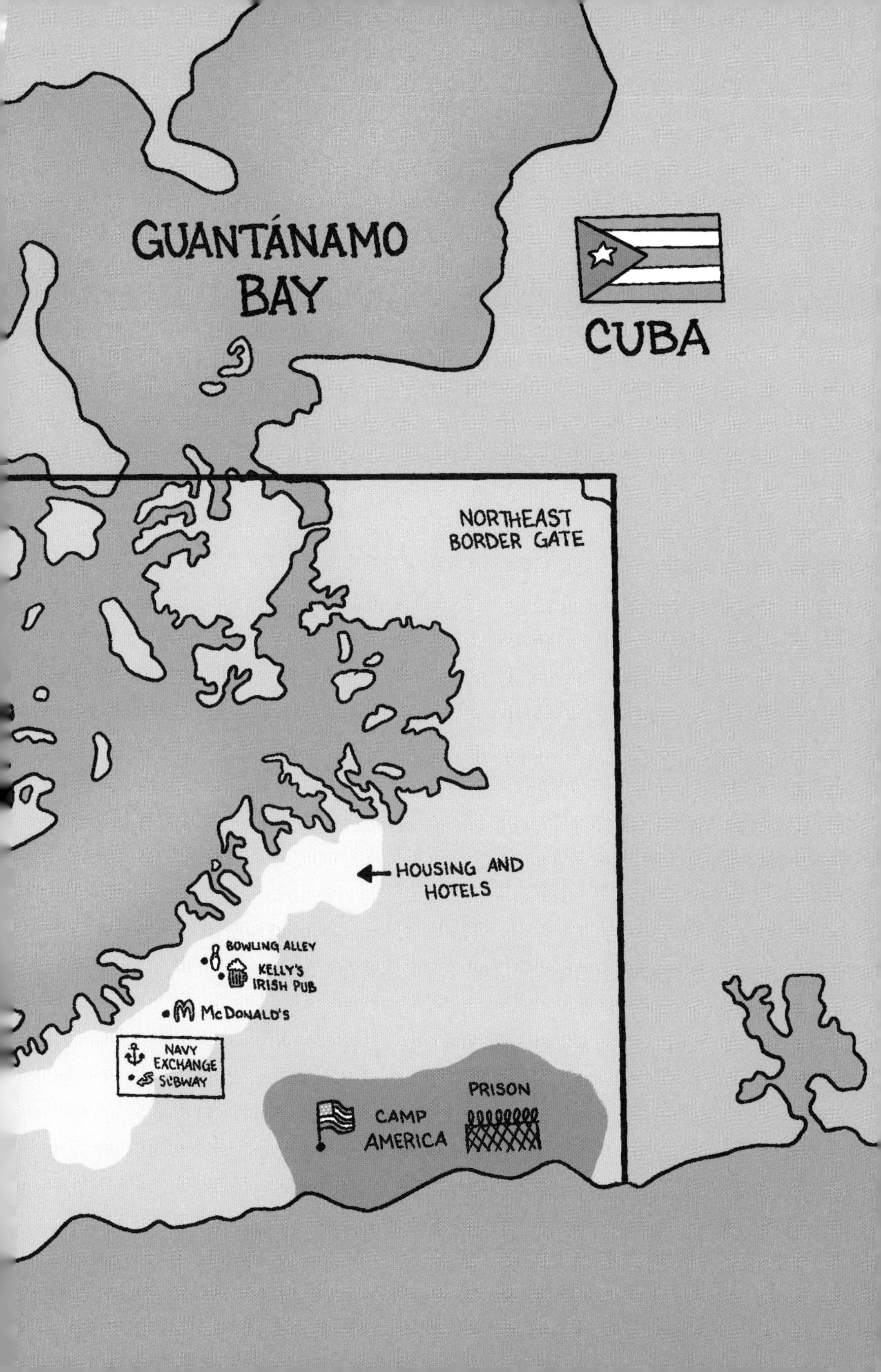
GUANTÁNAMO BAY
CUBA
NORTHEAST BORDER GATE
HOUSING AND HOTELS
BOWLING ALLEY
KELLY'S IRISH PUB
McDONALD'S
NAVY EXCHANGE
SUBWAY
CAMP AMERICA
PRISON

GUANTÁNAMO FACTS

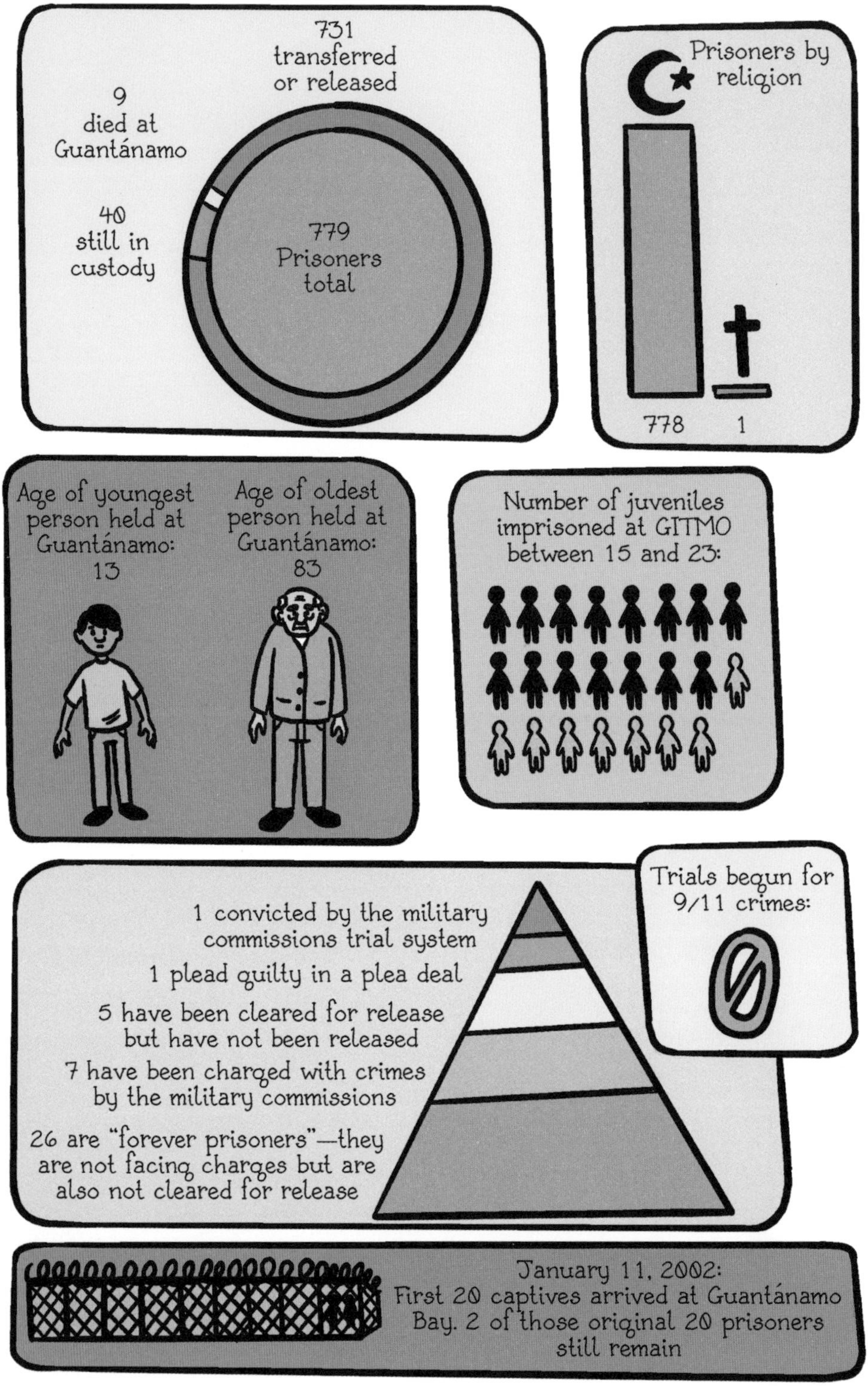
731
transferred
or released
9
died at
Guantánamo
40
still in
custody
779
Prisoners
total
Prisoners by
religion
778
1
Age of youngest
person held at
Guantánamo:
13
Age of oldest
person held at
Guantánamo:
83
Number of juveniles
imprisoned at GITMO
between 15 and 23:
1 convicted by the military
commissions trial system
1 plead guilty in a plea deal
5 have been cleared for release
but have not been released
7 have been charged with crimes
by the military commissions
26 are "forever prisoners"—they
are not facing charges but are
also not cleared for release
Trials begun for
9/11 crimes:
0
January 11, 2002:
First 20 captives arrived at Guantánamo
Bay. 2 of those original 20 prisoners
still remain

Citizens of 49 countries have been held in Guantánamo.

Afghanistan: 220 people

Saudi Arabia: 135 people

China: 22 people

Britain: 9 people

France: 7 people

Where do people go when they're released from Guantánamo? Do people released from Guantánamo join terrorist groups? The data is incomplete and ambiguous. The most thorough reports say 6 to 9 percent of prisoners "actively engaged on the battlefield" after their release.

Percent of Guantánamo prisoners turned over to the U.S. for bounties:

80%

Bounties the U.S. government paid Pakistani and Afghani citizens for individuals they suspected to be part of the Taliban:

$3,000 to $30,000

Number of people working at the detention camp:

1,800

Ratio of workers to prisoners:

1 : 45

Cost to run GITMO per year: $445 million

Cost per prisoner per year: $11 million

Average cost of holding someone in federal prison per year: $36,299

For a list of sources for these numbers, see the endnotes.

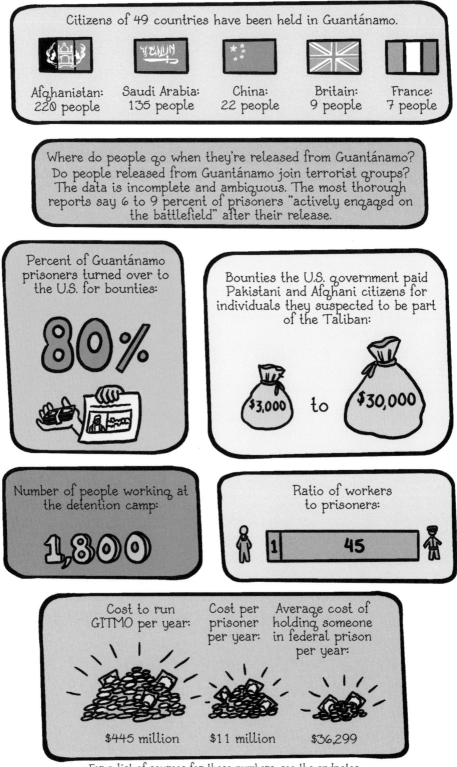

TIMELINE

1903: The United States asks to lease the strategically important bay on the south side of Cuba for a naval station. The $3,386 annual lease has no expiration date.

1944: During the peak of WWII, 9,000 Cubans and 4,000 Americans work at the Naval Station at Guantánamo Bay.

1958: Cuban Revolution

1959: Fidel Castro demands the return of Guantánamo Bay

1960s: 50,000 mines are placed around Guantánamo's fence, creating the largest minefield in the Western Hemisphere.

1991–92: 34,000 Haitian refugees are held at GITMO in makeshift camps while they apply for asylum.

1994–96: GITMO continues to detain Cuban and Haitian refugees who are picked up at sea on their way to the U.S.

January 2002: The first 20 War on Terror prisoners are sent to Camp X-Ray.

April 2002: Camp X-Ray is closed and prisoners are relocated to the prison building Camp Delta.

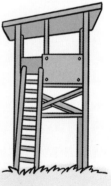

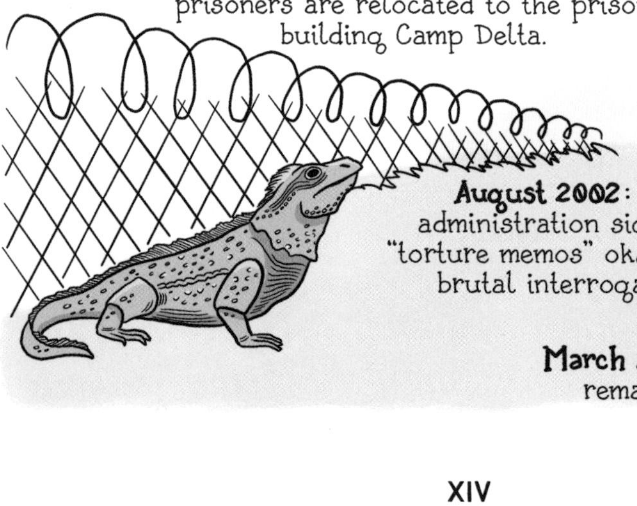

August 2002: The Bush administration signs off on the "torture memos" okaying the use of brutal interrogation tactics.

March 2003: 665 prisoners remain in Guantánamo.

April 2004: The Supreme Court rules that prisoners at Guantanámo Bay have a right to habeas corpus—the reasons for each person's imprisonment must be reviewed.

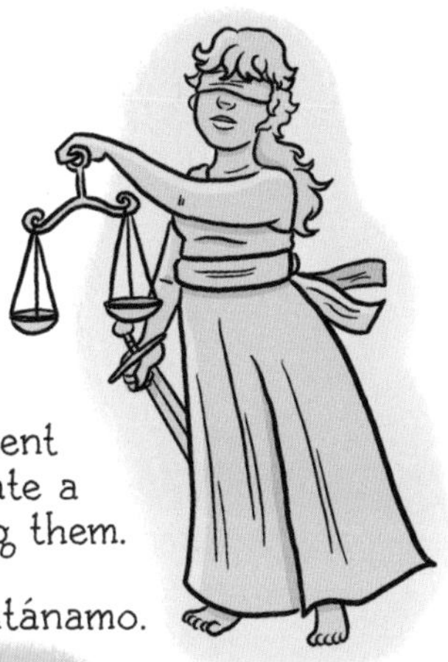

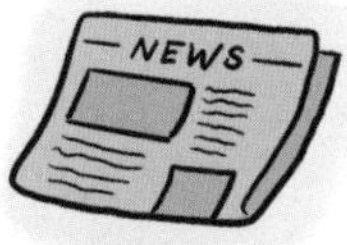
NEWS

April 2004: Media outlets publish photos of horrific abuse at Abu Ghraib prison.

2005: To protest their continued imprisonment without trial, 50 Guantánamo prisoners initiate a hunger strike. The military begins force-feeding them.

January 2006: 496 prisoners remain in Guantánamo.

June 2006: In a coordinated act, three prisoners at Guantánamo commit suicide on the same day.

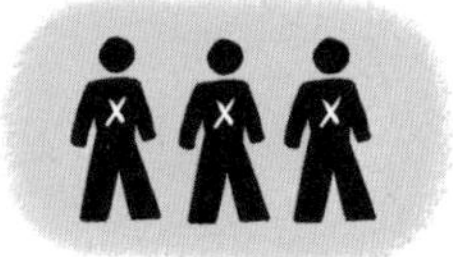

December 2007: 277 prisoners remain in Guantánamo.

January 2009: On his first day in office, President Obama orders Guantanamo to close within a year. (His efforts are subverted by Congress.)

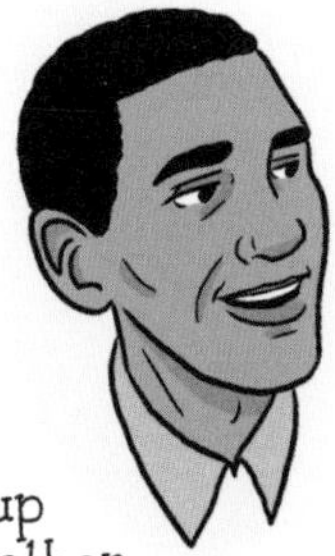

2010: Congress writes a provision into a defense spending bill that says Guantánamo prisoners cannot be brought to the U.S. mainland for trial or imprisonment.

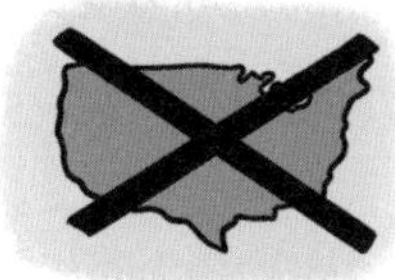

2011: The Obama administration sets up "periodic review boards" to determine whether individual prisoners should be transferred or continue to be imprisoned without charge.

January 2012: 171 prisoners remain in Guantánamo.

2012: The Senate finishes a 6,700-page report on abuse of prisoners in U.S. custody after 9/11.

April 2013: 106 of the remaining 166 prisoners go on hunger strike. In December, the government changes it policy and refuses to disclose any information about hunger strikes.

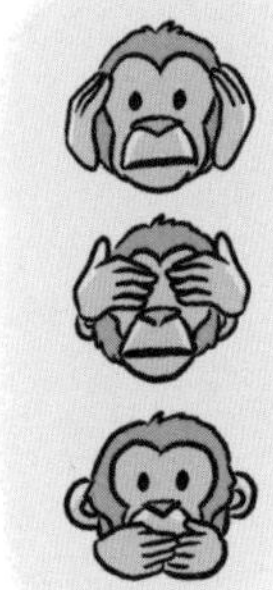

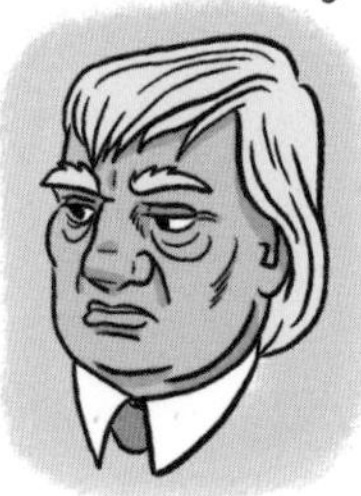

January 2018: President Trump signs an order keeping the prison open indefinitely.

January 2019: 40 prisoners remain in Guantánamo.

"YOUR OPPONENTS WOULD LOVE YOU TO
BELIEVE THAT IT'S HOPELESS, THAT YOU
HAVE NO POWER, THAT THERE'S NO REASON
TO ACT, THAT YOU CAN'T WIN. HOPE IS A
GIFT YOU DON'T HAVE TO SURRENDER, A
POWER YOU DON'T HAVE TO THROW AWAY."
—REBECCA SOLNIT

CHAPTER ONE

WELCOME TO GUANTÁNAMO

ILLUSTRATED BY HAZEL NEWLEVANT

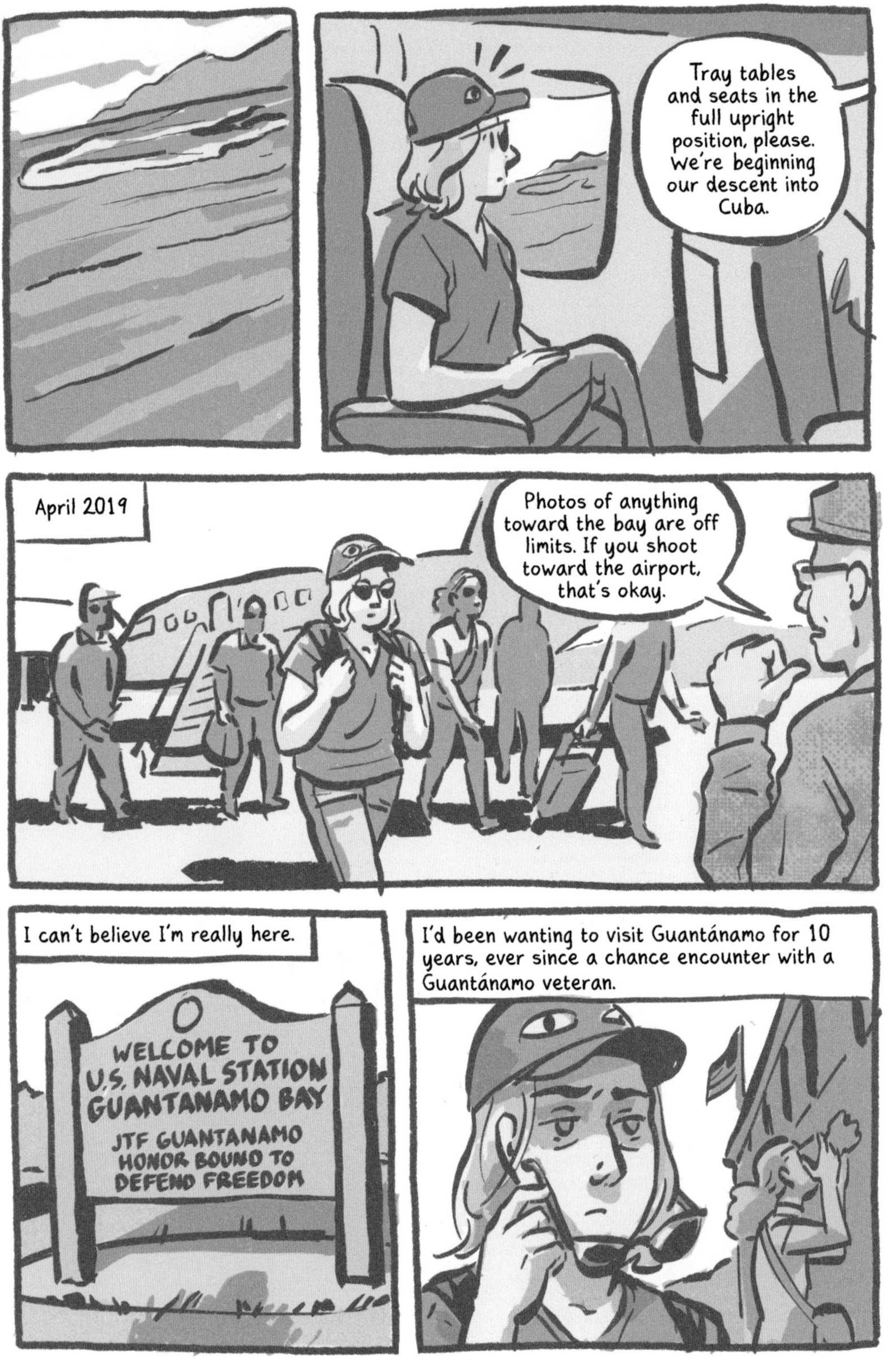
Tray tables and seats in the full upright position, please. We're beginning our descent into Cuba.
April 2019
Photos of anything toward the bay are off limits. If you shoot toward the airport, that's okay.
I can't believe I'm really here.
WELCOME TO U.S. NAVAL STATION GUANTANAMO BAY
JTF GUANTANAMO HONOR BOUND TO DEFEND FREEDOM
I'd been wanting to visit Guantánamo for 10 years, ever since a chance encounter with a Guantánamo veteran.

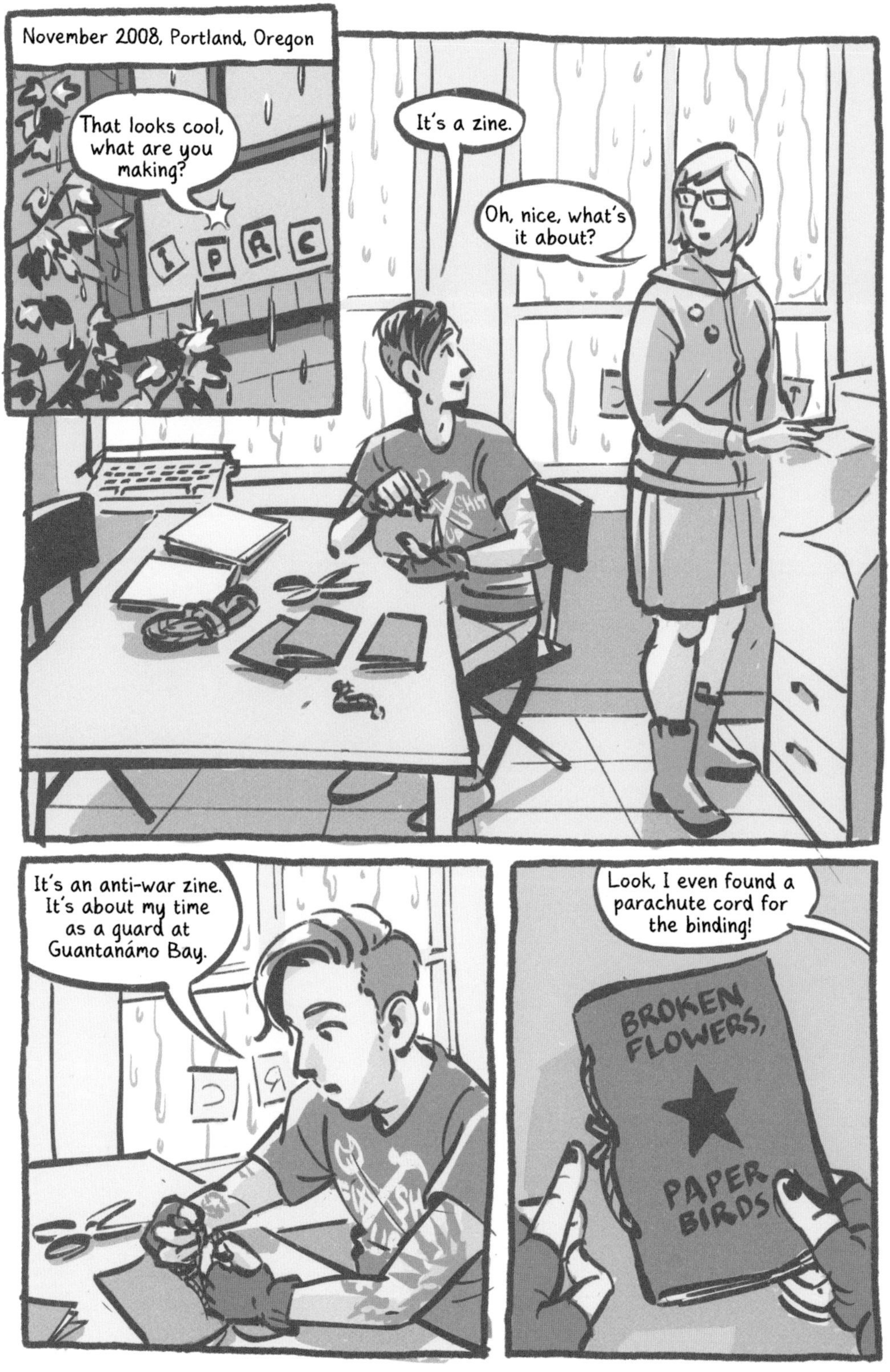
November 2008, Portland, Oregon
That looks cool, what are you making?
IPRC
It's a zine.
Oh, nice, what's it about?
It's an anti-war zine. It's about my time as a guard at Guantanámo Bay.
Look, I even found a parachute cord for the binding!
BROKEN FLOWERS, PAPER BIRDS

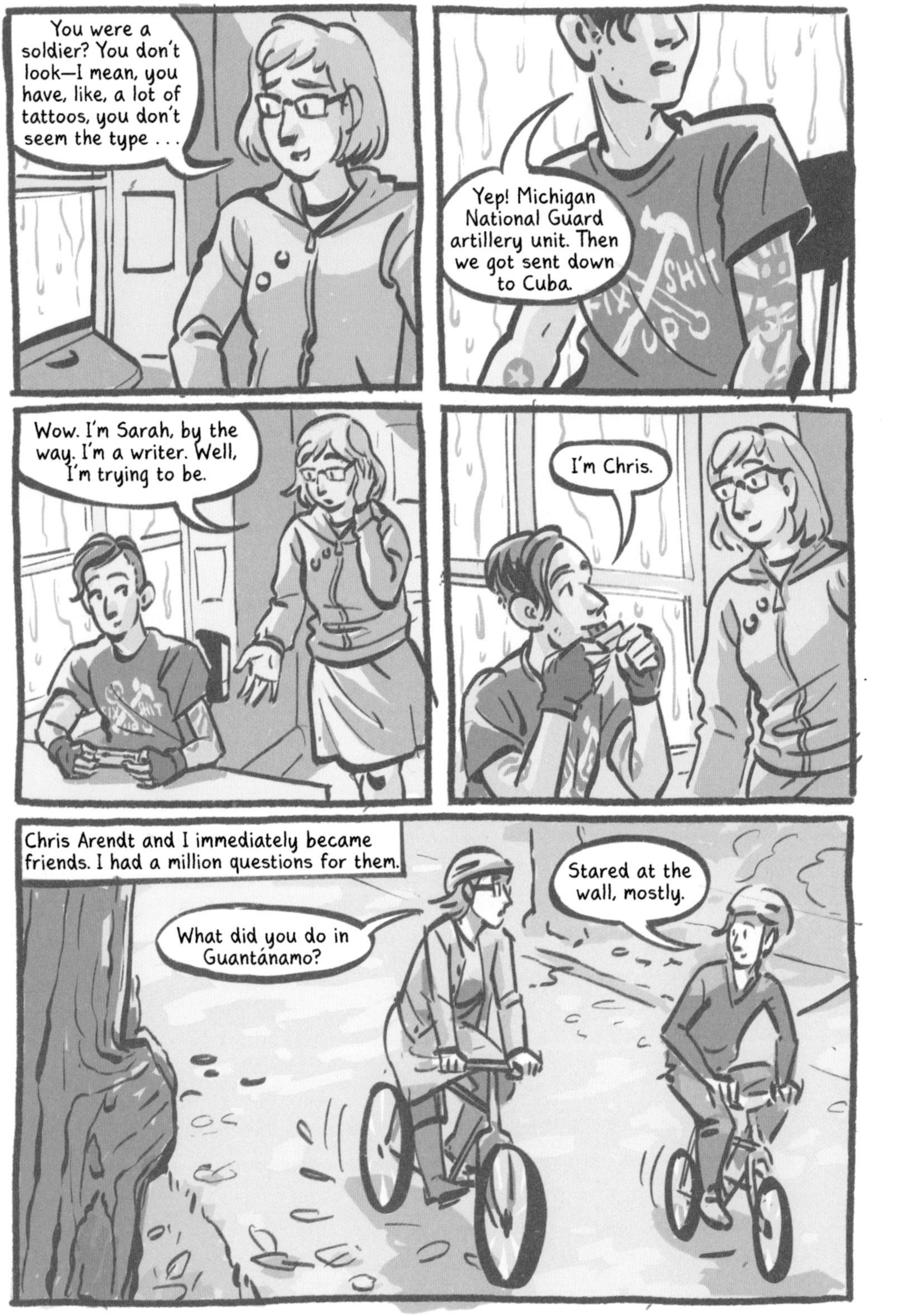
You were a soldier? You don't look—I mean, you have, like, a lot of tattoos, you don't seem the type . . .
Yep! Michigan National Guard artillery unit. Then we got sent down to Cuba.
FIX SHIT UP
Wow. I'm Sarah, by the way. I'm a writer. Well, I'm trying to be.
I'm Chris.
Chris Arendt and I immediately became friends. I had a million questions for them.
What did you do in Guantánamo?
Stared at the wall, mostly.

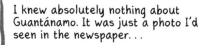

I knew absolutely nothing about Guantánamo. It was just a photo I'd seen in the newspaper. . .
NO WAR FOR OIL
WAR CRIMINALS
CLOSE GITMO
NO WAR
. . . a word in a headline about torture. While known around the world, to me at age 22, it was a mostly invisible, very confusing place.
It wasn't a real place, full of real people.
I was working as an unpaid intern at a newspaper. I wanted to be a journalist. Through getting to know Chris, I interviewed former Guantánamo prisoners.
And eventually other Guantánamo veterans.

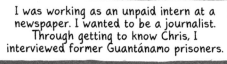

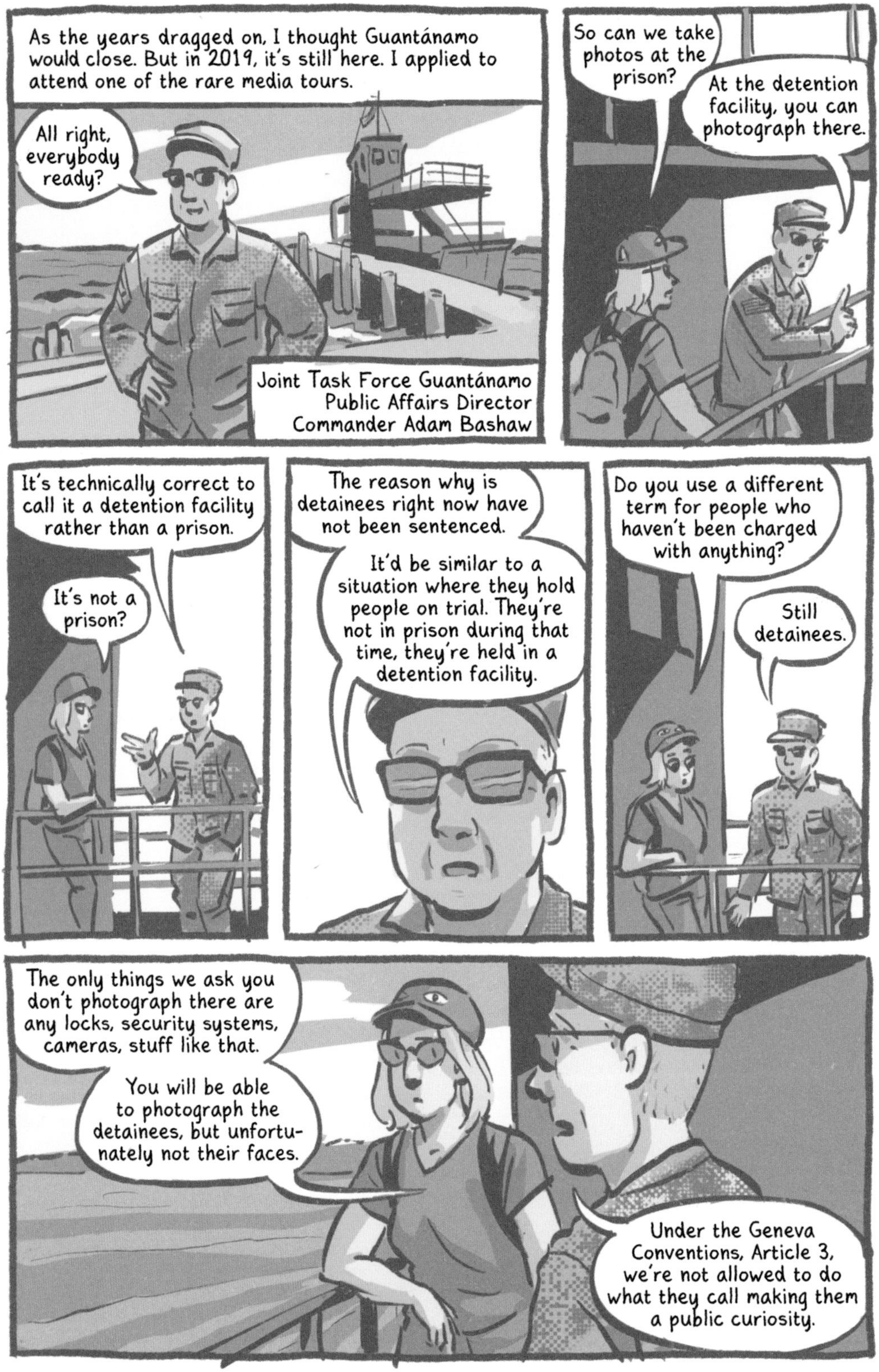

As the years dragged on, I thought Guantánamo would close. But in 2019, it's still here. I applied to attend one of the rare media tours.
All right, everybody ready?
Joint Task Force Guantánamo Public Affairs Director Commander Adam Bashaw
So can we take photos at the prison?
At the detention facility, you can photograph there.
It's technically correct to call it a detention facility rather than a prison.
It's not a prison?
The reason why is detainees right now have not been sentenced.
It'd be similar to a situation where they hold people on trial. They're not in prison during that time, they're held in a detention facility.
Do you use a different term for people who haven't been charged with anything?
Still detainees.
The only things we ask you don't photograph there are any locks, security systems, cameras, stuff like that.
You will be able to photograph the detainees, but unfortunately not their faces.
Under the Geneva Conventions, Article 3, we're not allowed to do what they call making them a public curiosity.

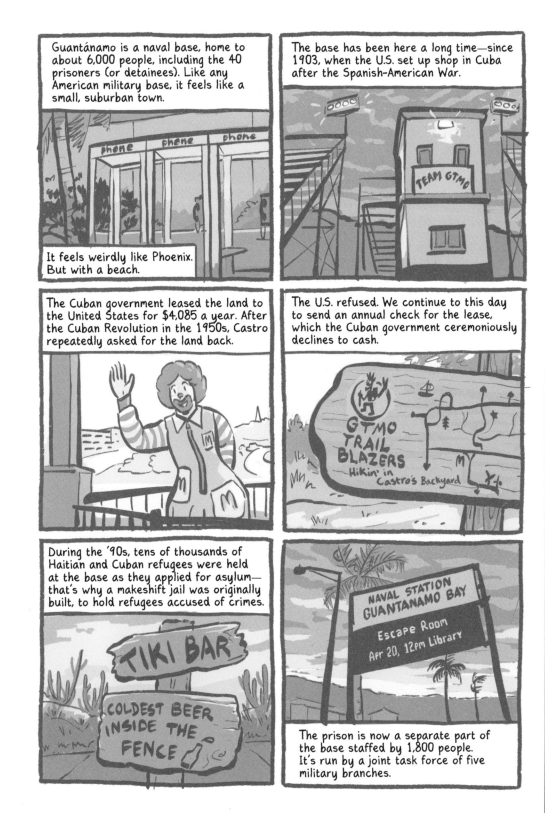

Guantánamo is a naval base, home to about 6,000 people, including the 40 prisoners (or detainees). Like any American military base, it feels like a small, suburban town.

It feels weirdly like Phoenix. But with a beach.

The base has been here a long time—since 1903, when the U.S. set up shop in Cuba after the Spanish-American War.

The Cuban government leased the land to the United States for $4,085 a year. After the Cuban Revolution in the 1950s, Castro repeatedly asked for the land back.

The U.S. refused. We continue to this day to send an annual check for the lease, which the Cuban government ceremoniously declines to cash.

During the '90s, tens of thousands of Haitian and Cuban refugees were held at the base as they applied for asylum—that's why a makeshift jail was originally built, to hold refugees accused of crimes.

The prison is now a separate part of the base staffed by 1,800 people. It's run by a joint task force of five military branches.

TEAM GTMO

GTMO TRAIL BLAZERS
Hikin' in Castro's Backyard

TIKI BAR
COLDEST BEER INSIDE THE FENCE

NAVAL STATION GUANTANAMO BAY
Escape Room
Apr 20, 12pm Library

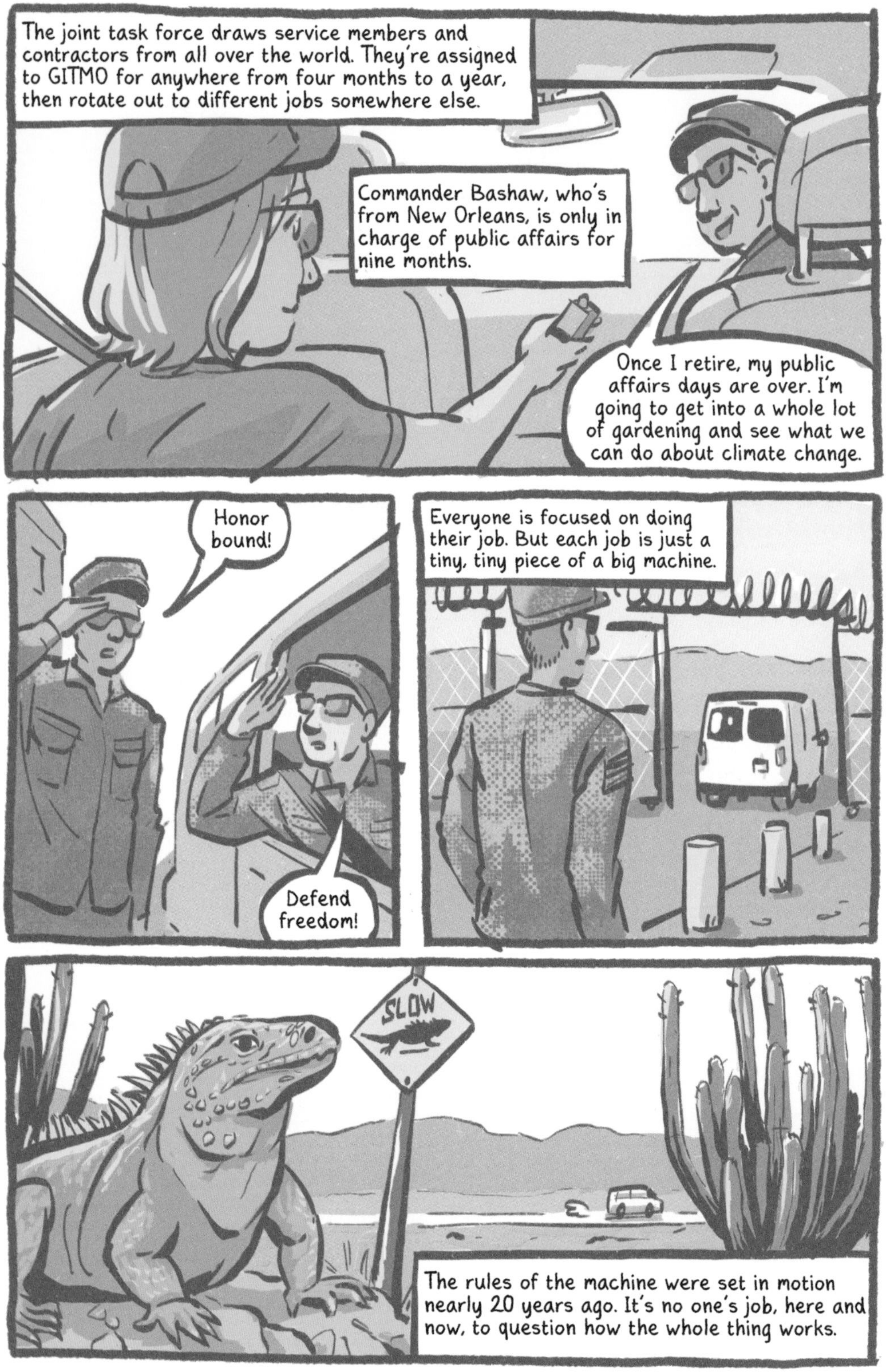
The joint task force draws service members and contractors from all over the world. They're assigned to GITMO for anywhere from four months to a year, then rotate out to different jobs somewhere else.
Commander Bashaw, who's from New Orleans, is only in charge of public affairs for nine months.
Once I retire, my public affairs days are over. I'm going to get into a whole lot of gardening and see what we can do about climate change.
Honor bound!
Defend freedom!
Everyone is focused on doing their job. But each job is just a tiny, tiny piece of a big machine.
SLOW
The rules of the machine were set in motion nearly 20 years ago. It's no one's job, here and now, to question how the whole thing works.

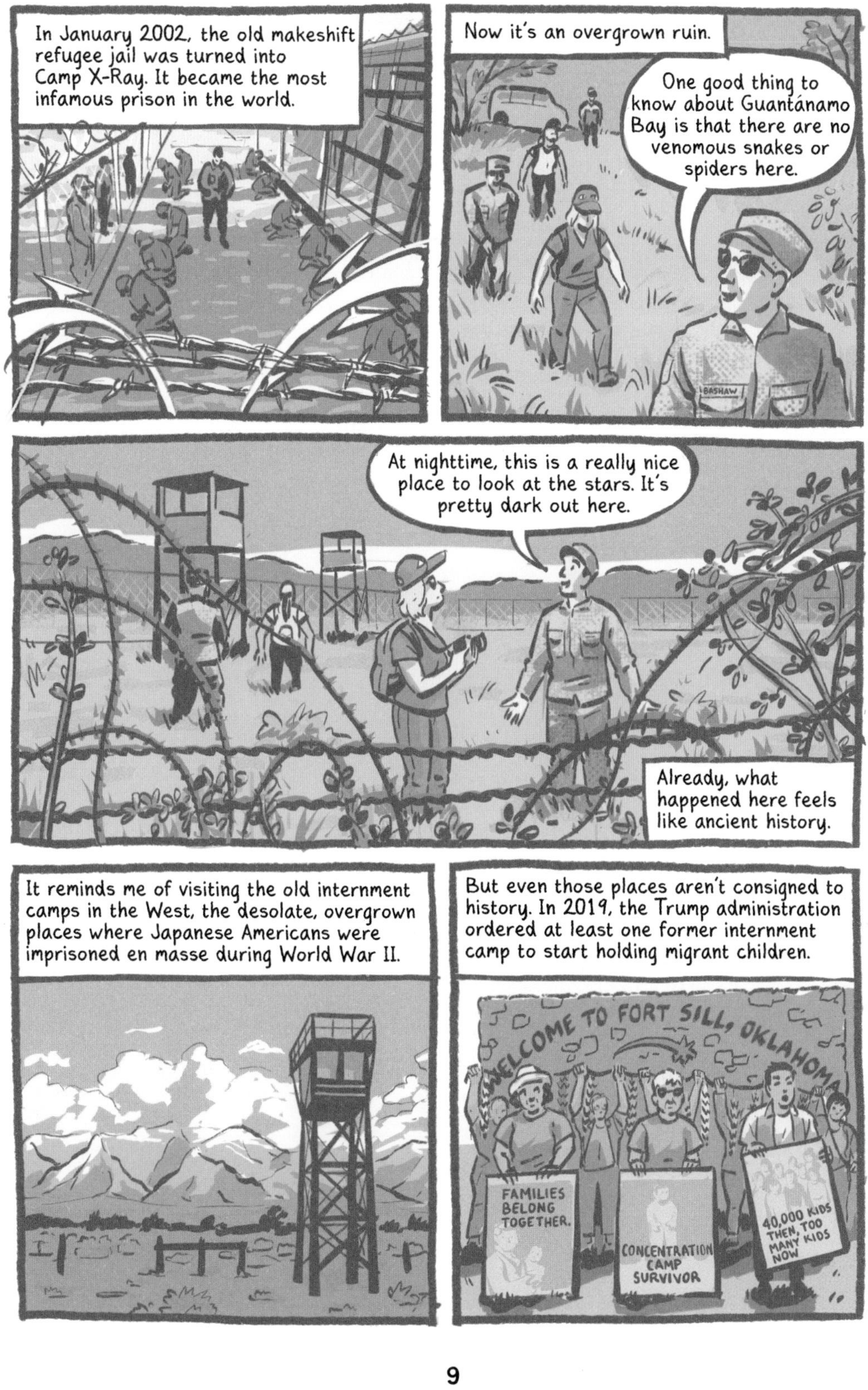
In January 2002, the old makeshift refugee jail was turned into Camp X-Ray. It became the most infamous prison in the world.
Now it's an overgrown ruin.
One good thing to know about Guantánamo Bay is that there are no venomous snakes or spiders here.
BASHAW
At nighttime, this is a really nice place to look at the stars. It's pretty dark out here.
Already, what happened here feels like ancient history.
It reminds me of visiting the old internment camps in the West, the desolate, overgrown places where Japanese Americans were imprisoned en masse during World War II.
But even those places aren't consigned to history. In 2019, the Trump administration ordered at least one former internment camp to start holding migrant children.
WELCOME TO FORT SILL, OKLAHOMA
FAMILIES BELONG TOGETHER.
CONCENTRATION CAMP SURVIVOR
40,000 KIDS THEN, TOO MANY KIDS NOW

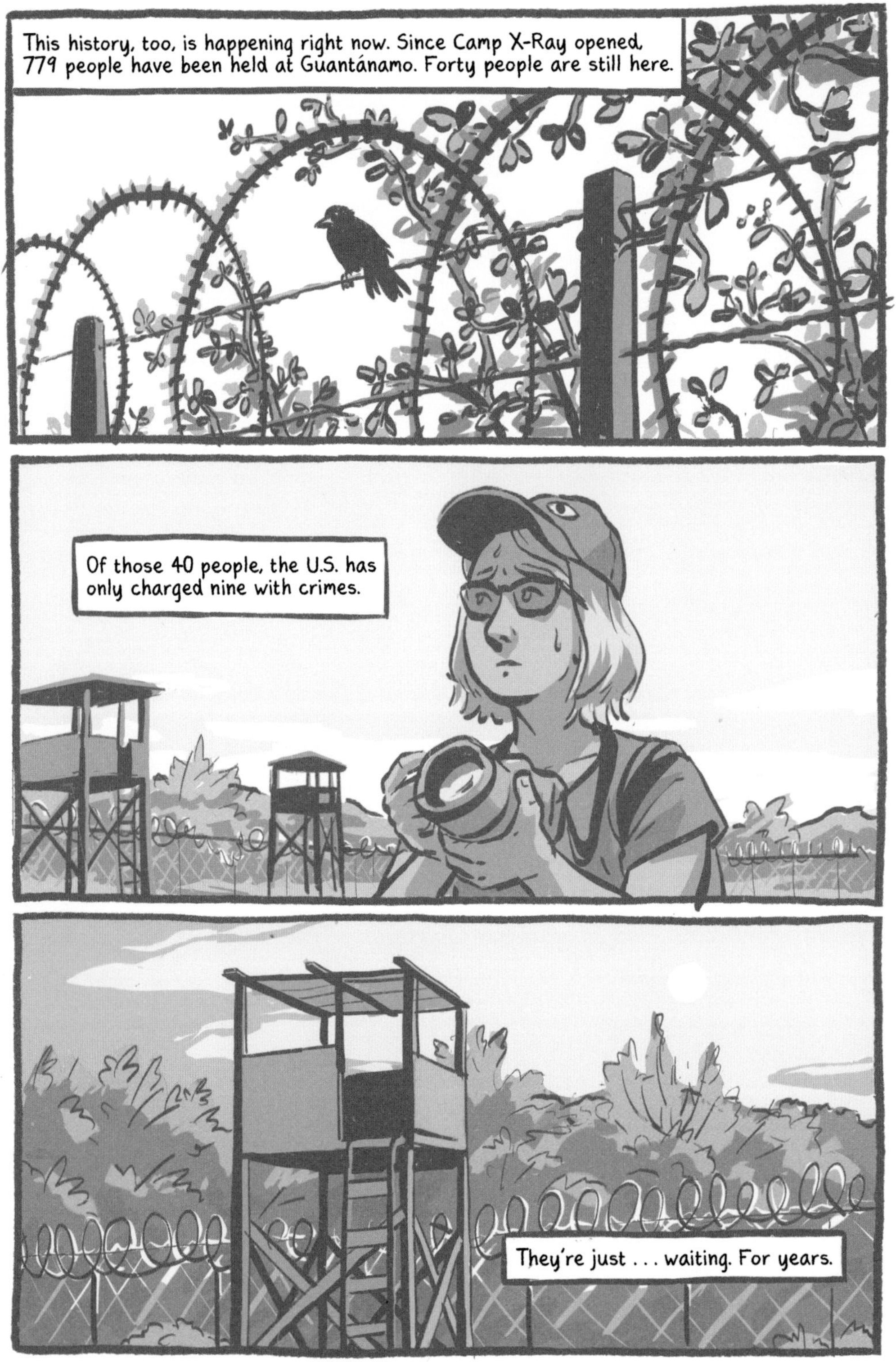
This history, too, is happening right now. Since Camp X-Ray opened, 779 people have been held at Guantánamo. Forty people are still here.
Of those 40 people, the U.S. has only charged nine with crimes.
They're just . . . waiting. For years.

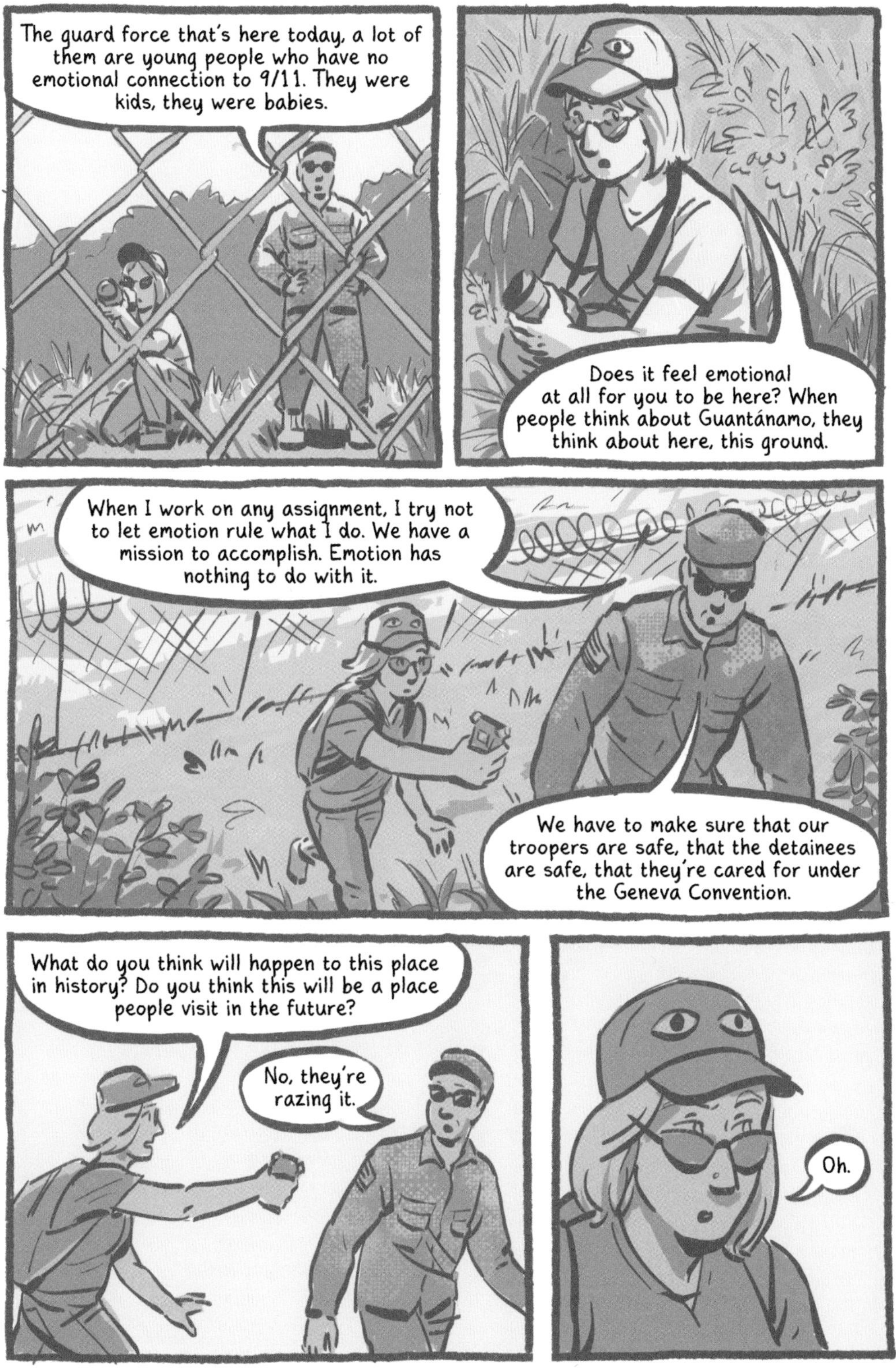
The guard force that's here today, a lot of them are young people who have no emotional connection to 9/11. They were kids, they were babies.
Does it feel emotional at all for you to be here? When people think about Guantánamo, they think about here, this ground.
When I work on any assignment, I try not to let emotion rule what I do. We have a mission to accomplish. Emotion has nothing to do with it.
We have to make sure that our troopers are safe, that the detainees are safe, that they're cared for under the Geneva Convention.
What do you think will happen to this place in history? Do you think this will be a place people visit in the future?
No, they're razing it.
Oh.

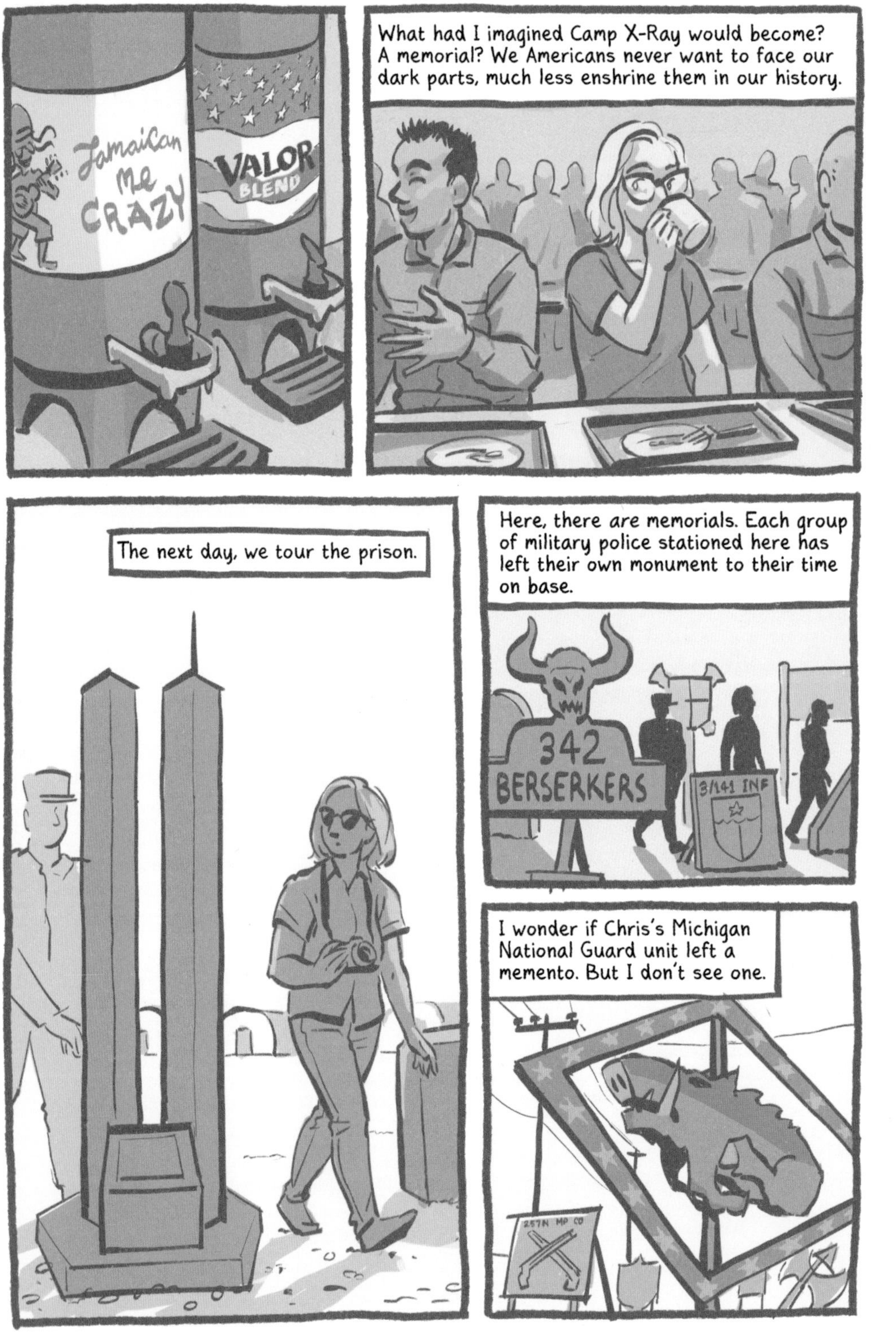
Jamaican me CRAZY
VALOR BLEND
What had I imagined Camp X-Ray would become? A memorial? We Americans never want to face our dark parts, much less enshrine them in our history.
The next day, we tour the prison.
Here, there are memorials. Each group of military police stationed here has left their own monument to their time on base.
342 BERSERKERS
3/141 INF
I wonder if Chris's Michigan National Guard unit left a memento. But I don't see one.
257TH MP CO

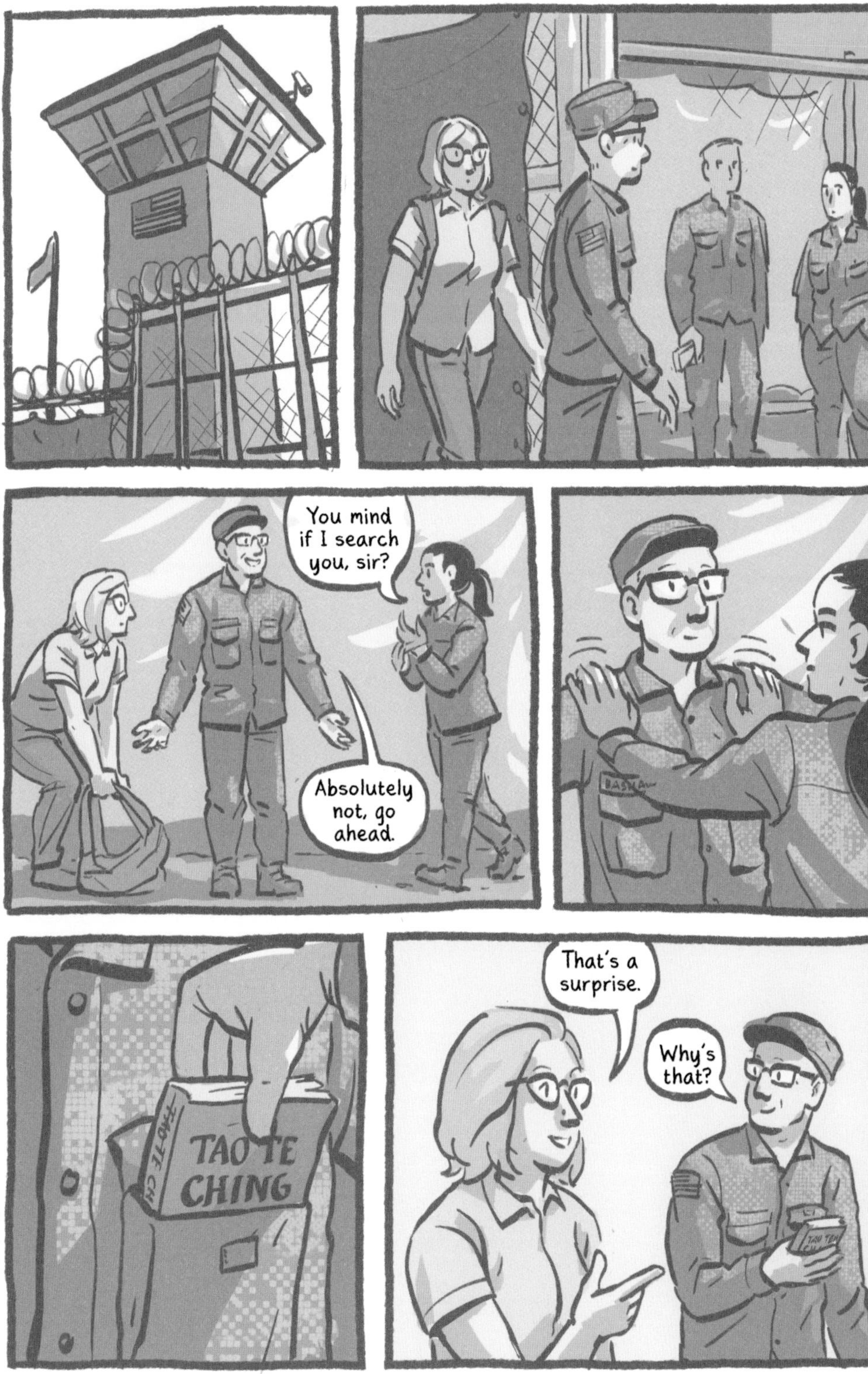
You mind if I search you, sir?
Absolutely not, go ahead.
TAO TE CHING
That's a surprise.
Why's that?

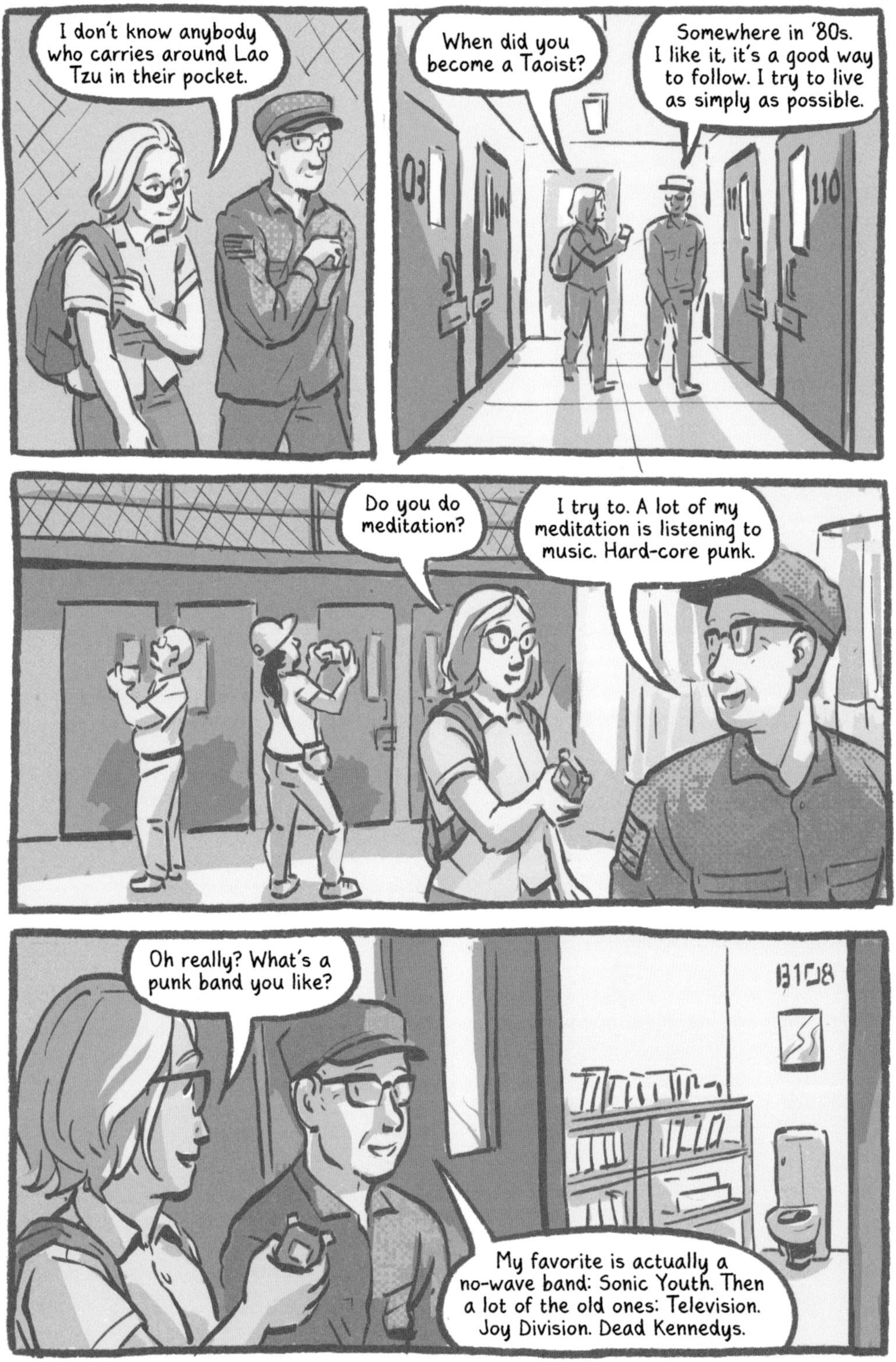
I don't know anybody who carries around Lao Tzu in their pocket.
When did you become a Taoist?
Somewhere in '80s. I like it, it's a good way to follow. I try to live as simply as possible.
03
110
Do you do meditation?
I try to. A lot of my meditation is listening to music. Hard-core punk.
Oh really? What's a punk band you like?
B108
My favorite is actually a no-wave band: Sonic Youth. Then a lot of the old ones: Television. Joy Division. Dead Kennedys.

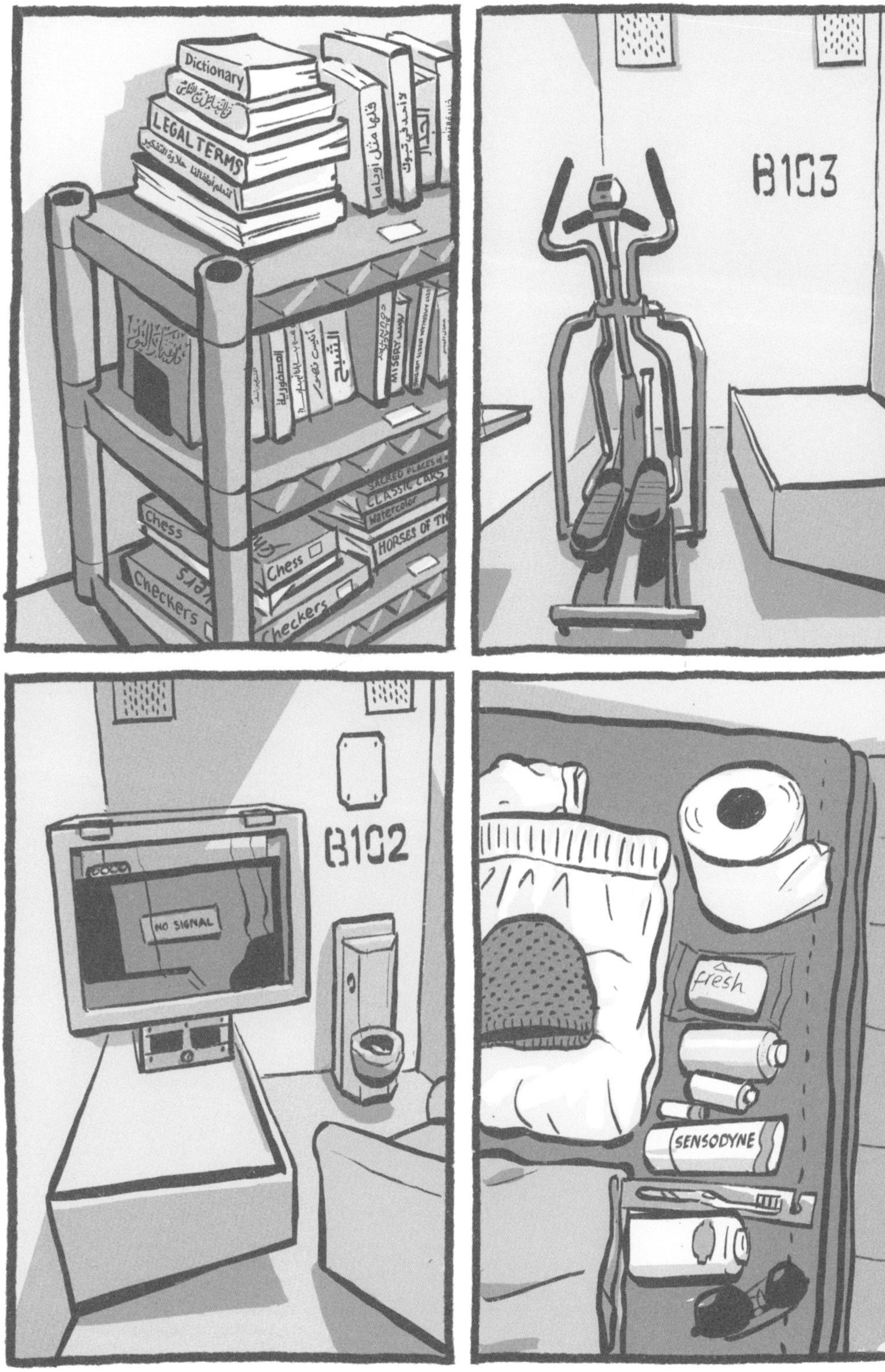
Dictionary
LEGAL TERMS
MISERY
CLASSIC CARS
Watercolor
Chess
Checkers
Chess
Checkers
B103
B102
NO SIGNAL
fresh
SENSODYNE

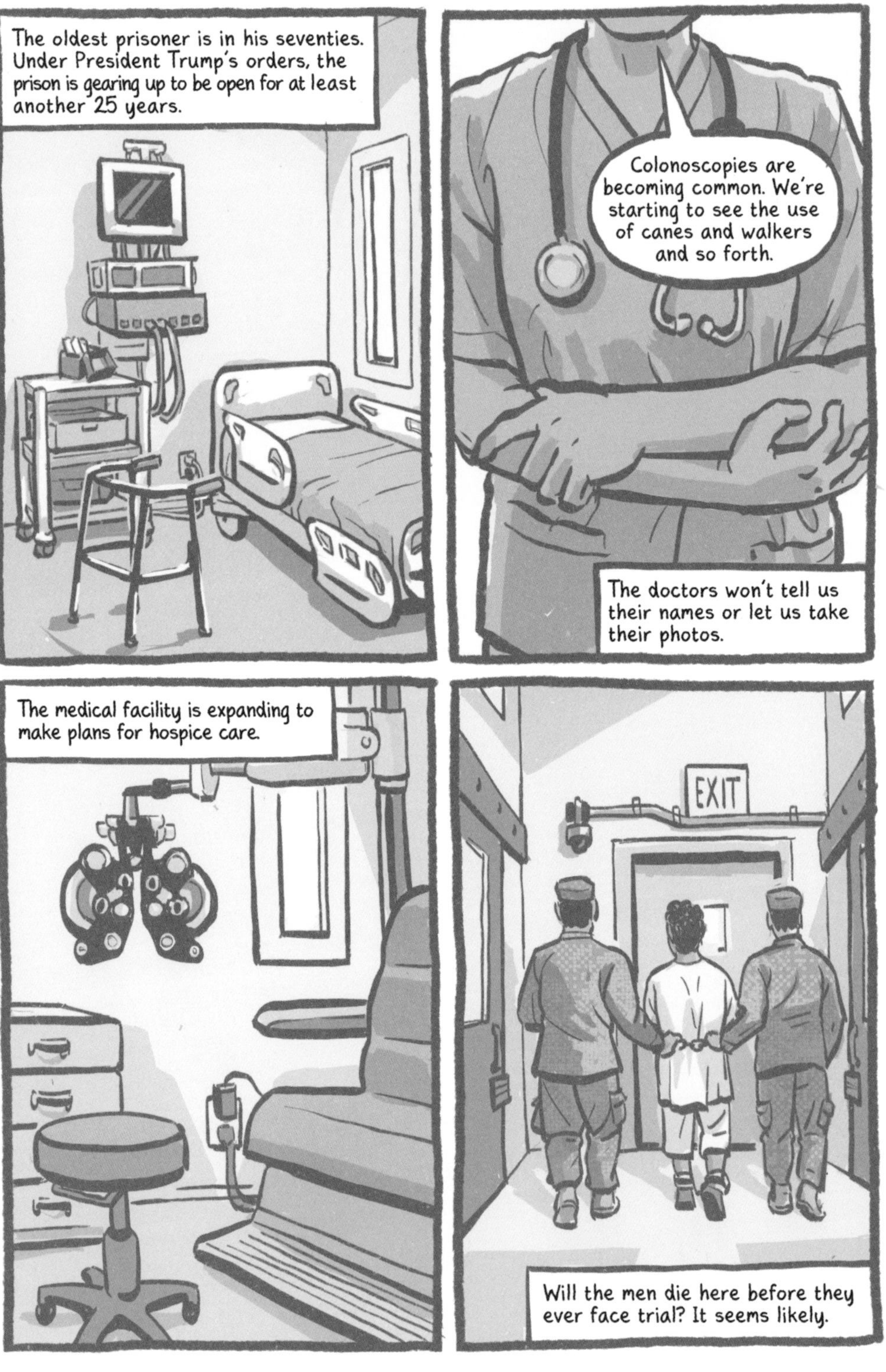
The oldest prisoner is in his seventies. Under President Trump's orders, the prison is gearing up to be open for at least another 25 years.
Colonoscopies are becoming common. We're starting to see the use of canes and walkers and so forth.
The doctors won't tell us their names or let us take their photos.
The medical facility is expanding to make plans for hospice care.
EXIT
Will the men die here before they ever face trial? It seems likely.

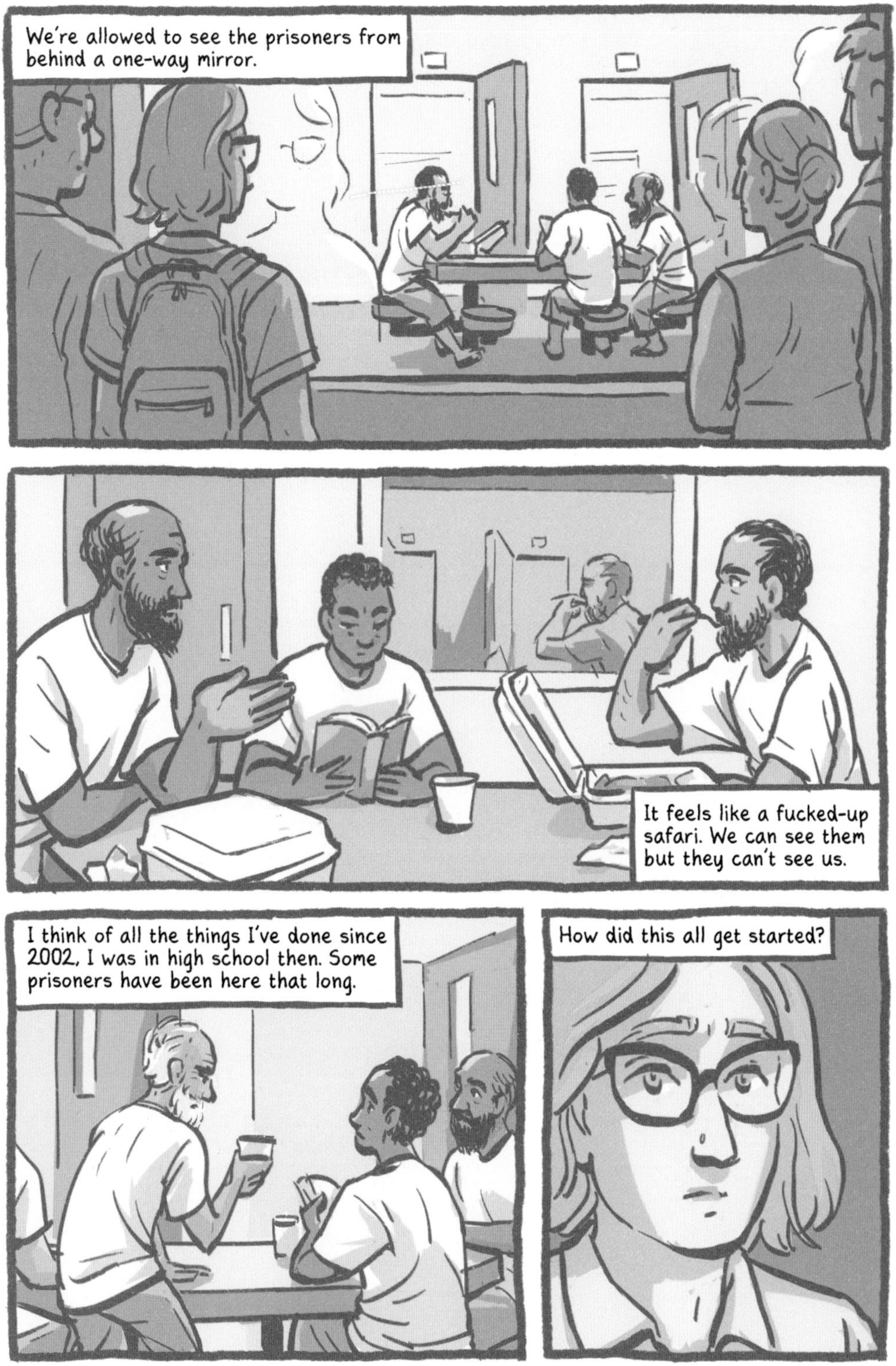
We're allowed to see the prisoners from behind a one-way mirror.
It feels like a fucked-up safari. We can see them but they can't see us.
I think of all the things I've done since 2002, I was in high school then. Some prisoners have been here that long.
How did this all get started?

CHAPTER TWO

MARK FALLON

FORMER CHIEF OF MIDDLE EAST COUNTERINTELLIGENCE OPERATIONS FOR NAVAL CRIMINAL INVESTIGATIVE SERVICE (NCIS)

ILLUSTRATED BY GERARDO ALBA

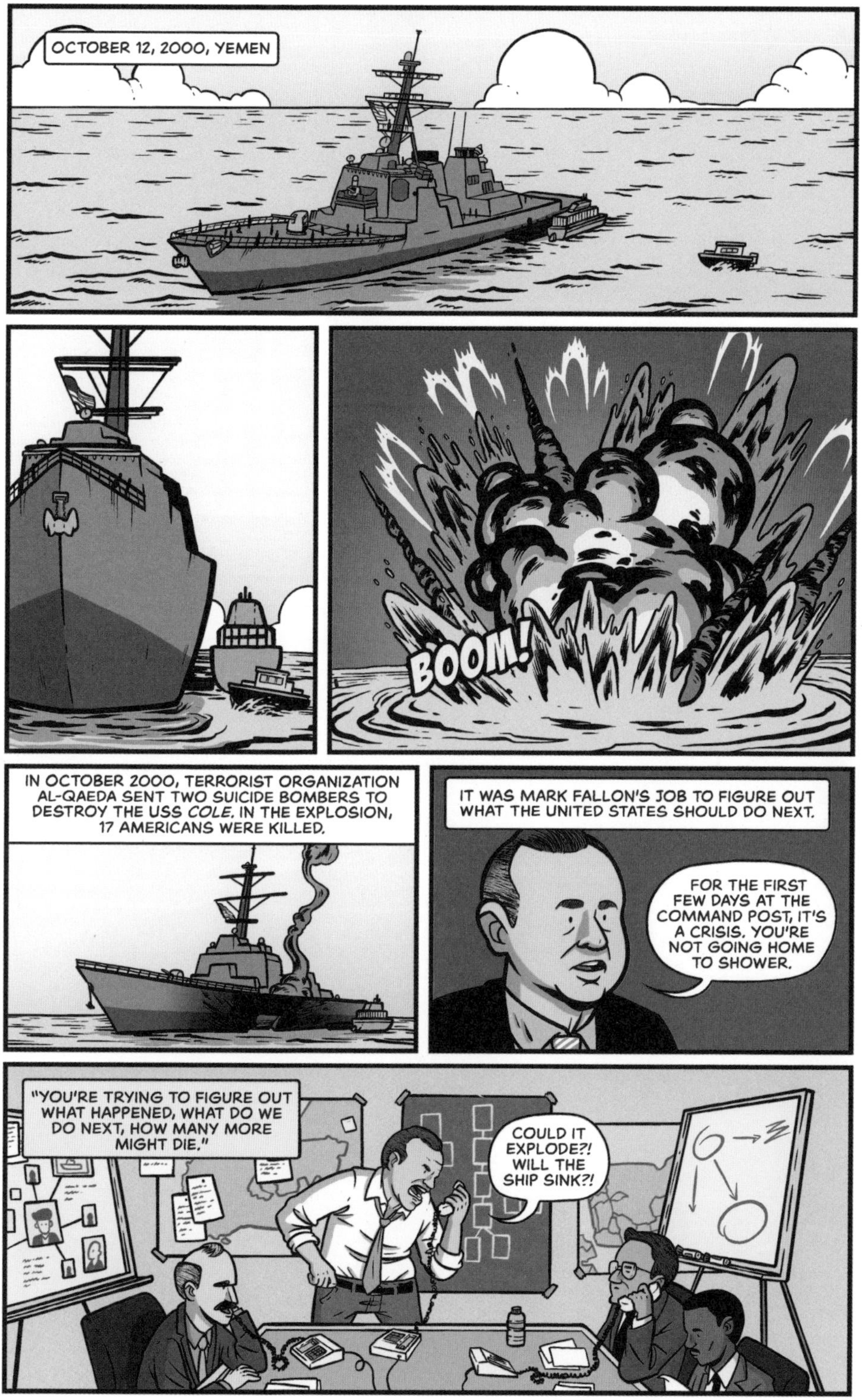
OCTOBER 12, 2000, YEMEN
BOOM!
IN OCTOBER 2000, TERRORIST ORGANIZATION AL-QAEDA SENT TWO SUICIDE BOMBERS TO DESTROY THE USS *COLE*. IN THE EXPLOSION, 17 AMERICANS WERE KILLED.
IT WAS MARK FALLON'S JOB TO FIGURE OUT WHAT THE UNITED STATES SHOULD DO NEXT.
FOR THE FIRST FEW DAYS AT THE COMMAND POST, IT'S A CRISIS. YOU'RE NOT GOING HOME TO SHOWER.
"YOU'RE TRYING TO FIGURE OUT WHAT HAPPENED, WHAT DO WE DO NEXT, HOW MANY MORE MIGHT DIE."
COULD IT EXPLODE?! WILL THE SHIP SINK?!

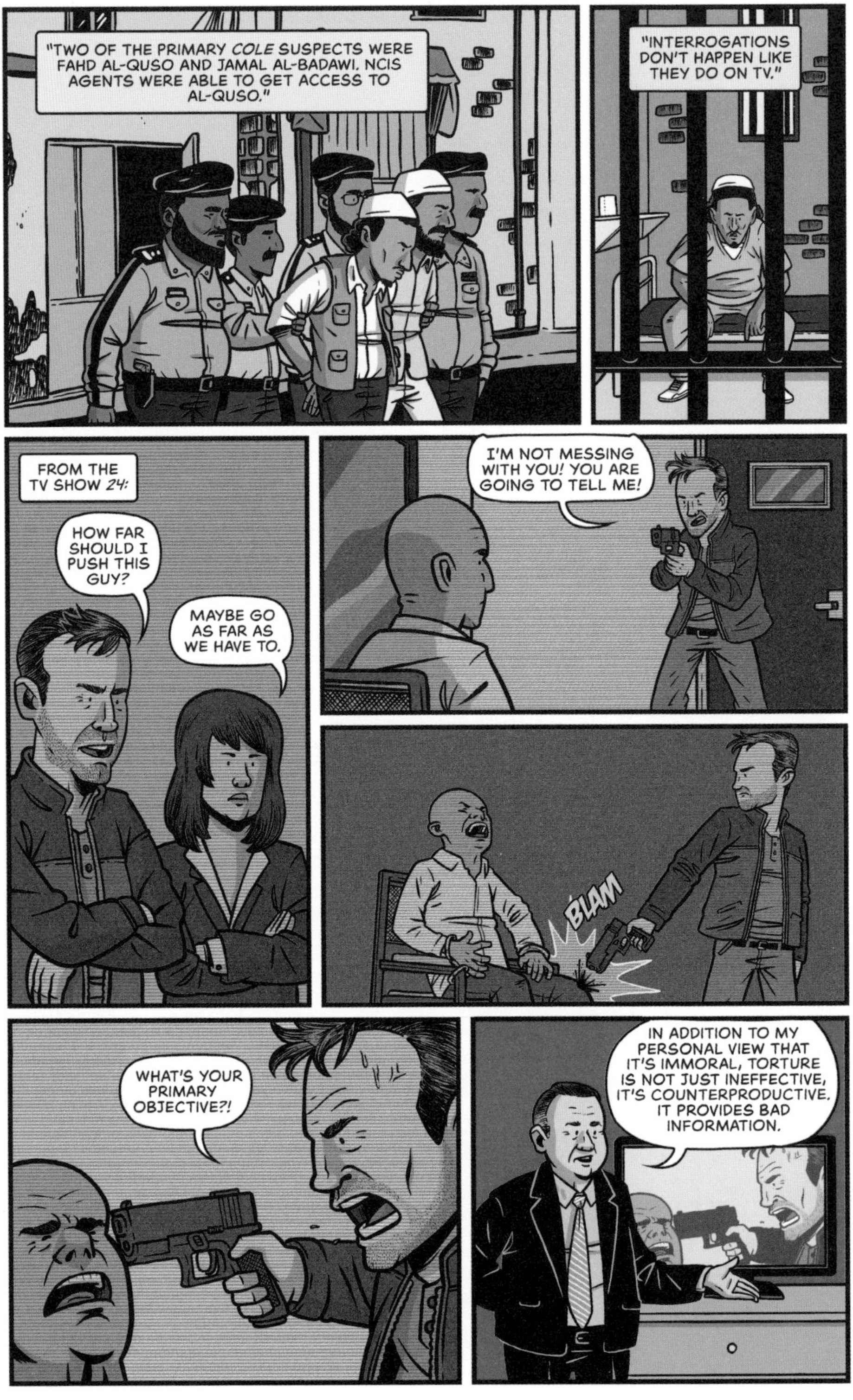
"TWO OF THE PRIMARY *COLE* SUSPECTS WERE FAHD AL-QUSO AND JAMAL AL-BADAWI. NCIS AGENTS WERE ABLE TO GET ACCESS TO AL-QUSO."
"INTERROGATIONS DON'T HAPPEN LIKE THEY DO ON TV."
FROM THE TV SHOW *24*:
HOW FAR SHOULD I PUSH THIS GUY?
MAYBE GO AS FAR AS WE HAVE TO.
I'M NOT MESSING WITH YOU! YOU ARE GOING TO TELL ME!
BLAM
WHAT'S YOUR PRIMARY OBJECTIVE?!
IN ADDITION TO MY PERSONAL VIEW THAT IT'S IMMORAL, TORTURE IS NOT JUST INEFFECTIVE, IT'S COUNTERPRODUCTIVE. IT PROVIDES BAD INFORMATION.

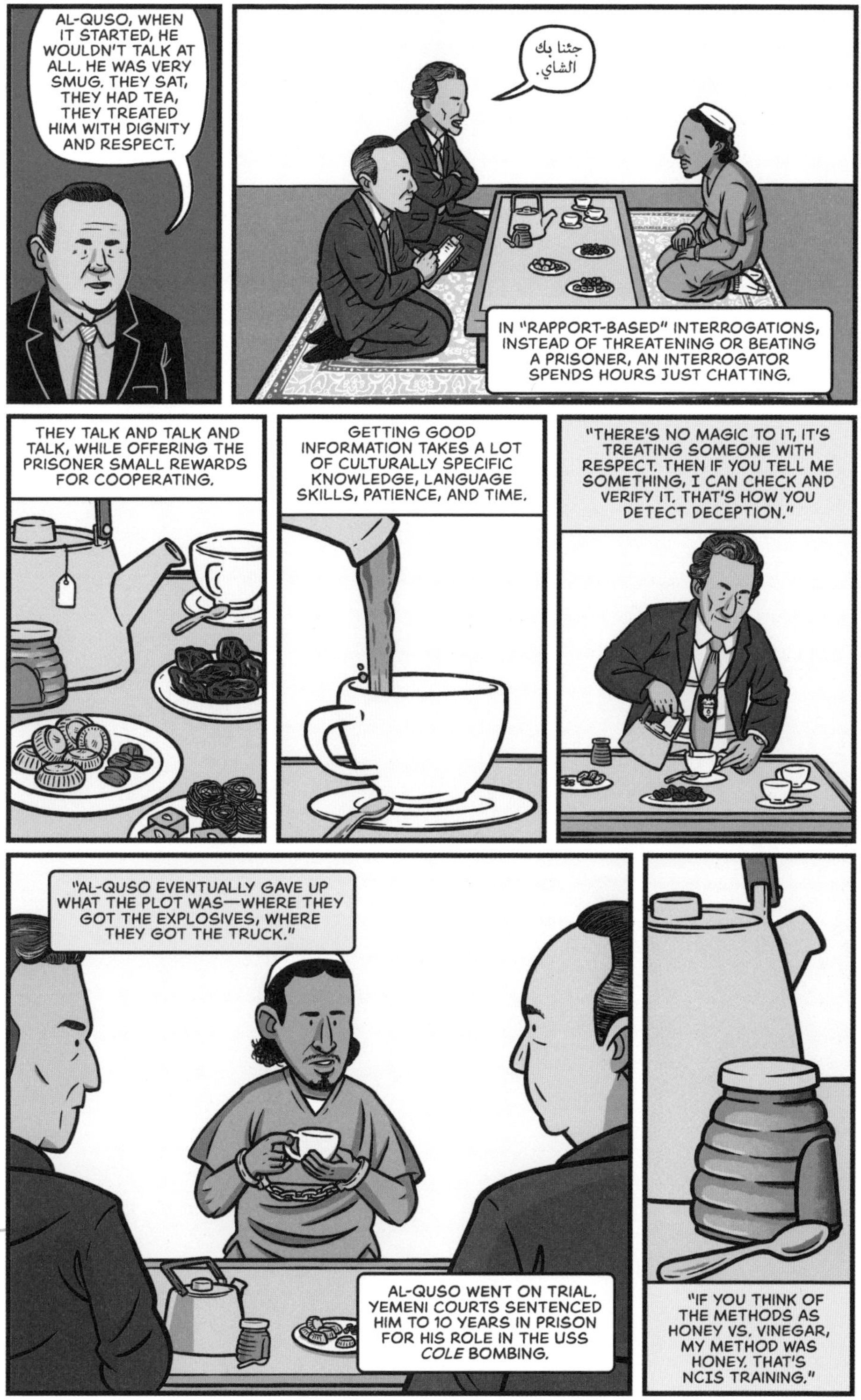
AL-QUSO, WHEN IT STARTED, HE WOULDN'T TALK AT ALL. HE WAS VERY SMUG. THEY SAT, THEY HAD TEA, THEY TREATED HIM WITH DIGNITY AND RESPECT.
جئنا بك الشاي.
IN "RAPPORT-BASED" INTERROGATIONS, INSTEAD OF THREATENING OR BEATING A PRISONER, AN INTERROGATOR SPENDS HOURS JUST CHATTING.
THEY TALK AND TALK AND TALK, WHILE OFFERING THE PRISONER SMALL REWARDS FOR COOPERATING.
GETTING GOOD INFORMATION TAKES A LOT OF CULTURALLY SPECIFIC KNOWLEDGE, LANGUAGE SKILLS, PATIENCE, AND TIME.
"THERE'S NO MAGIC TO IT, IT'S TREATING SOMEONE WITH RESPECT. THEN IF YOU TELL ME SOMETHING, I CAN CHECK AND VERIFY IT. THAT'S HOW YOU DETECT DECEPTION."
"AL-QUSO EVENTUALLY GAVE UP WHAT THE PLOT WAS—WHERE THEY GOT THE EXPLOSIVES, WHERE THEY GOT THE TRUCK."
AL-QUSO WENT ON TRIAL. YEMENI COURTS SENTENCED HIM TO 10 YEARS IN PRISON FOR HIS ROLE IN THE USS *COLE* BOMBING.
"IF YOU THINK OF THE METHODS AS HONEY VS. VINEGAR, MY METHOD WAS HONEY. THAT'S NCIS TRAINING."

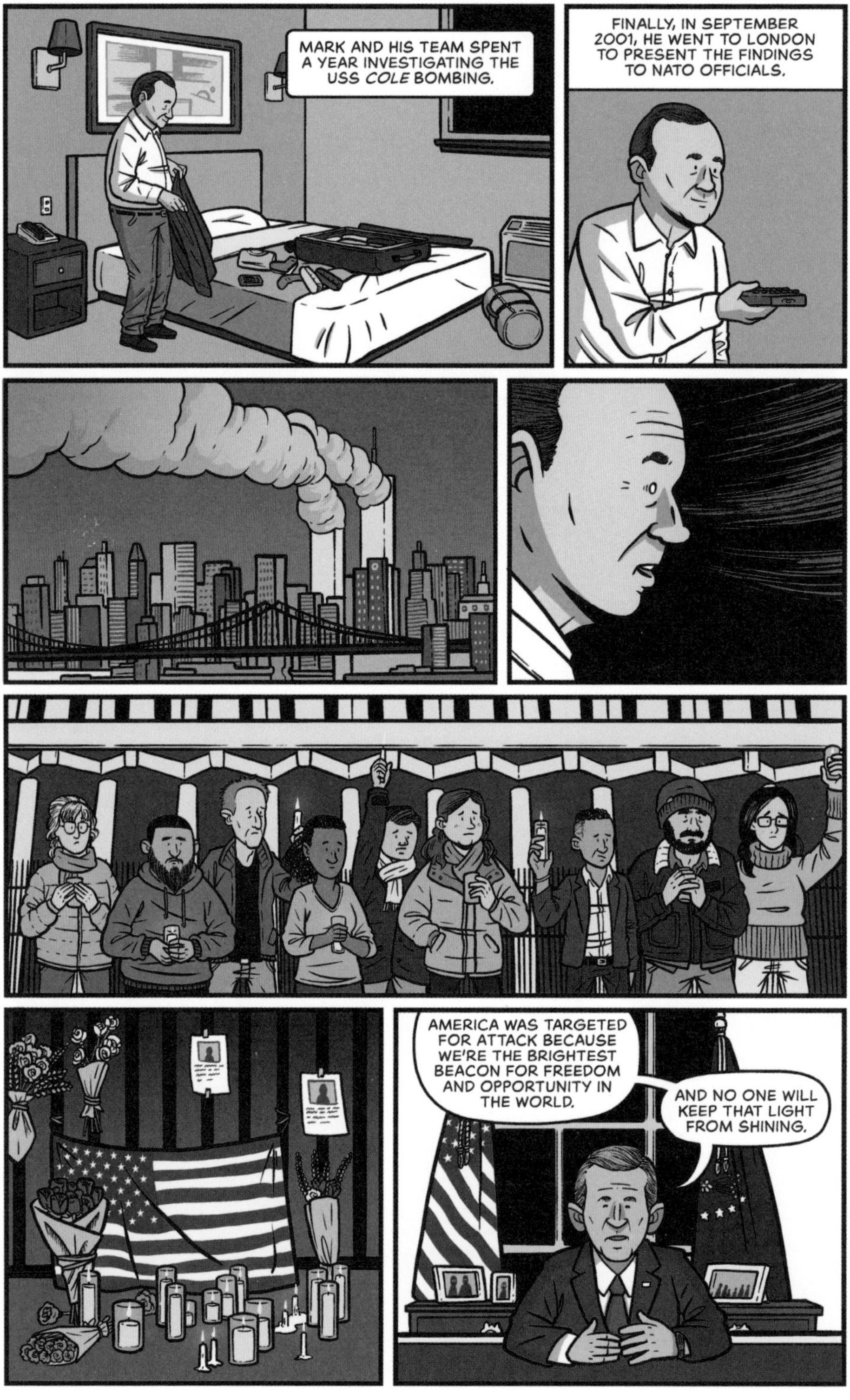
MARK AND HIS TEAM SPENT A YEAR INVESTIGATING THE USS *COLE* BOMBING.
FINALLY, IN SEPTEMBER 2001, HE WENT TO LONDON TO PRESENT THE FINDINGS TO NATO OFFICIALS.
AMERICA WAS TARGETED FOR ATTACK BECAUSE WE'RE THE BRIGHTEST BEACON FOR FREEDOM AND OPPORTUNITY IN THE WORLD.
AND NO ONE WILL KEEP THAT LIGHT FROM SHINING.

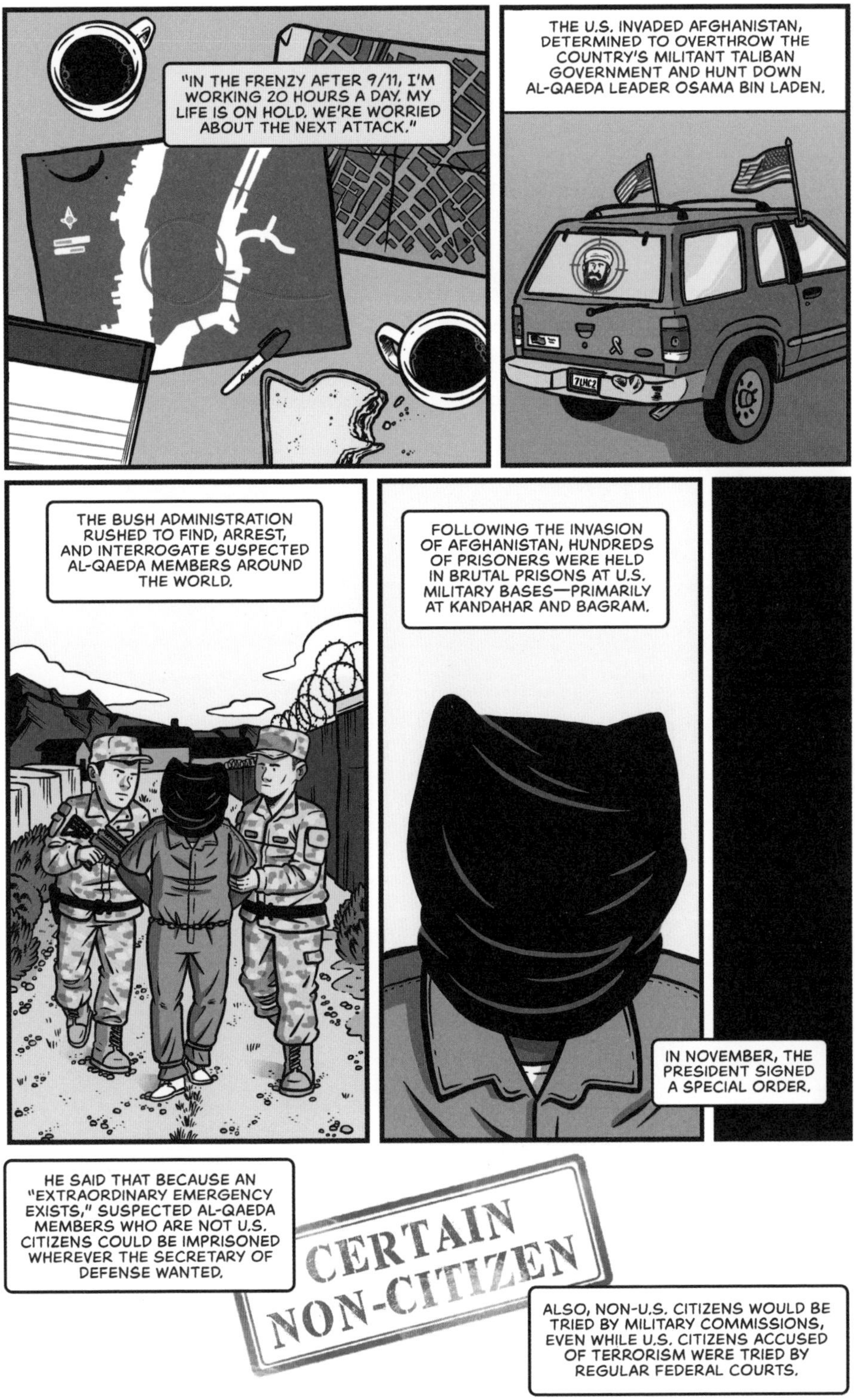
"IN THE FRENZY AFTER 9/11, I'M WORKING 20 HOURS A DAY. MY LIFE IS ON HOLD. WE'RE WORRIED ABOUT THE NEXT ATTACK."
THE U.S. INVADED AFGHANISTAN, DETERMINED TO OVERTHROW THE COUNTRY'S MILITANT TALIBAN GOVERNMENT AND HUNT DOWN AL-QAEDA LEADER OSAMA BIN LADEN.
THE BUSH ADMINISTRATION RUSHED TO FIND, ARREST, AND INTERROGATE SUSPECTED AL-QAEDA MEMBERS AROUND THE WORLD.
FOLLOWING THE INVASION OF AFGHANISTAN, HUNDREDS OF PRISONERS WERE HELD IN BRUTAL PRISONS AT U.S. MILITARY BASES—PRIMARILY AT KANDAHAR AND BAGRAM.
IN NOVEMBER, THE PRESIDENT SIGNED A SPECIAL ORDER.
HE SAID THAT BECAUSE AN "EXTRAORDINARY EMERGENCY EXISTS," SUSPECTED AL-QAEDA MEMBERS WHO ARE NOT U.S. CITIZENS COULD BE IMPRISONED WHEREVER THE SECRETARY OF DEFENSE WANTED.
CERTAIN NON-CITIZEN
ALSO, NON-U.S. CITIZENS WOULD BE TRIED BY MILITARY COMMISSIONS, EVEN WHILE U.S. CITIZENS ACCUSED OF TERRORISM WERE TRIED BY REGULAR FEDERAL COURTS.

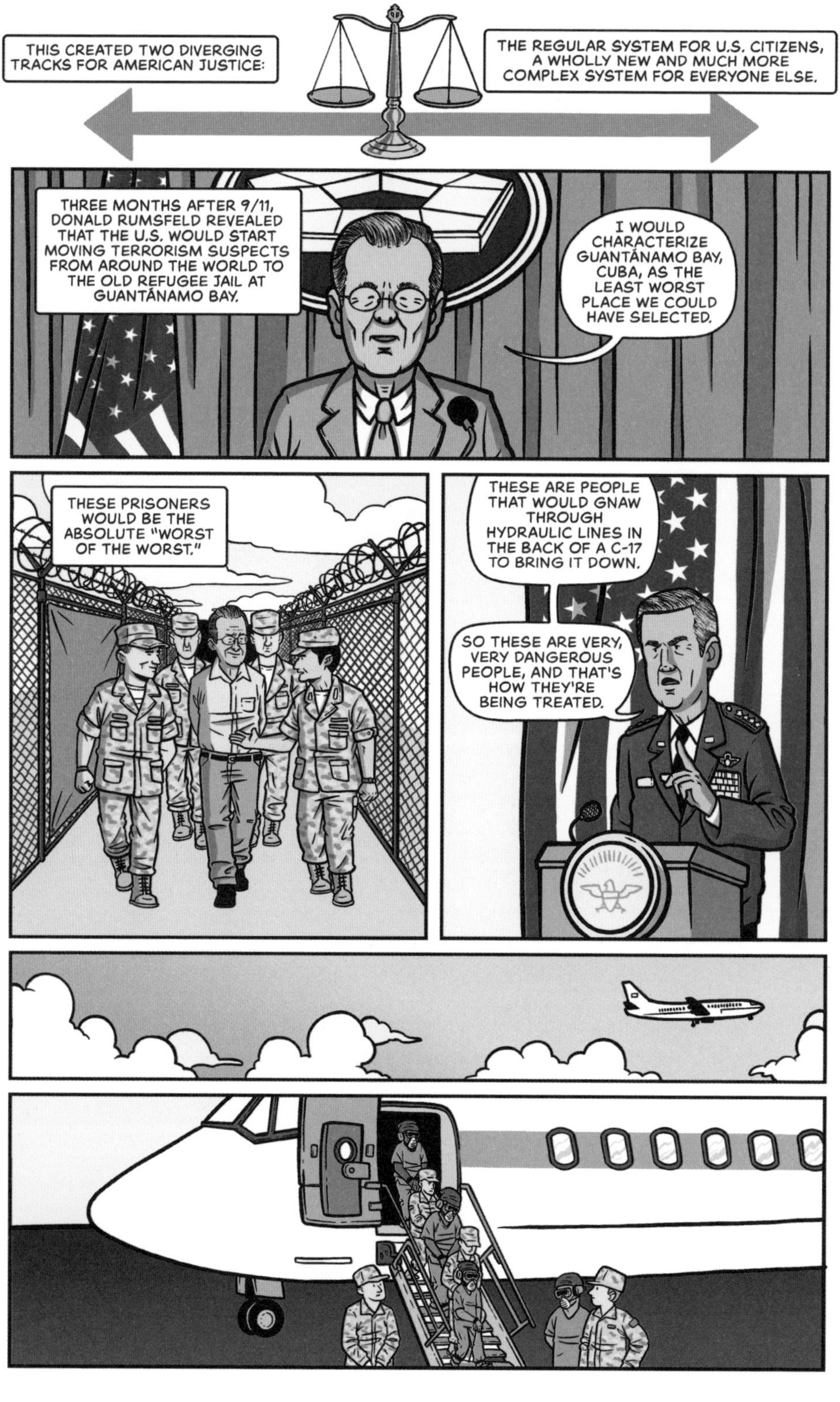
THIS CREATED TWO DIVERGING TRACKS FOR AMERICAN JUSTICE:
THE REGULAR SYSTEM FOR U.S. CITIZENS, A WHOLLY NEW AND MUCH MORE COMPLEX SYSTEM FOR EVERYONE ELSE.
THREE MONTHS AFTER 9/11, DONALD RUMSFELD REVEALED THAT THE U.S. WOULD START MOVING TERRORISM SUSPECTS FROM AROUND THE WORLD TO THE OLD REFUGEE JAIL AT GUANTÁNAMO BAY.
I WOULD CHARACTERIZE GUANTÁNAMO BAY, CUBA, AS THE LEAST WORST PLACE WE COULD HAVE SELECTED.
THESE PRISONERS WOULD BE THE ABSOLUTE "WORST OF THE WORST."
THESE ARE PEOPLE THAT WOULD GNAW THROUGH HYDRAULIC LINES IN THE BACK OF A C-17 TO BRING IT DOWN.
SO THESE ARE VERY, VERY DANGEROUS PEOPLE, AND THAT'S HOW THEY'RE BEING TREATED.

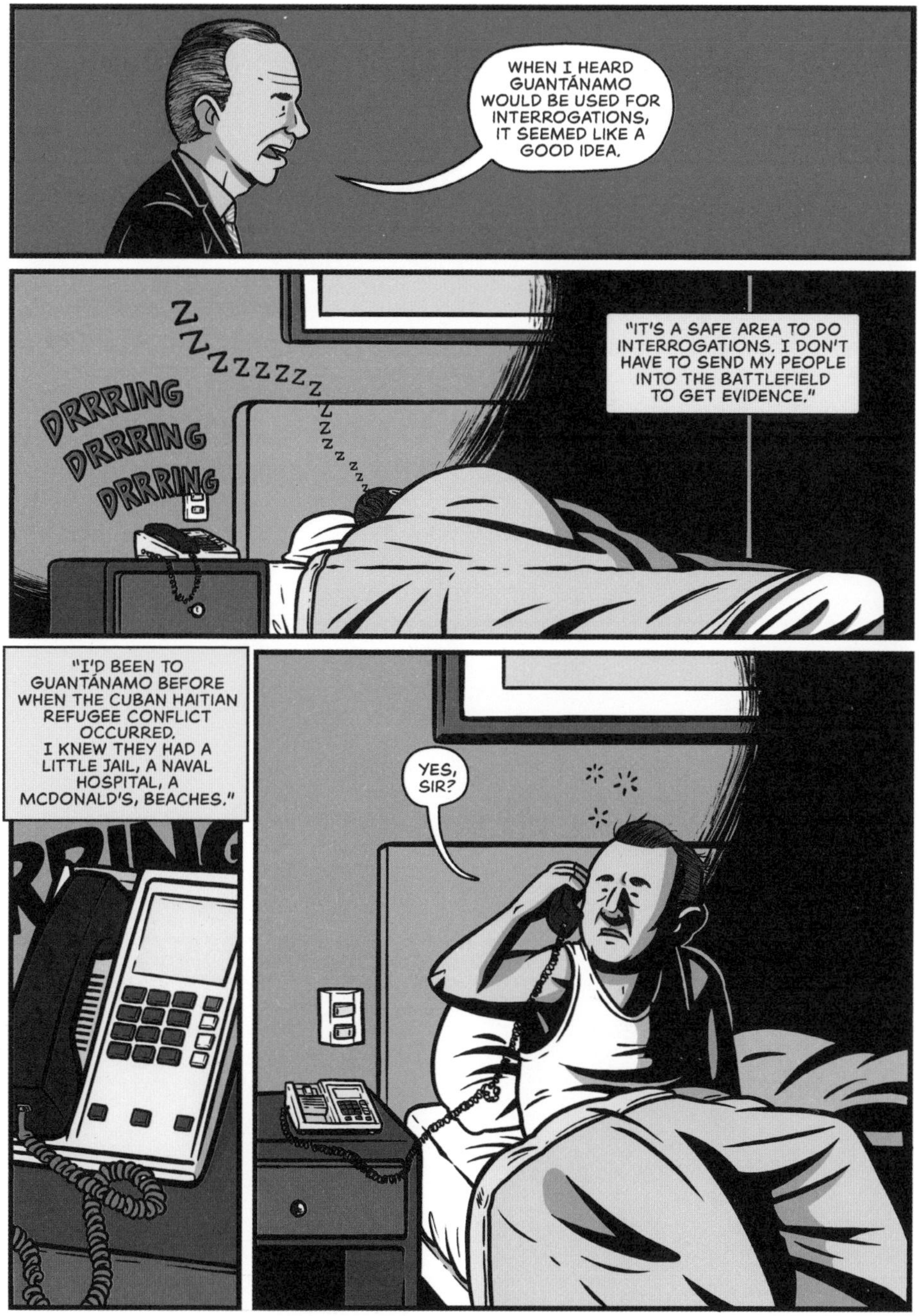
WHEN I HEARD GUANTÁNAMO WOULD BE USED FOR INTERROGATIONS, IT SEEMED LIKE A GOOD IDEA.
"IT'S A SAFE AREA TO DO INTERROGATIONS. I DON'T HAVE TO SEND MY PEOPLE INTO THE BATTLEFIELD TO GET EVIDENCE."
ZZZZZZZZZZZZZZ
DRRRING
DRRRING
DRRRING
"I'D BEEN TO GUANTÁNAMO BEFORE WHEN THE CUBAN HAITIAN REFUGEE CONFLICT OCCURRED. I KNEW THEY HAD A LITTLE JAIL, A NAVAL HOSPITAL, A MCDONALD'S, BEACHES."
YES, SIR?

MARK WAS ASKED TO BECOME CHIEF INVESTIGATOR FOR THE MILITARY COMMISSION PROCESS—BASICALLY, LEADING INVESTIGATIONS TO FIND EVIDENCE THAT COULD BE USED TO PROSECUTE GUANTÁNAMO PRISONERS IN MILITARY COURTS.

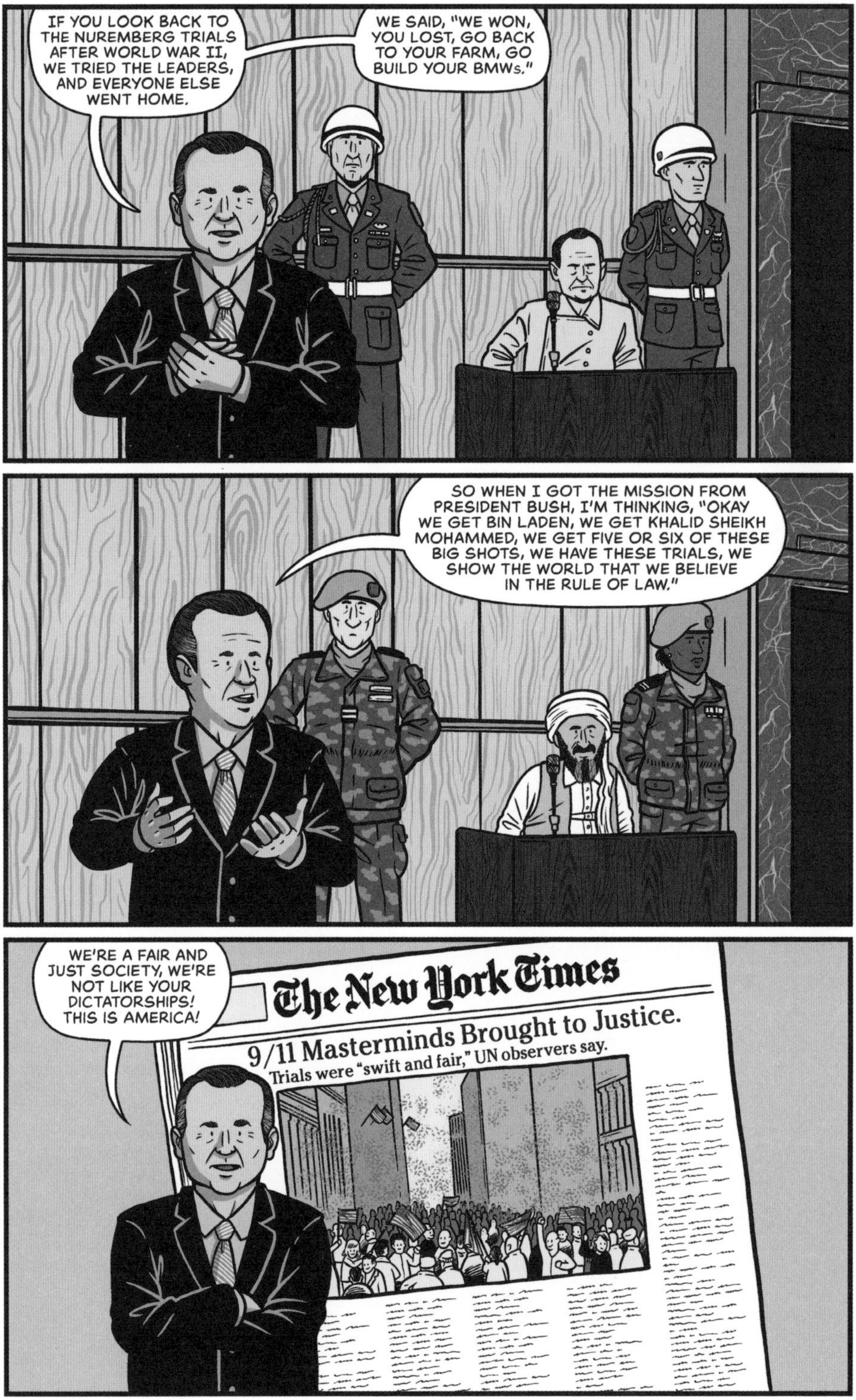
IF YOU LOOK BACK TO THE NUREMBERG TRIALS AFTER WORLD WAR II, WE TRIED THE LEADERS, AND EVERYONE ELSE WENT HOME.
WE SAID, "WE WON, YOU LOST, GO BACK TO YOUR FARM, GO BUILD YOUR BMWs."
SO WHEN I GOT THE MISSION FROM PRESIDENT BUSH, I'M THINKING, "OKAY WE GET BIN LADEN, WE GET KHALID SHEIKH MOHAMMED, WE GET FIVE OR SIX OF THESE BIG SHOTS, WE HAVE THESE TRIALS, WE SHOW THE WORLD THAT WE BELIEVE IN THE RULE OF LAW."
WE'RE A FAIR AND JUST SOCIETY, WE'RE NOT LIKE YOUR DICTATORSHIPS! THIS IS AMERICA!
The New York Times
9/11 Masterminds Brought to Justice.
Trials were "swift and fair," UN observers say.

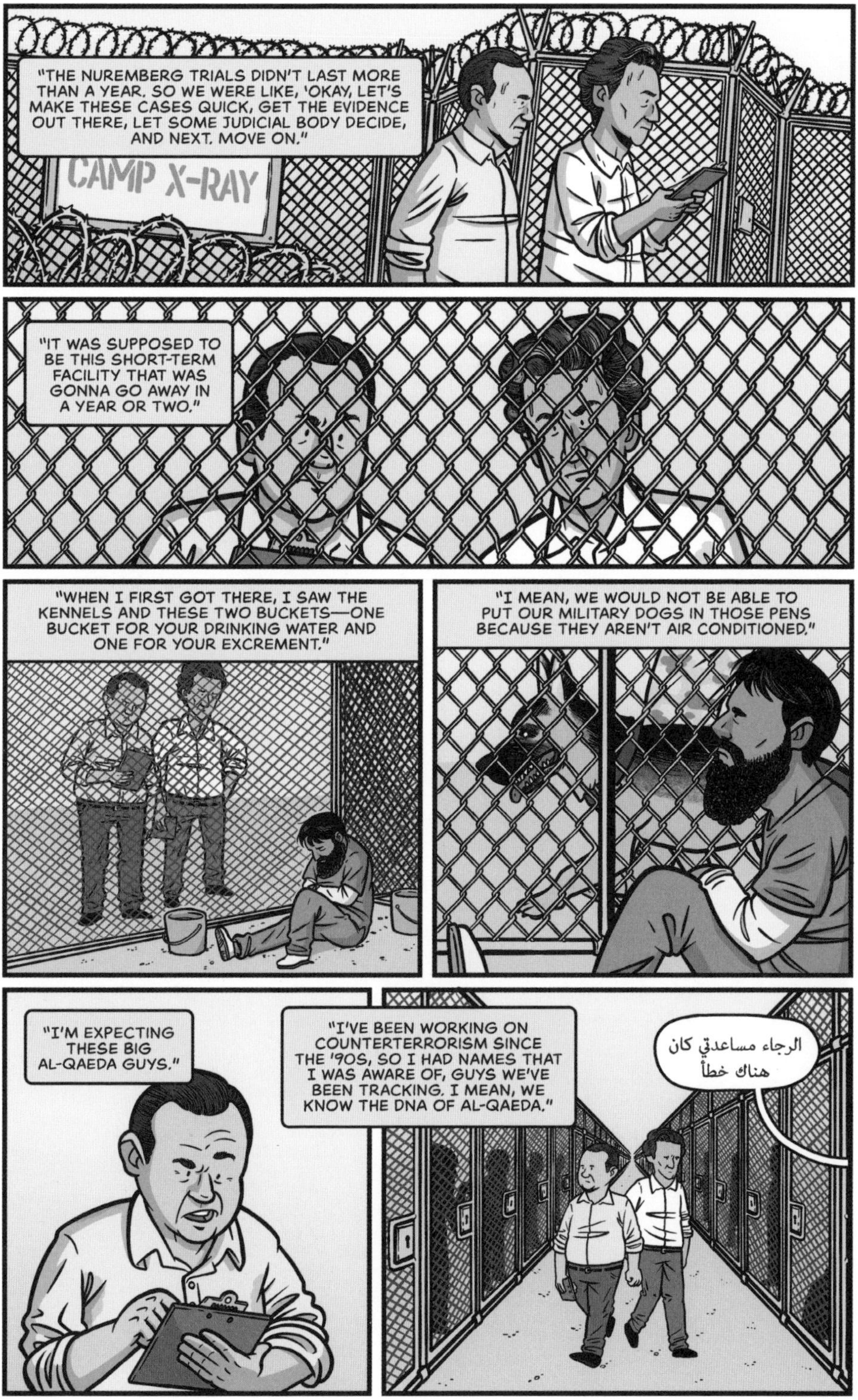
"THE NUREMBERG TRIALS DIDN'T LAST MORE THAN A YEAR. SO WE WERE LIKE, 'OKAY, LET'S MAKE THESE CASES QUICK, GET THE EVIDENCE OUT THERE, LET SOME JUDICIAL BODY DECIDE, AND NEXT. MOVE ON."
CAMP X-RAY
"IT WAS SUPPOSED TO BE THIS SHORT-TERM FACILITY THAT WAS GONNA GO AWAY IN A YEAR OR TWO."
"WHEN I FIRST GOT THERE, I SAW THE KENNELS AND THESE TWO BUCKETS—ONE BUCKET FOR YOUR DRINKING WATER AND ONE FOR YOUR EXCREMENT."
"I MEAN, WE WOULD NOT BE ABLE TO PUT OUR MILITARY DOGS IN THOSE PENS BECAUSE THEY AREN'T AIR CONDITIONED."
"I'M EXPECTING THESE BIG AL-QAEDA GUYS."
"I'VE BEEN WORKING ON COUNTERTERRORISM SINCE THE '90S, SO I HAD NAMES THAT I WAS AWARE OF, GUYS WE'VE BEEN TRACKING. I MEAN, WE KNOW THE DNA OF AL-QAEDA."
الرجاء مساعدتي كان هناك خطأ

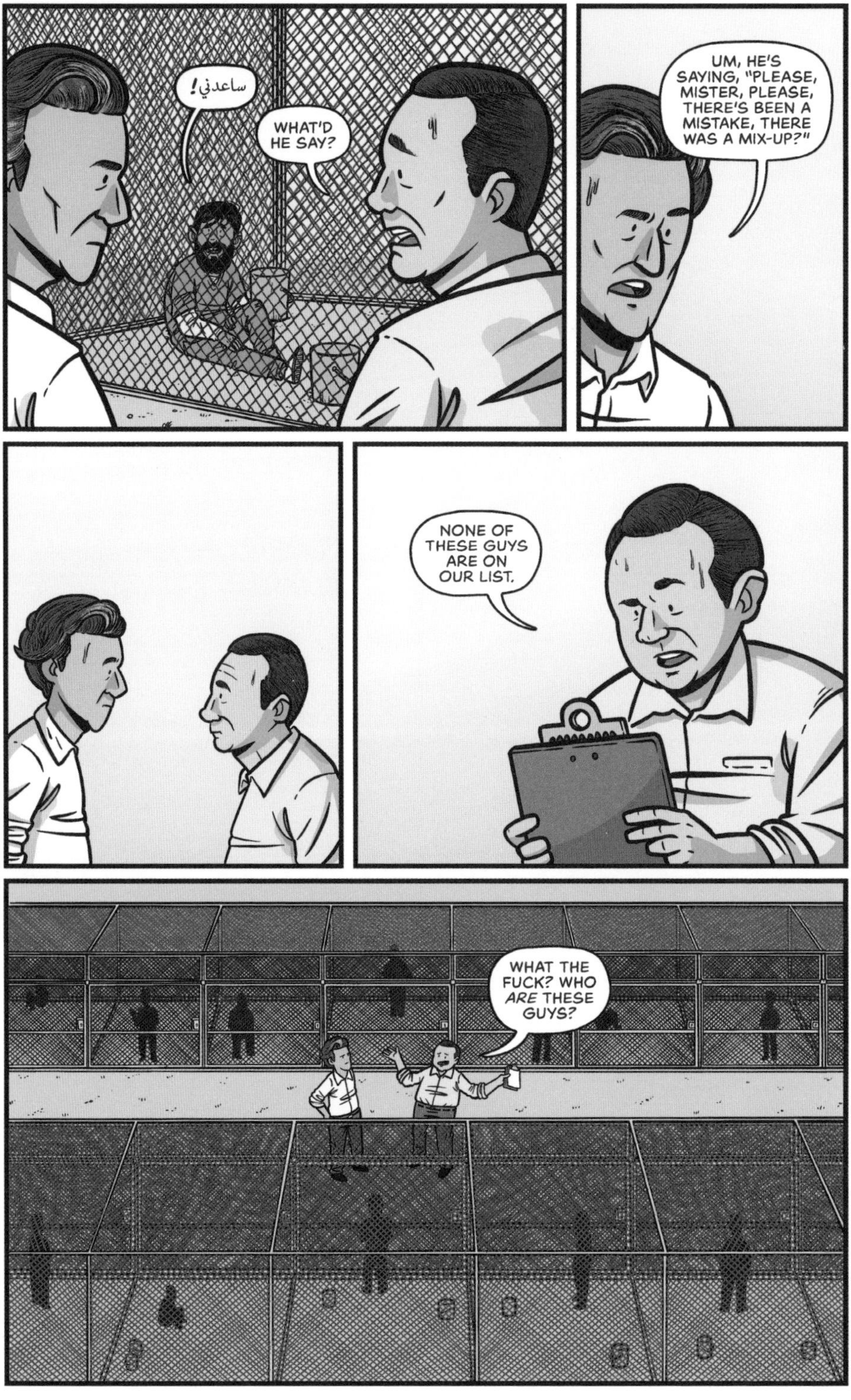

ساعدني!
WHAT'D HE SAY?
UM, HE'S SAYING, "PLEASE, MISTER, PLEASE, THERE'S BEEN A MISTAKE, THERE WAS A MIX-UP?"
NONE OF THESE GUYS ARE ON OUR LIST.
WHAT THE FUCK? WHO *ARE* THESE GUYS?

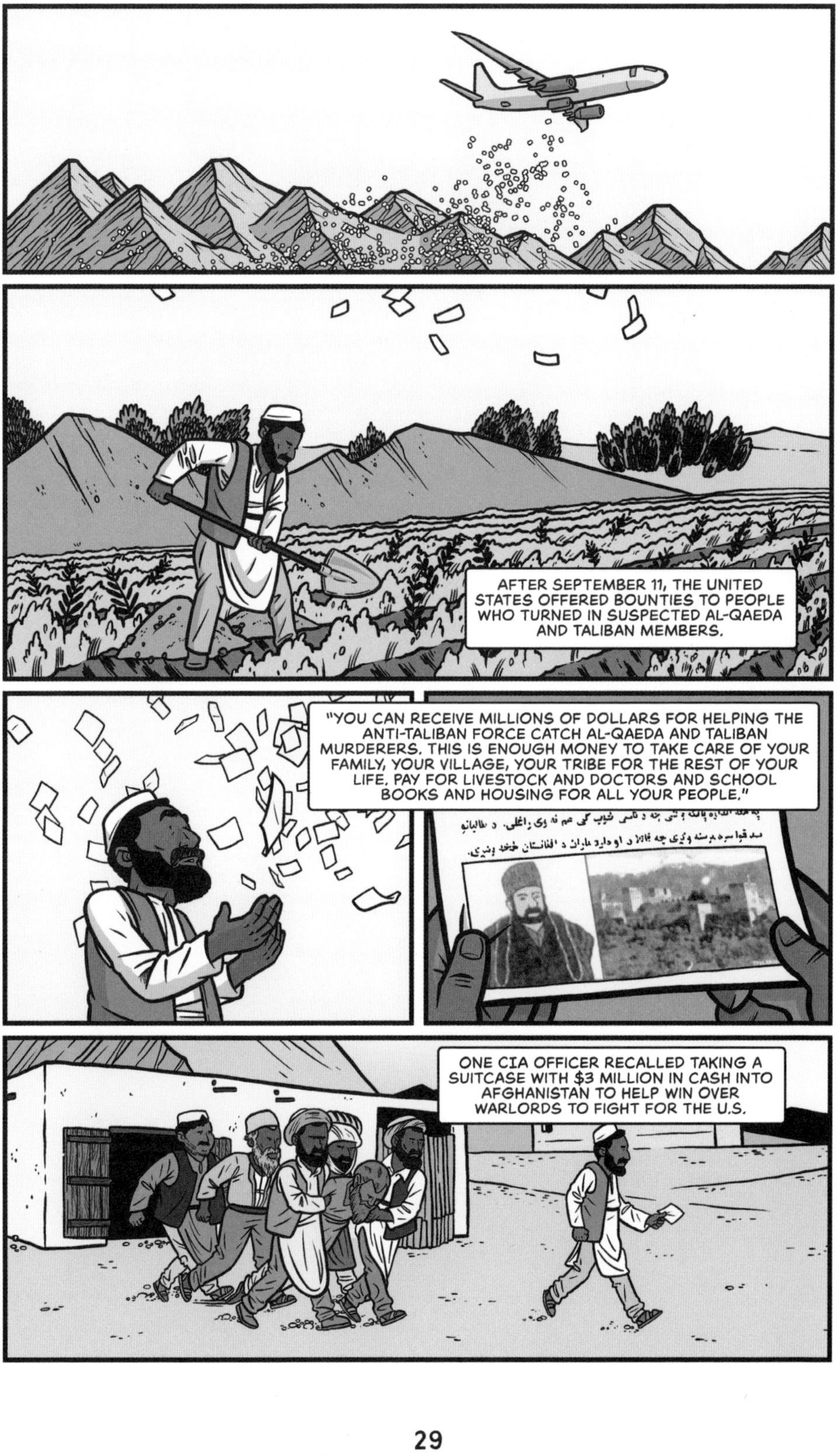
AFTER SEPTEMBER 11, THE UNITED STATES OFFERED BOUNTIES TO PEOPLE WHO TURNED IN SUSPECTED AL-QAEDA AND TALIBAN MEMBERS.
"YOU CAN RECEIVE MILLIONS OF DOLLARS FOR HELPING THE ANTI-TALIBAN FORCE CATCH AL-QAEDA AND TALIBAN MURDERERS. THIS IS ENOUGH MONEY TO TAKE CARE OF YOUR FAMILY, YOUR VILLAGE, YOUR TRIBE FOR THE REST OF YOUR LIFE. PAY FOR LIVESTOCK AND DOCTORS AND SCHOOL BOOKS AND HOUSING FOR ALL YOUR PEOPLE."
ONE CIA OFFICER RECALLED TAKING A SUITCASE WITH $3 MILLION IN CASH INTO AFGHANISTAN TO HELP WIN OVER WARLORDS TO FIGHT FOR THE U.S.

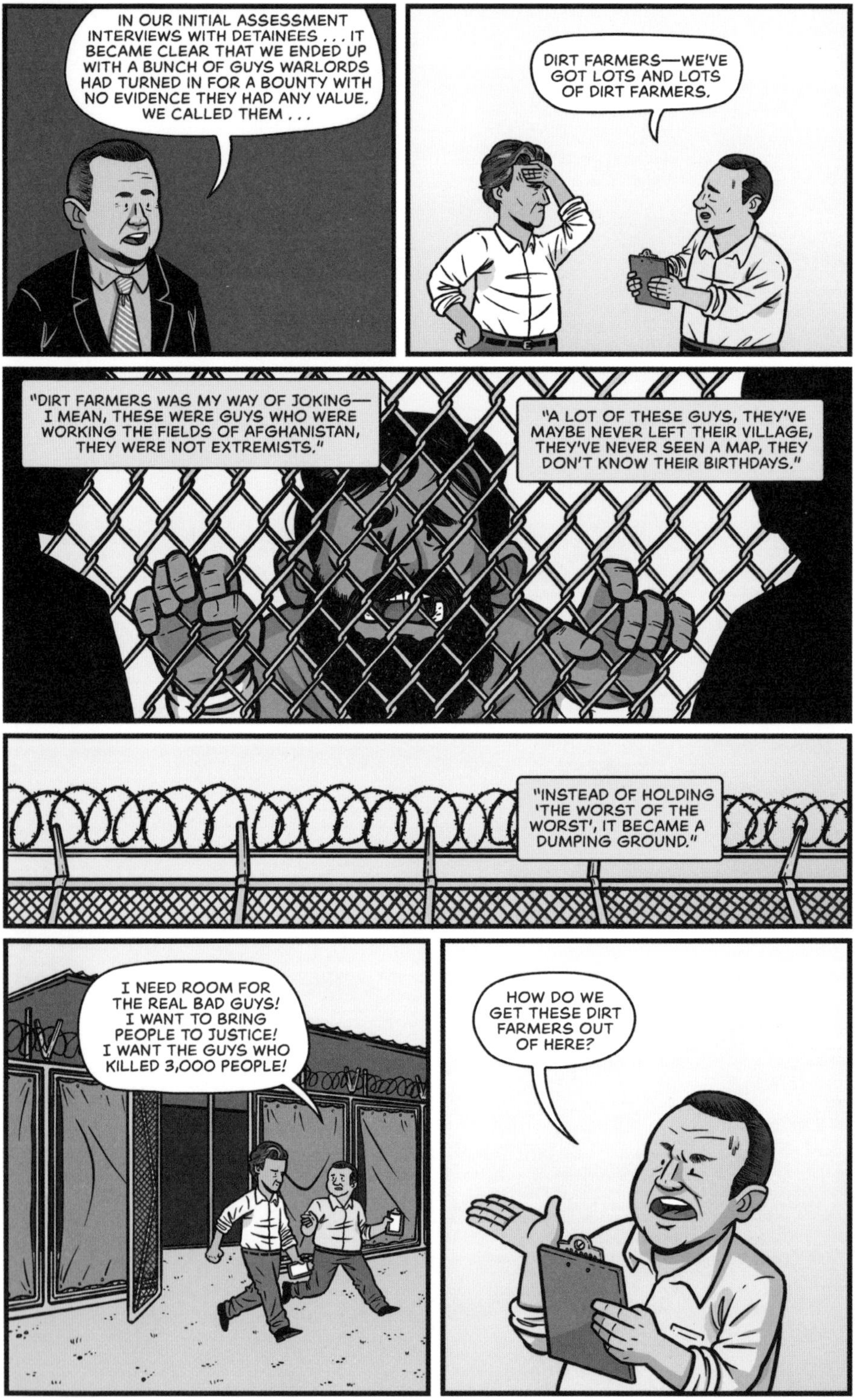
IN OUR INITIAL ASSESSMENT INTERVIEWS WITH DETAINEES . . . IT BECAME CLEAR THAT WE ENDED UP WITH A BUNCH OF GUYS WARLORDS HAD TURNED IN FOR A BOUNTY WITH NO EVIDENCE THEY HAD ANY VALUE. WE CALLED THEM . . .
DIRT FARMERS—WE'VE GOT LOTS AND LOTS OF DIRT FARMERS.
"DIRT FARMERS WAS MY WAY OF JOKING—I MEAN, THESE WERE GUYS WHO WERE WORKING THE FIELDS OF AFGHANISTAN, THEY WERE NOT EXTREMISTS."
"A LOT OF THESE GUYS, THEY'VE MAYBE NEVER LEFT THEIR VILLAGE, THEY'VE NEVER SEEN A MAP, THEY DON'T KNOW THEIR BIRTHDAYS."
"INSTEAD OF HOLDING 'THE WORST OF THE WORST', IT BECAME A DUMPING GROUND."
I NEED ROOM FOR THE REAL BAD GUYS! I WANT TO BRING PEOPLE TO JUSTICE! I WANT THE GUYS WHO KILLED 3,000 PEOPLE!
HOW DO WE GET THESE DIRT FARMERS OUT OF HERE?

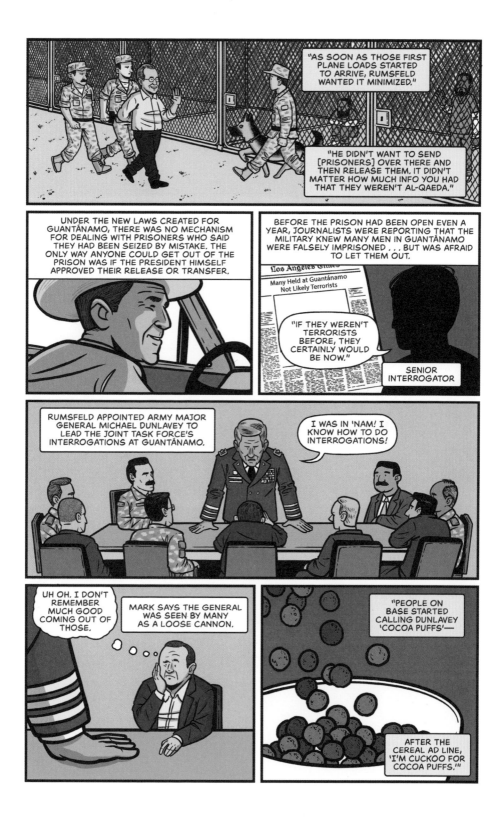

"AS SOON AS THOSE FIRST PLANE LOADS STARTED TO ARRIVE, RUMSFELD WANTED IT MINIMIZED."

"HE DIDN'T WANT TO SEND [PRISONERS] OVER THERE AND THEN RELEASE THEM. IT DIDN'T MATTER HOW MUCH INFO YOU HAD THAT THEY WEREN'T AL-QAEDA."

UNDER THE NEW LAWS CREATED FOR GUANTÁNAMO, THERE WAS NO MECHANISM FOR DEALING WITH PRISONERS WHO SAID THEY HAD BEEN SEIZED BY MISTAKE. THE ONLY WAY ANYONE COULD GET OUT OF THE PRISON WAS IF THE PRESIDENT HIMSELF APPROVED THEIR RELEASE OR TRANSFER.

BEFORE THE PRISON HAD BEEN OPEN EVEN A YEAR, JOURNALISTS WERE REPORTING THAT THE MILITARY KNEW MANY MEN IN GUANTÁNAMO WERE FALSELY IMPRISONED . . . BUT WAS AFRAID TO LET THEM OUT.

Los Angeles Times

Many Held at Guantánamo Not Likely Terrorists

"IF THEY WEREN'T TERRORISTS BEFORE, THEY CERTAINLY WOULD BE NOW."

SENIOR INTERROGATOR

RUMSFELD APPOINTED ARMY MAJOR GENERAL MICHAEL DUNLAVEY TO LEAD THE JOINT TASK FORCE'S INTERROGATIONS AT GUANTÁNAMO.

I WAS IN 'NAM! I KNOW HOW TO DO INTERROGATIONS!

UH OH. I DON'T REMEMBER MUCH GOOD COMING OUT OF THOSE.

MARK SAYS THE GENERAL WAS SEEN BY MANY AS A LOOSE CANNON.

"PEOPLE ON BASE STARTED CALLING DUNLAVEY 'COCOA PUFFS'—

AFTER THE CEREAL AD LINE, 'I'M CUCKOO FOR COCOA PUFFS.'"

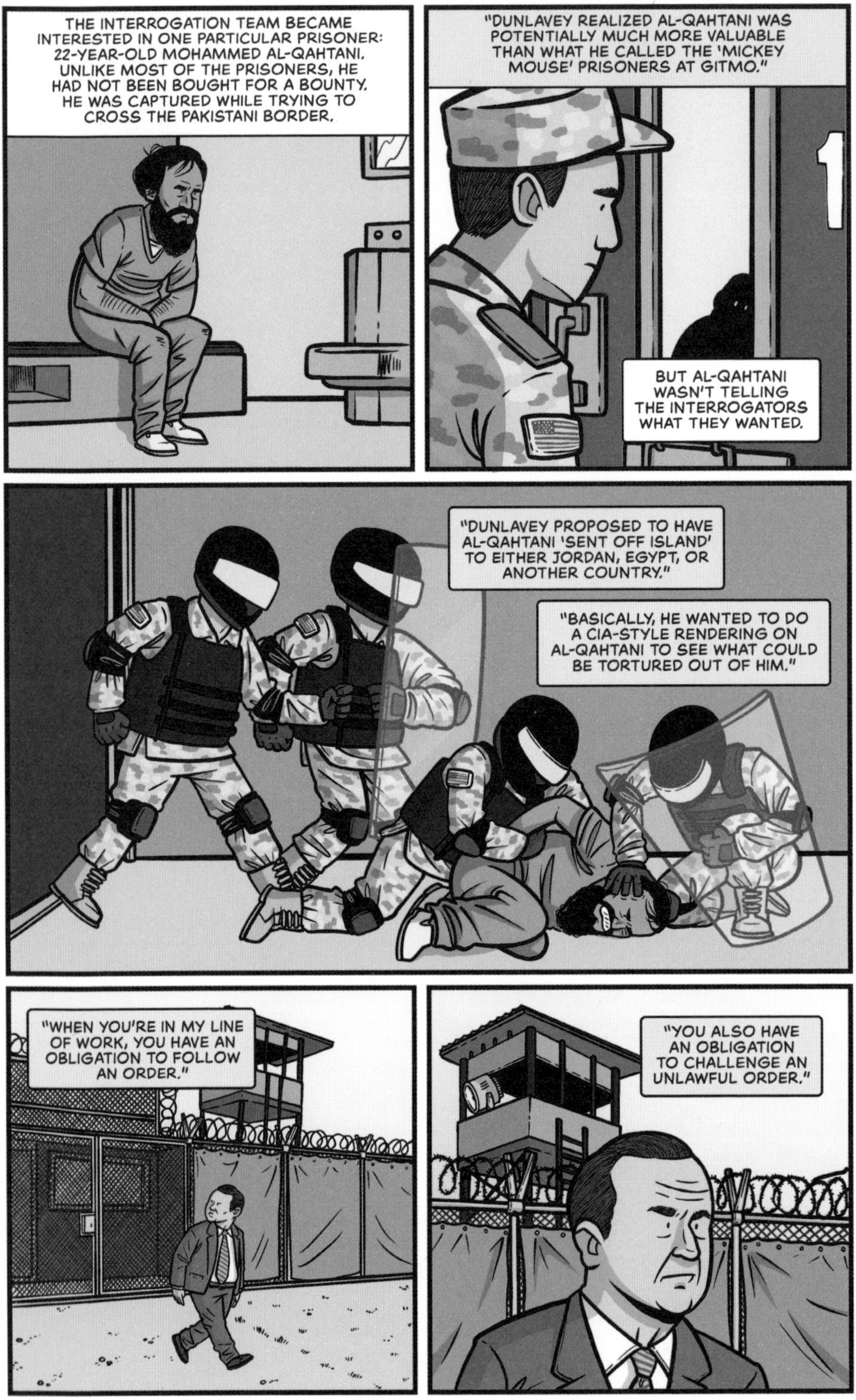
THE INTERROGATION TEAM BECAME INTERESTED IN ONE PARTICULAR PRISONER: 22-YEAR-OLD MOHAMMED AL-QAHTANI. UNLIKE MOST OF THE PRISONERS, HE HAD NOT BEEN BOUGHT FOR A BOUNTY. HE WAS CAPTURED WHILE TRYING TO CROSS THE PAKISTANI BORDER.
"DUNLAVEY REALIZED AL-QAHTANI WAS POTENTIALLY MUCH MORE VALUABLE THAN WHAT HE CALLED THE 'MICKEY MOUSE' PRISONERS AT GITMO."
1
BUT AL-QAHTANI WASN'T TELLING THE INTERROGATORS WHAT THEY WANTED.
"DUNLAVEY PROPOSED TO HAVE AL-QAHTANI 'SENT OFF ISLAND' TO EITHER JORDAN, EGYPT, OR ANOTHER COUNTRY."
"BASICALLY, HE WANTED TO DO A CIA-STYLE RENDERING ON AL-QAHTANI TO SEE WHAT COULD BE TORTURED OUT OF HIM."
"WHEN YOU'RE IN MY LINE OF WORK, YOU HAVE AN OBLIGATION TO FOLLOW AN ORDER."
"YOU ALSO HAVE AN OBLIGATION TO CHALLENGE AN UNLAWFUL ORDER."

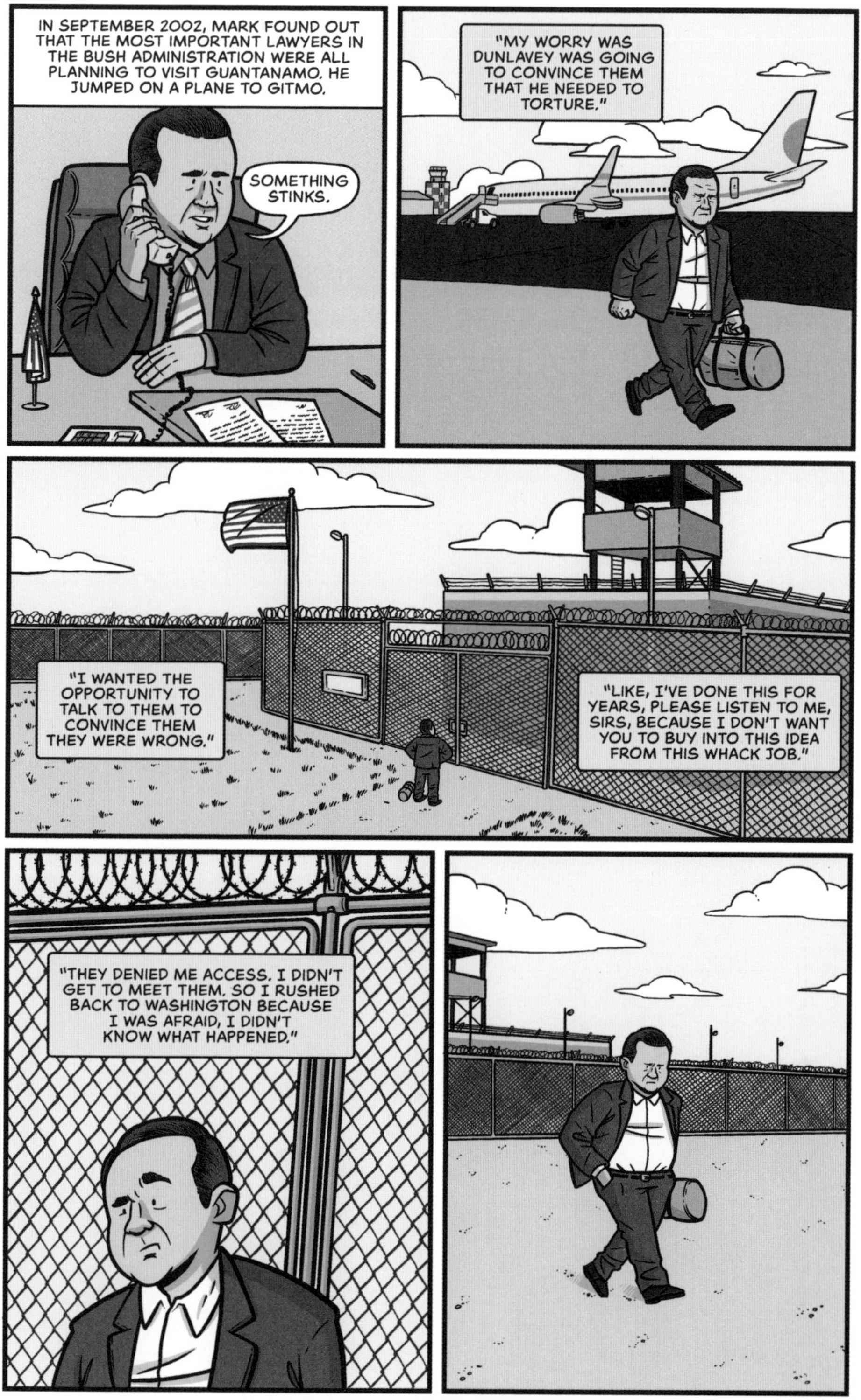
IN SEPTEMBER 2002, MARK FOUND OUT THAT THE MOST IMPORTANT LAWYERS IN THE BUSH ADMINISTRATION WERE ALL PLANNING TO VISIT GUANTANAMO. HE JUMPED ON A PLANE TO GITMO.
SOMETHING STINKS.
"MY WORRY WAS DUNLAVEY WAS GOING TO CONVINCE THEM THAT HE NEEDED TO TORTURE."
"I WANTED THE OPPORTUNITY TO TALK TO THEM TO CONVINCE THEM THEY WERE WRONG."
"LIKE, I'VE DONE THIS FOR YEARS, PLEASE LISTEN TO ME, SIRS, BECAUSE I DON'T WANT YOU TO BUY INTO THIS IDEA FROM THIS WHACK JOB."
"THEY DENIED ME ACCESS. I DIDN'T GET TO MEET THEM. SO I RUSHED BACK TO WASHINGTON BECAUSE I WAS AFRAID, I DIDN'T KNOW WHAT HAPPENED."

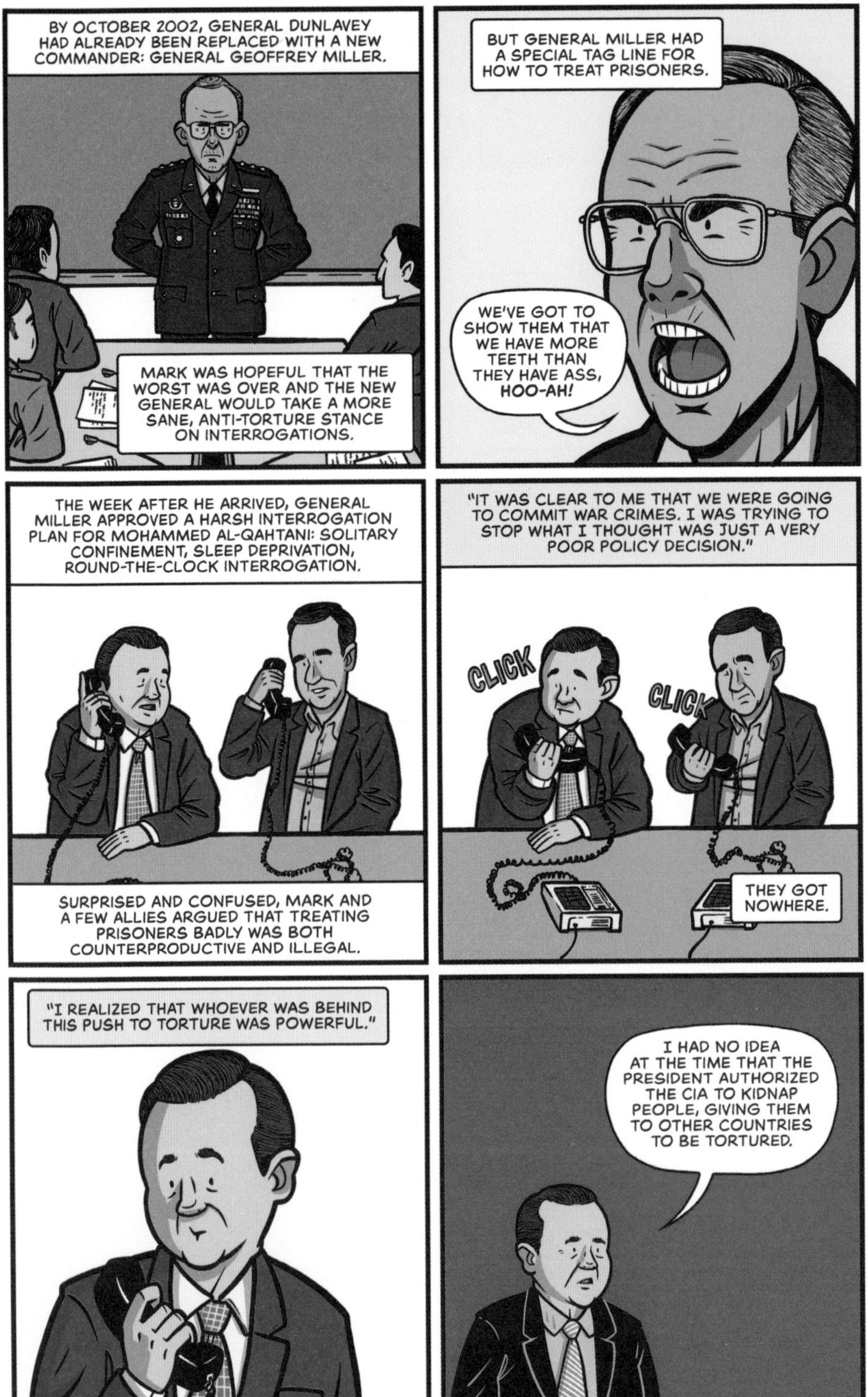
BY OCTOBER 2002, GENERAL DUNLAVEY HAD ALREADY BEEN REPLACED WITH A NEW COMMANDER: GENERAL GEOFFREY MILLER.
MARK WAS HOPEFUL THAT THE WORST WAS OVER AND THE NEW GENERAL WOULD TAKE A MORE SANE, ANTI-TORTURE STANCE ON INTERROGATIONS.
BUT GENERAL MILLER HAD A SPECIAL TAG LINE FOR HOW TO TREAT PRISONERS.
WE'VE GOT TO SHOW THEM THAT WE HAVE MORE TEETH THAN THEY HAVE ASS, HOO-AH!
THE WEEK AFTER HE ARRIVED, GENERAL MILLER APPROVED A HARSH INTERROGATION PLAN FOR MOHAMMED AL-QAHTANI: SOLITARY CONFINEMENT, SLEEP DEPRIVATION, ROUND-THE-CLOCK INTERROGATION.
SURPRISED AND CONFUSED, MARK AND A FEW ALLIES ARGUED THAT TREATING PRISONERS BADLY WAS BOTH COUNTERPRODUCTIVE AND ILLEGAL.
"IT WAS CLEAR TO ME THAT WE WERE GOING TO COMMIT WAR CRIMES. I WAS TRYING TO STOP WHAT I THOUGHT WAS JUST A VERY POOR POLICY DECISION."
CLICK
CLICK
THEY GOT NOWHERE.
"I REALIZED THAT WHOEVER WAS BEHIND THIS PUSH TO TORTURE WAS POWERFUL."
I HAD NO IDEA AT THE TIME THAT THE PRESIDENT AUTHORIZED THE CIA TO KIDNAP PEOPLE, GIVING THEM TO OTHER COUNTRIES TO BE TORTURED.

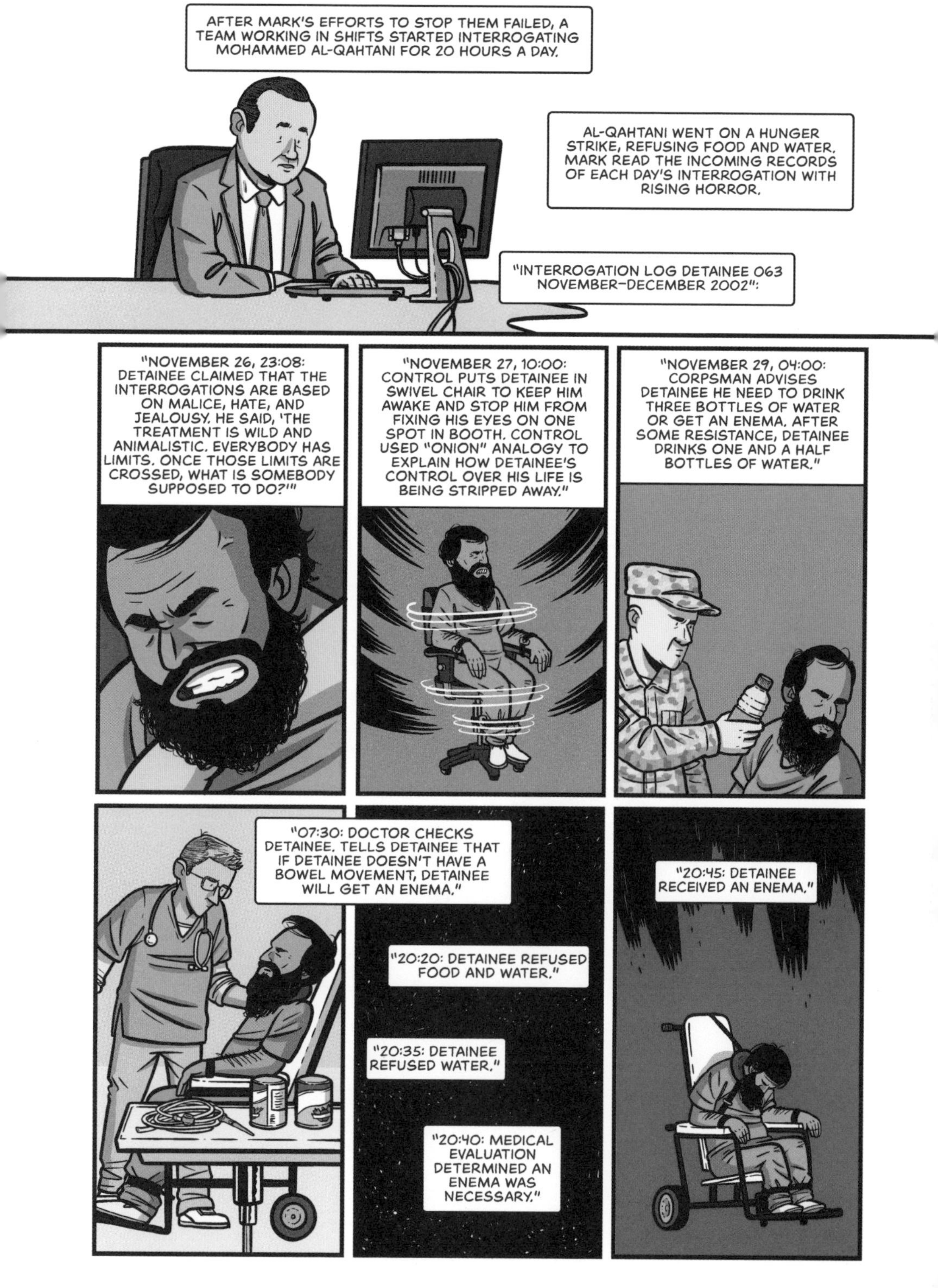
AFTER MARK'S EFFORTS TO STOP THEM FAILED, A TEAM WORKING IN SHIFTS STARTED INTERROGATING MOHAMMED AL-QAHTANI FOR 20 HOURS A DAY.
AL-QAHTANI WENT ON A HUNGER STRIKE, REFUSING FOOD AND WATER. MARK READ THE INCOMING RECORDS OF EACH DAY'S INTERROGATION WITH RISING HORROR.
"INTERROGATION LOG DETAINEE 063 NOVEMBER–DECEMBER 2002":
"NOVEMBER 26, 23:08: DETAINEE CLAIMED THAT THE INTERROGATIONS ARE BASED ON MALICE, HATE, AND JEALOUSY. HE SAID, 'THE TREATMENT IS WILD AND ANIMALISTIC. EVERYBODY HAS LIMITS. ONCE THOSE LIMITS ARE CROSSED, WHAT IS SOMEBODY SUPPOSED TO DO?'"
"NOVEMBER 27, 10:00: CONTROL PUTS DETAINEE IN SWIVEL CHAIR TO KEEP HIM AWAKE AND STOP HIM FROM FIXING HIS EYES ON ONE SPOT IN BOOTH. CONTROL USED "ONION" ANALOGY TO EXPLAIN HOW DETAINEE'S CONTROL OVER HIS LIFE IS BEING STRIPPED AWAY."
"NOVEMBER 29, 04:00: CORPSMAN ADVISES DETAINEE HE NEED TO DRINK THREE BOTTLES OF WATER OR GET AN ENEMA. AFTER SOME RESISTANCE, DETAINEE DRINKS ONE AND A HALF BOTTLES OF WATER."
"07:30: DOCTOR CHECKS DETAINEE. TELLS DETAINEE THAT IF DETAINEE DOESN'T HAVE A BOWEL MOVEMENT, DETAINEE WILL GET AN ENEMA."
"20:20: DETAINEE REFUSED FOOD AND WATER."
"20:35: DETAINEE REFUSED WATER."
"20:40: MEDICAL EVALUATION DETERMINED AN ENEMA WAS NECESSARY."
"20:45: DETAINEE RECEIVED AN ENEMA."

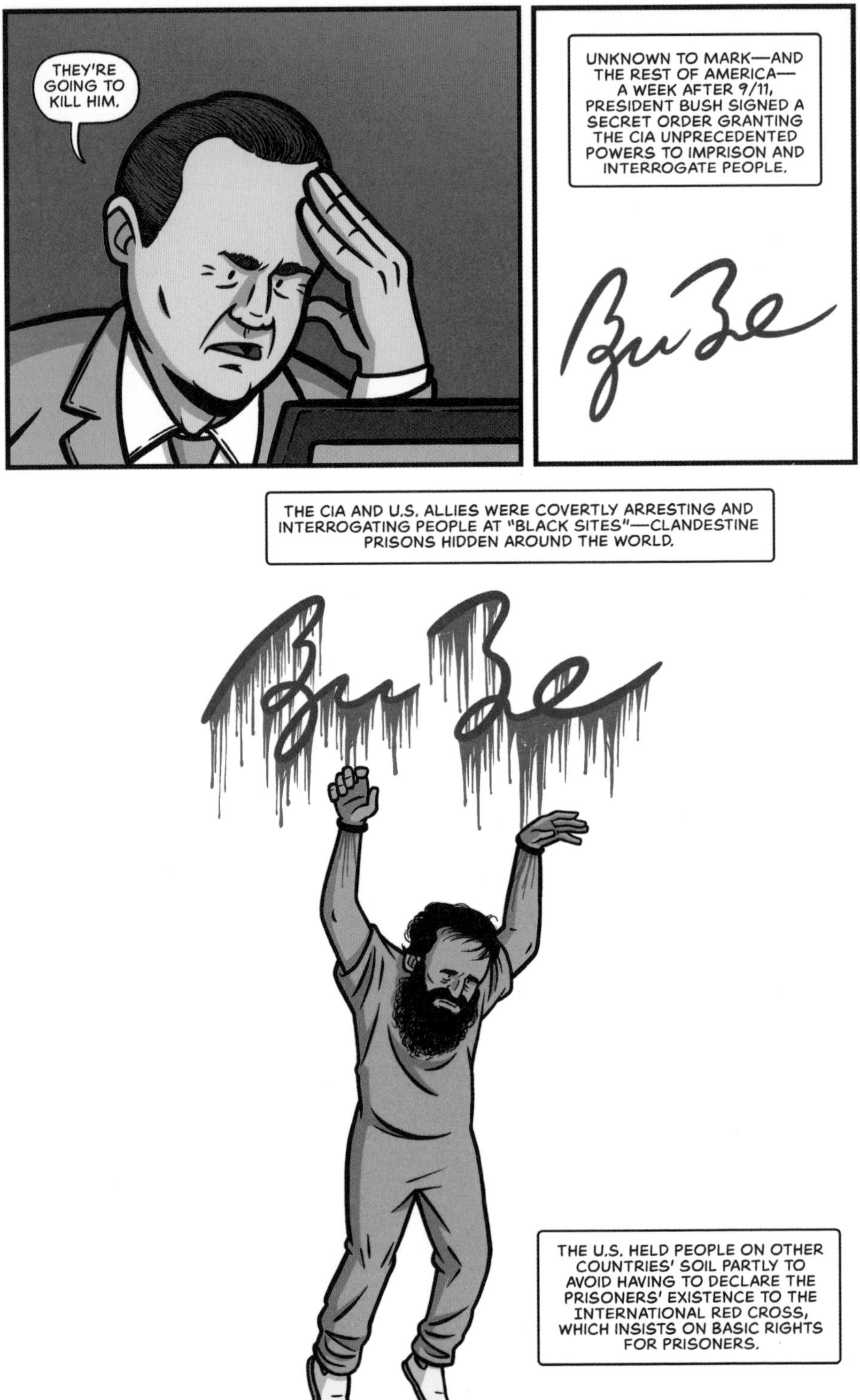
THEY'RE GOING TO KILL HIM.
UNKNOWN TO MARK—AND THE REST OF AMERICA—A WEEK AFTER 9/11, PRESIDENT BUSH SIGNED A SECRET ORDER GRANTING THE CIA UNPRECEDENTED POWERS TO IMPRISON AND INTERROGATE PEOPLE.
THE CIA AND U.S. ALLIES WERE COVERTLY ARRESTING AND INTERROGATING PEOPLE AT "BLACK SITES"—CLANDESTINE PRISONS HIDDEN AROUND THE WORLD.
THE U.S. HELD PEOPLE ON OTHER COUNTRIES' SOIL PARTLY TO AVOID HAVING TO DECLARE THE PRISONERS' EXISTENCE TO THE INTERNATIONAL RED CROSS, WHICH INSISTS ON BASIC RIGHTS FOR PRISONERS.

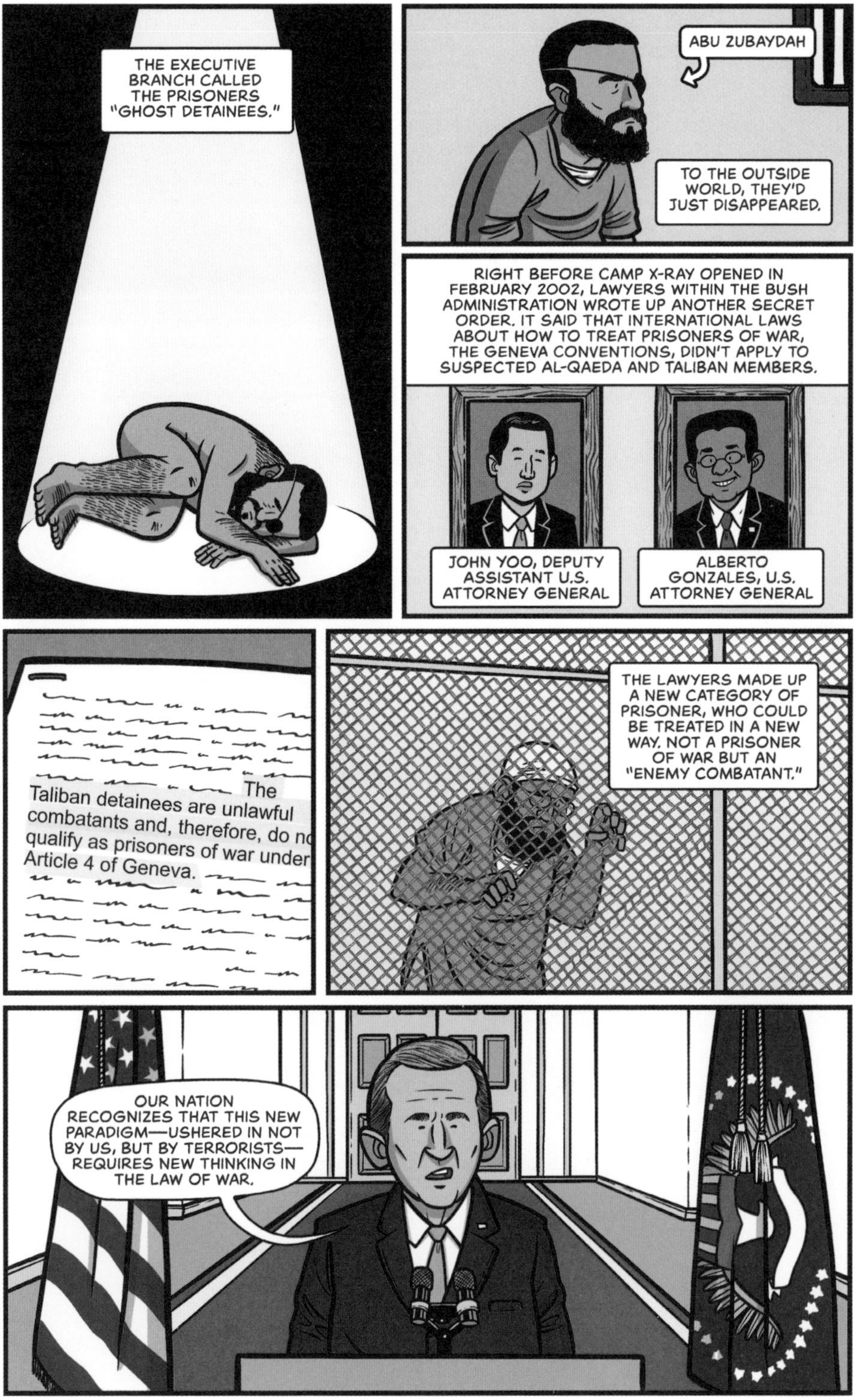
THE EXECUTIVE BRANCH CALLED THE PRISONERS "GHOST DETAINEES."
ABU ZUBAYDAH
TO THE OUTSIDE WORLD, THEY'D JUST DISAPPEARED.
RIGHT BEFORE CAMP X-RAY OPENED IN FEBRUARY 2002, LAWYERS WITHIN THE BUSH ADMINISTRATION WROTE UP ANOTHER SECRET ORDER. IT SAID THAT INTERNATIONAL LAWS ABOUT HOW TO TREAT PRISONERS OF WAR, THE GENEVA CONVENTIONS, DIDN'T APPLY TO SUSPECTED AL-QAEDA AND TALIBAN MEMBERS.
JOHN YOO, DEPUTY ASSISTANT U.S. ATTORNEY GENERAL
ALBERTO GONZALES, U.S. ATTORNEY GENERAL
The Taliban detainees are unlawful combatants and, therefore, do no
qualify as prisoners of war under Article 4 of Geneva.
THE LAWYERS MADE UP A NEW CATEGORY OF PRISONER, WHO COULD BE TREATED IN A NEW WAY. NOT A PRISONER OF WAR BUT AN "ENEMY COMBATANT."
OUR NATION RECOGNIZES THAT THIS NEW PARADIGM—USHERED IN NOT BY US, BUT BY TERRORISTS—REQUIRES NEW THINKING IN THE LAW OF WAR.

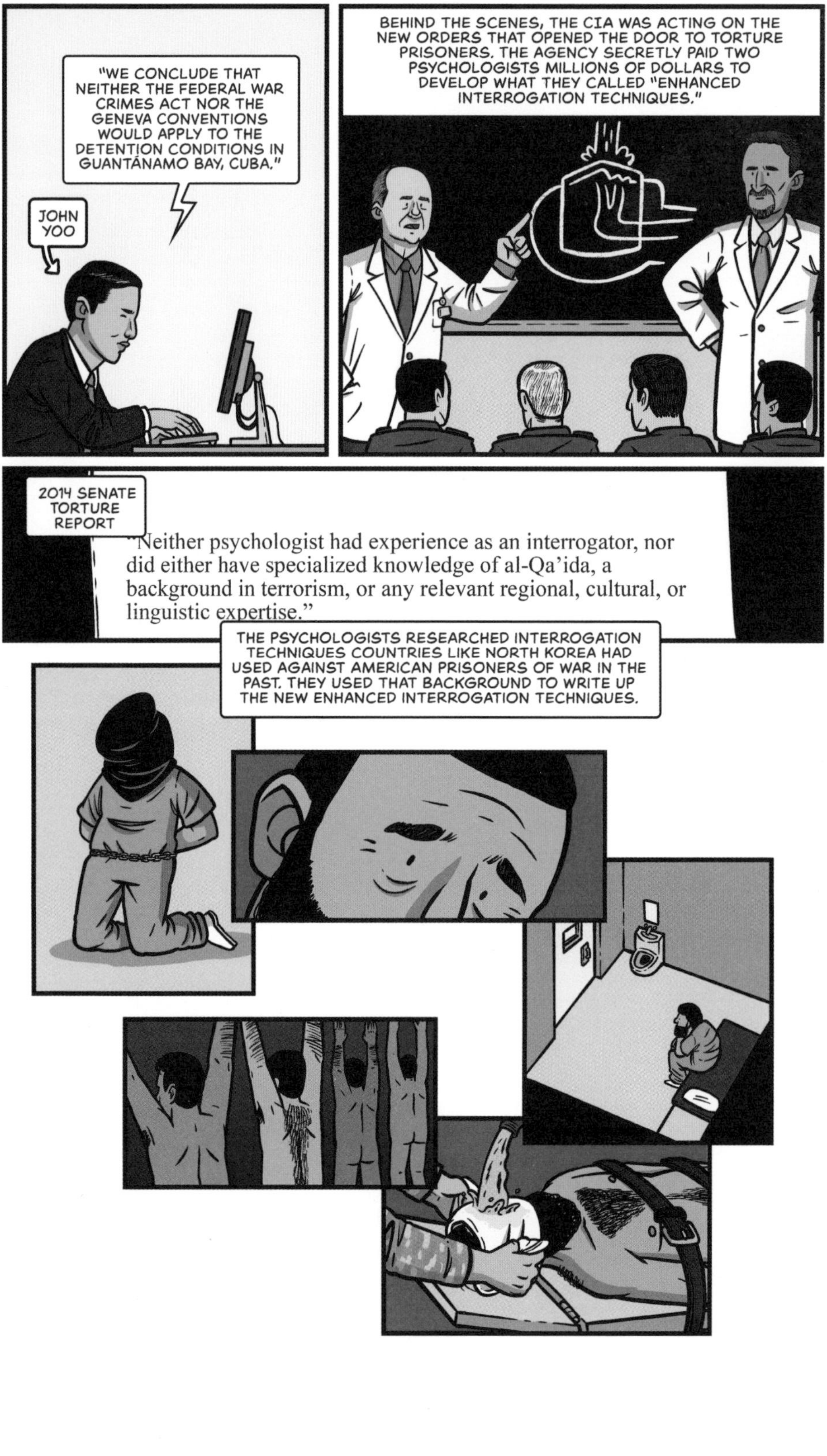
"WE CONCLUDE THAT NEITHER THE FEDERAL WAR CRIMES ACT NOR THE GENEVA CONVENTIONS WOULD APPLY TO THE DETENTION CONDITIONS IN GUANTÁNAMO BAY, CUBA."
JOHN YOO
BEHIND THE SCENES, THE CIA WAS ACTING ON THE NEW ORDERS THAT OPENED THE DOOR TO TORTURE PRISONERS. THE AGENCY SECRETLY PAID TWO PSYCHOLOGISTS MILLIONS OF DOLLARS TO DEVELOP WHAT THEY CALLED "ENHANCED INTERROGATION TECHNIQUES."
2014 SENATE TORTURE REPORT
"Neither psychologist had experience as an interrogator, nor did either have specialized knowledge of al-Qa'ida, a background in terrorism, or any relevant regional, cultural, or linguistic expertise."
THE PSYCHOLOGISTS RESEARCHED INTERROGATION TECHNIQUES COUNTRIES LIKE NORTH KOREA HAD USED AGAINST AMERICAN PRISONERS OF WAR IN THE PAST. THEY USED THAT BACKGROUND TO WRITE UP THE NEW ENHANCED INTERROGATION TECHNIQUES.

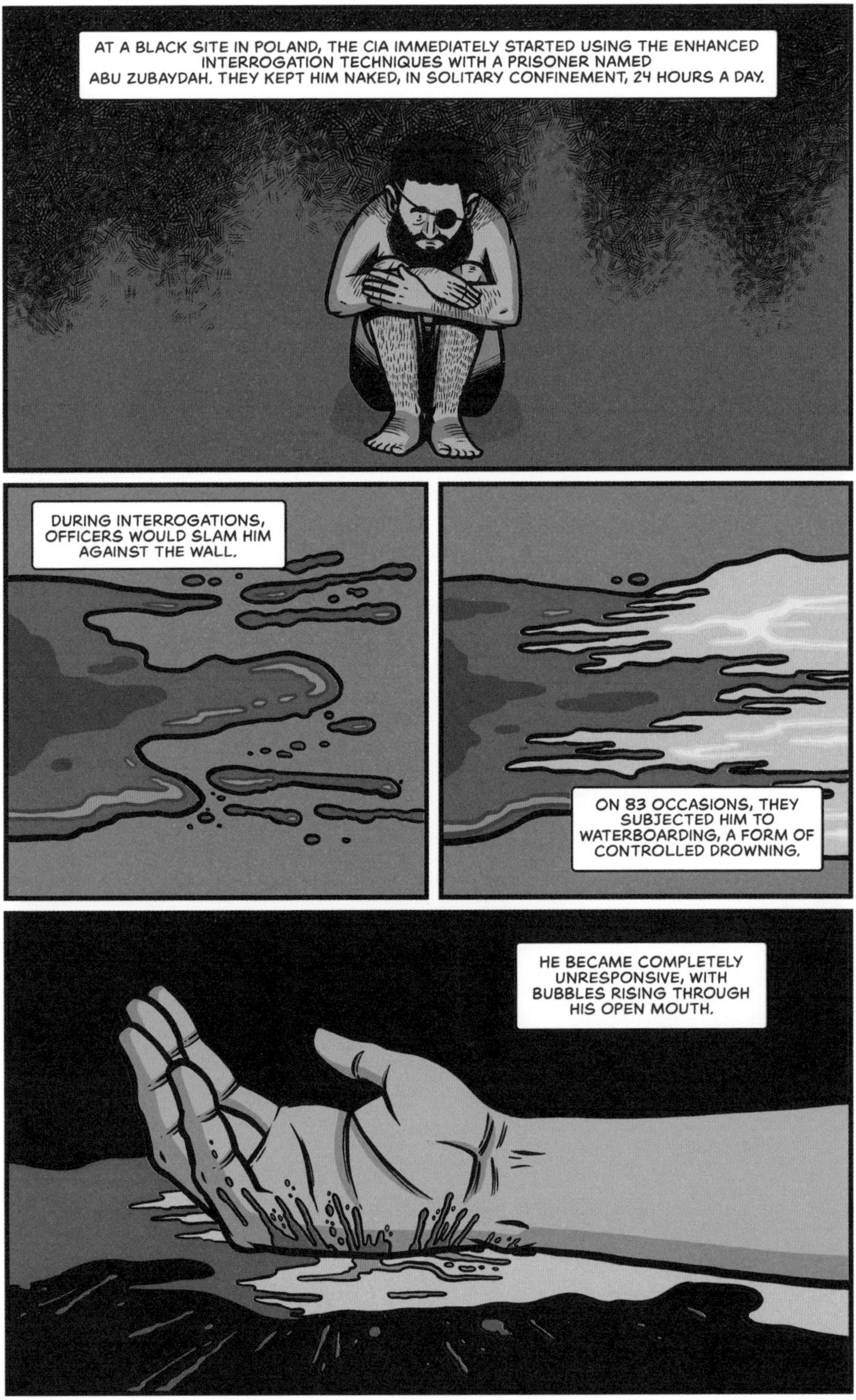
AT A BLACK SITE IN POLAND, THE CIA IMMEDIATELY STARTED USING THE ENHANCED INTERROGATION TECHNIQUES WITH A PRISONER NAMED ABU ZUBAYDAH. THEY KEPT HIM NAKED, IN SOLITARY CONFINEMENT, 24 HOURS A DAY.
DURING INTERROGATIONS, OFFICERS WOULD SLAM HIM AGAINST THE WALL.
ON 83 OCCASIONS, THEY SUBJECTED HIM TO WATERBOARDING, A FORM OF CONTROLLED DROWNING.
HE BECAME COMPLETELY UNRESPONSIVE, WITH BUBBLES RISING THROUGH HIS OPEN MOUTH.

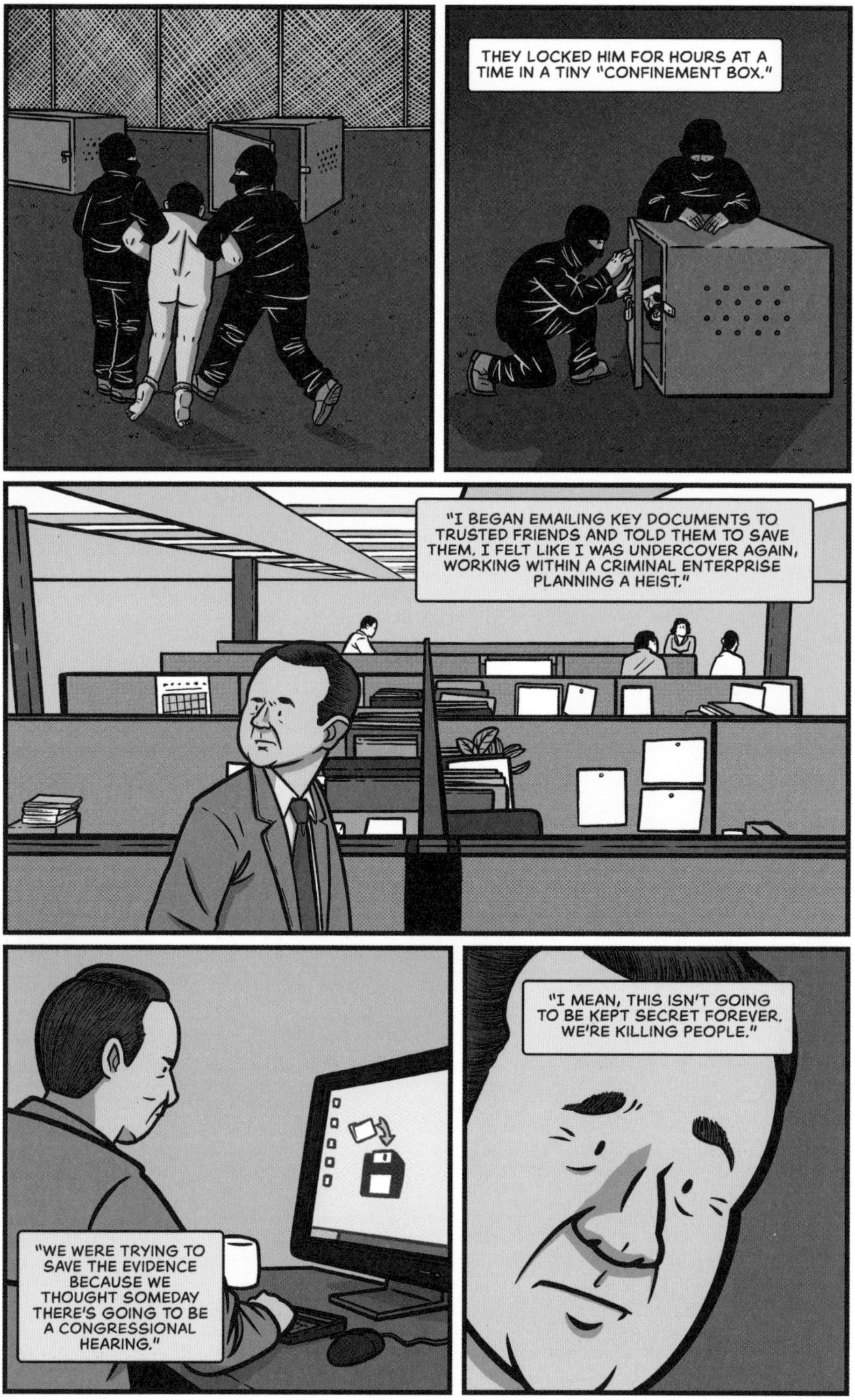
THEY LOCKED HIM FOR HOURS AT A TIME IN A TINY "CONFINEMENT BOX."
"I BEGAN EMAILING KEY DOCUMENTS TO TRUSTED FRIENDS AND TOLD THEM TO SAVE THEM. I FELT LIKE I WAS UNDERCOVER AGAIN, WORKING WITHIN A CRIMINAL ENTERPRISE PLANNING A HEIST."
"WE WERE TRYING TO SAVE THE EVIDENCE BECAUSE WE THOUGHT SOMEDAY THERE'S GOING TO BE A CONGRESSIONAL HEARING."
"I MEAN, THIS ISN'T GOING TO BE KEPT SECRET FOREVER. WE'RE KILLING PEOPLE."

THE CIA DID DESTROY EVIDENCE, AS MARK FEARED. IN 2005, AGENTS DESTROYED VIDEOTAPES OF INTERROGATIONS OF ZUBAYDAH AND ANOTHER MAN.

AT THE SAME TIME, THE CIA HAD BUILT A SECRET COMPOUND AT GUANTÁNAMO AND TRANSFERRED "HIGH-VALUE" DETAINEES LIKE ZUBAYDAH THERE FROM THE OTHER BLACK SITES AROUND THE WORLD. THE SITE'S CODE NAME WAS STRAWBERRY FIELDS . . .

. . . BECAUSE, CIA OFFICIALS SAID, THE MEN WOULD BE THERE FOREVER.

2006

FOR YEARS, PRESIDENT BUSH DEFENDED TORTURE AS NECESSARY TO SAVE AMERICAN LIVES.

WE KNEW THAT ZUBAYDAH HAD MORE INFORMATION THAT COULD SAVE INNOCENT LIVES, BUT HE STOPPED TALKING . . . AND SO THE CIA USED AN ALTERNATIVE SET OF PROCEDURES.

THE PROCEDURES WERE TOUGH, AND THEY WERE SAFE, AND LAWFUL, AND NECESSARY.

THE CIA'S CLAIMS THAT TORTURING PRISONERS RESULTED IN "OTHERWISE UNAVAILABLE" INTELLIGENCE THAT "SAVED LIVES" WAS INACCURATE IN EVERY SINGLE CASE. THE INVESTIGATION ALSO NOTED THAT THE CIA EVENTUALLY CONCLUDED THAT ABU ZUBAYDAH WAS NOT ACTUALLY A MEMBER OF AL-QAEDA.

BUT A MASSIVE, 6,700-PAGE SENATE INVESTIGATION FINISHED IN 2012 FOUND THE OPPOSITE.

ABU ZUBAYDAH IS STILL IN GUANTÁNAMO.

HE'S NEVER BEEN CHARGED WITH A CRIME.

CHAPTER THREE

MATTHEW DIAZ

FORMER NAVY JUDGE ADVOCATE GENERAL CORPS OFFICER (LAWYER) AND 20-YEAR VETERAN: 8.5 YEARS ARMY, 12 YEARS NAVY

ILLUSTRATED BY
ALEX BEGUEZ

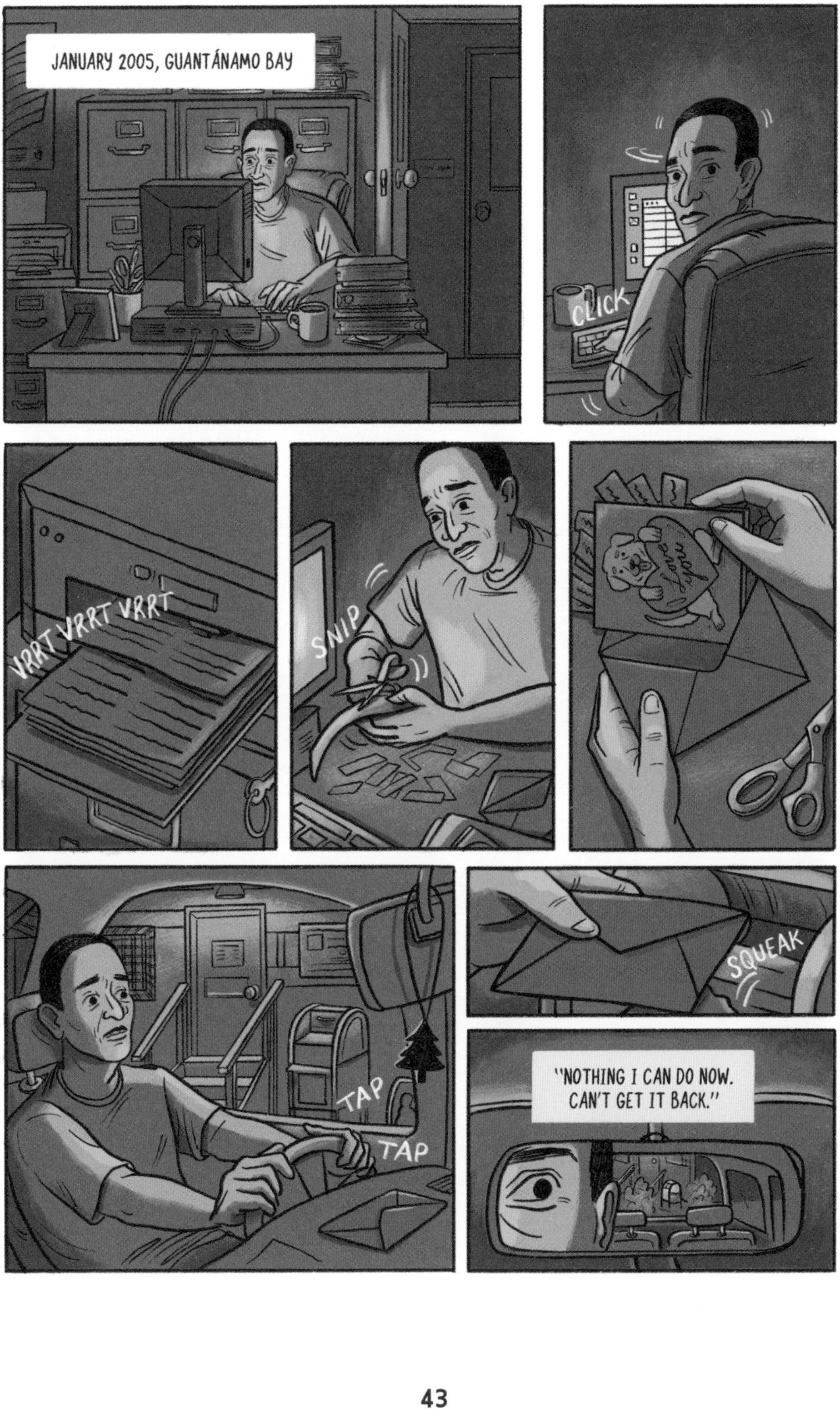
JANUARY 2005, GUANTÁNAMO BAY
CLICK
VRRT VRRT VRRT
SNIP
TAP
TAP
SQUEAK
"NOTHING I CAN DO NOW. CAN'T GET IT BACK."

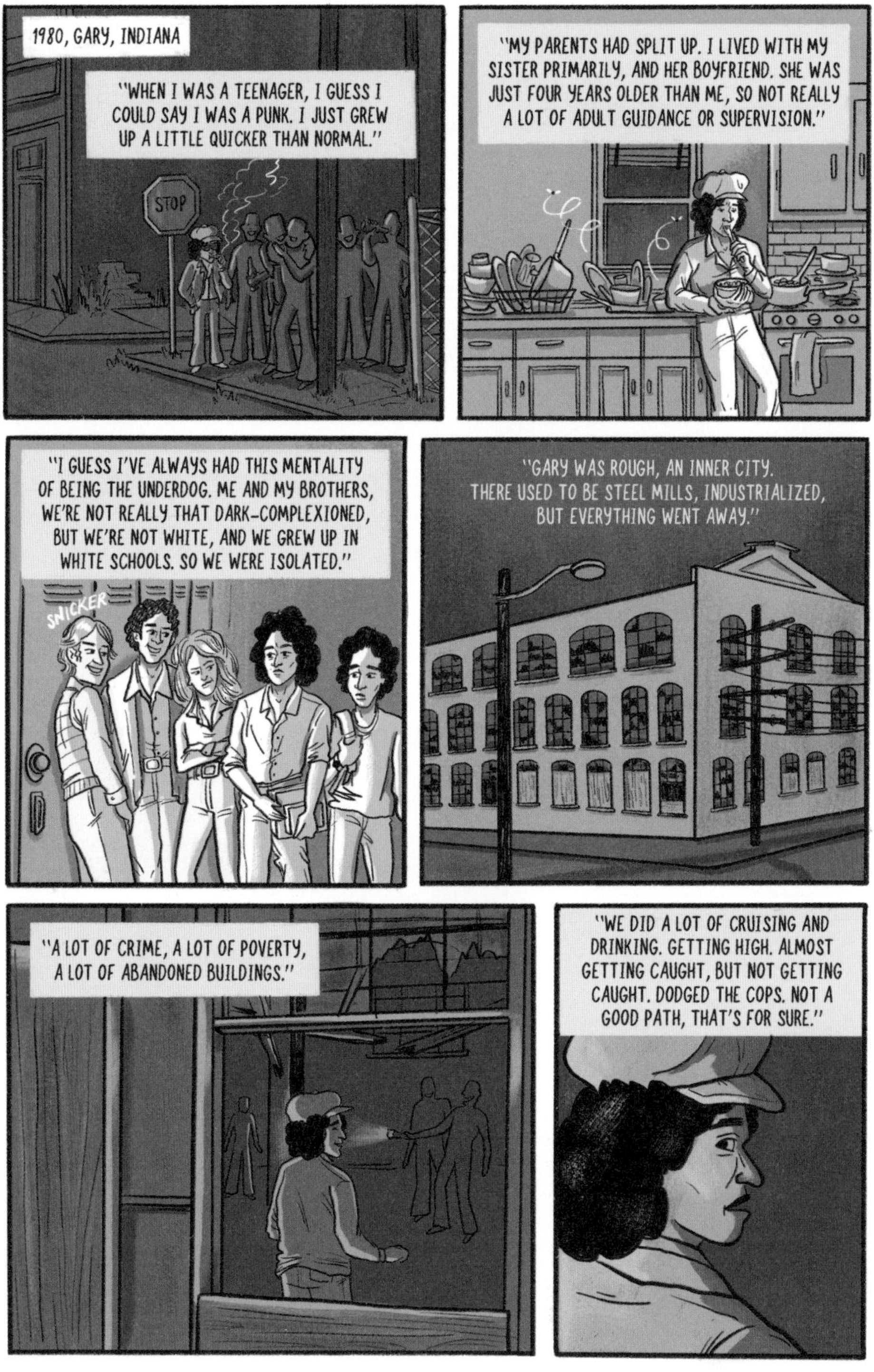
1980, GARY, INDIANA
"WHEN I WAS A TEENAGER, I GUESS I COULD SAY I WAS A PUNK. I JUST GREW UP A LITTLE QUICKER THAN NORMAL."
STOP
"MY PARENTS HAD SPLIT UP. I LIVED WITH MY SISTER PRIMARILY, AND HER BOYFRIEND. SHE WAS JUST FOUR YEARS OLDER THAN ME, SO NOT REALLY A LOT OF ADULT GUIDANCE OR SUPERVISION."
"I GUESS I'VE ALWAYS HAD THIS MENTALITY OF BEING THE UNDERDOG. ME AND MY BROTHERS, WE'RE NOT REALLY THAT DARK-COMPLEXIONED, BUT WE'RE NOT WHITE, AND WE GREW UP IN WHITE SCHOOLS. SO WE WERE ISOLATED."
SNICKER
"GARY WAS ROUGH, AN INNER CITY. THERE USED TO BE STEEL MILLS, INDUSTRIALIZED, BUT EVERYTHING WENT AWAY."
"A LOT OF CRIME, A LOT OF POVERTY, A LOT OF ABANDONED BUILDINGS."
"WE DID A LOT OF CRUISING AND DRINKING. GETTING HIGH. ALMOST GETTING CAUGHT, BUT NOT GETTING CAUGHT. DODGED THE COPS. NOT A GOOD PATH, THAT'S FOR SURE."

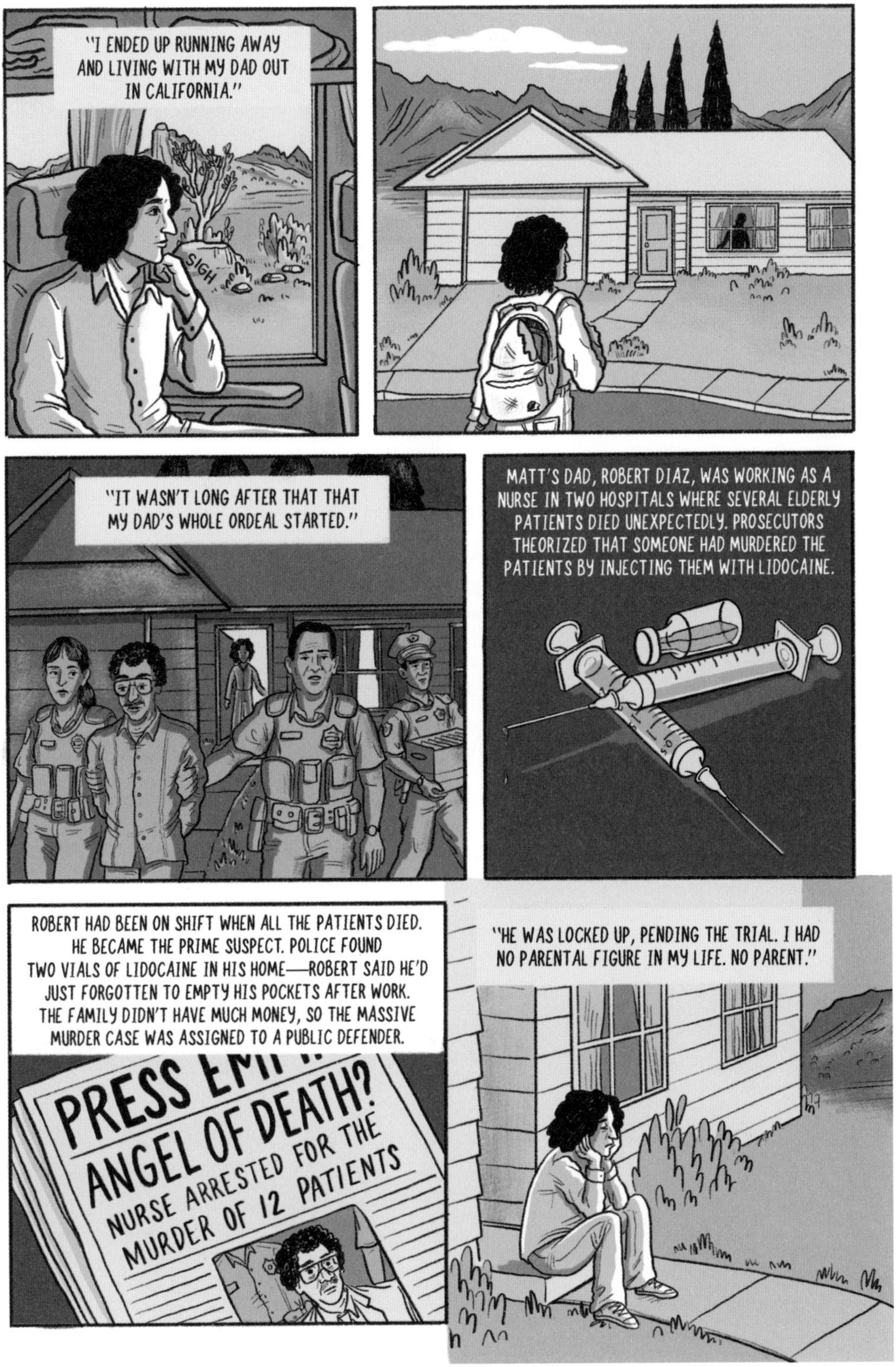
"I ENDED UP RUNNING AWAY AND LIVING WITH MY DAD OUT IN CALIFORNIA."
SIGH
"IT WASN'T LONG AFTER THAT THAT MY DAD'S WHOLE ORDEAL STARTED."
MATT'S DAD, ROBERT DIAZ, WAS WORKING AS A NURSE IN TWO HOSPITALS WHERE SEVERAL ELDERLY PATIENTS DIED UNEXPECTEDLY. PROSECUTORS THEORIZED THAT SOMEONE HAD MURDERED THE PATIENTS BY INJECTING THEM WITH LIDOCAINE.
ROBERT HAD BEEN ON SHIFT WHEN ALL THE PATIENTS DIED. HE BECAME THE PRIME SUSPECT. POLICE FOUND TWO VIALS OF LIDOCAINE IN HIS HOME—ROBERT SAID HE'D JUST FORGOTTEN TO EMPTY HIS POCKETS AFTER WORK. THE FAMILY DIDN'T HAVE MUCH MONEY, SO THE MASSIVE MURDER CASE WAS ASSIGNED TO A PUBLIC DEFENDER.
ANGEL OF DEATH?
NURSE ARRESTED FOR THE MURDER OF 12 PATIENTS
"HE WAS LOCKED UP, PENDING THE TRIAL. I HAD NO PARENTAL FIGURE IN MY LIFE. NO PARENT."

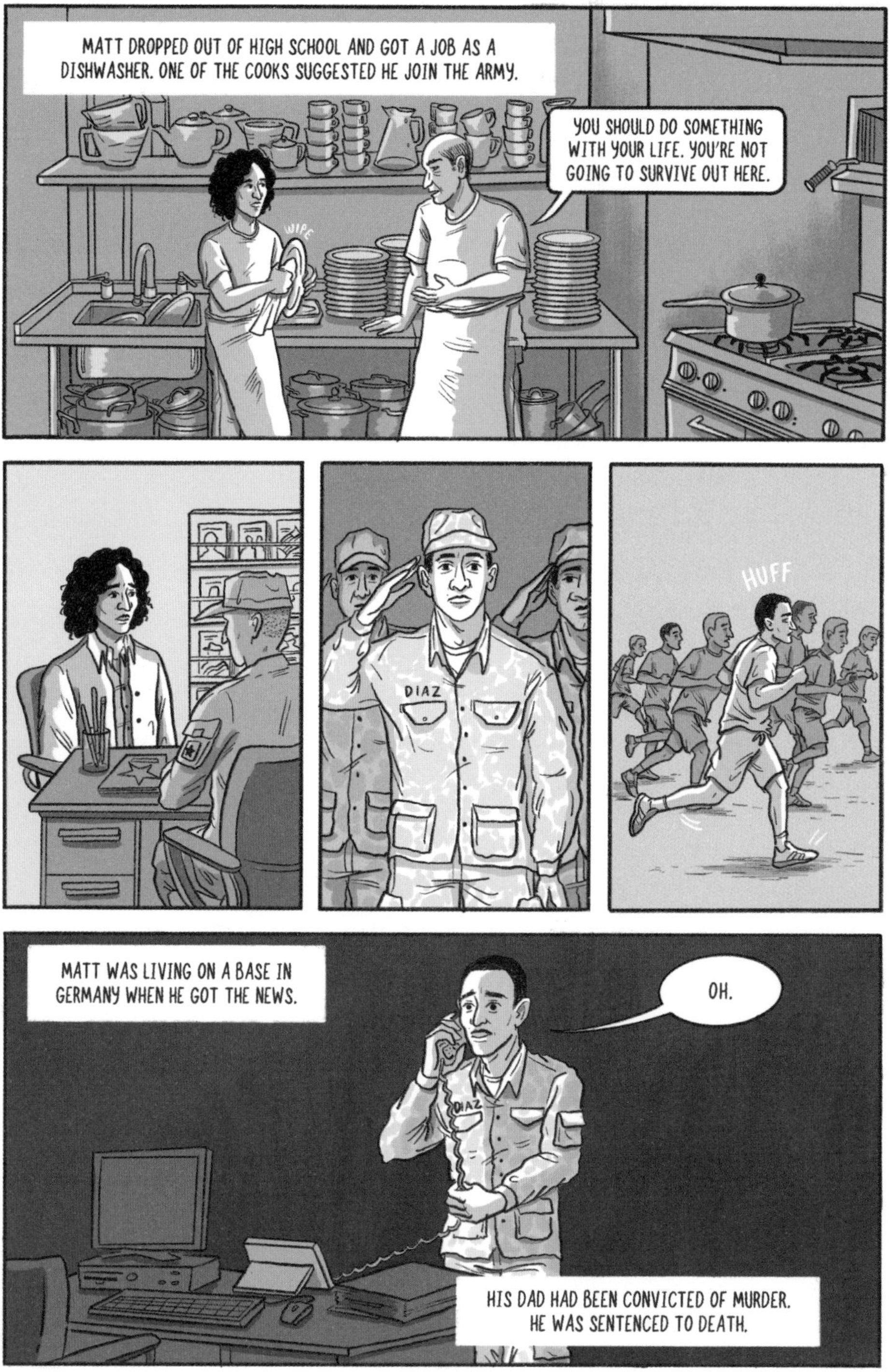
MATT DROPPED OUT OF HIGH SCHOOL AND GOT A JOB AS A DISHWASHER. ONE OF THE COOKS SUGGESTED HE JOIN THE ARMY.
WIPE
YOU SHOULD DO SOMETHING WITH YOUR LIFE. YOU'RE NOT GOING TO SURVIVE OUT HERE.
DIAZ
HUFF
MATT WAS LIVING ON A BASE IN GERMANY WHEN HE GOT THE NEWS.
OH.
DIAZ
HIS DAD HAD BEEN CONVICTED OF MURDER. HE WAS SENTENCED TO DEATH.

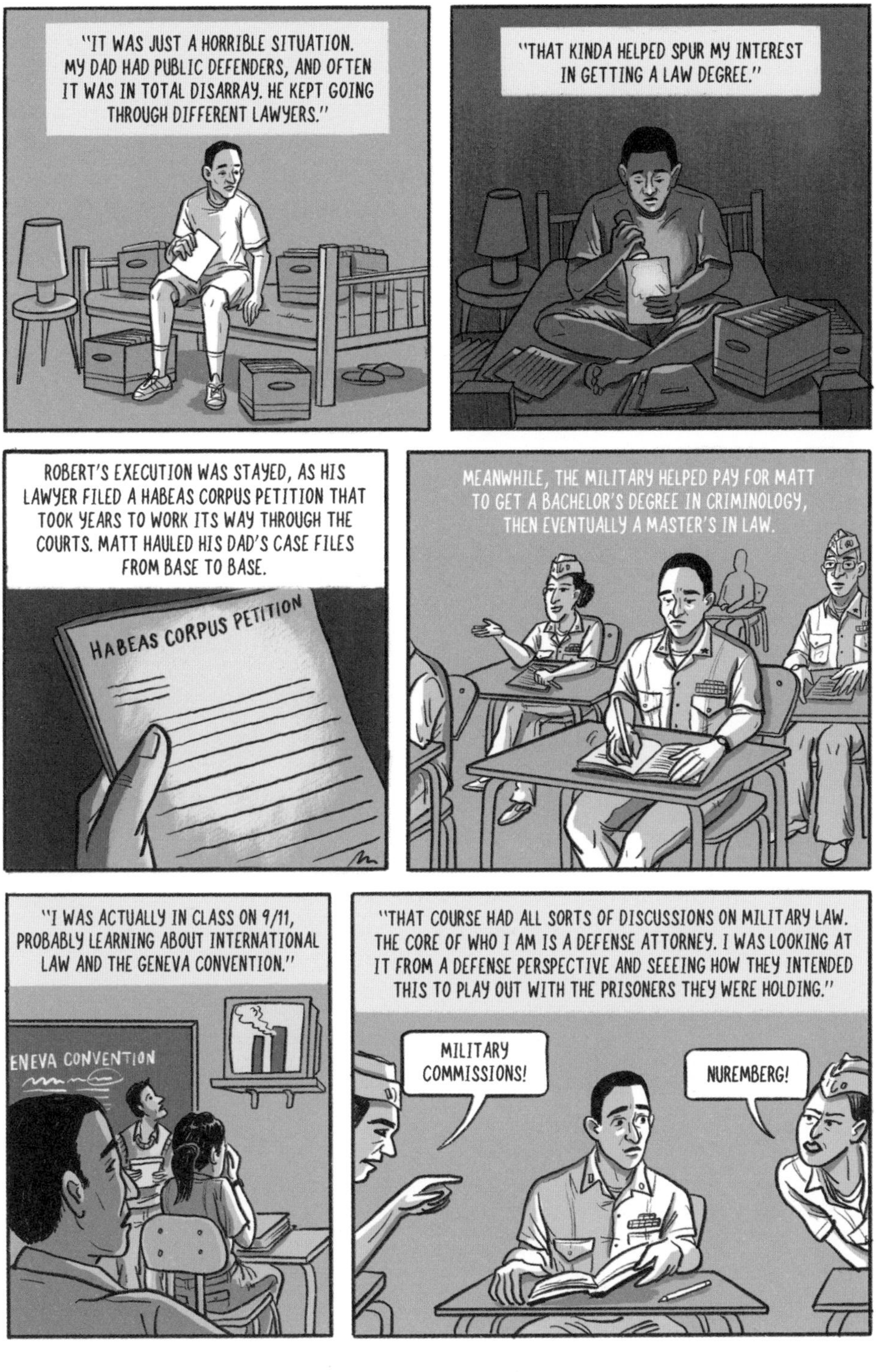
"IT WAS JUST A HORRIBLE SITUATION. MY DAD HAD PUBLIC DEFENDERS, AND OFTEN IT WAS IN TOTAL DISARRAY. HE KEPT GOING THROUGH DIFFERENT LAWYERS."
"THAT KINDA HELPED SPUR MY INTEREST IN GETTING A LAW DEGREE."
ROBERT'S EXECUTION WAS STAYED, AS HIS LAWYER FILED A HABEAS CORPUS PETITION THAT TOOK YEARS TO WORK ITS WAY THROUGH THE COURTS. MATT HAULED HIS DAD'S CASE FILES FROM BASE TO BASE.
HABEAS CORPUS PETITION
MEANWHILE, THE MILITARY HELPED PAY FOR MATT TO GET A BACHELOR'S DEGREE IN CRIMINOLOGY, THEN EVENTUALLY A MASTER'S IN LAW.
"I WAS ACTUALLY IN CLASS ON 9/11, PROBABLY LEARNING ABOUT INTERNATIONAL LAW AND THE GENEVA CONVENTION."
ENEVA CONVENTION
"THAT COURSE HAD ALL SORTS OF DISCUSSIONS ON MILITARY LAW. THE CORE OF WHO I AM IS A DEFENSE ATTORNEY. I WAS LOOKING AT IT FROM A DEFENSE PERSPECTIVE AND SEEING HOW THEY INTENDED THIS TO PLAY OUT WITH THE PRISONERS THEY WERE HOLDING."
MILITARY COMMISSIONS!
NUREMBERG!

WHEN HE GRADUATED, MATT TOOK A JOB DEFENDING SERVICE MEMBERS WHO WERE STANDING TRIAL IN MILITARY COURT. THEIR CRIMES RANGED FROM MARIJUANA USE TO SEXUAL ASSAULTS.

NAVAL BRIG

IN SPRING 2004, MATT GOT THREE CHOICES FOR WHERE TO BE DEPLOYED FOR A NEW JOB.

IRAQ, AFGHANISTAN, OR GUANTÁNAMO?

HE CHOSE GUANTÁNAMO.

"I HAD BEEN THERE BACK IN 1998 AND WAS VERY FAMILIAR WITH THE BASE. BUT I DIDN'T KNOW THE DETAILS OF JTF (JOINT TASK FORCE) OPERATION. I WAS LOOSELY FOLLOWING THE NEWS."

HMMM

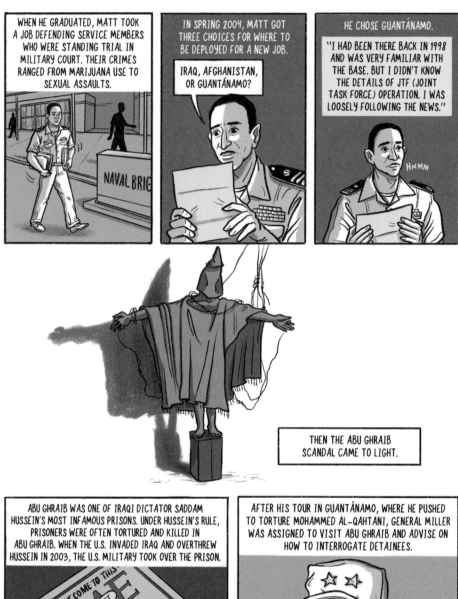

THEN THE ABU GHRAIB SCANDAL CAME TO LIGHT.

ABU GHRAIB WAS ONE OF IRAQI DICTATOR SADDAM HUSSEIN'S MOST INFAMOUS PRISONS. UNDER HUSSEIN'S RULE, PRISONERS WERE OFTEN TORTURED AND KILLED IN ABU GHRAIB. WHEN THE U.S. INVADED IRAQ AND OVERTHREW HUSSEIN IN 2003, THE U.S. MILITARY TOOK OVER THE PRISON.

IRAQ: HOW DID IT COME TO THIS
TIME
SPECIAL REPORT

AFTER HIS TOUR IN GUANTÁNAMO, WHERE HE PUSHED TO TORTURE MOHAMMED AL-QAHTANI, GENERAL MILLER WAS ASSIGNED TO VISIT ABU GHRAIB AND ADVISE ON HOW TO INTERROGATE DETAINEES.

48

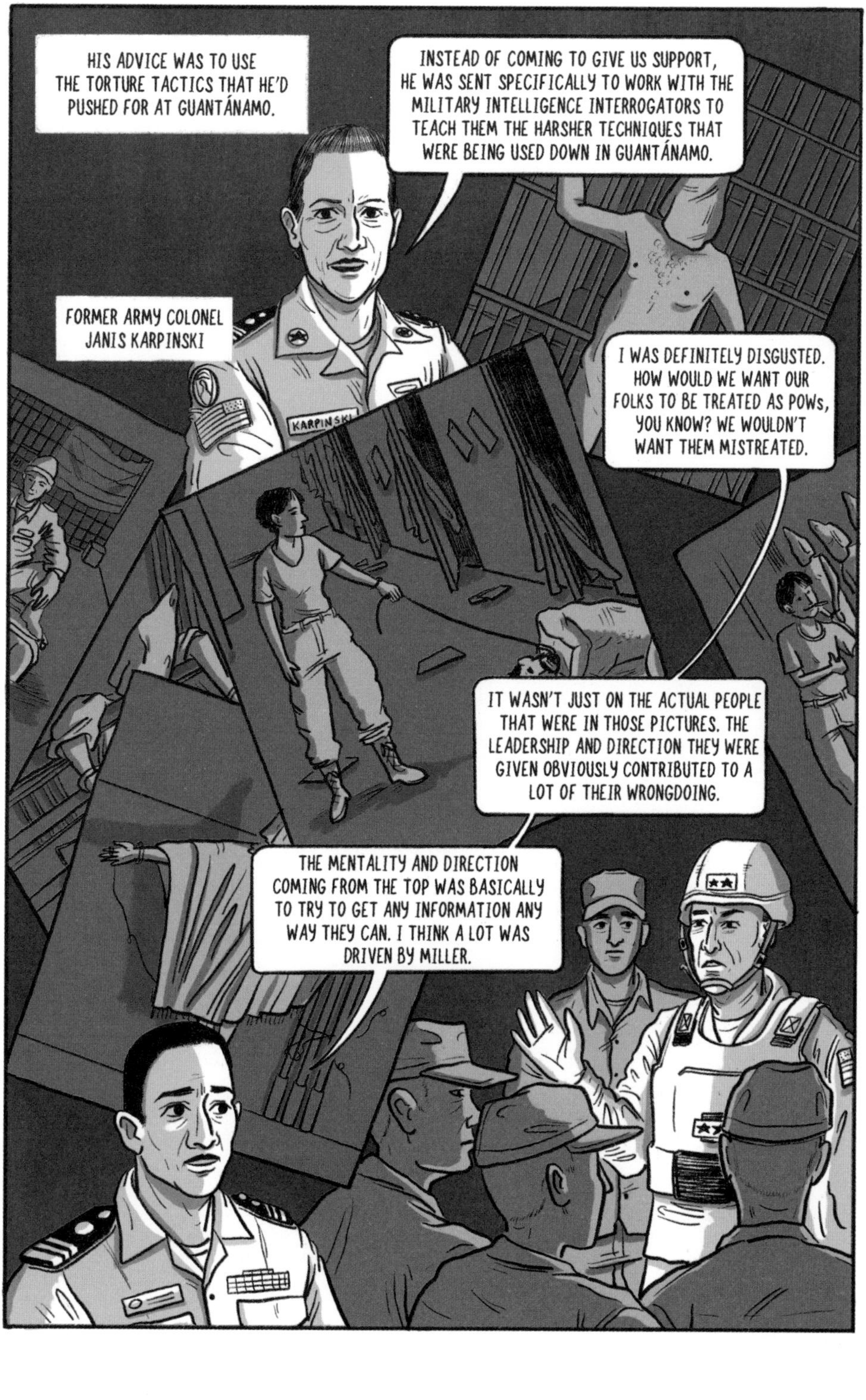
HIS ADVICE WAS TO USE THE TORTURE TACTICS THAT HE'D PUSHED FOR AT GUANTÁNAMO.
INSTEAD OF COMING TO GIVE US SUPPORT, HE WAS SENT SPECIFICALLY TO WORK WITH THE MILITARY INTELLIGENCE INTERROGATORS TO TEACH THEM THE HARSHER TECHNIQUES THAT WERE BEING USED DOWN IN GUANTÁNAMO.
FORMER ARMY COLONEL JANIS KARPINSKI
KARPINSKI
I WAS DEFINITELY DISGUSTED. HOW WOULD WE WANT OUR FOLKS TO BE TREATED AS POWs, YOU KNOW? WE WOULDN'T WANT THEM MISTREATED.
IT WASN'T JUST ON THE ACTUAL PEOPLE THAT WERE IN THOSE PICTURES. THE LEADERSHIP AND DIRECTION THEY WERE GIVEN OBVIOUSLY CONTRIBUTED TO A LOT OF THEIR WRONGDOING.
THE MENTALITY AND DIRECTION COMING FROM THE TOP WAS BASICALLY TO TRY TO GET ANY INFORMATION ANY WAY THEY CAN. I THINK A LOT WAS DRIVEN BY MILLER.

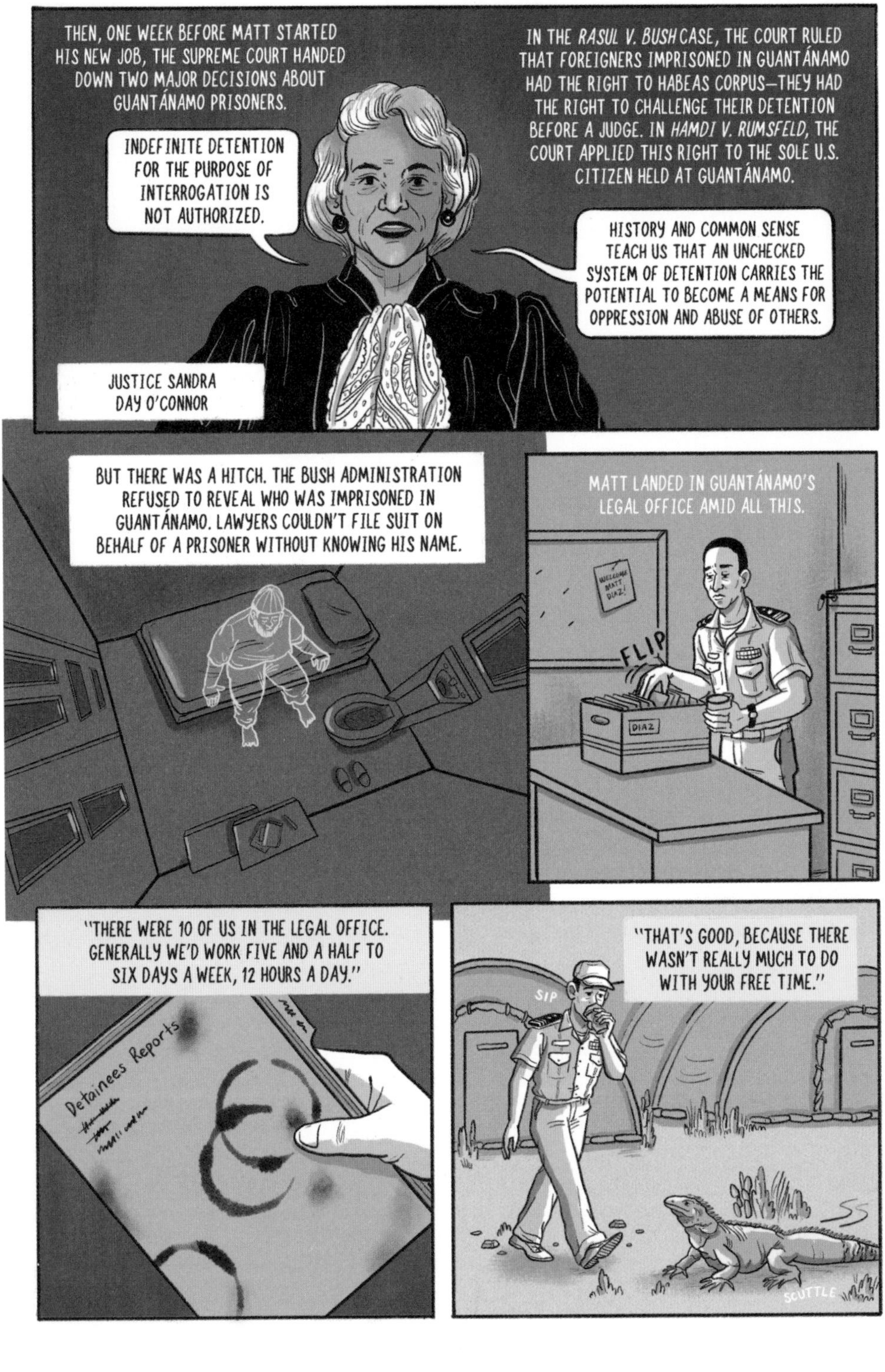
THEN, ONE WEEK BEFORE MATT STARTED HIS NEW JOB, THE SUPREME COURT HANDED DOWN TWO MAJOR DECISIONS ABOUT GUANTÁNAMO PRISONERS.
IN THE RASUL V. BUSH CASE, THE COURT RULED THAT FOREIGNERS IMPRISONED IN GUANTÁNAMO HAD THE RIGHT TO HABEAS CORPUS—THEY HAD THE RIGHT TO CHALLENGE THEIR DETENTION BEFORE A JUDGE. IN HAMDI V. RUMSFELD, THE COURT APPLIED THIS RIGHT TO THE SOLE U.S. CITIZEN HELD AT GUANTÁNAMO.
INDEFINITE DETENTION FOR THE PURPOSE OF INTERROGATION IS NOT AUTHORIZED.
HISTORY AND COMMON SENSE TEACH US THAT AN UNCHECKED SYSTEM OF DETENTION CARRIES THE POTENTIAL TO BECOME A MEANS FOR OPPRESSION AND ABUSE OF OTHERS.
JUSTICE SANDRA DAY O'CONNOR
BUT THERE WAS A HITCH. THE BUSH ADMINISTRATION REFUSED TO REVEAL WHO WAS IMPRISONED IN GUANTÁNAMO. LAWYERS COULDN'T FILE SUIT ON BEHALF OF A PRISONER WITHOUT KNOWING HIS NAME.
MATT LANDED IN GUANTÁNAMO'S LEGAL OFFICE AMID ALL THIS.
WELCOME MATT DIAZ!
FLIP
DIAZ
"THERE WERE 10 OF US IN THE LEGAL OFFICE. GENERALLY WE'D WORK FIVE AND A HALF TO SIX DAYS A WEEK, 12 HOURS A DAY."
Detainees Reports
"THAT'S GOOD, BECAUSE THERE WASN'T REALLY MUCH TO DO WITH YOUR FREE TIME."
SIP
SCUTTLE

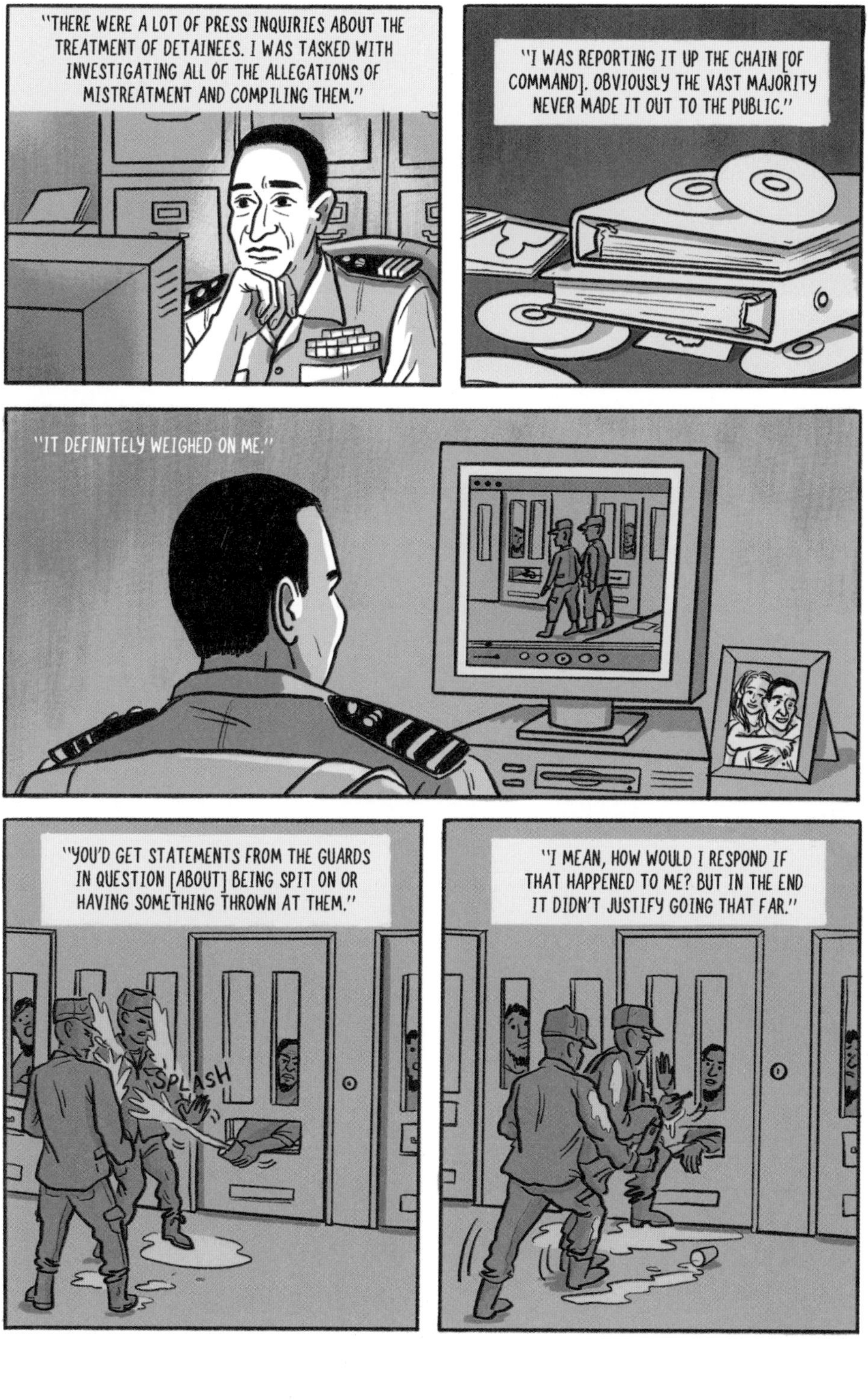
"THERE WERE A LOT OF PRESS INQUIRIES ABOUT THE TREATMENT OF DETAINEES. I WAS TASKED WITH INVESTIGATING ALL OF THE ALLEGATIONS OF MISTREATMENT AND COMPILING THEM."
"I WAS REPORTING IT UP THE CHAIN [OF COMMAND]. OBVIOUSLY THE VAST MAJORITY NEVER MADE IT OUT TO THE PUBLIC."
"IT DEFINITELY WEIGHED ON ME."
"YOU'D GET STATEMENTS FROM THE GUARDS IN QUESTION [ABOUT] BEING SPIT ON OR HAVING SOMETHING THROWN AT THEM."
SPLASH
"I MEAN, HOW WOULD I RESPOND IF THAT HAPPENED TO ME? BUT IN THE END IT DIDN'T JUSTIFY GOING THAT FAR."

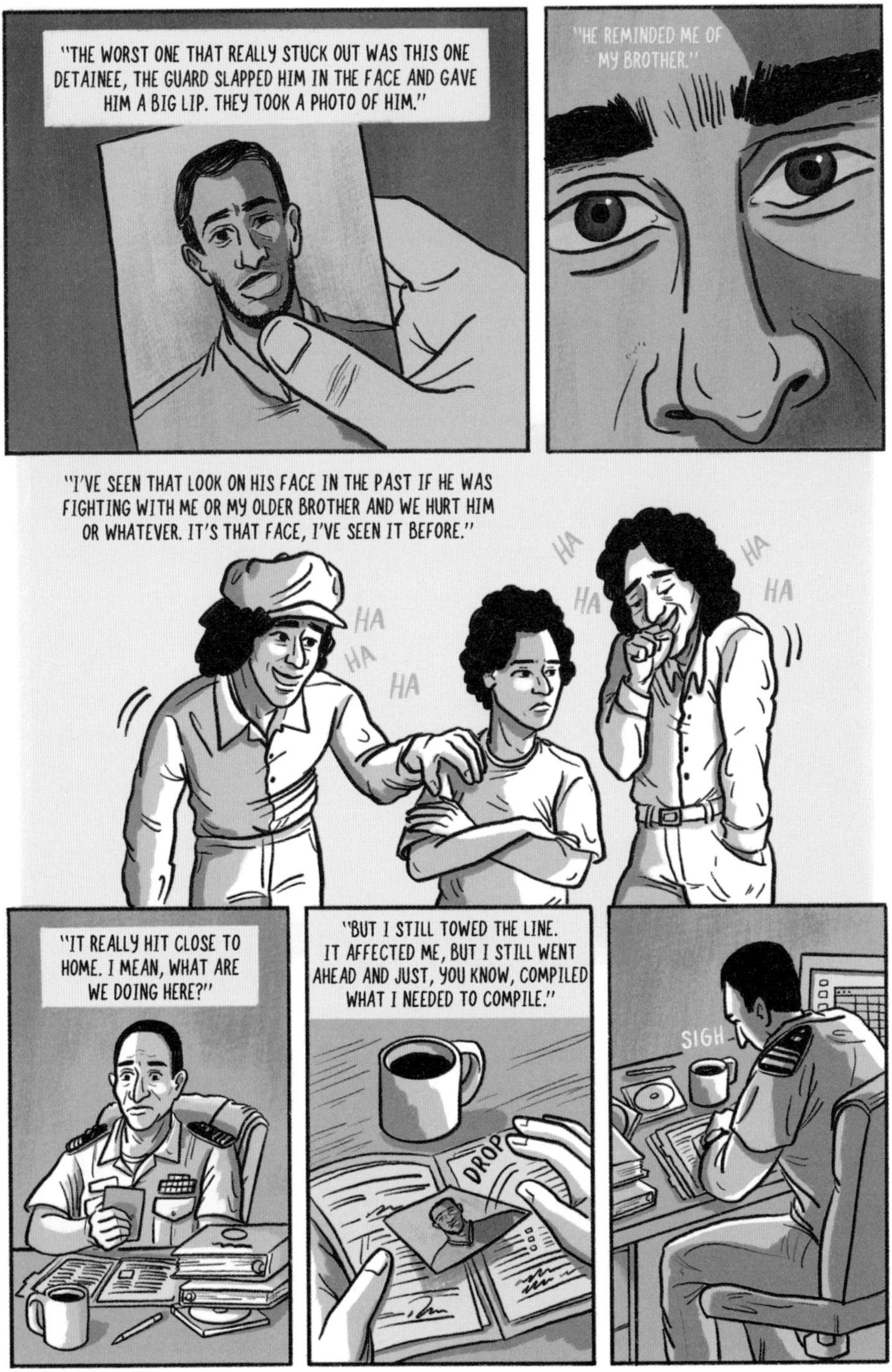
"THE WORST ONE THAT REALLY STUCK OUT WAS THIS ONE DETAINEE, THE GUARD SLAPPED HIM IN THE FACE AND GAVE HIM A BIG LIP. THEY TOOK A PHOTO OF HIM."
"HE REMINDED ME OF MY BROTHER."
"I'VE SEEN THAT LOOK ON HIS FACE IN THE PAST IF HE WAS FIGHTING WITH ME OR MY OLDER BROTHER AND WE HURT HIM OR WHATEVER. IT'S THAT FACE, I'VE SEEN IT BEFORE."
HA
HA
HA
HA
HA
HA
HA
"IT REALLY HIT CLOSE TO HOME. I MEAN, WHAT ARE WE DOING HERE?"
"BUT I STILL TOWED THE LINE. IT AFFECTED ME, BUT I STILL WENT AHEAD AND JUST, YOU KNOW, COMPILED WHAT I NEEDED TO COMPILE."
DROP
SIGH

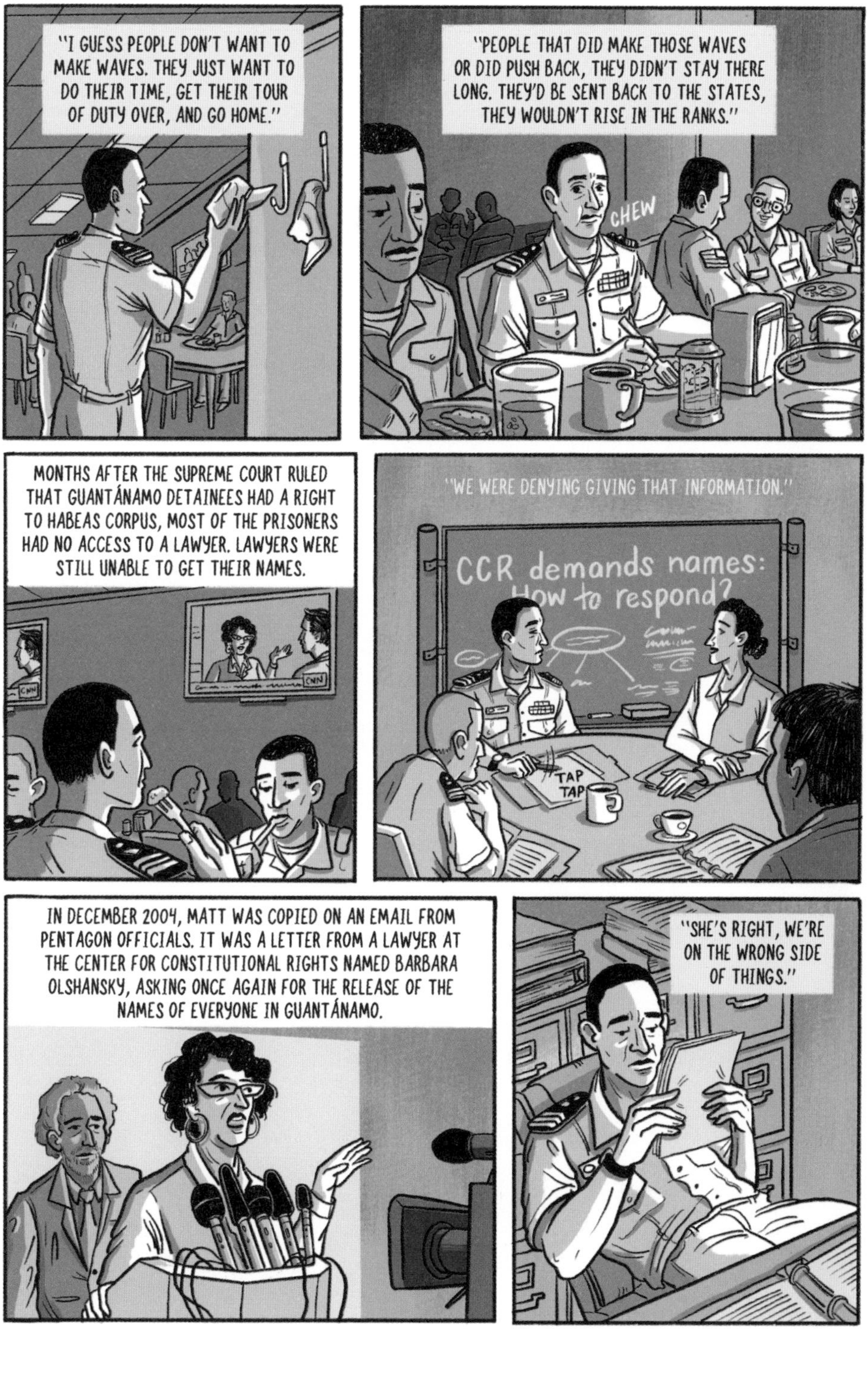
"I GUESS PEOPLE DON'T WANT TO MAKE WAVES. THEY JUST WANT TO DO THEIR TIME, GET THEIR TOUR OF DUTY OVER, AND GO HOME."
"PEOPLE THAT DID MAKE THOSE WAVES OR DID PUSH BACK, THEY DIDN'T STAY THERE LONG. THEY'D BE SENT BACK TO THE STATES, THEY WOULDN'T RISE IN THE RANKS."
CHEW
MONTHS AFTER THE SUPREME COURT RULED THAT GUANTÁNAMO DETAINEES HAD A RIGHT TO HABEAS CORPUS, MOST OF THE PRISONERS HAD NO ACCESS TO A LAWYER. LAWYERS WERE STILL UNABLE TO GET THEIR NAMES.
CNN
CNN
"WE WERE DENYING GIVING THAT INFORMATION."
CCR demands names:
How to respond?
TAP
TAP
IN DECEMBER 2004, MATT WAS COPIED ON AN EMAIL FROM PENTAGON OFFICIALS. IT WAS A LETTER FROM A LAWYER AT THE CENTER FOR CONSTITUTIONAL RIGHTS NAMED BARBARA OLSHANSKY, ASKING ONCE AGAIN FOR THE RELEASE OF THE NAMES OF EVERYONE IN GUANTÁNAMO.
"SHE'S RIGHT, WE'RE ON THE WRONG SIDE OF THINGS."

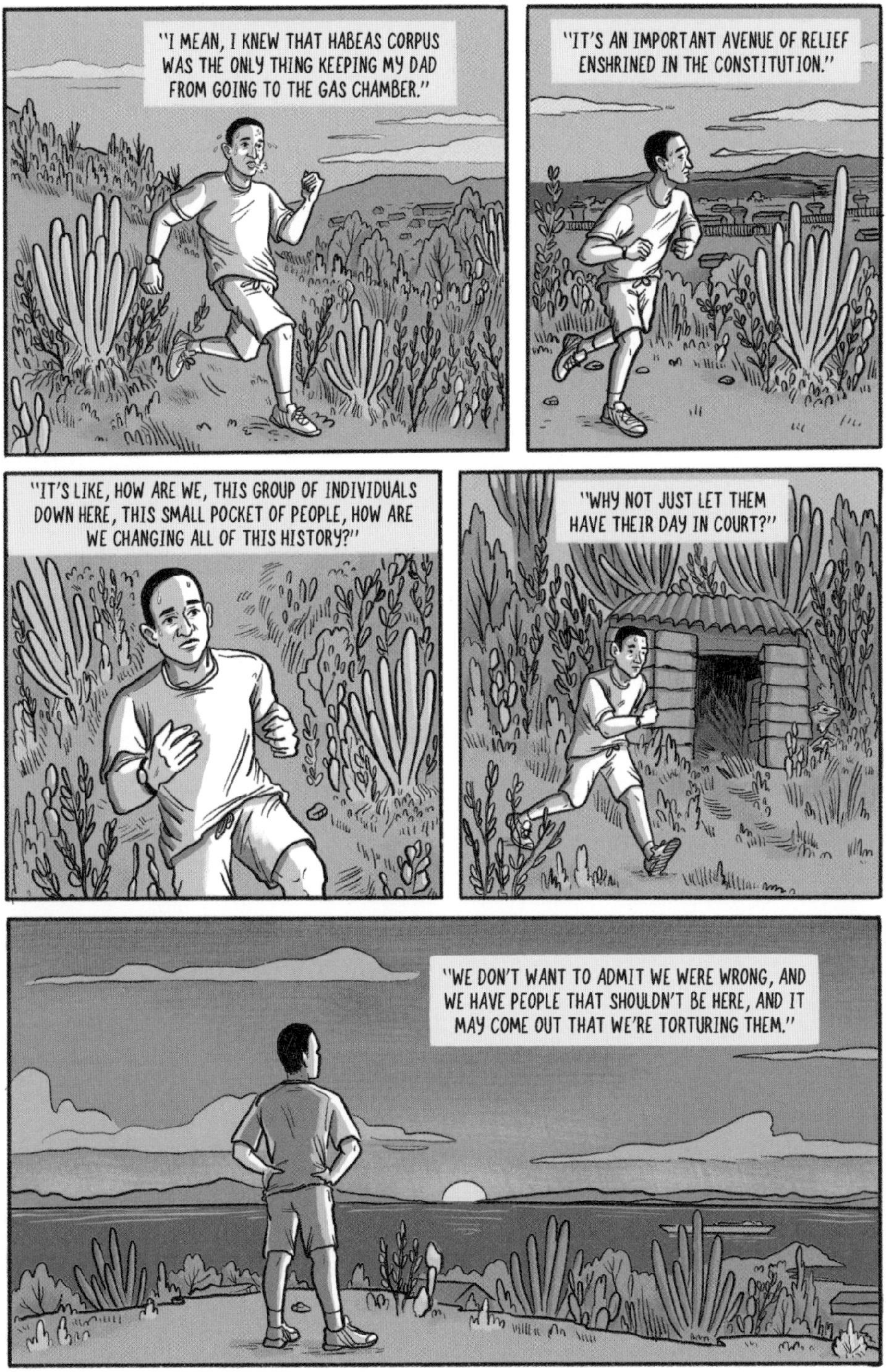
"I MEAN, I KNEW THAT HABEAS CORPUS WAS THE ONLY THING KEEPING MY DAD FROM GOING TO THE GAS CHAMBER."
"IT'S AN IMPORTANT AVENUE OF RELIEF ENSHRINED IN THE CONSTITUTION."
"IT'S LIKE, HOW ARE WE, THIS GROUP OF INDIVIDUALS DOWN HERE, THIS SMALL POCKET OF PEOPLE, HOW ARE WE CHANGING ALL OF THIS HISTORY?"
"WHY NOT JUST LET THEM HAVE THEIR DAY IN COURT?"
"WE DON'T WANT TO ADMIT WE WERE WRONG, AND WE HAVE PEOPLE THAT SHOULDN'T BE HERE, AND IT MAY COME OUT THAT WE'RE TORTURING THEM."

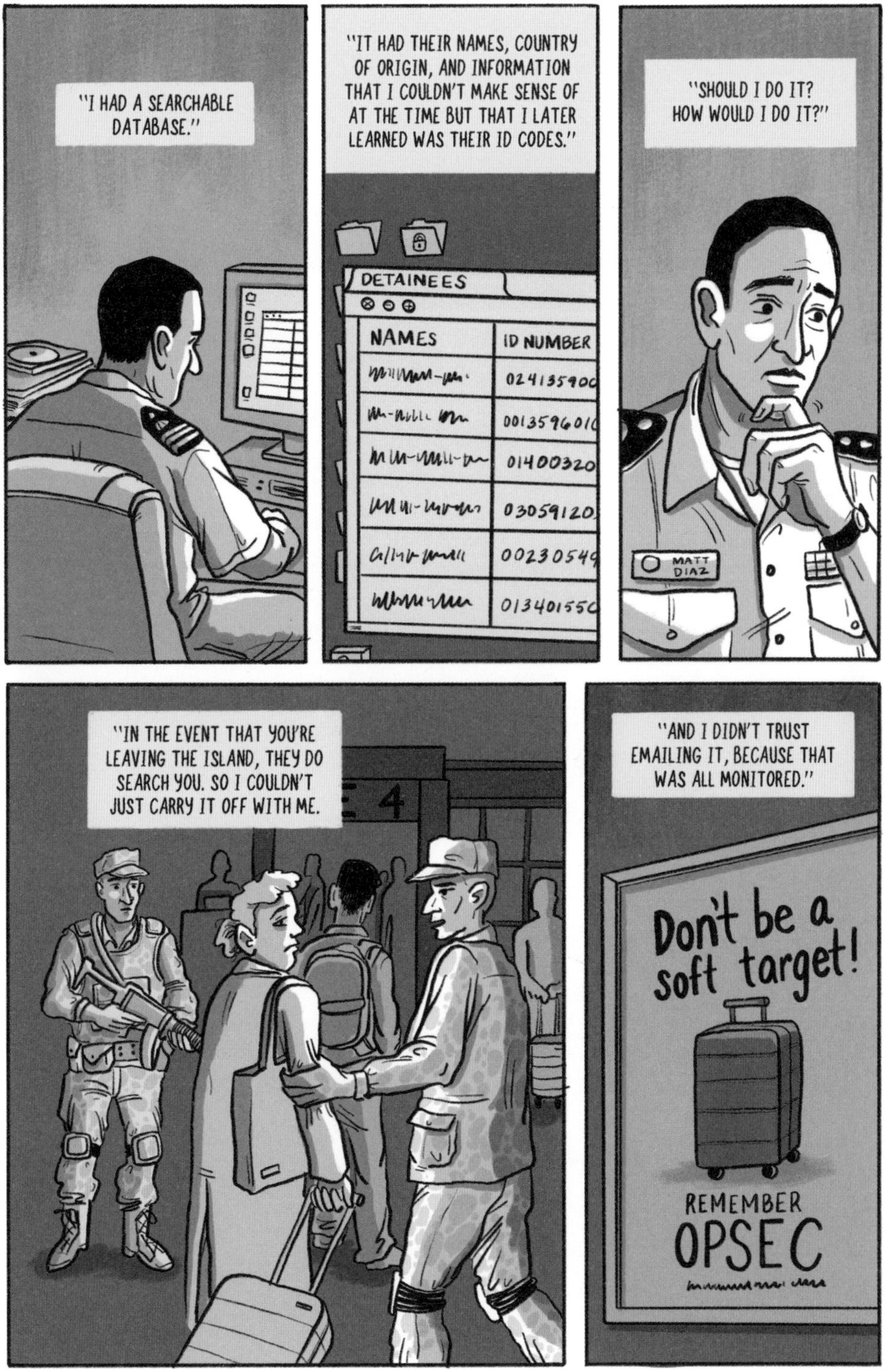
"I HAD A SEARCHABLE DATABASE."
"IT HAD THEIR NAMES, COUNTRY OF ORIGIN, AND INFORMATION THAT I COULDN'T MAKE SENSE OF AT THE TIME BUT THAT I LATER LEARNED WAS THEIR ID CODES."
DETAINEES
NAMES
ID NUMBER
"SHOULD I DO IT? HOW WOULD I DO IT?"
MATT DIAZ
"IN THE EVENT THAT YOU'RE LEAVING THE ISLAND, THEY DO SEARCH YOU. SO I COULDN'T JUST CARRY IT OFF WITH ME.
"AND I DIDN'T TRUST EMAILING IT, BECAUSE THAT WAS ALL MONITORED."
Don't be a soft target!
REMEMBER
OPSEC

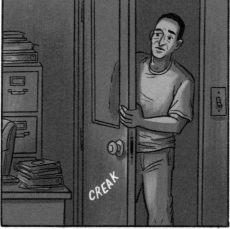

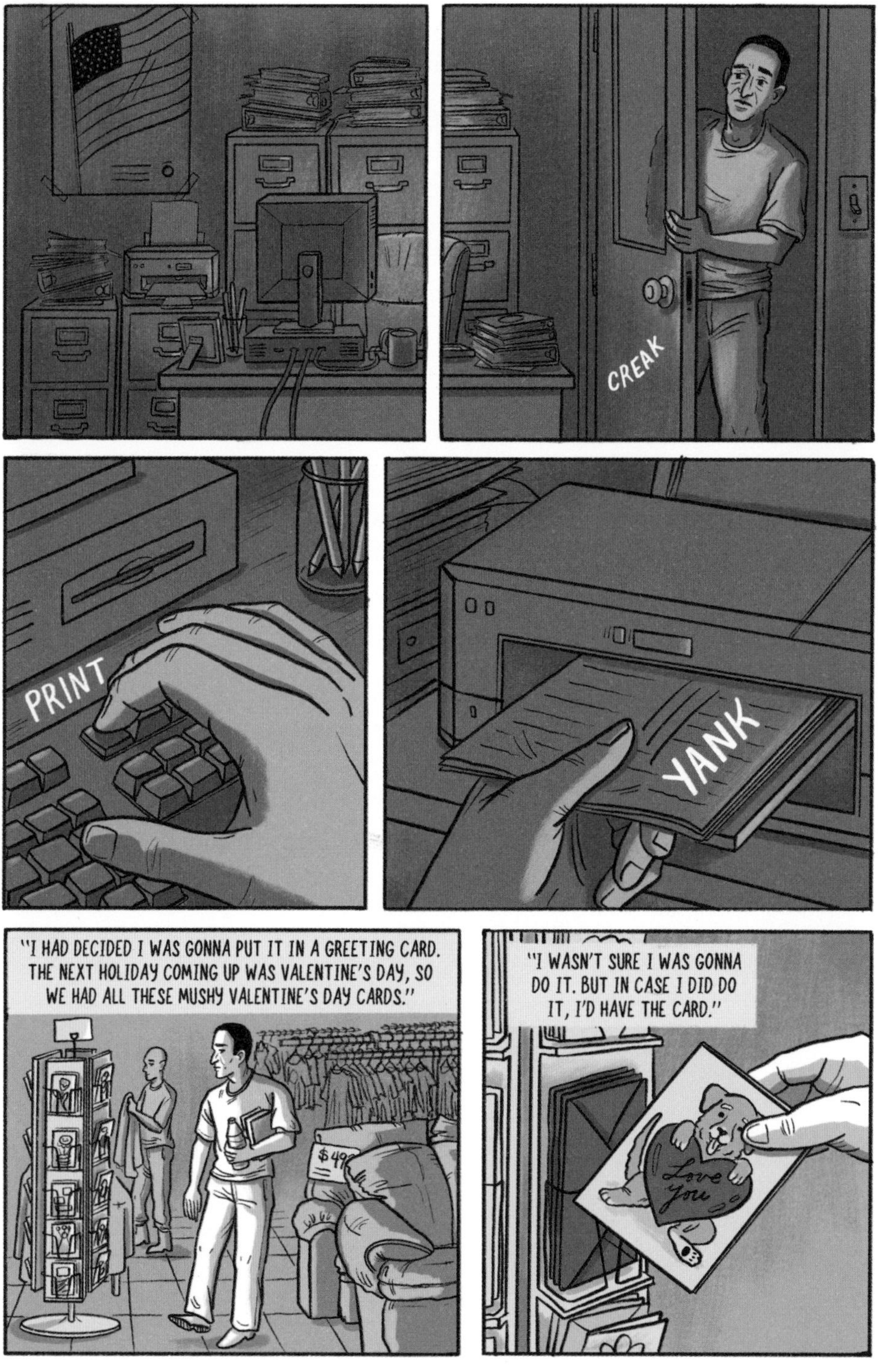
CREAK
PRINT
YANK
"I HAD DECIDED I WAS GONNA PUT IT IN A GREETING CARD. THE NEXT HOLIDAY COMING UP WAS VALENTINE'S DAY, SO WE HAD ALL THESE MUSHY VALENTINE'S DAY CARDS."
"I WASN'T SURE I WAS GONNA DO IT. BUT IN CASE I DID DO IT, I'D HAVE THE CARD."
Love you

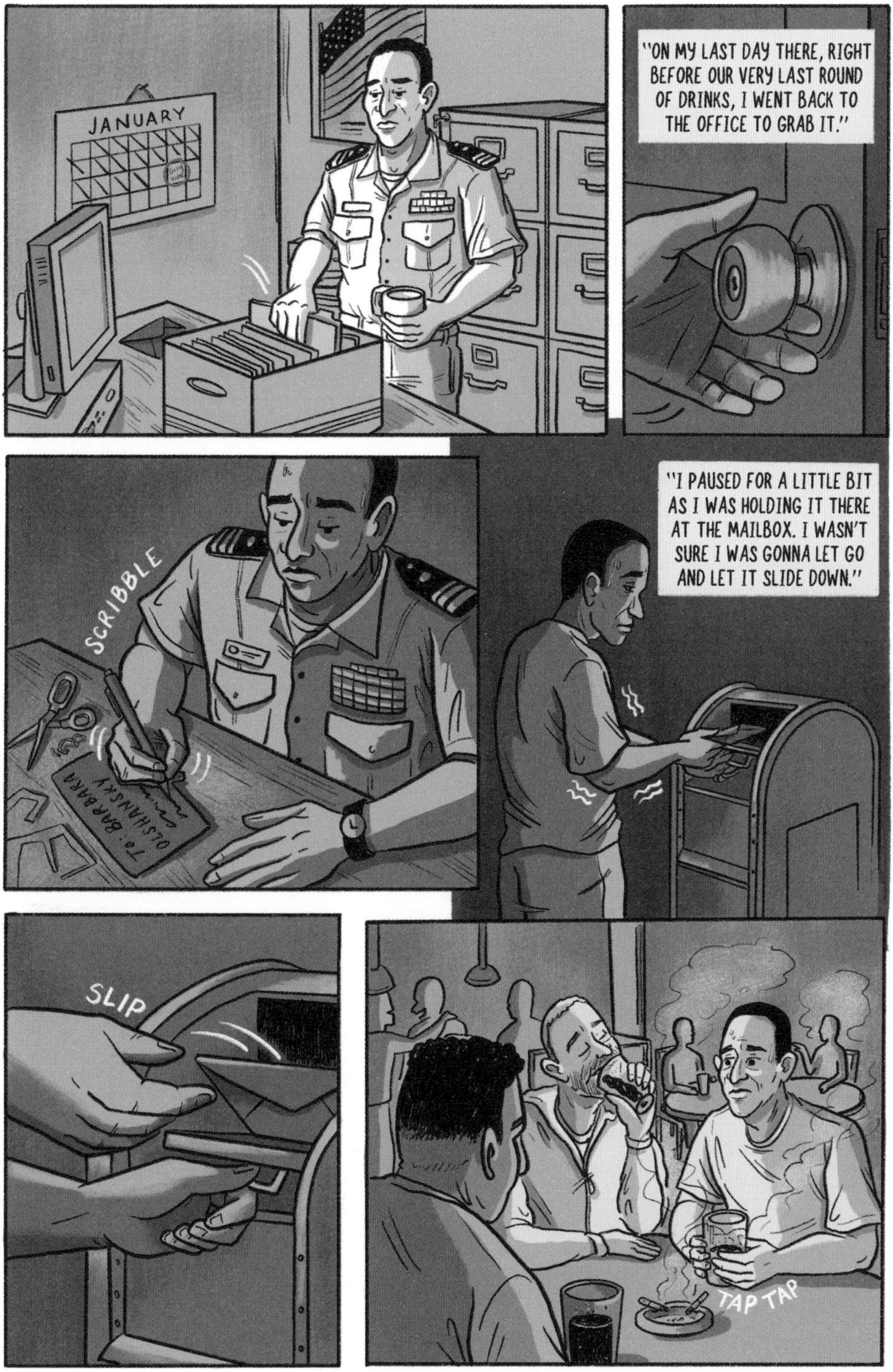
JANUARY
"ON MY LAST DAY THERE, RIGHT BEFORE OUR VERY LAST ROUND OF DRINKS, I WENT BACK TO THE OFFICE TO GRAB IT."
SCRIBBLE
TO: BARBARA OLSHANSKY
"I PAUSED FOR A LITTLE BIT AS I WAS HOLDING IT THERE AT THE MAILBOX. I WASN'T SURE I WAS GONNA LET GO AND LET IT SLIDE DOWN."
SLIP
TAP TAP

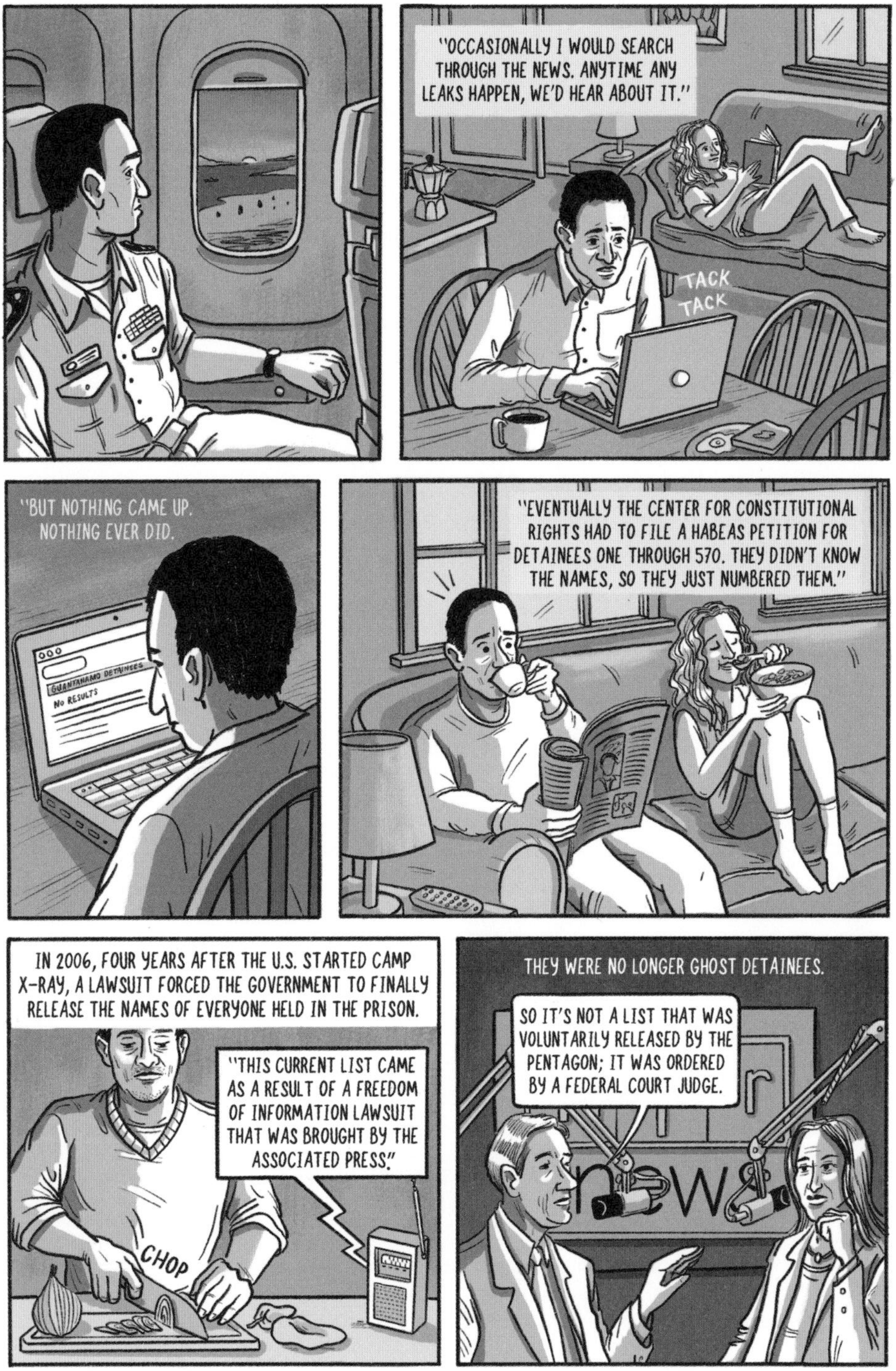
"OCCASIONALLY I WOULD SEARCH THROUGH THE NEWS. ANYTIME ANY LEAKS HAPPEN, WE'D HEAR ABOUT IT."
TACK TACK
"BUT NOTHING CAME UP. NOTHING EVER DID.
GUANTANAMO DETAINEES
NO RESULTS
"EVENTUALLY THE CENTER FOR CONSTITUTIONAL RIGHTS HAD TO FILE A HABEAS PETITION FOR DETAINEES ONE THROUGH 570. THEY DIDN'T KNOW THE NAMES, SO THEY JUST NUMBERED THEM."
IN 2006, FOUR YEARS AFTER THE U.S. STARTED CAMP X-RAY, A LAWSUIT FORCED THE GOVERNMENT TO FINALLY RELEASE THE NAMES OF EVERYONE HELD IN THE PRISON.
"THIS CURRENT LIST CAME AS A RESULT OF A FREEDOM OF INFORMATION LAWSUIT THAT WAS BROUGHT BY THE ASSOCIATED PRESS."
CHOP
THEY WERE NO LONGER GHOST DETAINEES.
SO IT'S NOT A LIST THAT WAS VOLUNTARILY RELEASED BY THE PENTAGON; IT WAS ORDERED BY A FEDERAL COURT JUDGE.

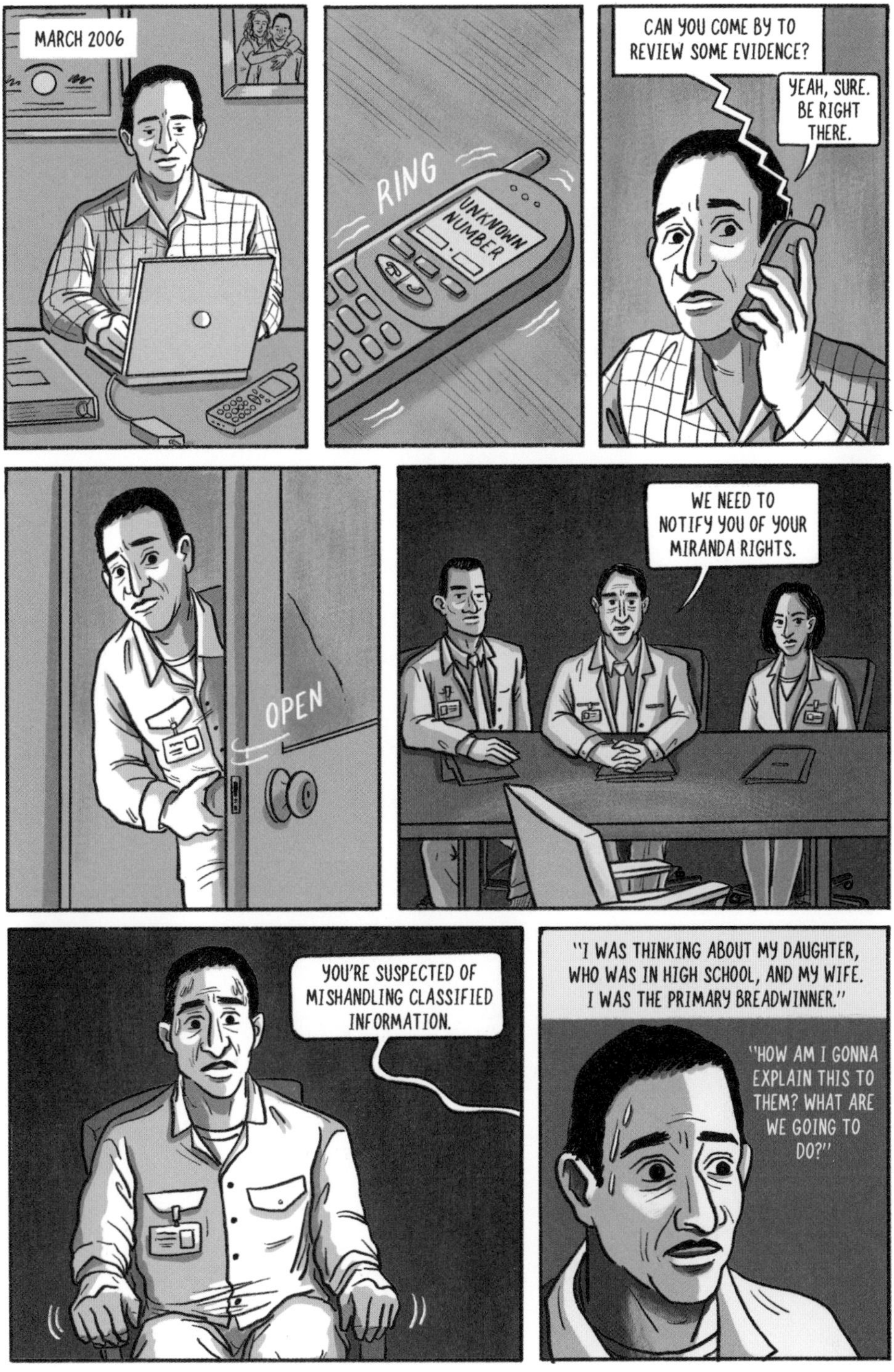
MARCH 2006
RING
UNKNOWN NUMBER
CAN YOU COME BY TO REVIEW SOME EVIDENCE?
YEAH, SURE. BE RIGHT THERE.
OPEN
WE NEED TO NOTIFY YOU OF YOUR MIRANDA RIGHTS.
YOU'RE SUSPECTED OF MISHANDLING CLASSIFIED INFORMATION.
"I WAS THINKING ABOUT MY DAUGHTER, WHO WAS IN HIGH SCHOOL, AND MY WIFE. I WAS THE PRIMARY BREADWINNER."
"HOW AM I GONNA EXPLAIN THIS TO THEM? WHAT ARE WE GOING TO DO?"

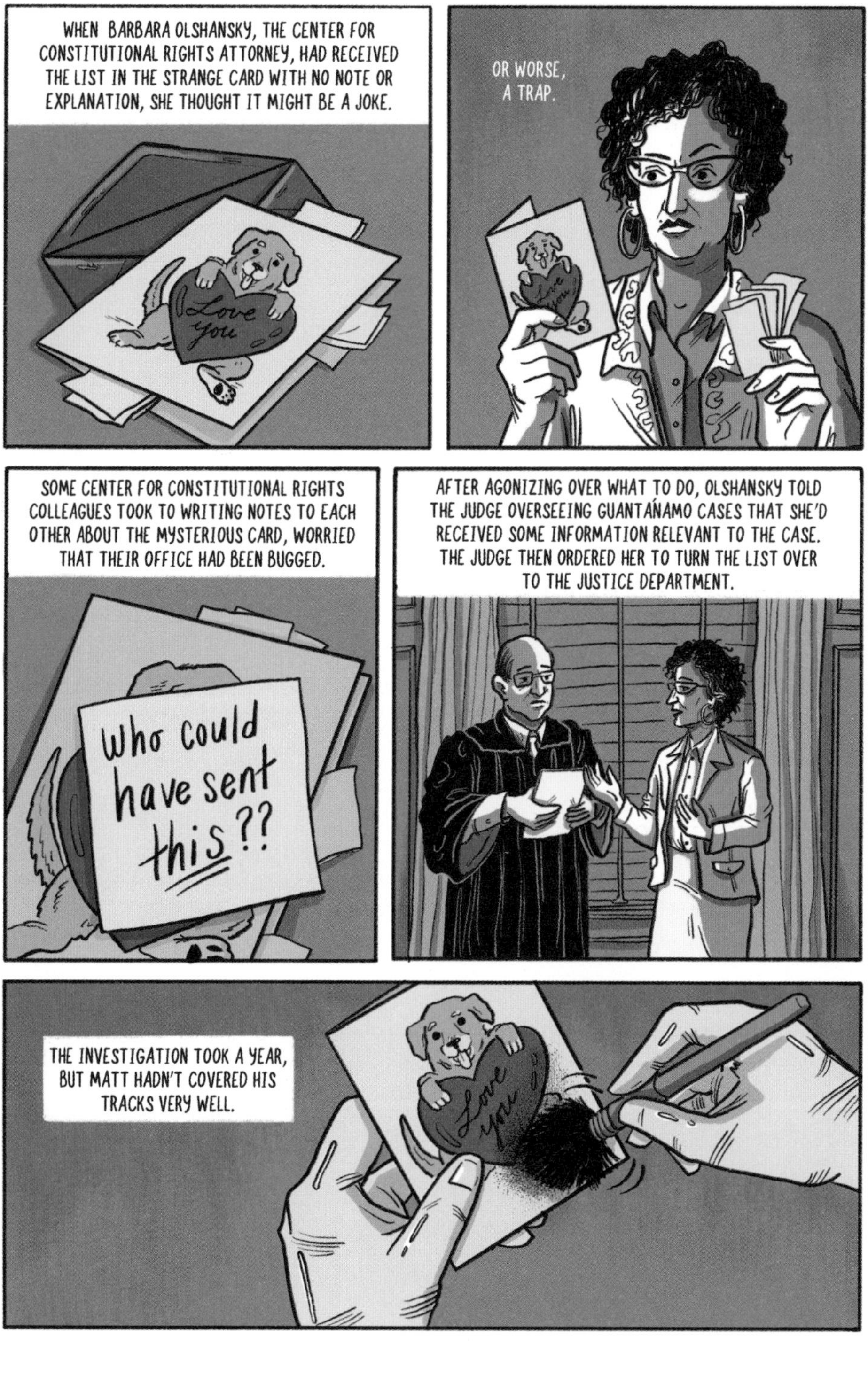
WHEN BARBARA OLSHANSKY, THE CENTER FOR CONSTITUTIONAL RIGHTS ATTORNEY, HAD RECEIVED THE LIST IN THE STRANGE CARD WITH NO NOTE OR EXPLANATION, SHE THOUGHT IT MIGHT BE A JOKE.
Love you
OR WORSE, A TRAP.
Love you
SOME CENTER FOR CONSTITUTIONAL RIGHTS COLLEAGUES TOOK TO WRITING NOTES TO EACH OTHER ABOUT THE MYSTERIOUS CARD, WORRIED THAT THEIR OFFICE HAD BEEN BUGGED.
Who could have sent this??
AFTER AGONIZING OVER WHAT TO DO, OLSHANSKY TOLD THE JUDGE OVERSEEING GUANTÁNAMO CASES THAT SHE'D RECEIVED SOME INFORMATION RELEVANT TO THE CASE. THE JUDGE THEN ORDERED HER TO TURN THE LIST OVER TO THE JUSTICE DEPARTMENT.
THE INVESTIGATION TOOK A YEAR, BUT MATT HADN'T COVERED HIS TRACKS VERY WELL.
Love you

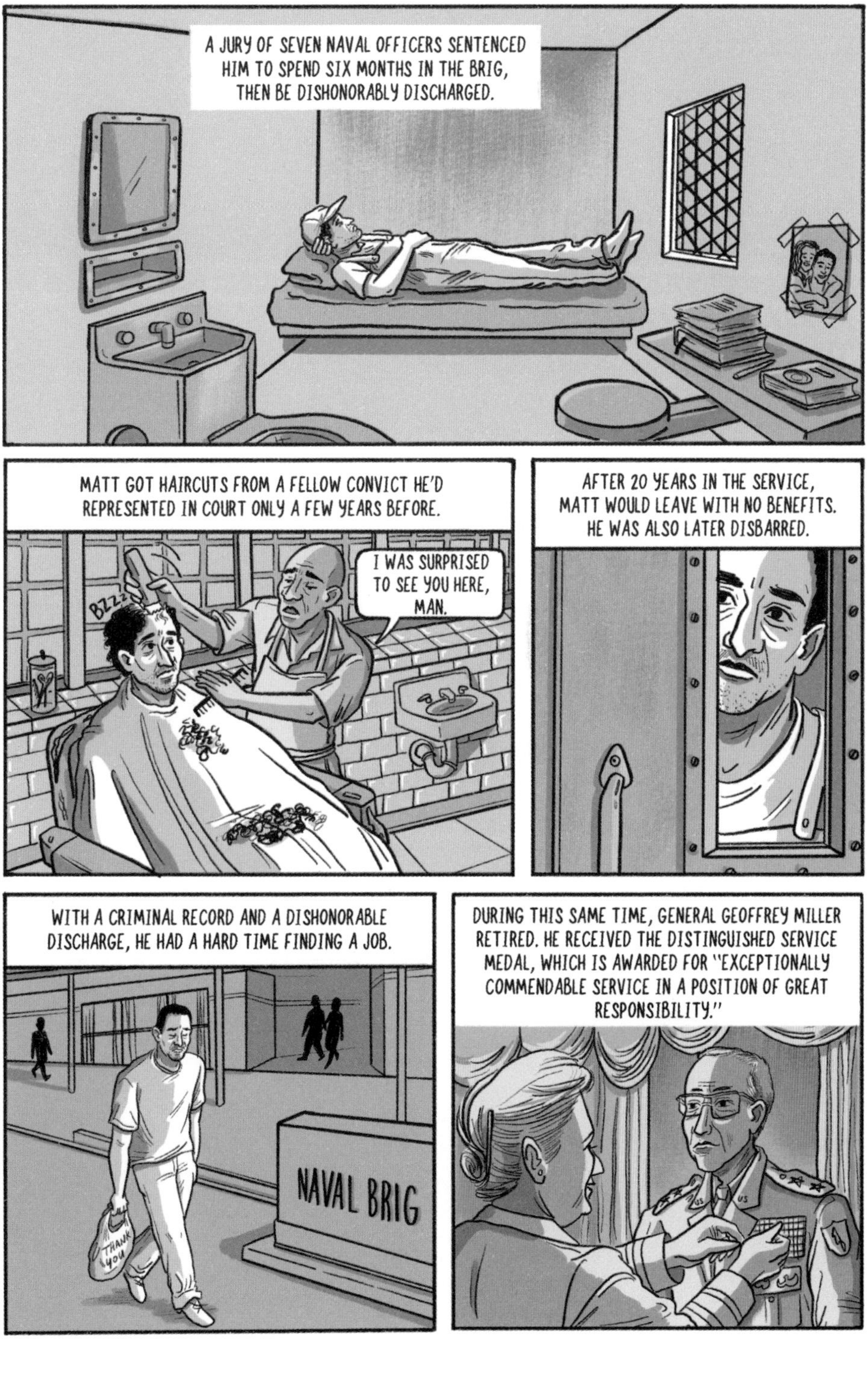
A JURY OF SEVEN NAVAL OFFICERS SENTENCED HIM TO SPEND SIX MONTHS IN THE BRIG, THEN BE DISHONORABLY DISCHARGED.
MATT GOT HAIRCUTS FROM A FELLOW CONVICT HE'D REPRESENTED IN COURT ONLY A FEW YEARS BEFORE.
BZZZ
I WAS SURPRISED TO SEE YOU HERE, MAN.
AFTER 20 YEARS IN THE SERVICE, MATT WOULD LEAVE WITH NO BENEFITS. HE WAS ALSO LATER DISBARRED.
WITH A CRIMINAL RECORD AND A DISHONORABLE DISCHARGE, HE HAD A HARD TIME FINDING A JOB.
THANK YOU
NAVAL BRIG
DURING THIS SAME TIME, GENERAL GEOFFREY MILLER RETIRED. HE RECEIVED THE DISTINGUISHED SERVICE MEDAL, WHICH IS AWARDED FOR "EXCEPTIONALLY COMMENDABLE SERVICE IN A POSITION OF GREAT RESPONSIBILITY."

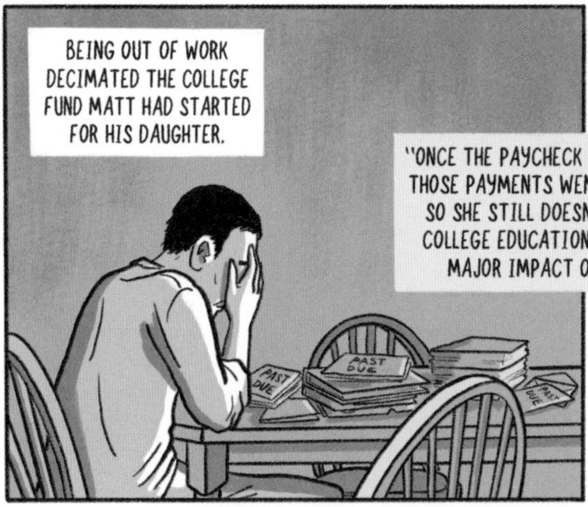
BEING OUT OF WORK DECIMATED THE COLLEGE FUND MATT HAD STARTED FOR HIS DAUGHTER.
"ONCE THE PAYCHECK WENT AWAY, THOSE PAYMENTS WENT AWAY . . . SO SHE STILL DOESN'T HAVE A COLLEGE EDUCATION. IT HAD A MAJOR IMPACT ON HER."
PAST DUE
PAST DUE
PAST DUE

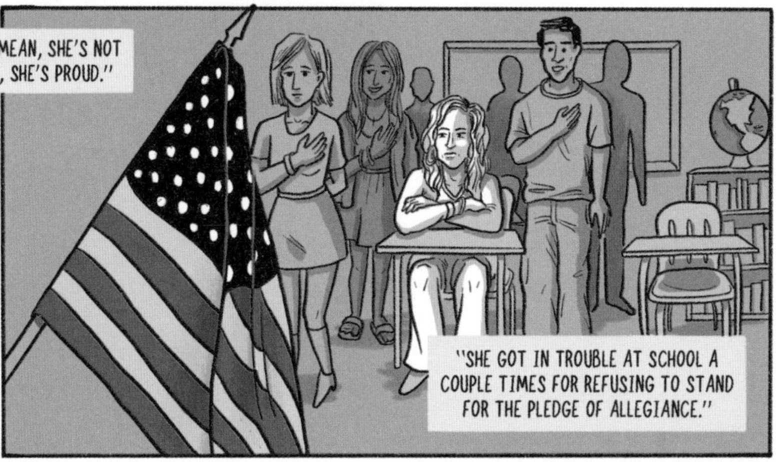
"BUT, I MEAN, SHE'S NOT BITTER, SHE'S PROUD."
"SHE GOT IN TROUBLE AT SCHOOL A COUPLE TIMES FOR REFUSING TO STAND FOR THE PLEDGE OF ALLEGIANCE."

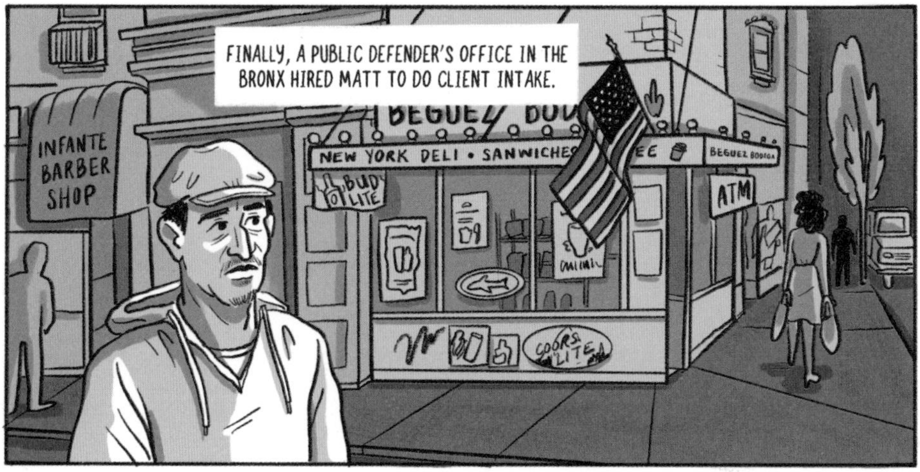
FINALLY, A PUBLIC DEFENDER'S OFFICE IN THE BRONX HIRED MATT TO DO CLIENT INTAKE.
INFANTE BARBER SHOP
NEW YORK DELI • SANWICHES
BUD LITE
ATM
COORS LITE

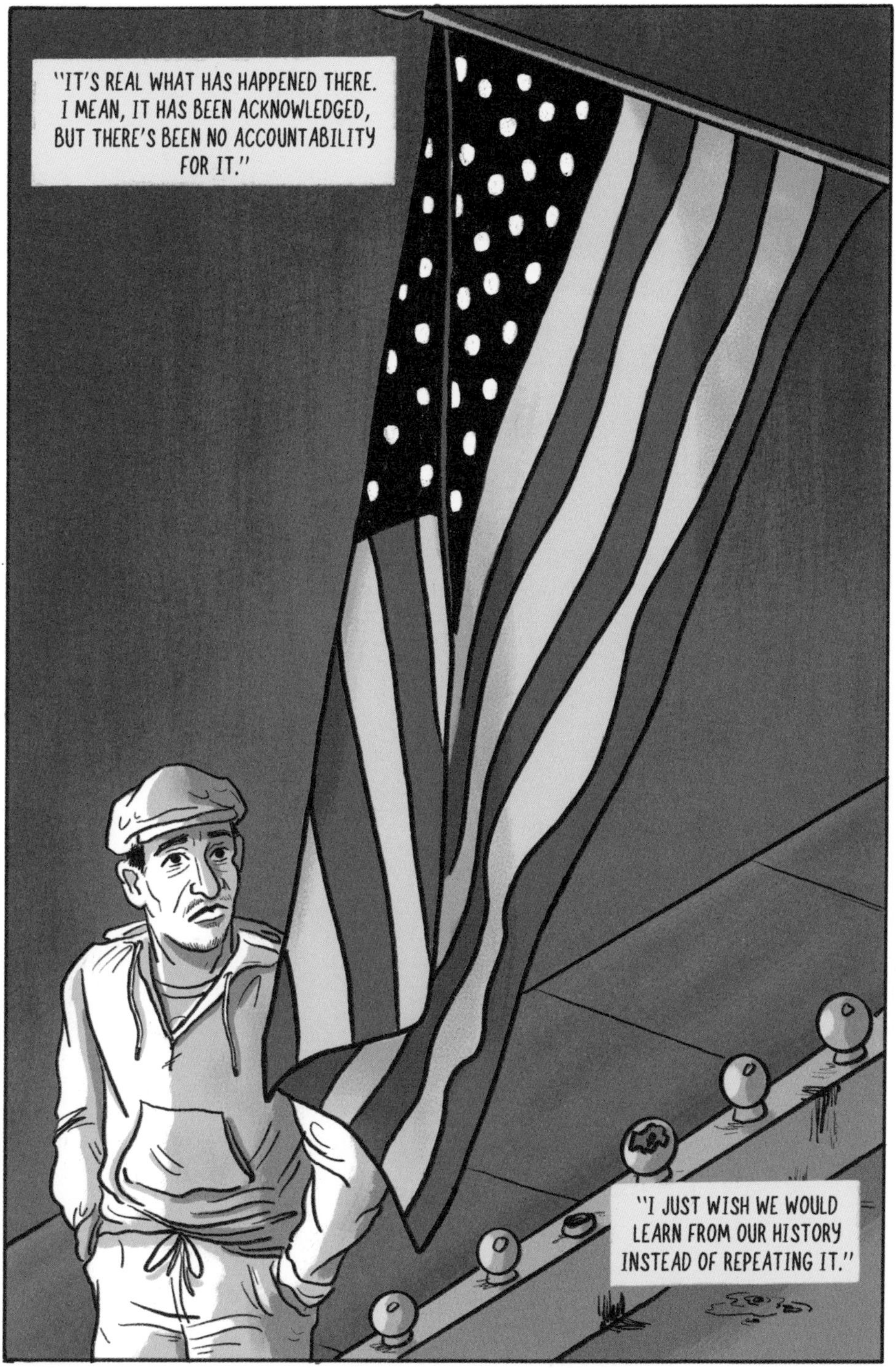
"IT'S REAL WHAT HAS HAPPENED THERE. I MEAN, IT HAS BEEN ACKNOWLEDGED, BUT THERE'S BEEN NO ACCOUNTABILITY FOR IT."
"I JUST WISH WE WOULD LEARN FROM OUR HISTORY INSTEAD OF REPEATING IT."

CHAPTER FOUR

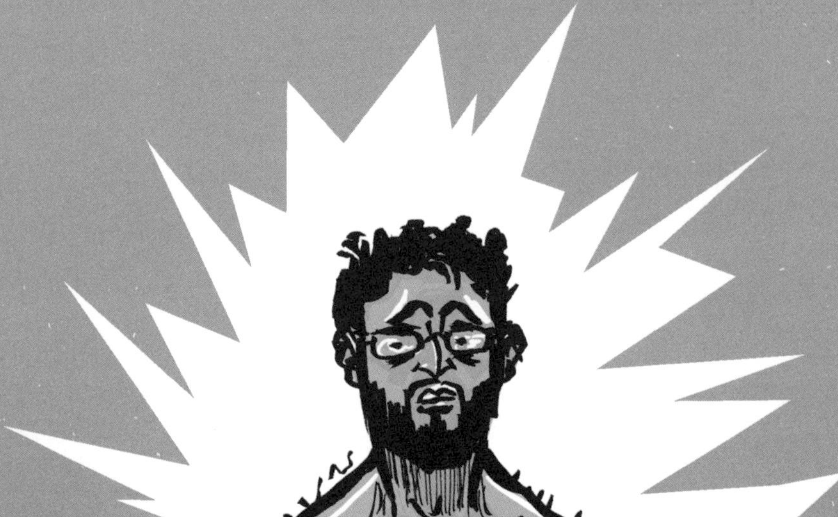
ENEMY PRISONER OF WAR
558

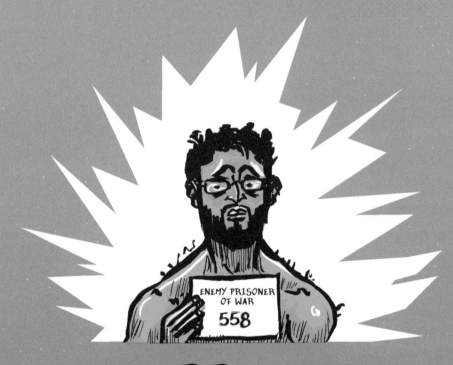

MOAZZAM BEGG

EDUCATOR AND
GUANTANAMO PRISONER 558,
FEBRUARY 2003 TO JANUARY 2005

ILLUSTRATED BY
OMAR KHOURI

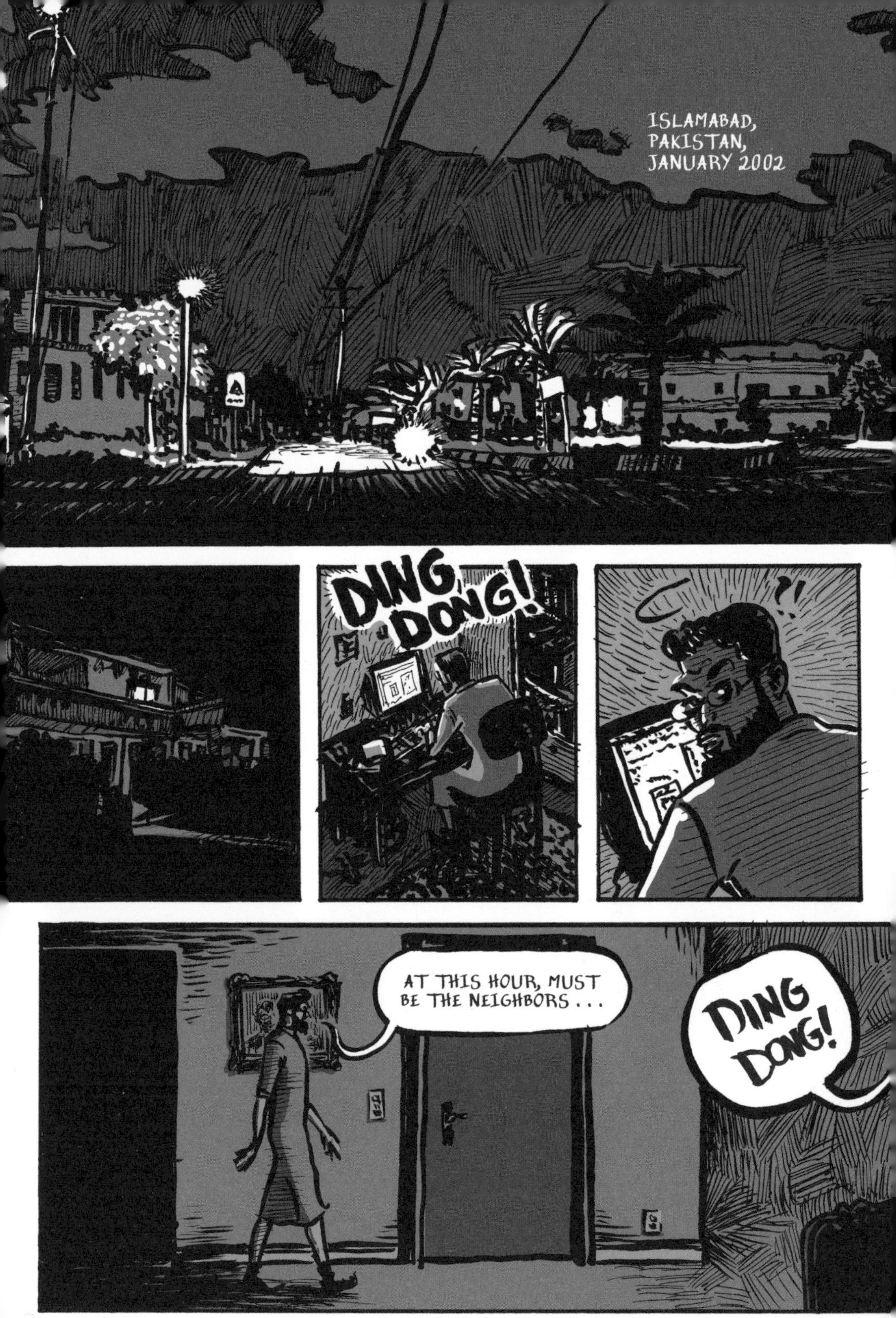
ISLAMABAD, PAKISTAN, JANUARY 2002
DING DONG!
?!
AT THIS HOUR, MUST BE THE NEIGHBORS . . .
DING DONG!

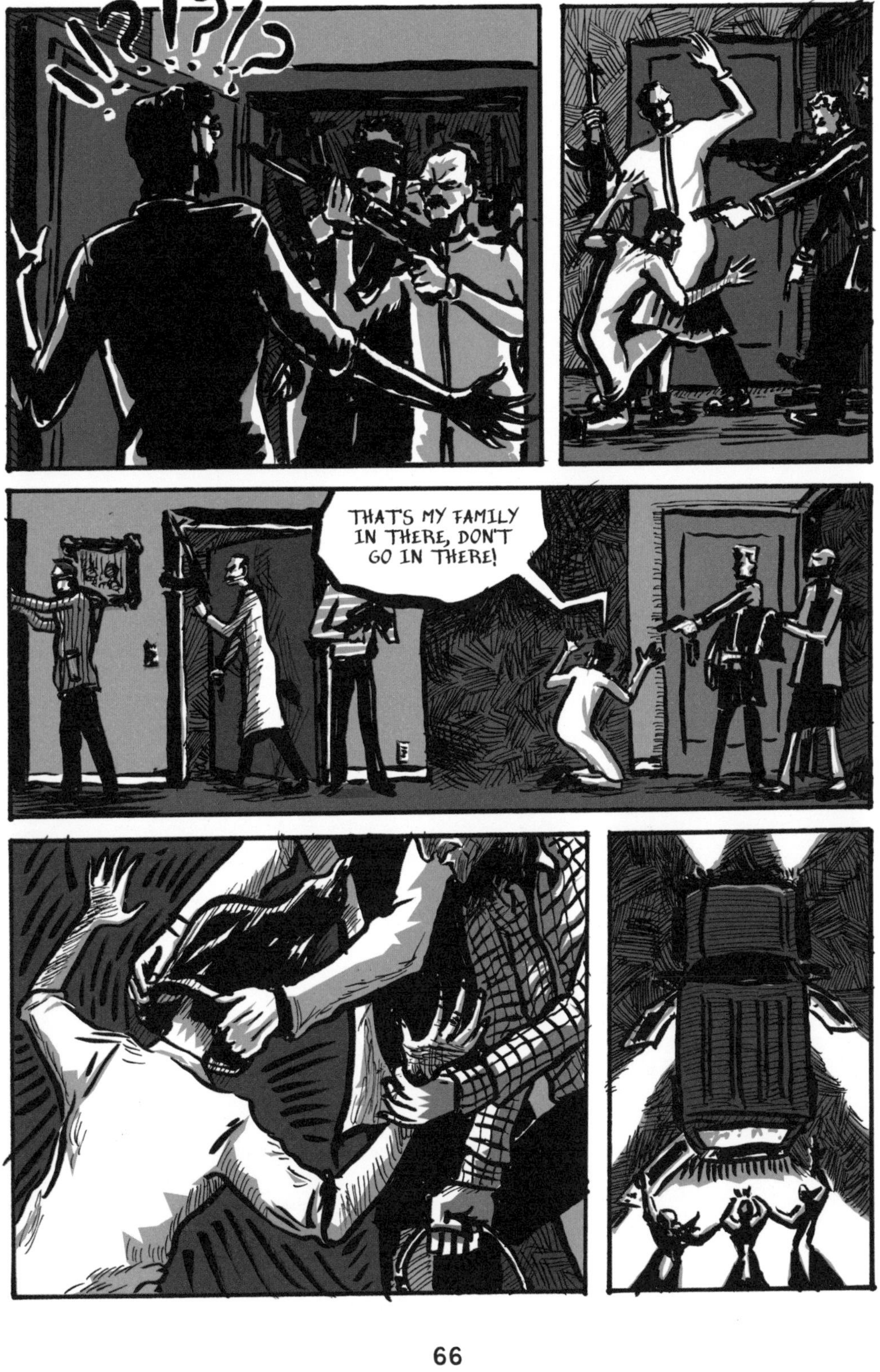
!!?!?!?
THAT'S MY FAMILY IN THERE, DON'T GO IN THERE!

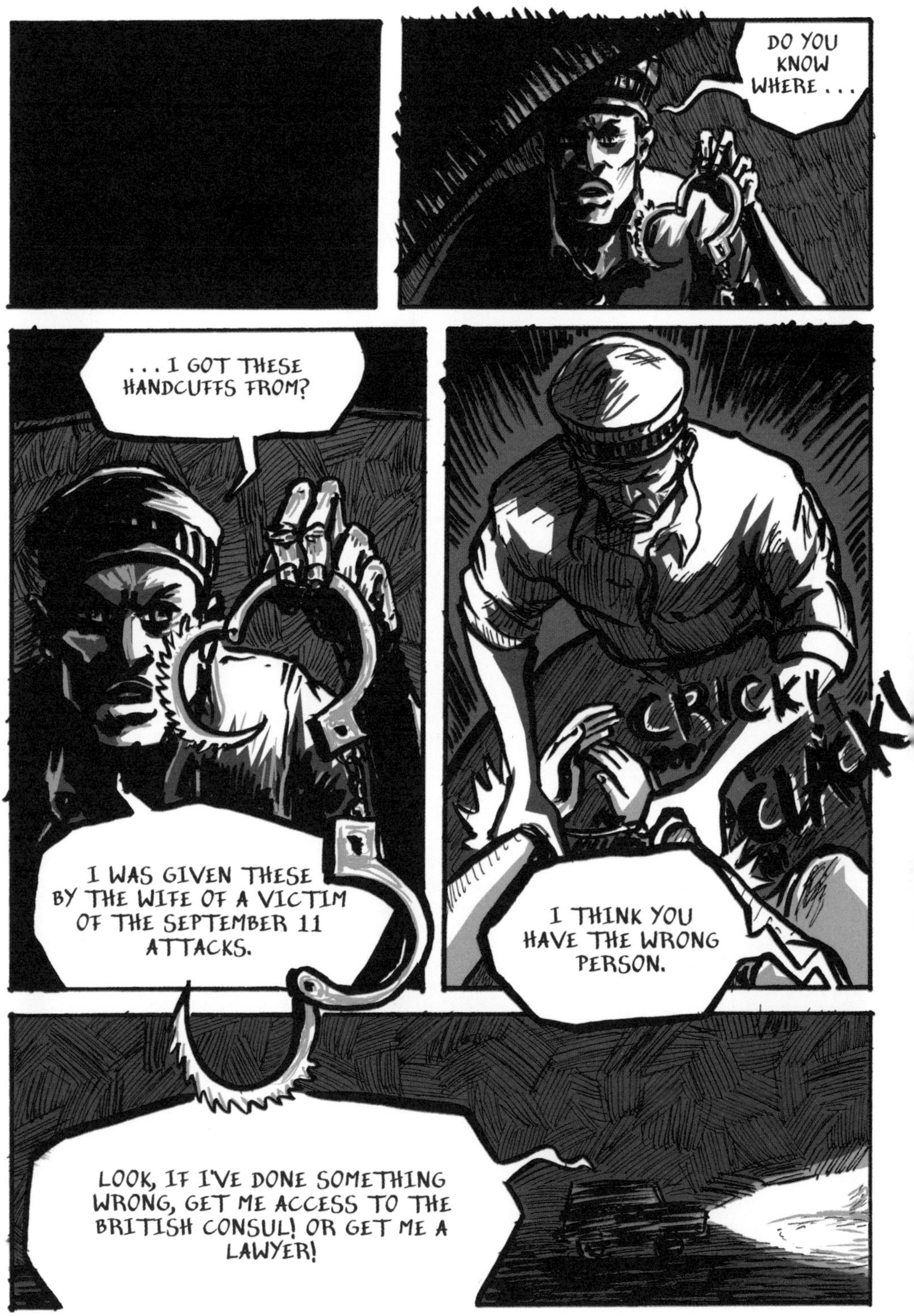
DO YOU KNOW WHERE . . .
. . . I GOT THESE HANDCUFFS FROM?
I WAS GIVEN THESE BY THE WIFE OF A VICTIM OF THE SEPTEMBER 11 ATTACKS.
CRICK!
CLACK!
I THINK YOU HAVE THE WRONG PERSON.
LOOK, IF I'VE DONE SOMETHING WRONG, GET ME ACCESS TO THE BRITISH CONSUL! OR GET ME A LAWYER!

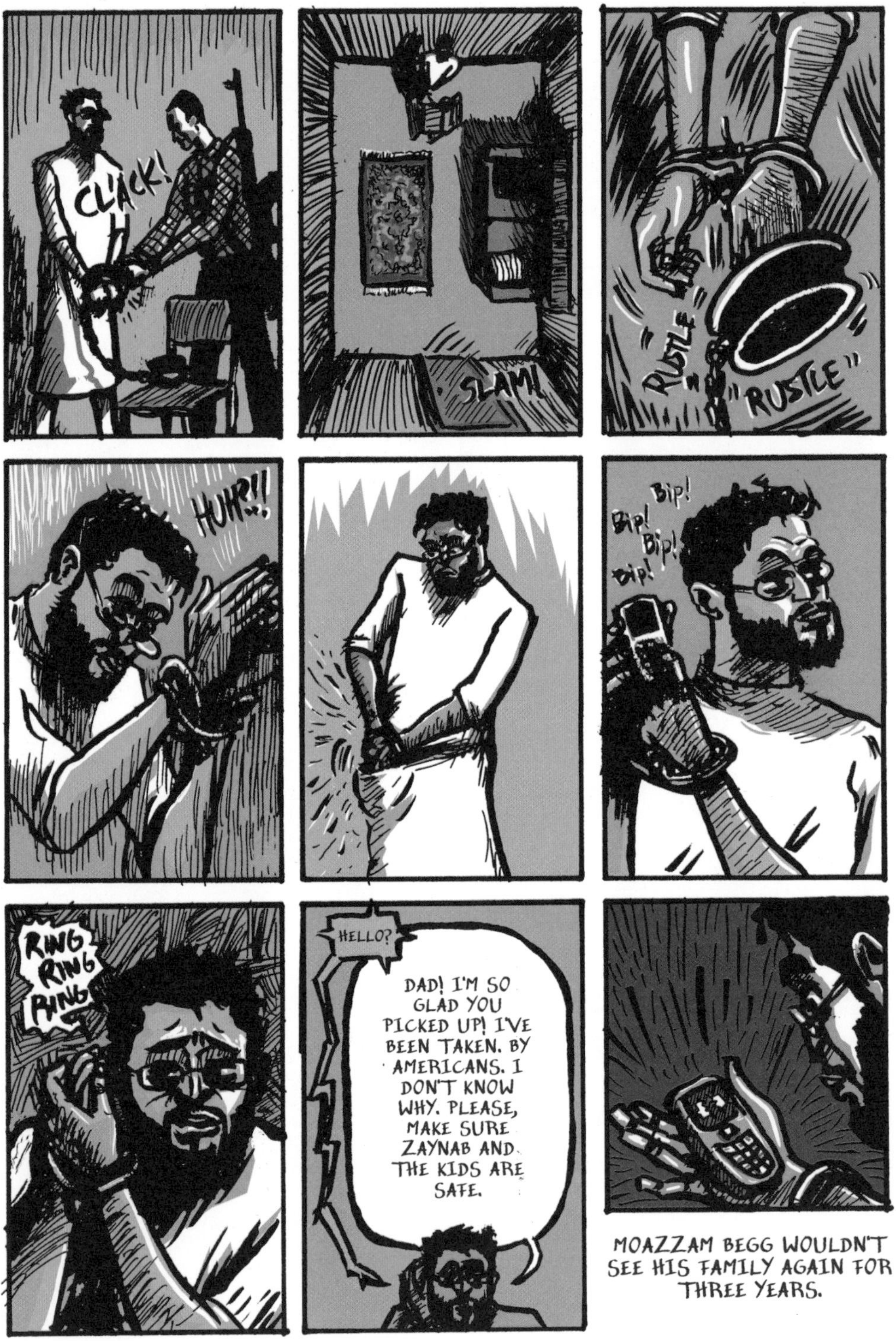
CLACK!
SLAM!
"RUSTLE"
"RUSTLE"
HUH?!!
Bip!
Bip!
Bip!
Bip!
RING RING RING
HELLO?
DAD! I'M SO GLAD YOU PICKED UP! I'VE BEEN TAKEN. BY AMERICANS. I DON'T KNOW WHY. PLEASE, MAKE SURE ZAYNAB AND THE KIDS ARE SAFE.

MOAZZAM BEGG WOULDN'T SEE HIS FAMILY AGAIN FOR THREE YEARS.

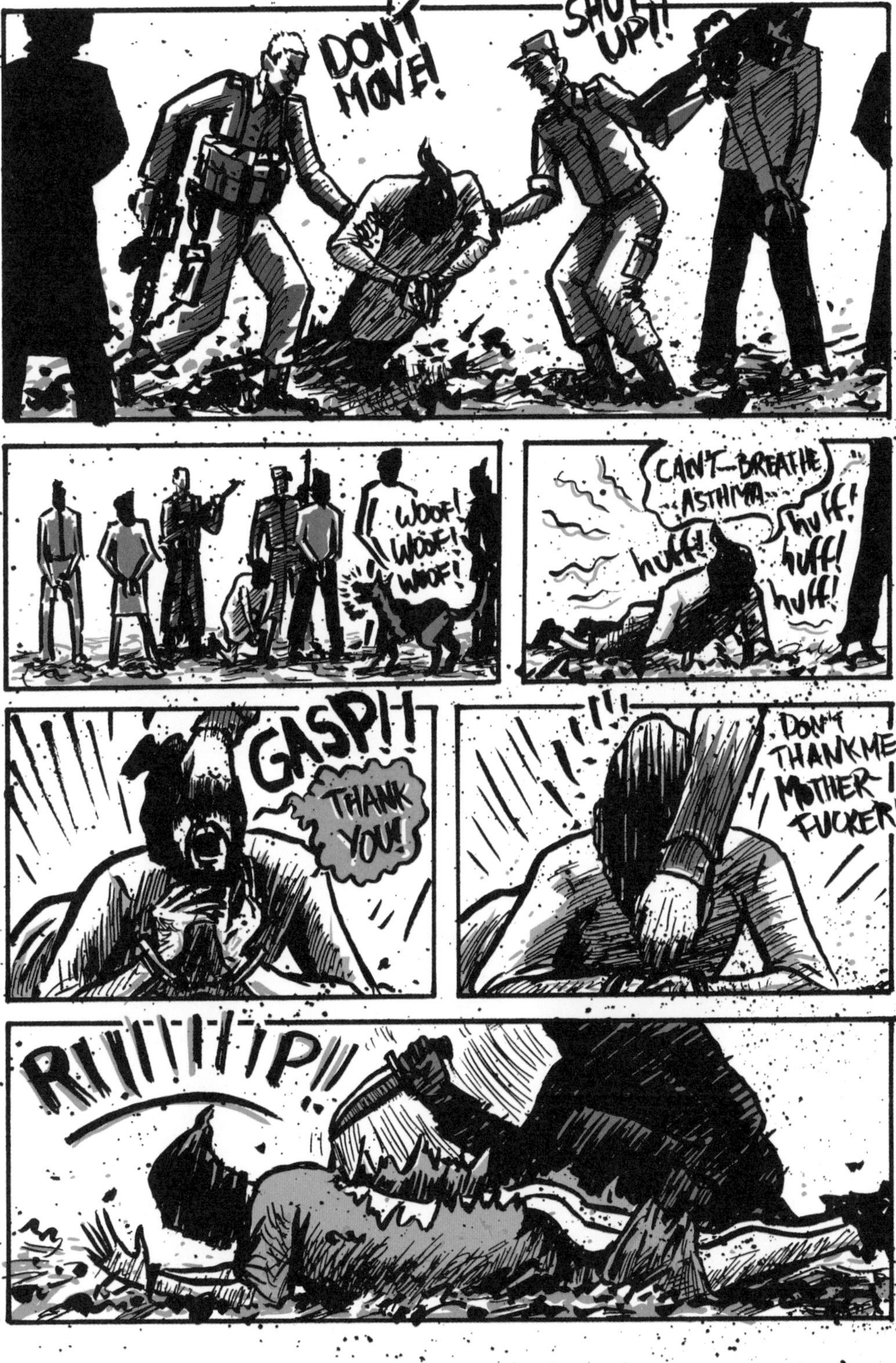
DON'T MOVE!
SHUT UP!!
WOOF! WOOF! WOOF!
CAN'T—BREATHE ...ASTHMA...
huff! huff! huff! huff!
GASP!!
THANK YOU!
!!!
DON'T THANK ME, MOTHER FUCKER!!
RIIIIIIP!

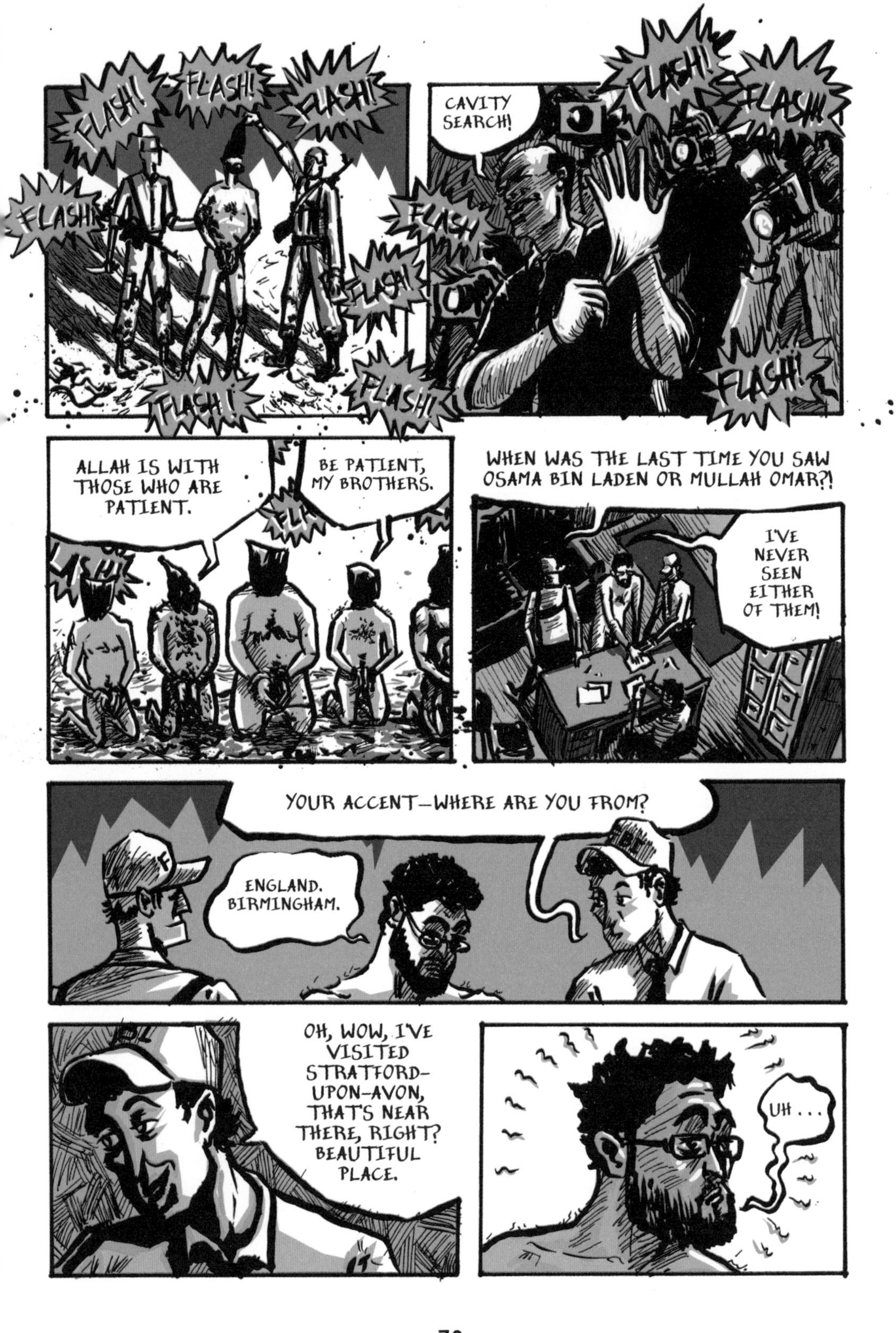
FLASH!
FLASH!
FLASH!
FLASH!
FLASH!
FLASH!
FLASH!
CAVITY SEARCH!
FLASH!
FLASH!
FLASH!
ALLAH IS WITH THOSE WHO ARE PATIENT.
BE PATIENT, MY BROTHERS.
WHEN WAS THE LAST TIME YOU SAW OSAMA BIN LADEN OR MULLAH OMAR?!
I'VE NEVER SEEN EITHER OF THEM!
YOUR ACCENT—WHERE ARE YOU FROM?
ENGLAND. BIRMINGHAM.
OH, WOW, I'VE VISITED STRATFORD-UPON-AVON, THAT'S NEAR THERE, RIGHT? BEAUTIFUL PLACE.
UH . . .

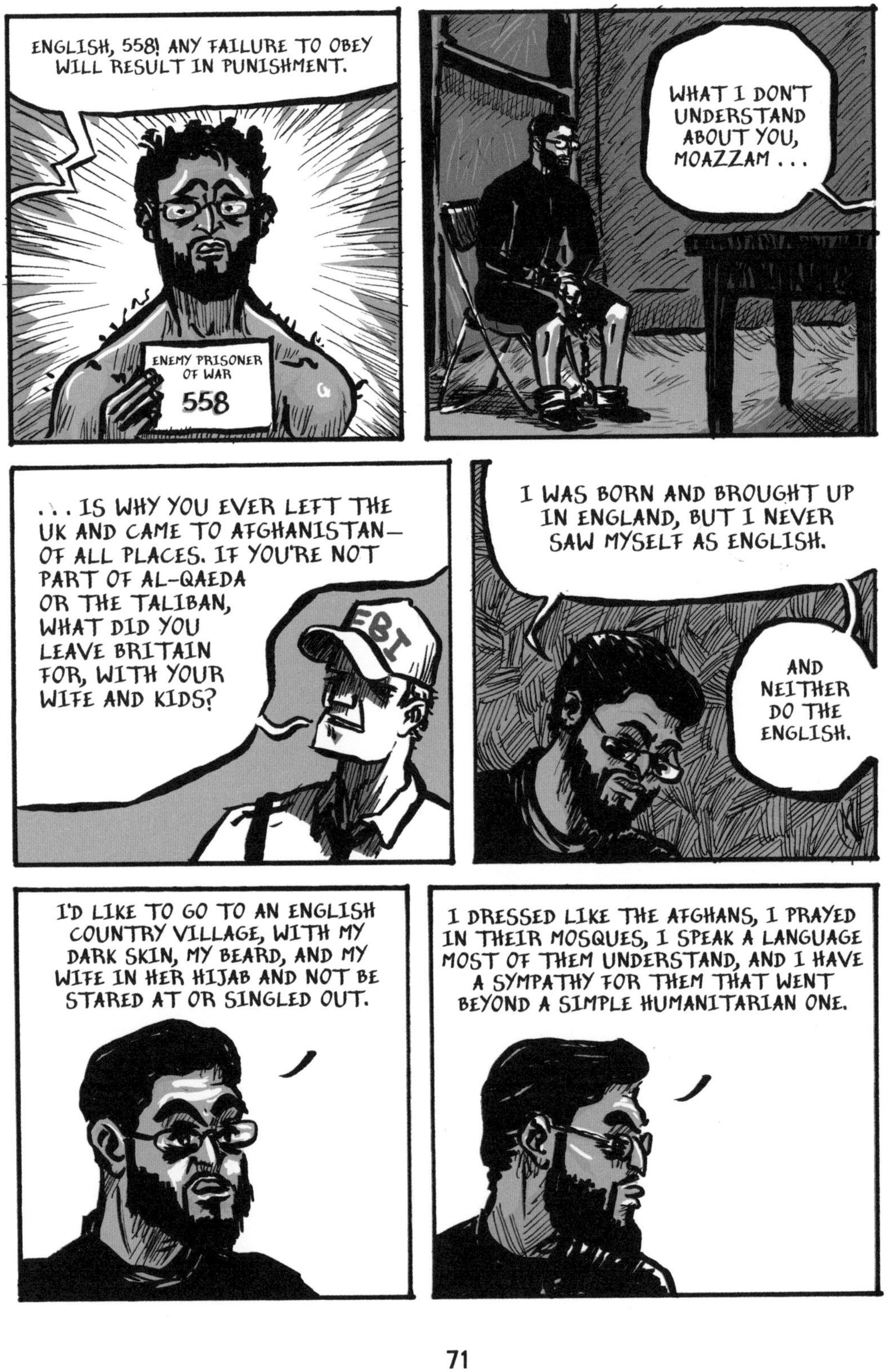
ENGLISH, 558! ANY FAILURE TO OBEY WILL RESULT IN PUNISHMENT.
ENEMY PRISONER OF WAR 558
WHAT I DON'T UNDERSTAND ABOUT YOU, MOAZZAM . . .
. . . IS WHY YOU EVER LEFT THE UK AND CAME TO AFGHANISTAN— OF ALL PLACES. IF YOU'RE NOT PART OF AL-QAEDA OR THE TALIBAN, WHAT DID YOU LEAVE BRITAIN FOR, WITH YOUR WIFE AND KIDS?
FBI
I WAS BORN AND BROUGHT UP IN ENGLAND, BUT I NEVER SAW MYSELF AS ENGLISH.
AND NEITHER DO THE ENGLISH.
I'D LIKE TO GO TO AN ENGLISH COUNTRY VILLAGE, WITH MY DARK SKIN, MY BEARD, AND MY WIFE IN HER HIJAB AND NOT BE STARED AT OR SINGLED OUT.
I DRESSED LIKE THE AFGHANS, I PRAYED IN THEIR MOSQUES, I SPEAK A LANGUAGE MOST OF THEM UNDERSTAND, AND I HAVE A SYMPATHY FOR THEM THAT WENT BEYOND A SIMPLE HUMANITARIAN ONE.

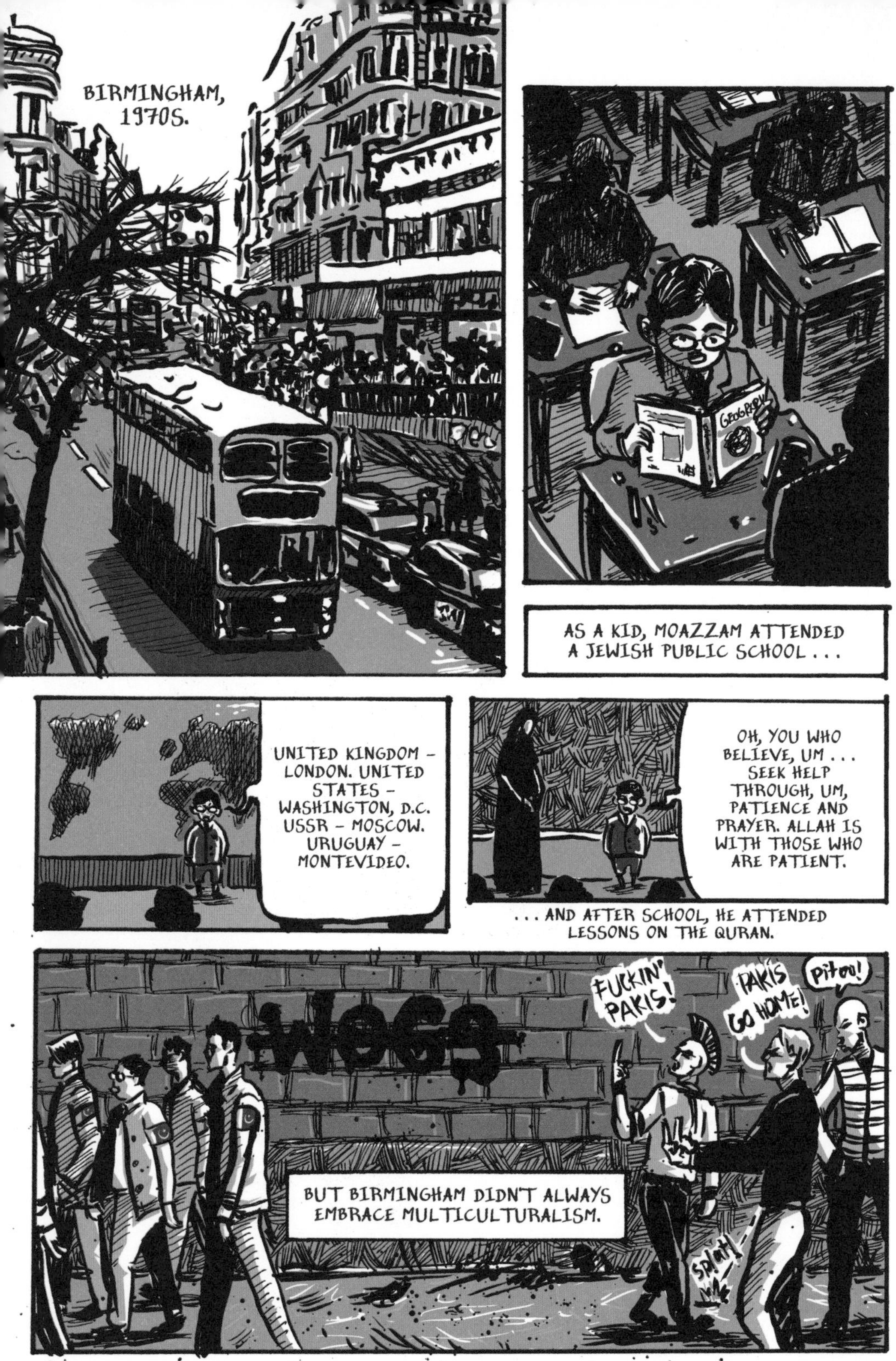
BIRMINGHAM, 1970S.
AS A KID, MOAZZAM ATTENDED A JEWISH PUBLIC SCHOOL . . .
UNITED KINGDOM – LONDON. UNITED STATES – WASHINGTON, D.C. USSR – MOSCOW. URUGUAY – MONTEVIDEO.
OH, YOU WHO BELIEVE, UM . . . SEEK HELP THROUGH, UM, PATIENCE AND PRAYER. ALLAH IS WITH THOSE WHO ARE PATIENT.
. . . AND AFTER SCHOOL, HE ATTENDED LESSONS ON THE QURAN.
WOGS
FUCKIN' PAKIS!
PAKIS GO HOME!
Pitoo!
BUT BIRMINGHAM DIDN'T ALWAYS EMBRACE MULTICULTURALISM.
splat!

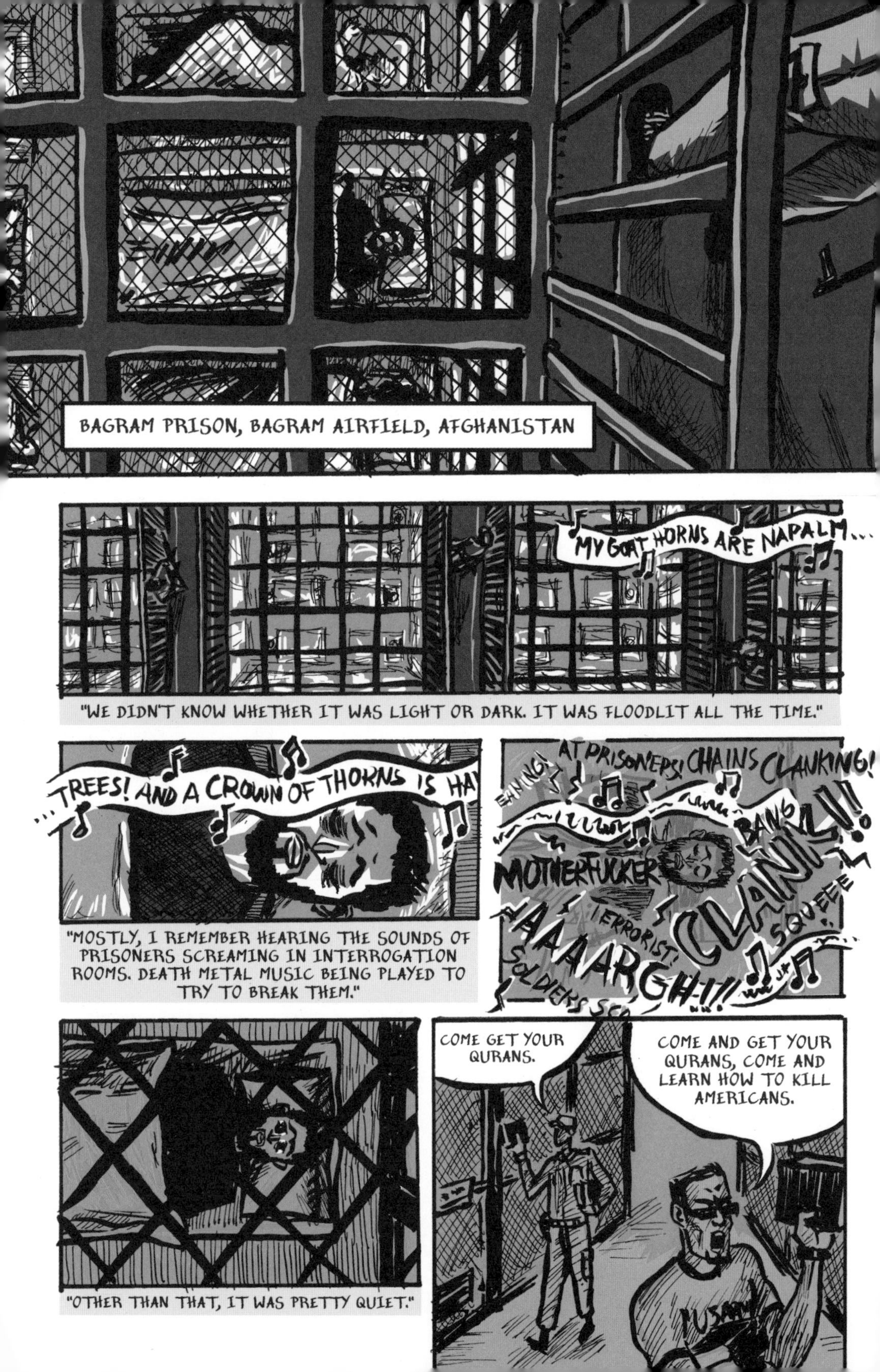
BAGRAM PRISON, BAGRAM AIRFIELD, AFGHANISTAN
MY GOAT HORNS ARE NAPALM...
"WE DIDN'T KNOW WHETHER IT WAS LIGHT OR DARK. IT WAS FLOODLIT ALL THE TIME."
...TREES! AND A CROWN OF THORNS IS HA
"MOSTLY, I REMEMBER HEARING THE SOUNDS OF PRISONERS SCREAMING IN INTERROGATION ROOMS. DEATH METAL MUSIC BEING PLAYED TO TRY TO BREAK THEM."
EAMING! AT PRISONERS! CHAINS CLANKING!
BANG
MOTHERFUCKER
CLANK!!
TERRORIST!
SQUEEE
AAAARGH!!
SOLDIERS SC
"OTHER THAN THAT, IT WAS PRETTY QUIET."
COME GET YOUR QURANS.
COME AND GET YOUR QURANS, COME AND LEARN HOW TO KILL AMERICANS.

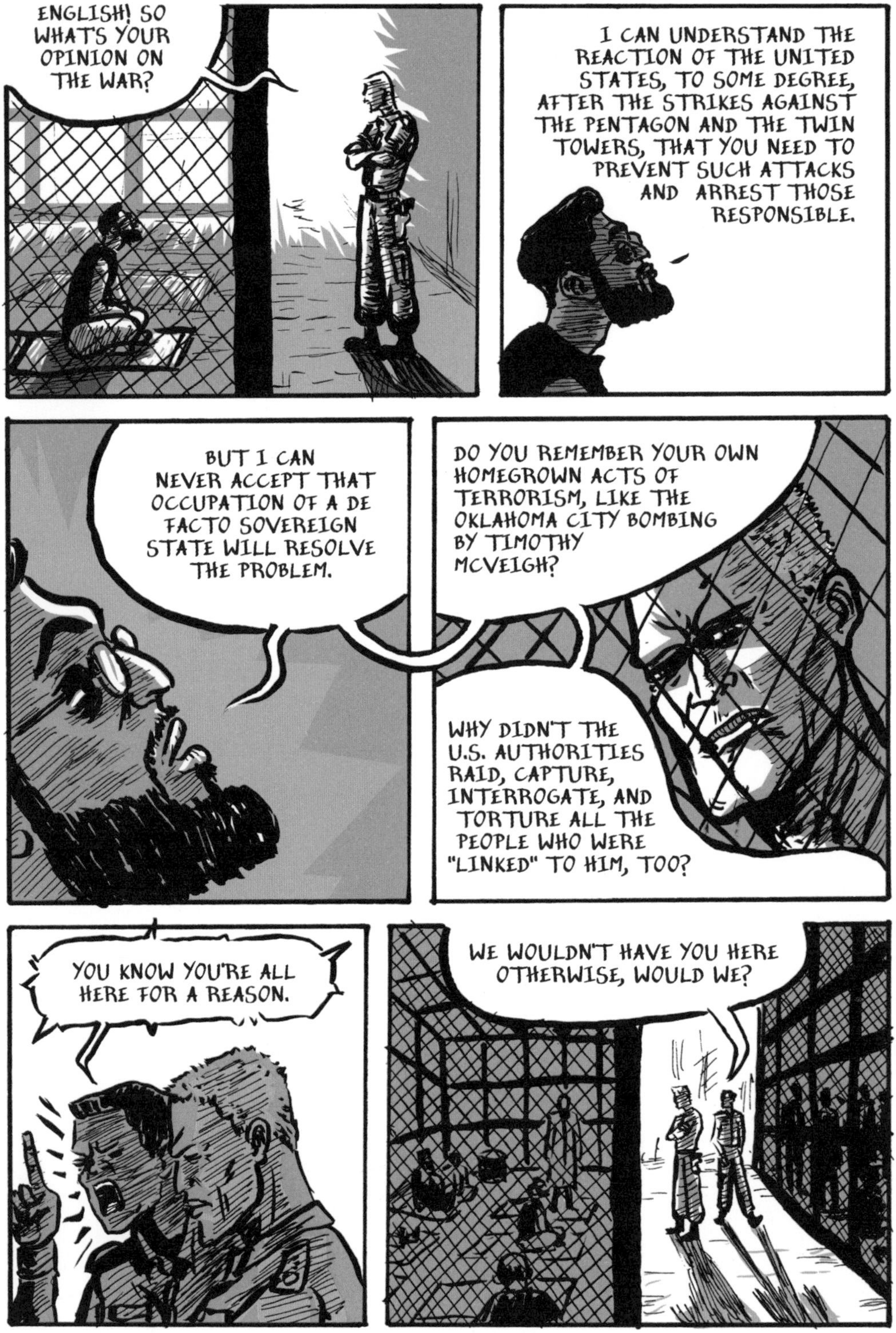
ENGLISH! SO WHAT'S YOUR OPINION ON THE WAR?
I CAN UNDERSTAND THE REACTION OF THE UNITED STATES, TO SOME DEGREE, AFTER THE STRIKES AGAINST THE PENTAGON AND THE TWIN TOWERS, THAT YOU NEED TO PREVENT SUCH ATTACKS AND ARREST THOSE RESPONSIBLE.
BUT I CAN NEVER ACCEPT THAT OCCUPATION OF A DE FACTO SOVEREIGN STATE WILL RESOLVE THE PROBLEM.
DO YOU REMEMBER YOUR OWN HOMEGROWN ACTS OF TERRORISM, LIKE THE OKLAHOMA CITY BOMBING BY TIMOTHY MCVEIGH?
WHY DIDN'T THE U.S. AUTHORITIES RAID, CAPTURE, INTERROGATE, AND TORTURE ALL THE PEOPLE WHO WERE "LINKED" TO HIM, TOO?
YOU KNOW YOU'RE ALL HERE FOR A REASON.
WE WOULDN'T HAVE YOU HERE OTHERWISE, WOULD WE?

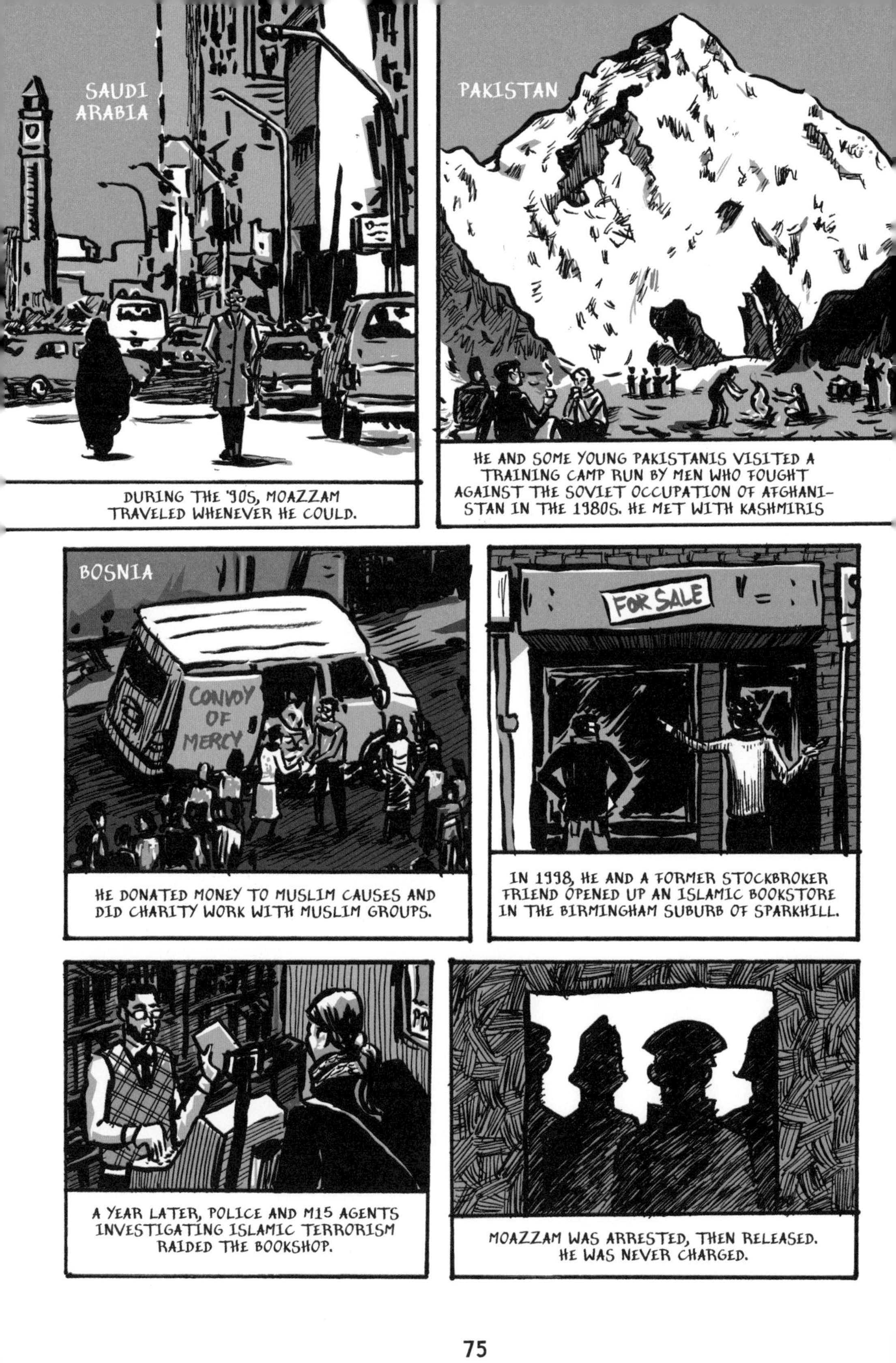
SAUDI ARABIA
DURING THE '90S, MOAZZAM TRAVELED WHENEVER HE COULD.
PAKISTAN
HE AND SOME YOUNG PAKISTANIS VISITED A TRAINING CAMP RUN BY MEN WHO FOUGHT AGAINST THE SOVIET OCCUPATION OF AFGHANI- STAN IN THE 1980S. HE MET WITH KASHMIRIS
BOSNIA
CONVOY OF MERCY
HE DONATED MONEY TO MUSLIM CAUSES AND DID CHARITY WORK WITH MUSLIM GROUPS.
FOR SALE
IN 1998, HE AND A FORMER STOCKBROKER FRIEND OPENED UP AN ISLAMIC BOOKSTORE IN THE BIRMINGHAM SUBURB OF SPARKHILL.
A YEAR LATER, POLICE AND M15 AGENTS INVESTIGATING ISLAMIC TERRORISM RAIDED THE BOOKSHOP.
MOAZZAM WAS ARRESTED, THEN RELEASED. HE WAS NEVER CHARGED.

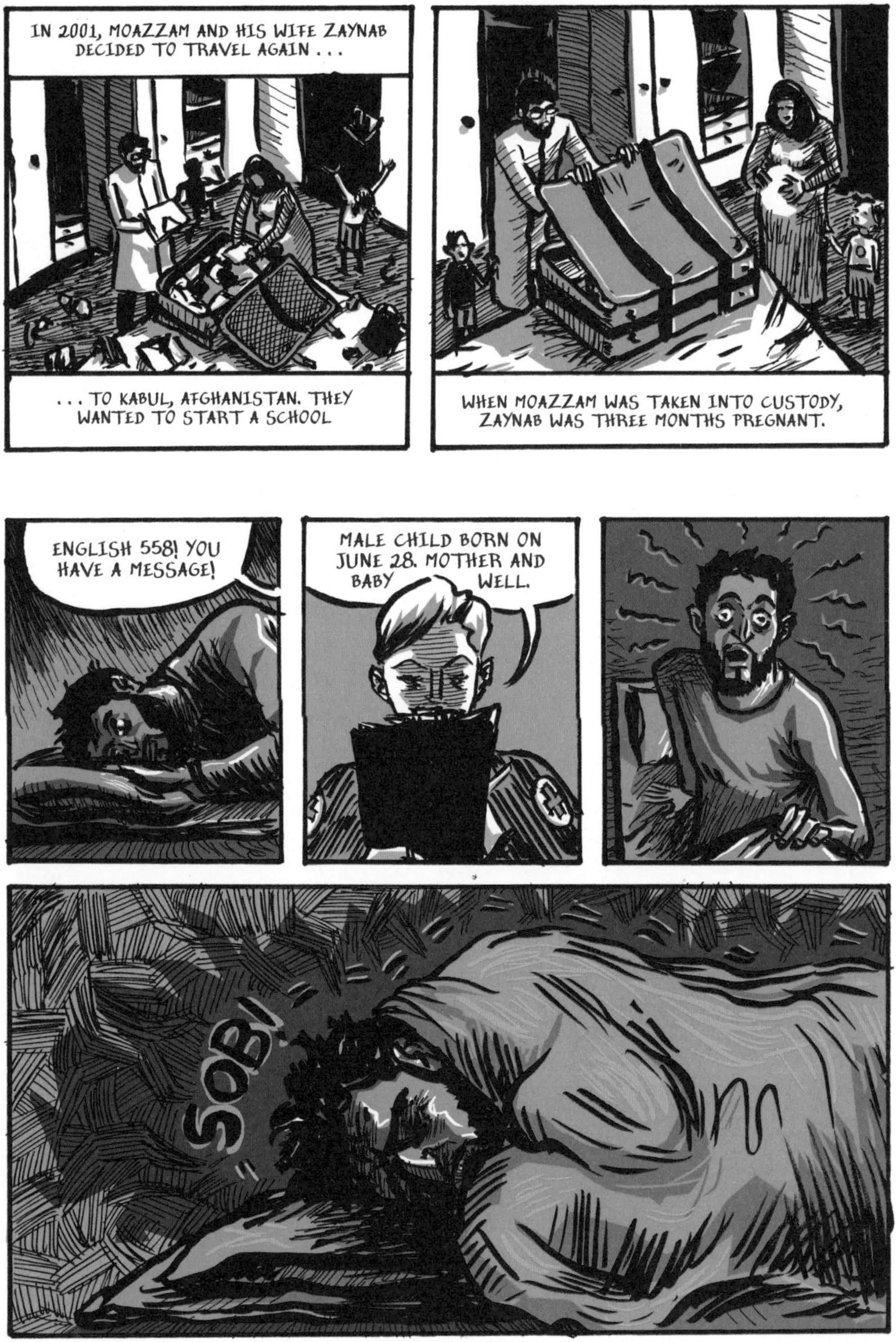
IN 2001, MOAZZAM AND HIS WIFE ZAYNAB DECIDED TO TRAVEL AGAIN . . .
. . . TO KABUL, AFGHANISTAN. THEY WANTED TO START A SCHOOL
WHEN MOAZZAM WAS TAKEN INTO CUSTODY, ZAYNAB WAS THREE MONTHS PREGNANT.
ENGLISH 558! YOU HAVE A MESSAGE!
MALE CHILD BORN ON JUNE 28. MOTHER AND BABY WELL.
SOB!

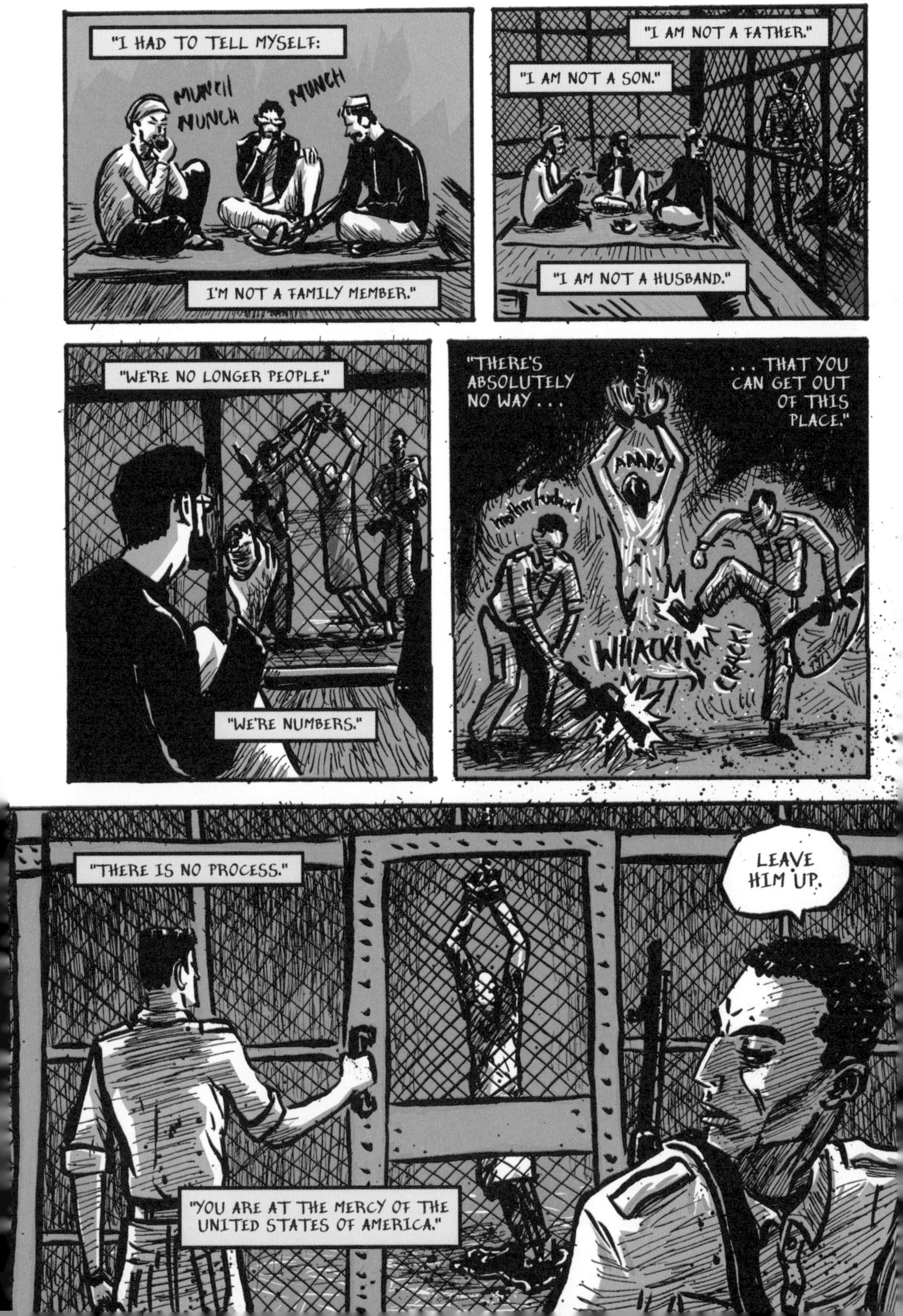

"I HAD TO TELL MYSELF:
MUNCH
MUNCH
MUNCH
I'M NOT A FAMILY MEMBER."
"I AM NOT A FATHER."
"I AM NOT A SON."
"I AM NOT A HUSBAND."
"WE'RE NO LONGER PEOPLE."
"WE'RE NUMBERS."
"THERE'S ABSOLUTELY NO WAY . . .
. . . THAT YOU CAN GET OUT OF THIS PLACE."
WHACK!
CRACK!
"THERE IS NO PROCESS."
LEAVE HIM UP.
"YOU ARE AT THE MERCY OF THE UNITED STATES OF AMERICA."

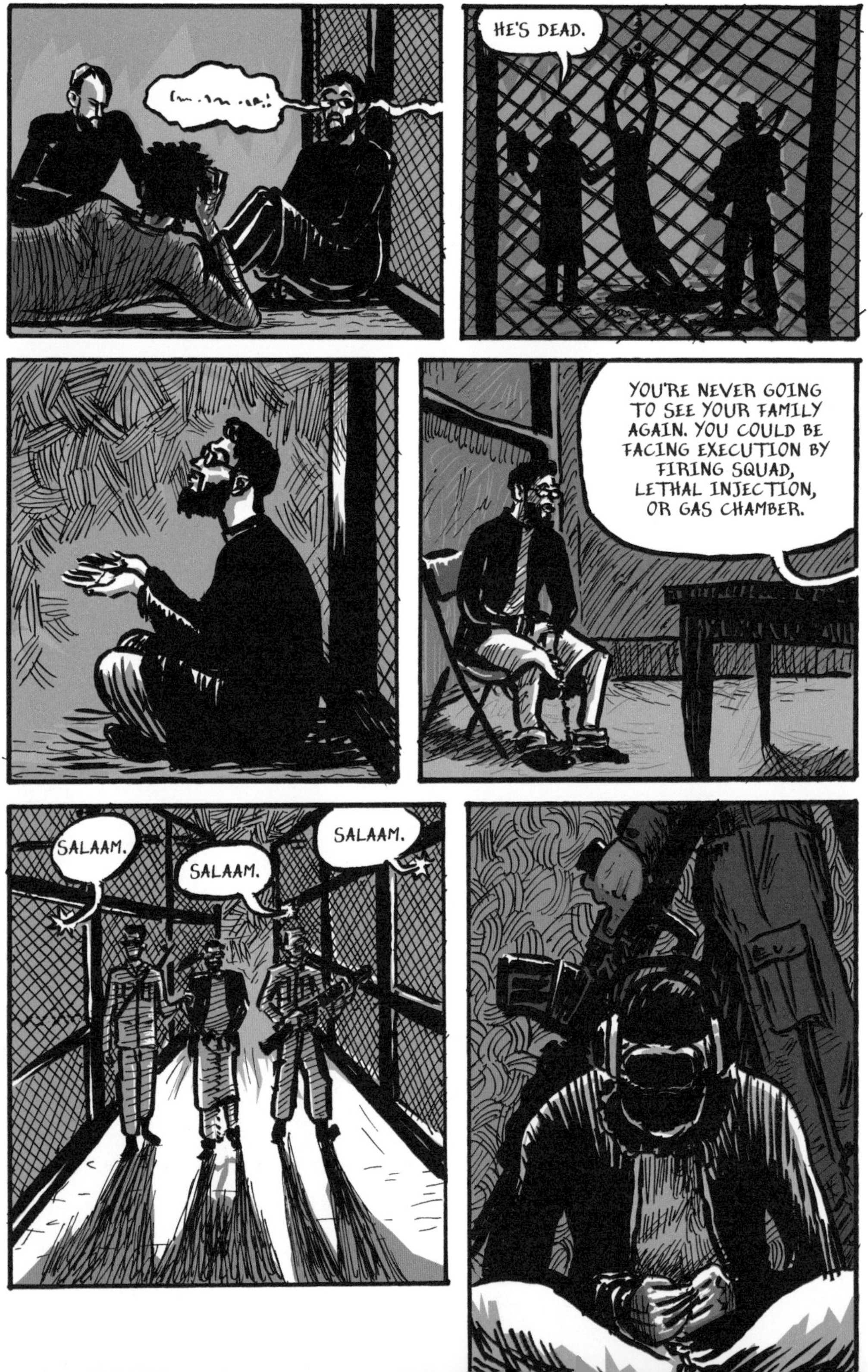
HE'S DEAD.
YOU'RE NEVER GOING TO SEE YOUR FAMILY AGAIN. YOU COULD BE FACING EXECUTION BY FIRING SQUAD, LETHAL INJECTION, OR GAS CHAMBER.
SALAAM.
SALAAM.
SALAAM.

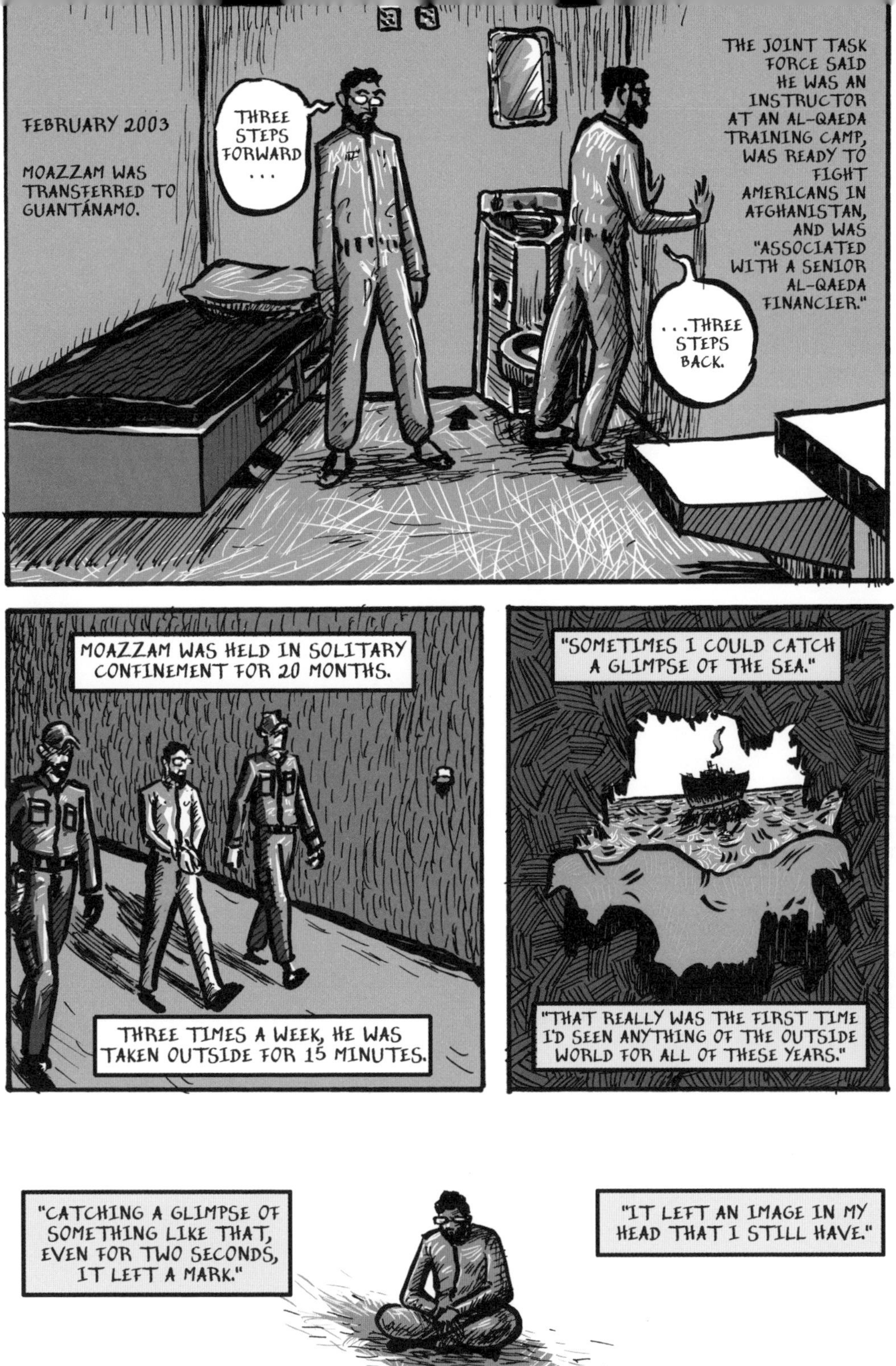
FEBRUARY 2003
MOAZZAM WAS TRANSFERRED TO GUANTÁNAMO.
THREE STEPS FORWARD . . .
THE JOINT TASK FORCE SAID HE WAS AN INSTRUCTOR AT AN AL-QAEDA TRAINING CAMP, WAS READY TO FIGHT AMERICANS IN AFGHANISTAN, AND WAS "ASSOCIATED WITH A SENIOR AL-QAEDA FINANCIER."
. . .THREE STEPS BACK.
MOAZZAM WAS HELD IN SOLITARY CONFINEMENT FOR 20 MONTHS.
THREE TIMES A WEEK, HE WAS TAKEN OUTSIDE FOR 15 MINUTES.
"SOMETIMES I COULD CATCH A GLIMPSE OF THE SEA."
"THAT REALLY WAS THE FIRST TIME I'D SEEN ANYTHING OF THE OUTSIDE WORLD FOR ALL OF THESE YEARS."
"CATCHING A GLIMPSE OF SOMETHING LIKE THAT, EVEN FOR TWO SECONDS, IT LEFT A MARK."
"IT LEFT AN IMAGE IN MY HEAD THAT I STILL HAVE."

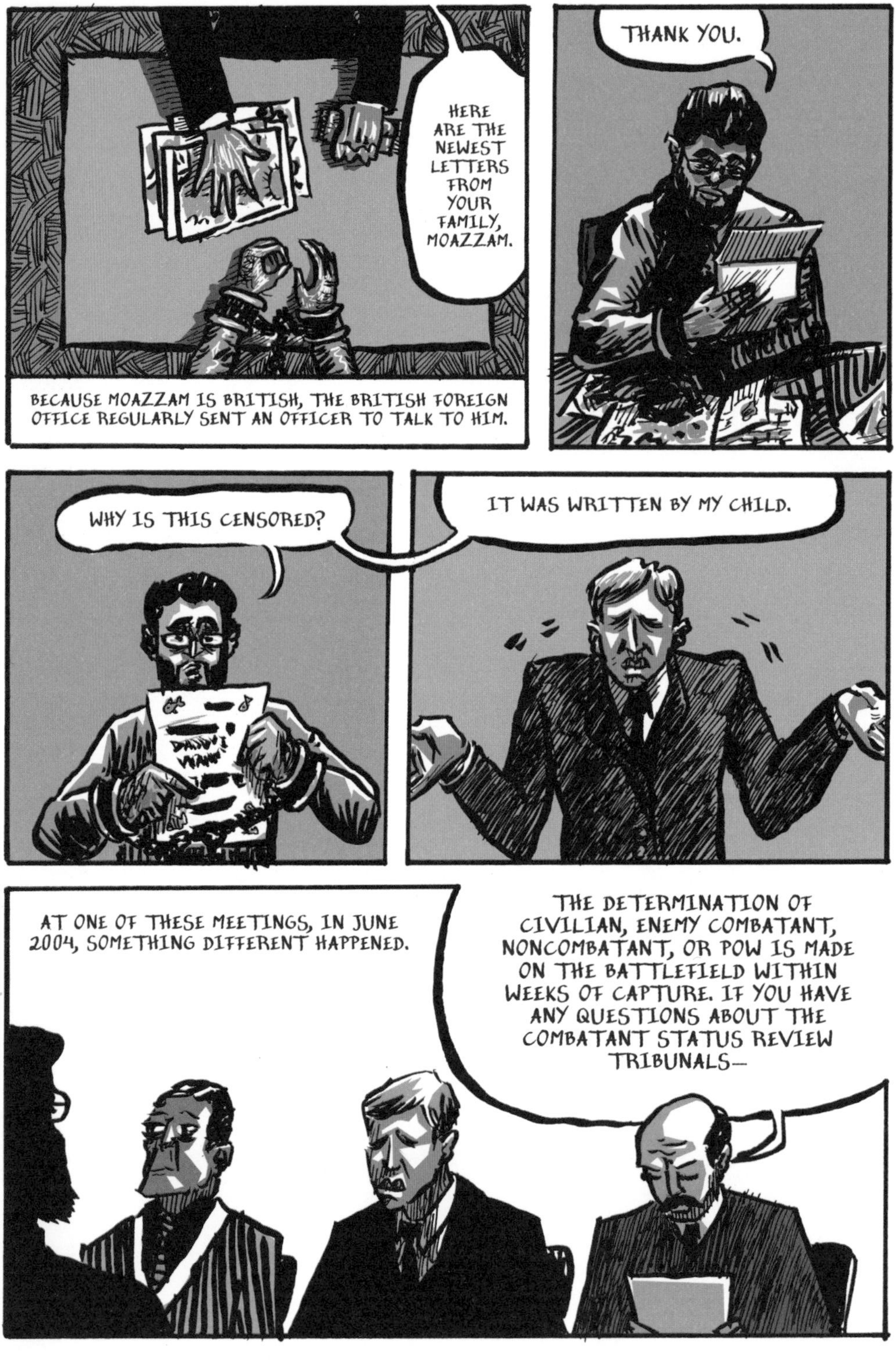
HERE ARE THE NEWEST LETTERS FROM YOUR FAMILY, MOAZZAM.
BECAUSE MOAZZAM IS BRITISH, THE BRITISH FOREIGN OFFICE REGULARLY SENT AN OFFICER TO TALK TO HIM.
THANK YOU.
WHY IS THIS CENSORED?
IT WAS WRITTEN BY MY CHILD.
AT ONE OF THESE MEETINGS, IN JUNE 2004, SOMETHING DIFFERENT HAPPENED.
THE DETERMINATION OF CIVILIAN, ENEMY COMBATANT, NONCOMBATANT, OR POW IS MADE ON THE BATTLEFIELD WITHIN WEEKS OF CAPTURE. IF YOU HAVE ANY QUESTIONS ABOUT THE COMBATANT STATUS REVIEW TRIBUNALS—

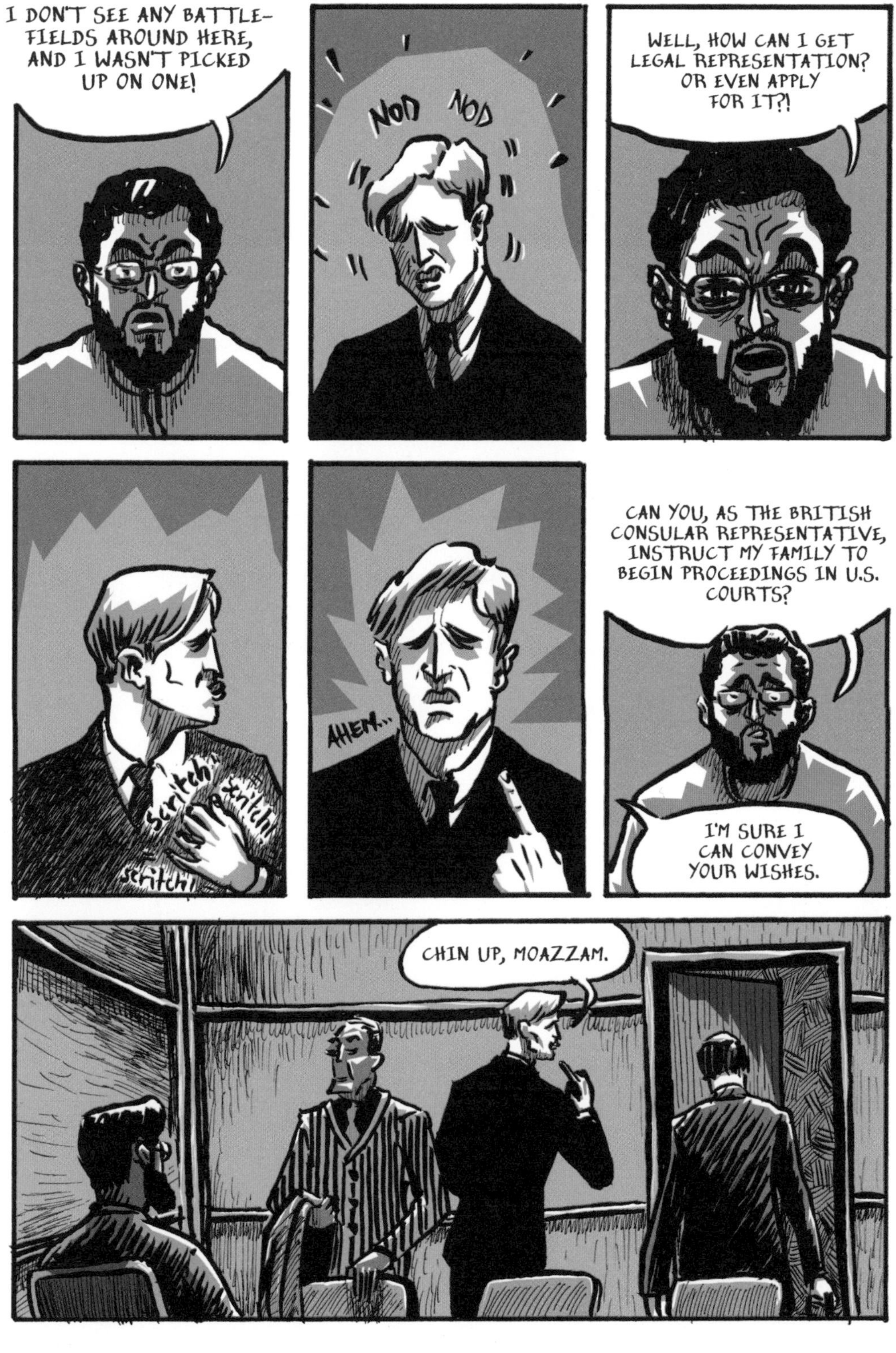
I DON'T SEE ANY BATTLE-FIELDS AROUND HERE, AND I WASN'T PICKED UP ON ONE!
NOD NOD
WELL, HOW CAN I GET LEGAL REPRESENTATION? OR EVEN APPLY FOR IT?!
scritch!
scritch!
scritch!
AHEM...
CAN YOU, AS THE BRITISH CONSULAR REPRESENTATIVE, INSTRUCT MY FAMILY TO BEGIN PROCEEDINGS IN U.S. COURTS?
I'M SURE I CAN CONVEY YOUR WISHES.
CHIN UP, MOAZZAM.

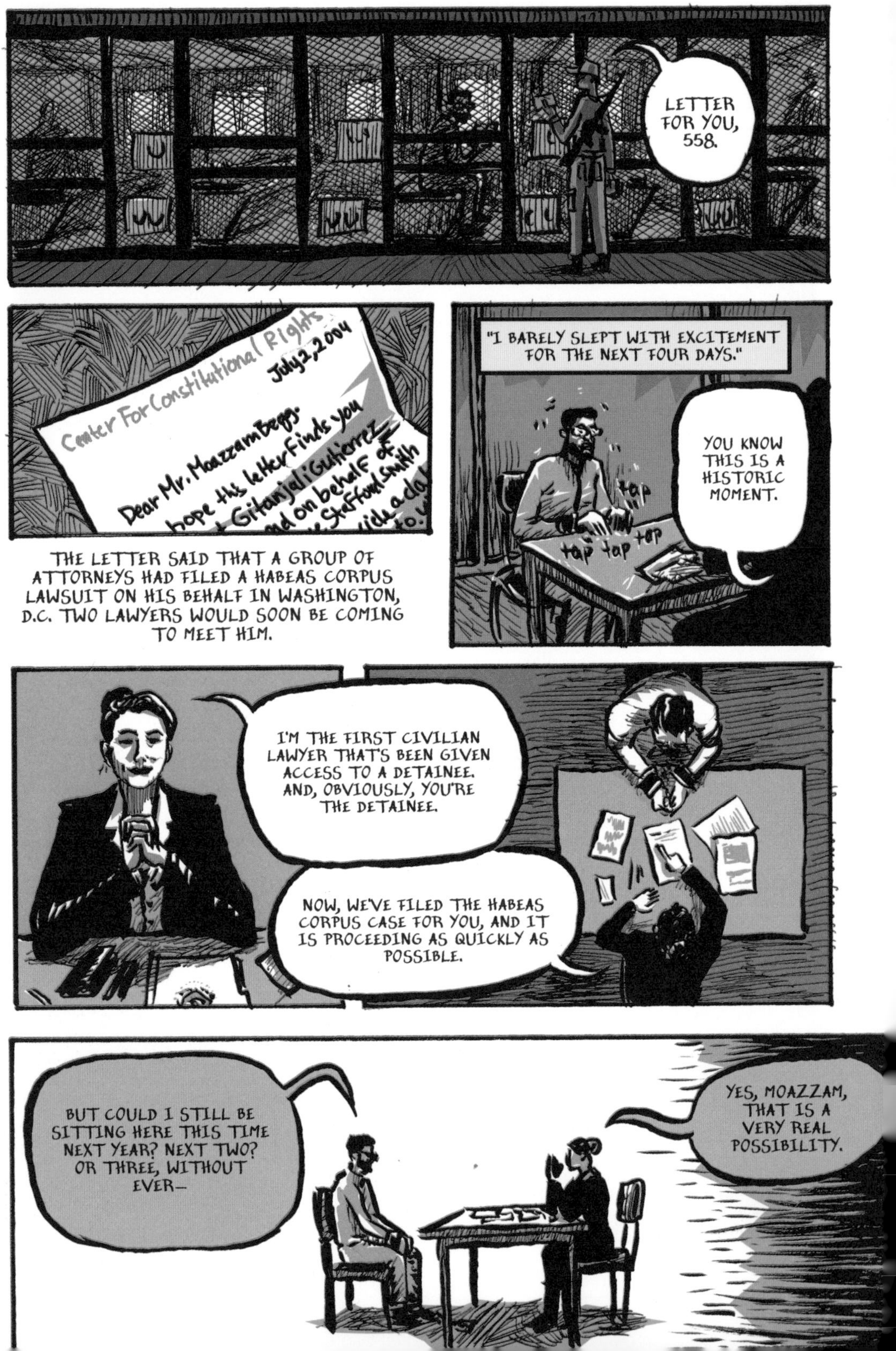

LETTER FOR YOU, 558.
Center For Constitutional Rights
July 2, 2004
Dear Mr. Moazzam Begg,
hope this letter finds you
Gitanjali Gutierrez
and on behalf of
Stafford Smith
THE LETTER SAID THAT A GROUP OF ATTORNEYS HAD FILED A HABEAS CORPUS LAWSUIT ON HIS BEHALF IN WASHINGTON, D.C. TWO LAWYERS WOULD SOON BE COMING TO MEET HIM.
"I BARELY SLEPT WITH EXCITEMENT FOR THE NEXT FOUR DAYS."
YOU KNOW THIS IS A HISTORIC MOMENT.
tap tap tap tap
I'M THE FIRST CIVILIAN LAWYER THAT'S BEEN GIVEN ACCESS TO A DETAINEE. AND, OBVIOUSLY, YOU'RE THE DETAINEE.
NOW, WE'VE FILED THE HABEAS CORPUS CASE FOR YOU, AND IT IS PROCEEDING AS QUICKLY AS POSSIBLE.
BUT COULD I STILL BE SITTING HERE THIS TIME NEXT YEAR? NEXT TWO? OR THREE, WITHOUT EVER—
YES, MOAZZAM, THAT IS A VERY REAL POSSIBILITY.

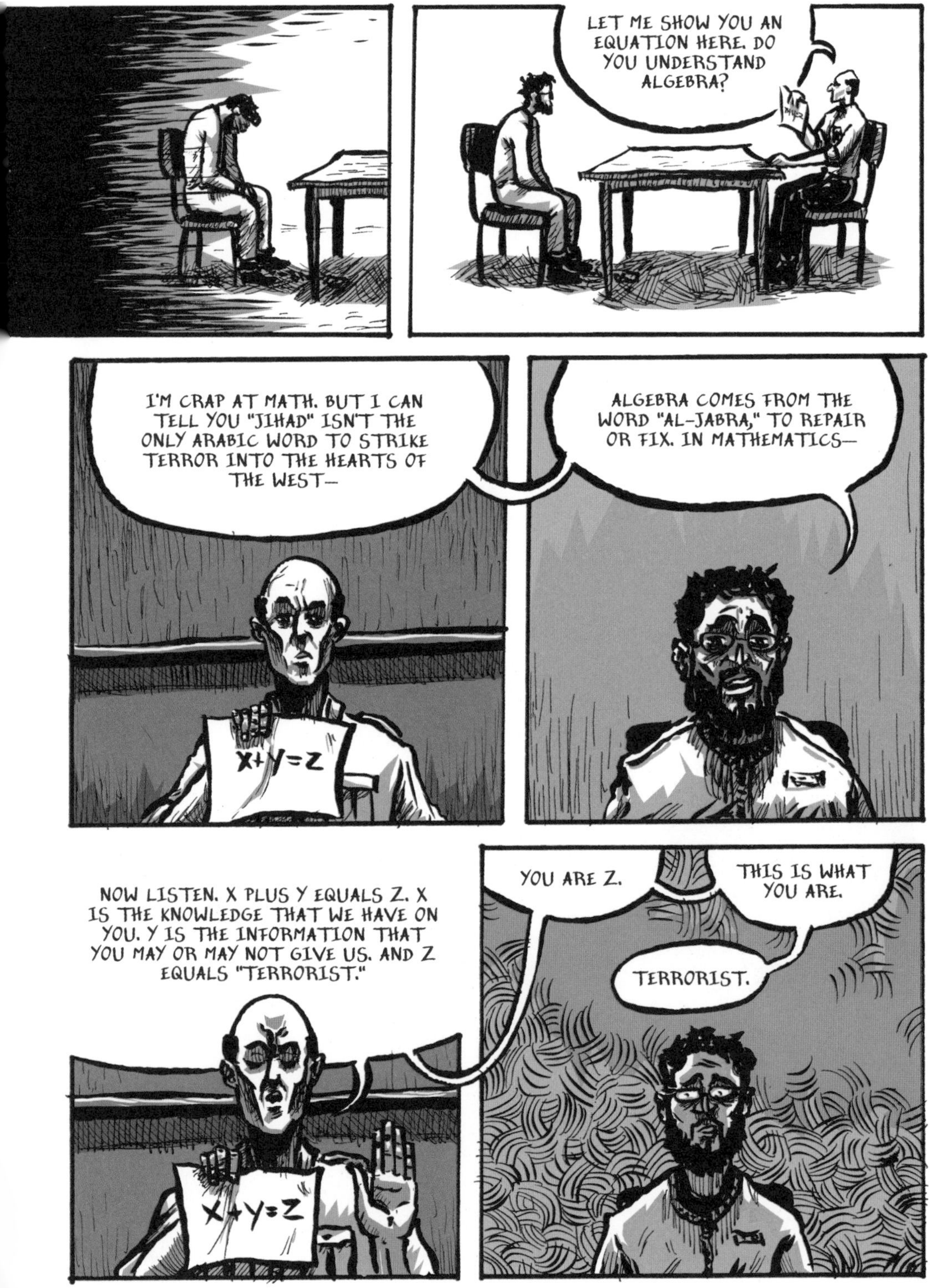
LET ME SHOW YOU AN EQUATION HERE. DO YOU UNDERSTAND ALGEBRA?
I'M CRAP AT MATH. BUT I CAN TELL YOU "JIHAD" ISN'T THE ONLY ARABIC WORD TO STRIKE TERROR INTO THE HEARTS OF THE WEST—
ALGEBRA COMES FROM THE WORD "AL-JABRA," TO REPAIR OR FIX. IN MATHEMATICS—
X+Y=Z
NOW LISTEN. X PLUS Y EQUALS Z. X IS THE KNOWLEDGE THAT WE HAVE ON YOU. Y IS THE INFORMATION THAT YOU MAY OR MAY NOT GIVE US. AND Z EQUALS "TERRORIST."
X+Y=Z
YOU ARE Z.
THIS IS WHAT YOU ARE.
TERRORIST.

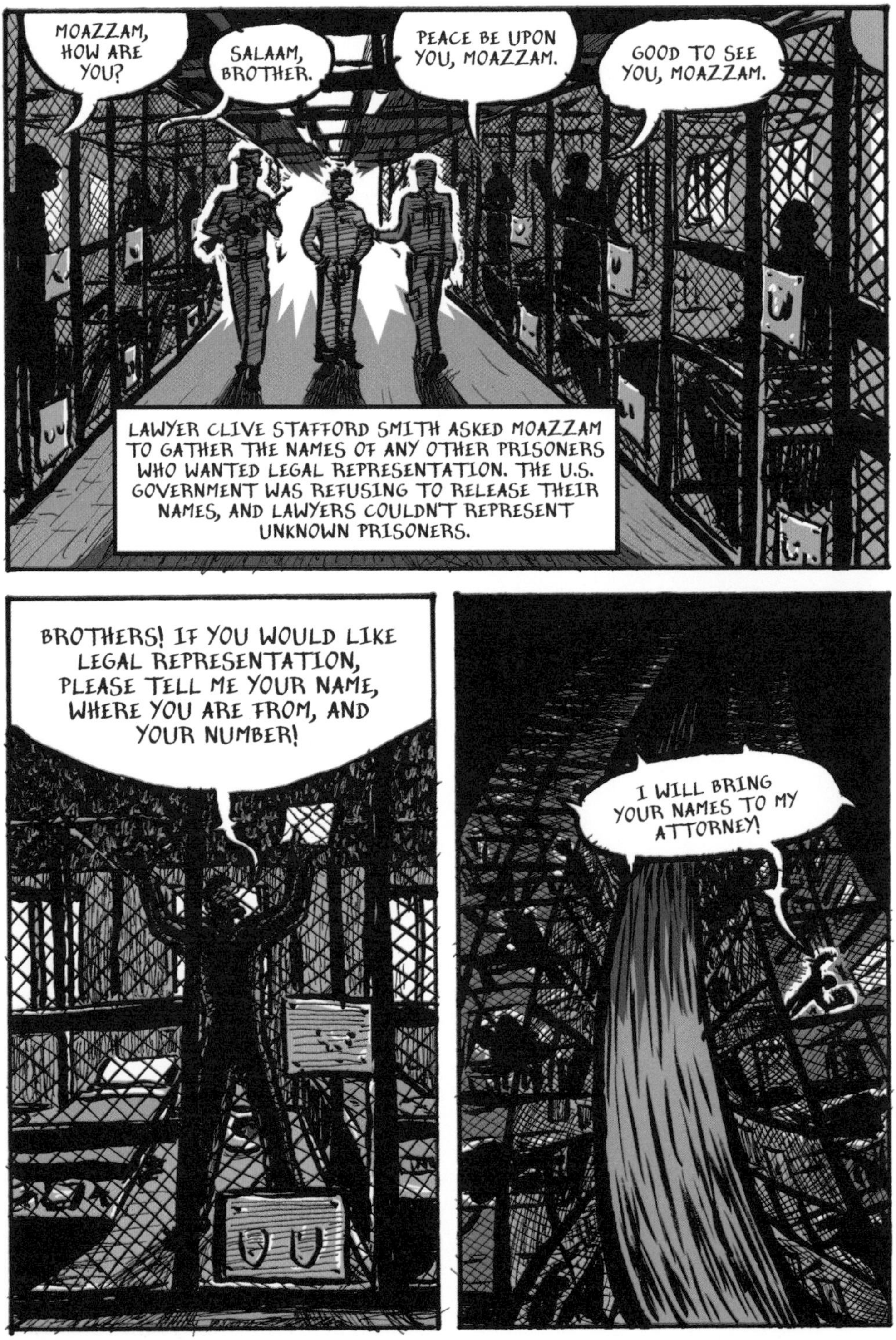
MOAZZAM, HOW ARE YOU?
SALAAM, BROTHER.
PEACE BE UPON YOU, MOAZZAM.
GOOD TO SEE YOU, MOAZZAM.
LAWYER CLIVE STAFFORD SMITH ASKED MOAZZAM TO GATHER THE NAMES OF ANY OTHER PRISONERS WHO WANTED LEGAL REPRESENTATION. THE U.S. GOVERNMENT WAS REFUSING TO RELEASE THEIR NAMES, AND LAWYERS COULDN'T REPRESENT UNKNOWN PRISONERS.
BROTHERS! IF YOU WOULD LIKE LEGAL REPRESENTATION, PLEASE TELL ME YOUR NAME, WHERE YOU ARE FROM, AND YOUR NUMBER!
I WILL BRING YOUR NAMES TO MY ATTORNEY!

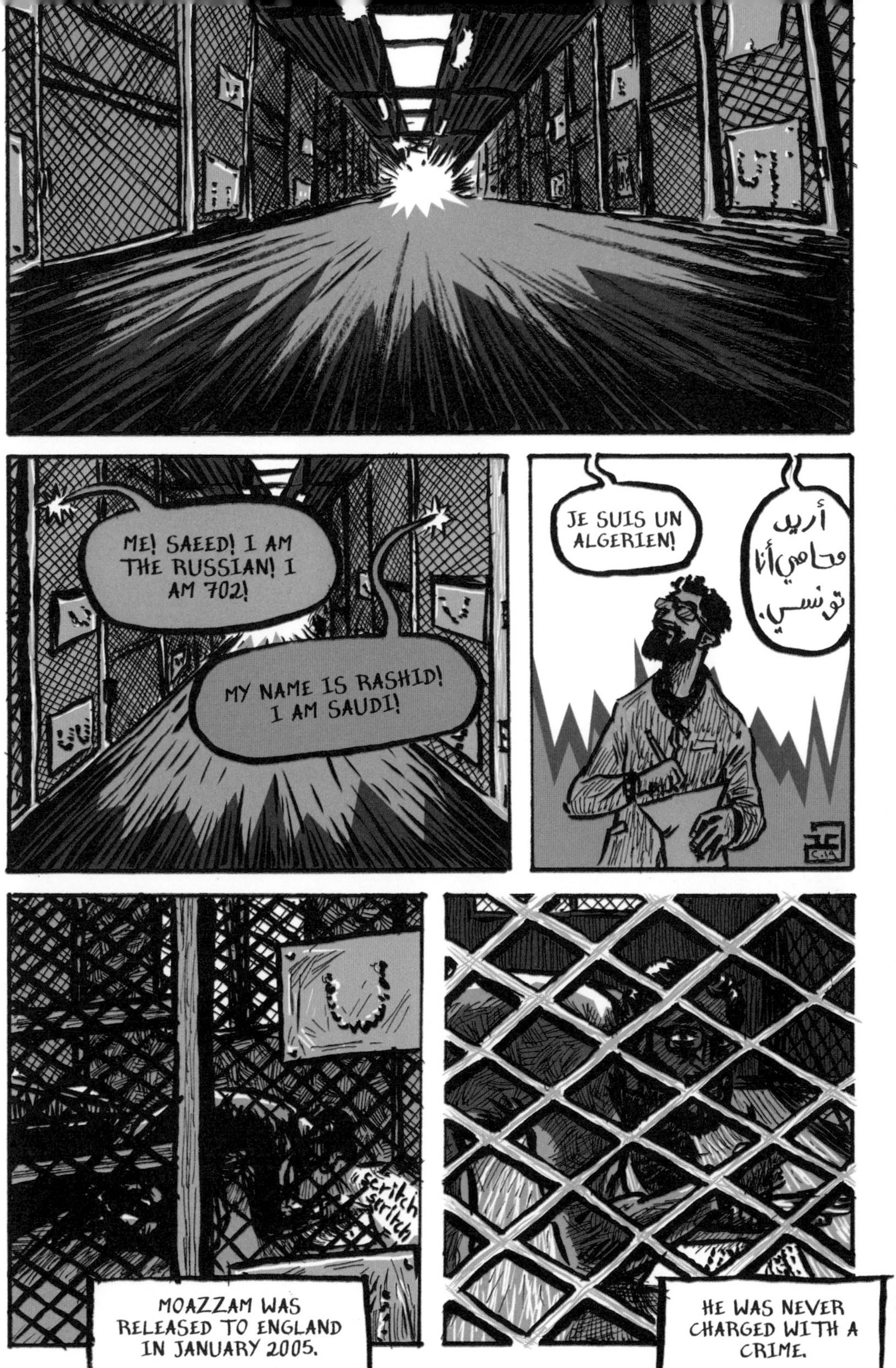

ME! SAEED! I AM THE RUSSIAN! I AM 702!
MY NAME IS RASHID! I AM SAUDI!
JE SUIS UN ALGERIEN!
أريد محامي أنا تونسي.
scritch scritch
MOAZZAM WAS RELEASED TO ENGLAND IN JANUARY 2005.
HE WAS NEVER CHARGED WITH A CRIME.

CHAPTER FIVE

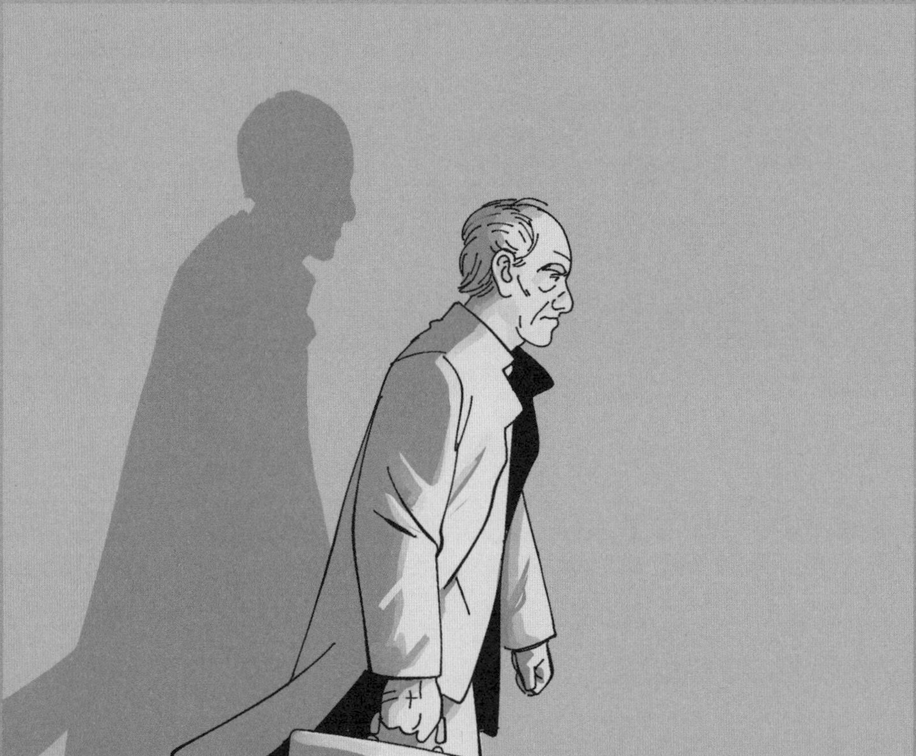

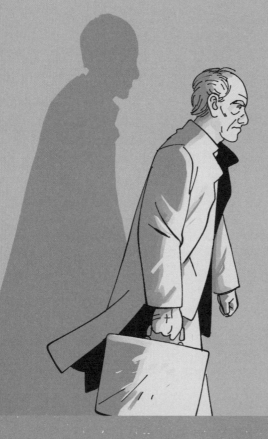

THOMAS WILNER

ATTORNEY REPRESENTING
GUANTÁNAMO PRISONERS

ILLUSTRATED BY MAKI NARO

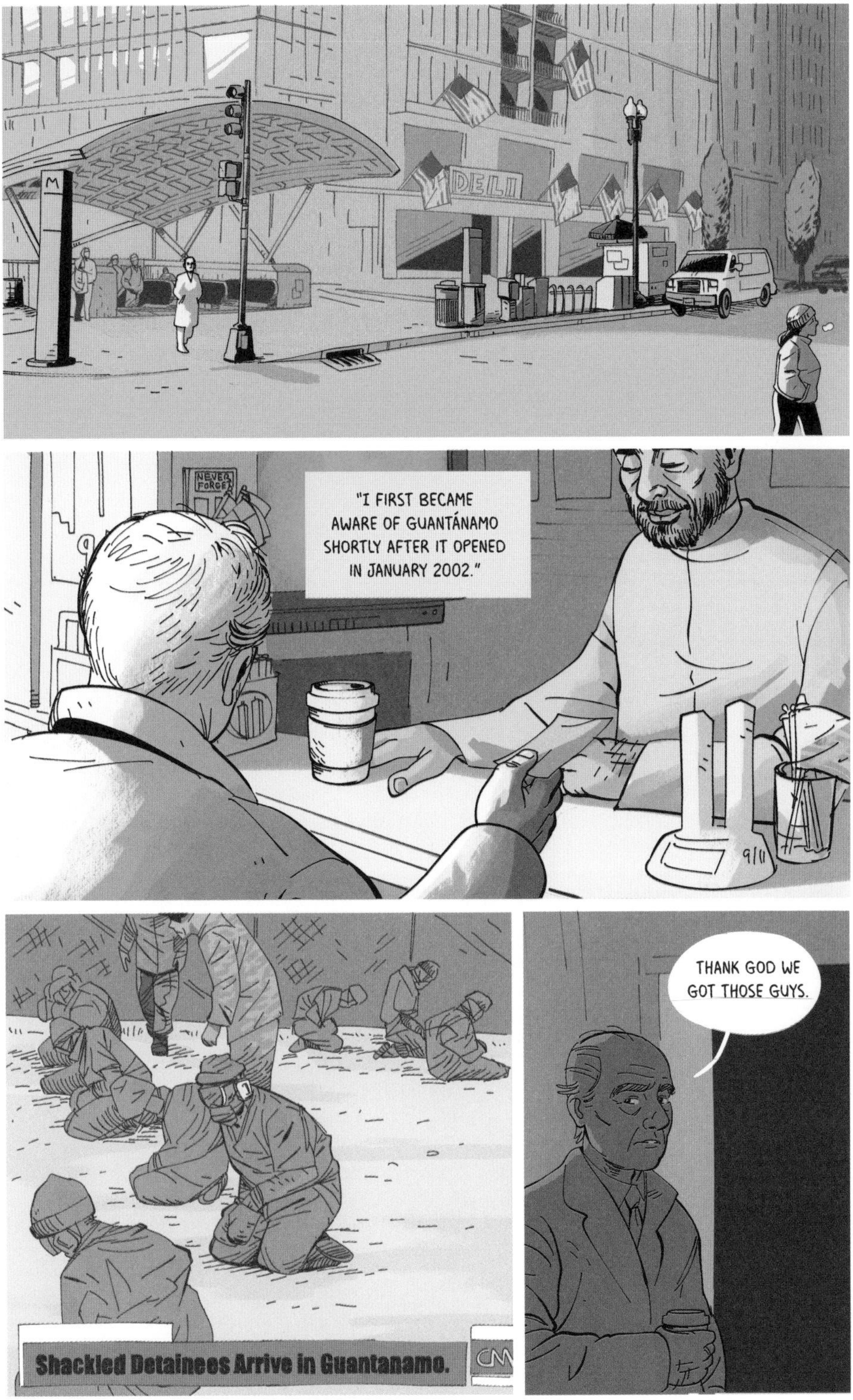
M
DELI
"I FIRST BECAME AWARE OF GUANTÁNAMO SHORTLY AFTER IT OPENED IN JANUARY 2002."
9/11
Shackled Detainees Arrive in Guantanamo.
THANK GOD WE GOT THOSE GUYS.

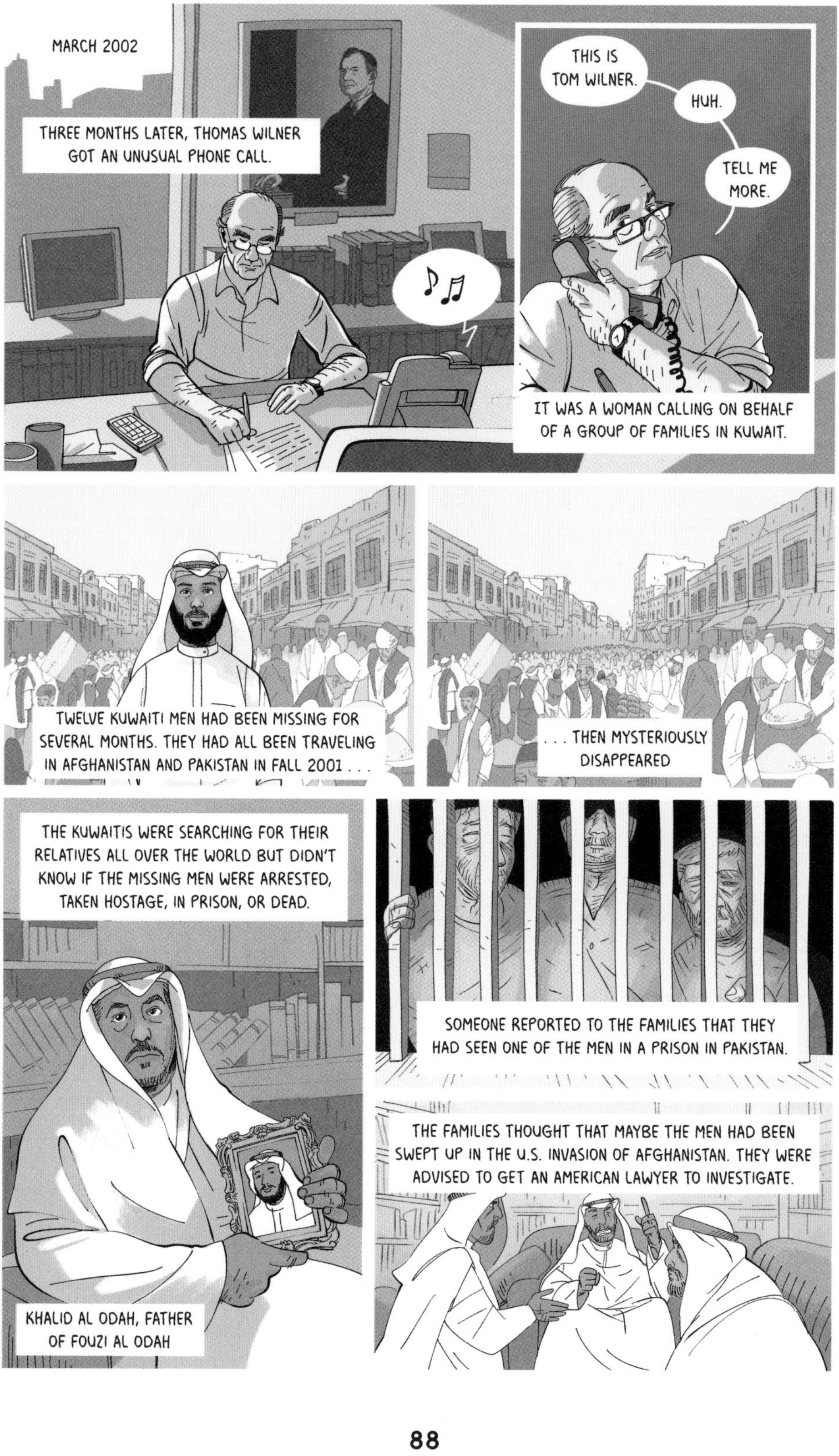
MARCH 2002
THREE MONTHS LATER, THOMAS WILNER GOT AN UNUSUAL PHONE CALL.
THIS IS TOM WILNER.
HUH.
TELL ME MORE.
IT WAS A WOMAN CALLING ON BEHALF OF A GROUP OF FAMILIES IN KUWAIT.
TWELVE KUWAITI MEN HAD BEEN MISSING FOR SEVERAL MONTHS. THEY HAD ALL BEEN TRAVELING IN AFGHANISTAN AND PAKISTAN IN FALL 2001 . . .
. . . THEN MYSTERIOUSLY DISAPPEARED
THE KUWAITIS WERE SEARCHING FOR THEIR RELATIVES ALL OVER THE WORLD BUT DIDN'T KNOW IF THE MISSING MEN WERE ARRESTED, TAKEN HOSTAGE, IN PRISON, OR DEAD.
KHALID AL ODAH, FATHER OF FOUZI AL ODAH
SOMEONE REPORTED TO THE FAMILIES THAT THEY HAD SEEN ONE OF THE MEN IN A PRISON IN PAKISTAN.
THE FAMILIES THOUGHT THAT MAYBE THE MEN HAD BEEN SWEPT UP IN THE U.S. INVASION OF AFGHANISTAN. THEY WERE ADVISED TO GET AN AMERICAN LAWYER TO INVESTIGATE.

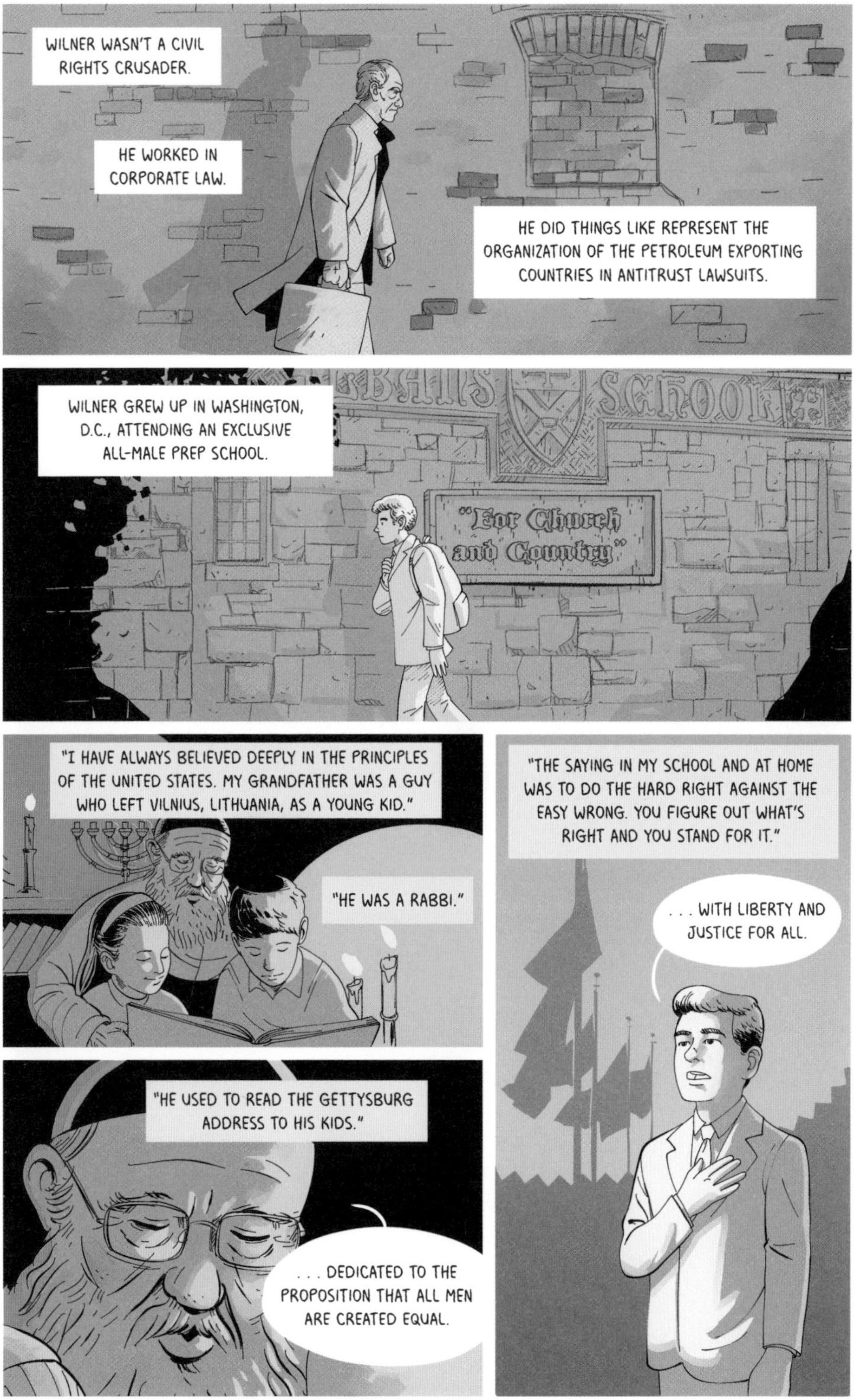
WILNER WASN'T A CIVIL RIGHTS CRUSADER.
HE WORKED IN CORPORATE LAW.
HE DID THINGS LIKE REPRESENT THE ORGANIZATION OF THE PETROLEUM EXPORTING COUNTRIES IN ANTITRUST LAWSUITS.
WILNER GREW UP IN WASHINGTON, D.C., ATTENDING AN EXCLUSIVE ALL-MALE PREP SCHOOL.
SCHOOL
"For Church and Country"
"I HAVE ALWAYS BELIEVED DEEPLY IN THE PRINCIPLES OF THE UNITED STATES. MY GRANDFATHER WAS A GUY WHO LEFT VILNIUS, LITHUANIA, AS A YOUNG KID."
"HE WAS A RABBI."
"HE USED TO READ THE GETTYSBURG ADDRESS TO HIS KIDS."
. . . DEDICATED TO THE PROPOSITION THAT ALL MEN ARE CREATED EQUAL.
"THE SAYING IN MY SCHOOL AND AT HOME WAS TO DO THE HARD RIGHT AGAINST THE EASY WRONG. YOU FIGURE OUT WHAT'S RIGHT AND YOU STAND FOR IT."
. . . WITH LIBERTY AND JUSTICE FOR ALL.

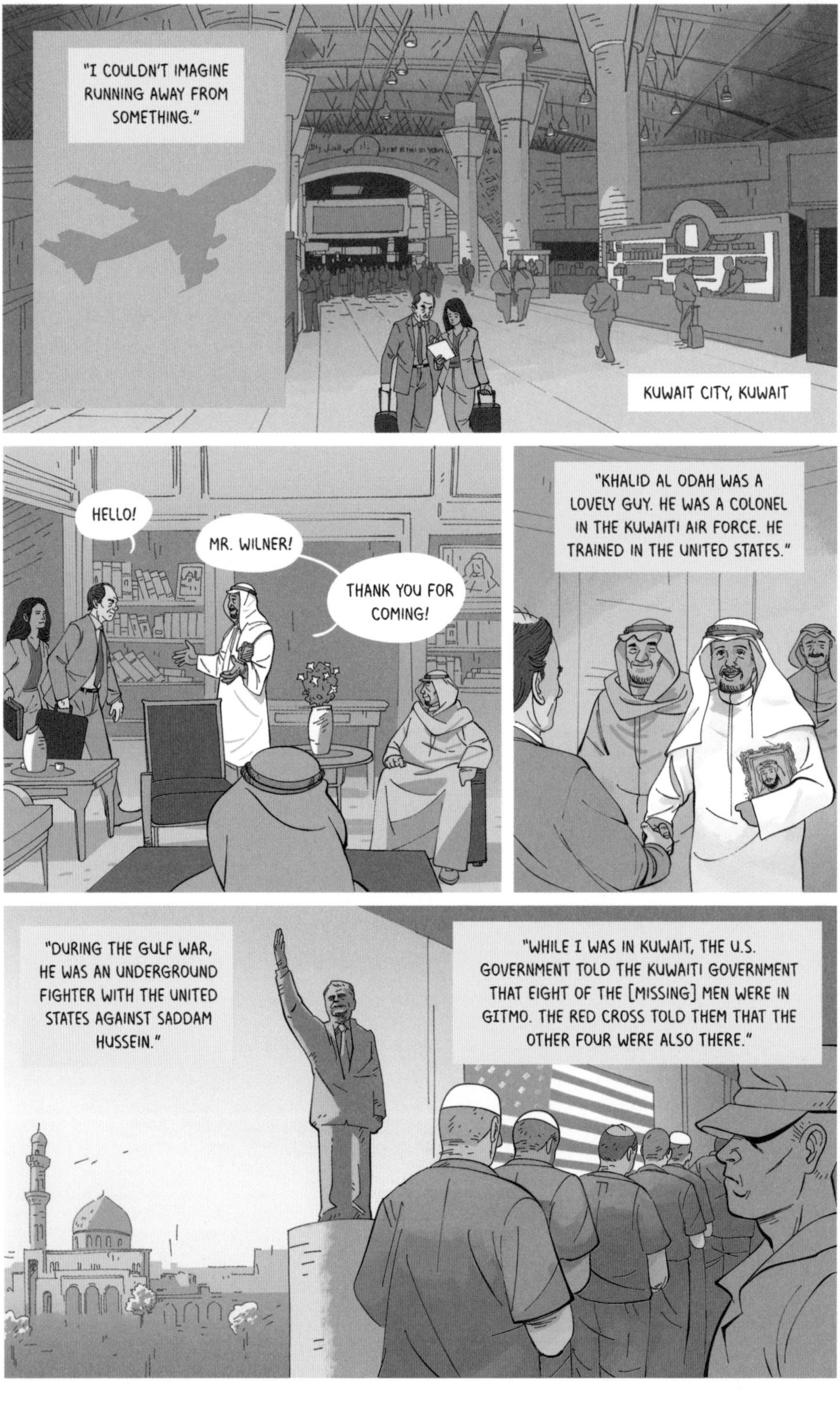
"I COULDN'T IMAGINE RUNNING AWAY FROM SOMETHING."
KUWAIT CITY, KUWAIT
HELLO!
MR. WILNER!
THANK YOU FOR COMING!
"KHALID AL ODAH WAS A LOVELY GUY. HE WAS A COLONEL IN THE KUWAITI AIR FORCE. HE TRAINED IN THE UNITED STATES."
"DURING THE GULF WAR, HE WAS AN UNDERGROUND FIGHTER WITH THE UNITED STATES AGAINST SADDAM HUSSEIN."
"WHILE I WAS IN KUWAIT, THE U.S. GOVERNMENT TOLD THE KUWAITI GOVERNMENT THAT EIGHT OF THE [MISSING] MEN WERE IN GITMO. THE RED CROSS TOLD THEM THAT THE OTHER FOUR WERE ALSO THERE."

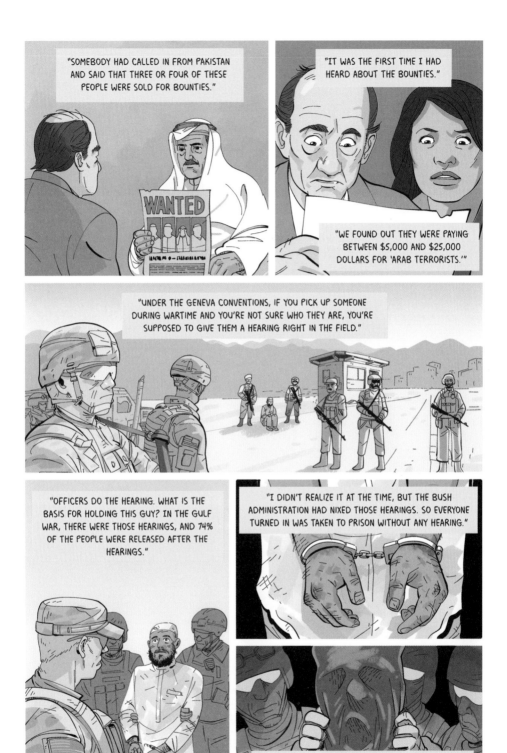

"SOMEBODY HAD CALLED IN FROM PAKISTAN AND SAID THAT THREE OR FOUR OF THESE PEOPLE WERE SOLD FOR BOUNTIES."

"IT WAS THE FIRST TIME I HAD HEARD ABOUT THE BOUNTIES."

"WE FOUND OUT THEY WERE PAYING BETWEEN $5,000 AND $25,000 DOLLARS FOR 'ARAB TERRORISTS.'"

"UNDER THE GENEVA CONVENTIONS, IF YOU PICK UP SOMEONE DURING WARTIME AND YOU'RE NOT SURE WHO THEY ARE, YOU'RE SUPPOSED TO GIVE THEM A HEARING RIGHT IN THE FIELD."

"OFFICERS DO THE HEARING. WHAT IS THE BASIS FOR HOLDING THIS GUY? IN THE GULF WAR, THERE WERE THOSE HEARINGS, AND 74% OF THE PEOPLE WERE RELEASED AFTER THE HEARINGS."

"I DIDN'T REALIZE IT AT THE TIME, BUT THE BUSH ADMINISTRATION HAD NIXED THOSE HEARINGS. SO EVERYONE TURNED IN WAS TAKEN TO PRISON WITHOUT ANY HEARING."

"AND ANY ARAB IN THE AREA WAS A VALUABLE COMMODITY WHO COULD BE TURNED IN FOR A BOUNTY."

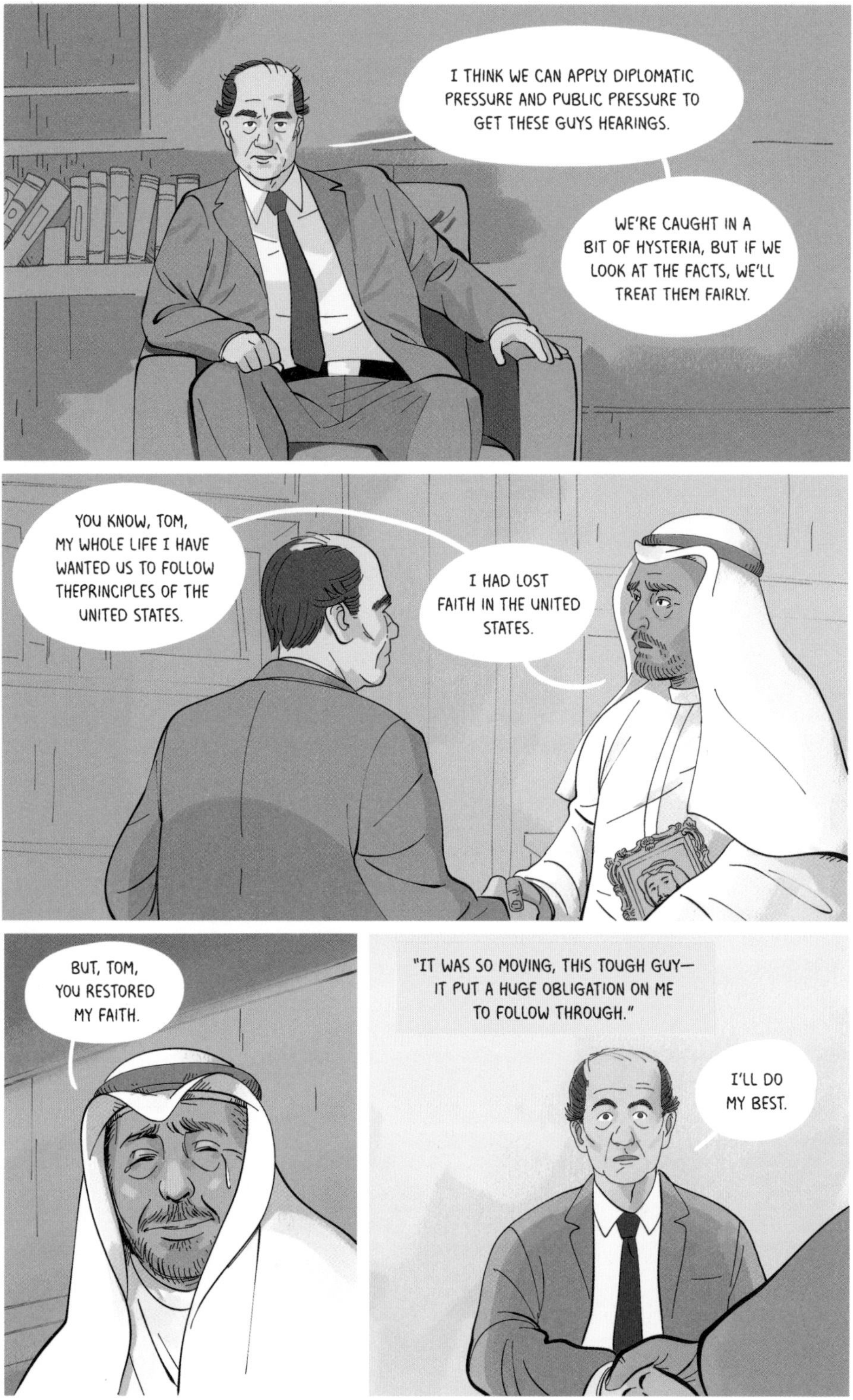
I THINK WE CAN APPLY DIPLOMATIC PRESSURE AND PUBLIC PRESSURE TO GET THESE GUYS HEARINGS.
WE'RE CAUGHT IN A BIT OF HYSTERIA, BUT IF WE LOOK AT THE FACTS, WE'LL TREAT THEM FAIRLY.
YOU KNOW, TOM, MY WHOLE LIFE I HAVE WANTED US TO FOLLOW THEPRINCIPLES OF THE UNITED STATES.
I HAD LOST FAITH IN THE UNITED STATES.
BUT, TOM, YOU RESTORED MY FAITH.
"IT WAS SO MOVING, THIS TOUGH GUY— IT PUT A HUGE OBLIGATION ON ME TO FOLLOW THROUGH."
I'LL DO MY BEST.

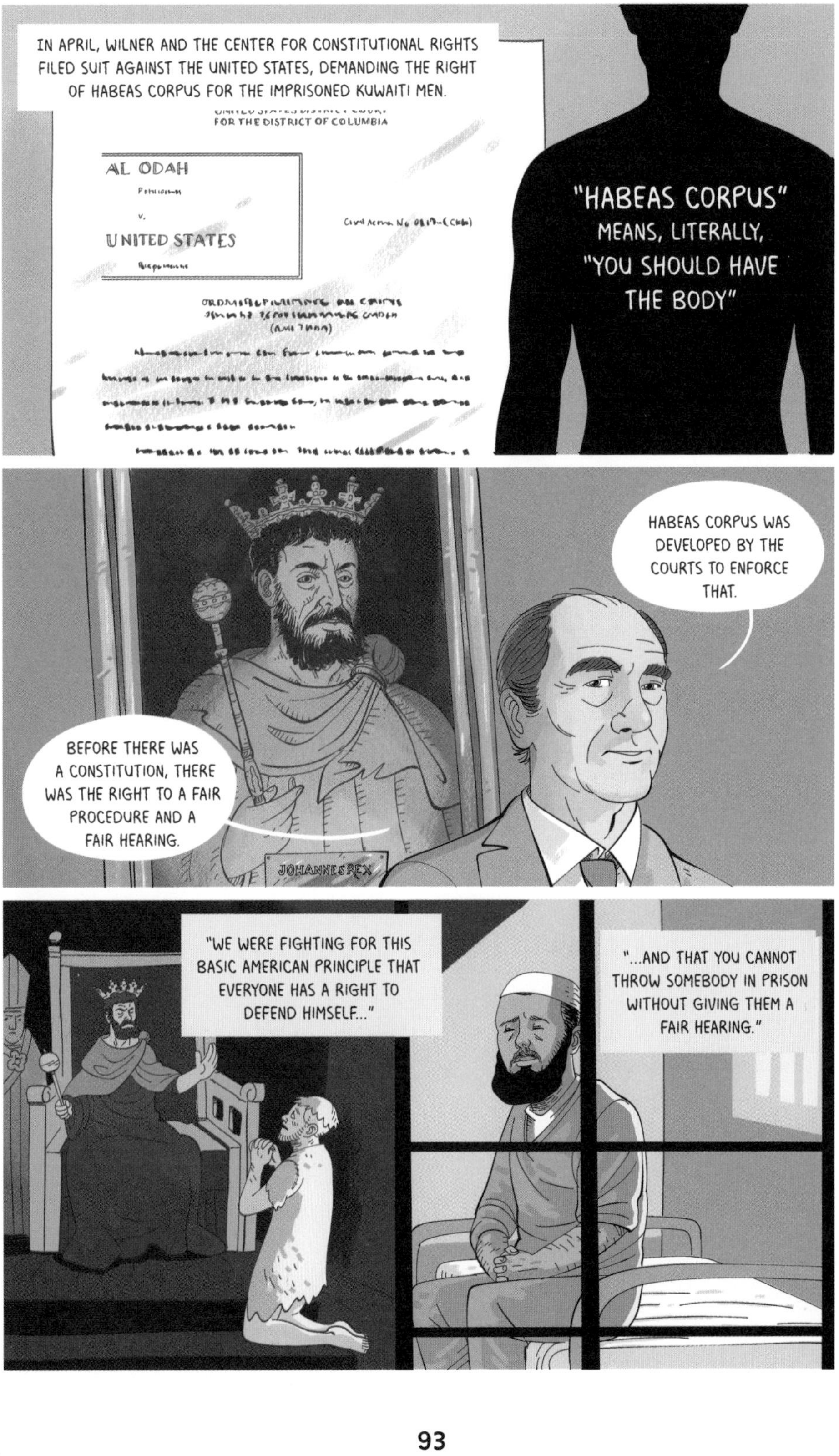
IN APRIL, WILNER AND THE CENTER FOR CONSTITUTIONAL RIGHTS FILED SUIT AGAINST THE UNITED STATES, DEMANDING THE RIGHT OF HABEAS CORPUS FOR THE IMPRISONED KUWAITI MEN.
FOR THE DISTRICT OF COLUMBIA
AL ODAH
v.
UNITED STATES
"HABEAS CORPUS" MEANS, LITERALLY, "YOU SHOULD HAVE THE BODY"
HABEAS CORPUS WAS DEVELOPED BY THE COURTS TO ENFORCE THAT.
BEFORE THERE WAS A CONSTITUTION, THERE WAS THE RIGHT TO A FAIR PROCEDURE AND A FAIR HEARING.
JOHANNES REX
"WE WERE FIGHTING FOR THIS BASIC AMERICAN PRINCIPLE THAT EVERYONE HAS A RIGHT TO DEFEND HIMSELF..."
"...AND THAT YOU CANNOT THROW SOMEBODY IN PRISON WITHOUT GIVING THEM A FAIR HEARING."

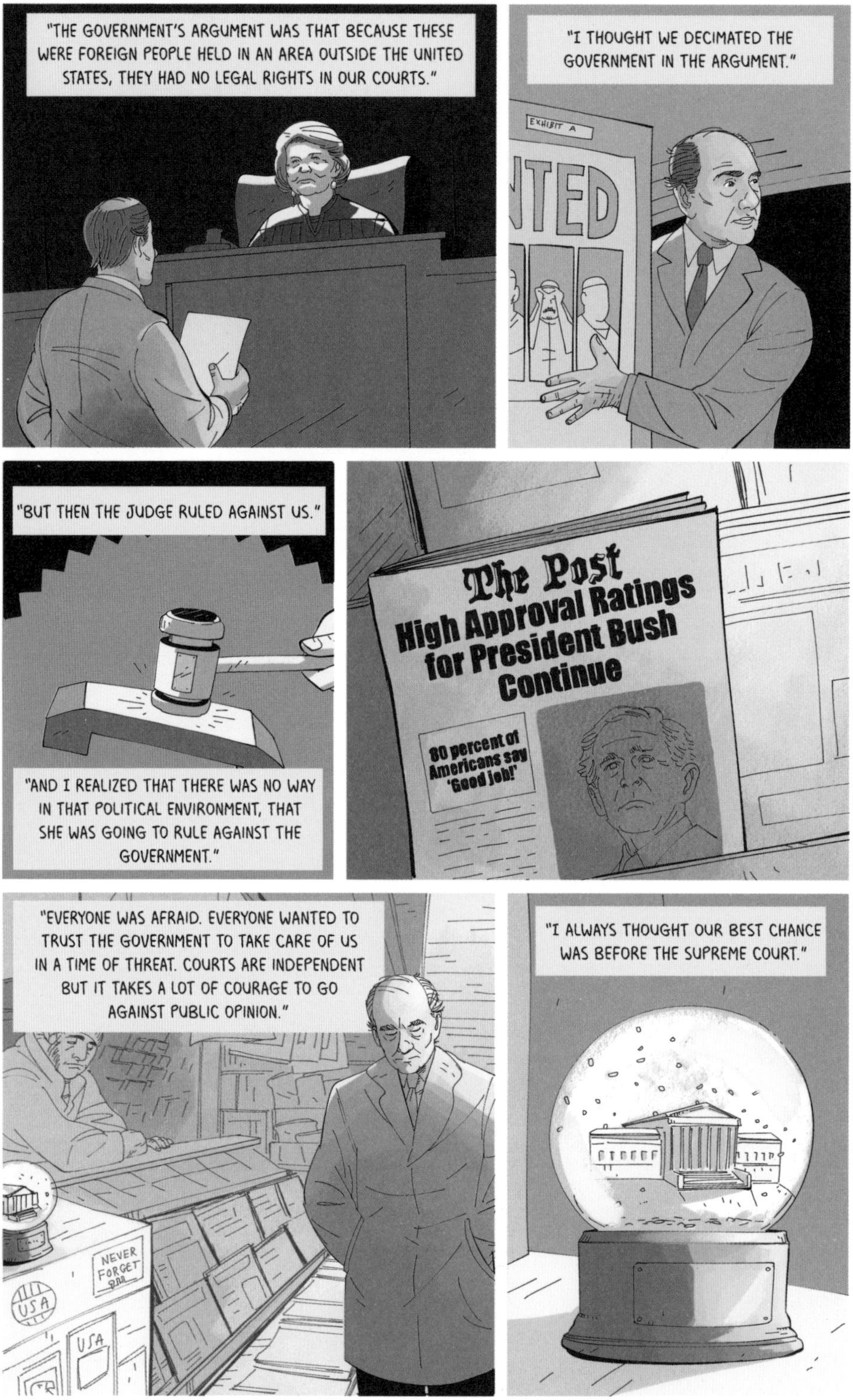
"THE GOVERNMENT'S ARGUMENT WAS THAT BECAUSE THESE WERE FOREIGN PEOPLE HELD IN AN AREA OUTSIDE THE UNITED STATES, THEY HAD NO LEGAL RIGHTS IN OUR COURTS."
"I THOUGHT WE DECIMATED THE GOVERNMENT IN THE ARGUMENT."
EXHIBIT A
NTED
"BUT THEN THE JUDGE RULED AGAINST US."
"AND I REALIZED THAT THERE WAS NO WAY IN THAT POLITICAL ENVIRONMENT, THAT SHE WAS GOING TO RULE AGAINST THE GOVERNMENT."
The Post
High Approval Ratings for President Bush Continue
80 percent of Americans say 'Good job!'
"EVERYONE WAS AFRAID. EVERYONE WANTED TO TRUST THE GOVERNMENT TO TAKE CARE OF US IN A TIME OF THREAT. COURTS ARE INDEPENDENT BUT IT TAKES A LOT OF COURAGE TO GO AGAINST PUBLIC OPINION."
NEVER FORGET
USA
USA
"I ALWAYS THOUGHT OUR BEST CHANCE WAS BEFORE THE SUPREME COURT."

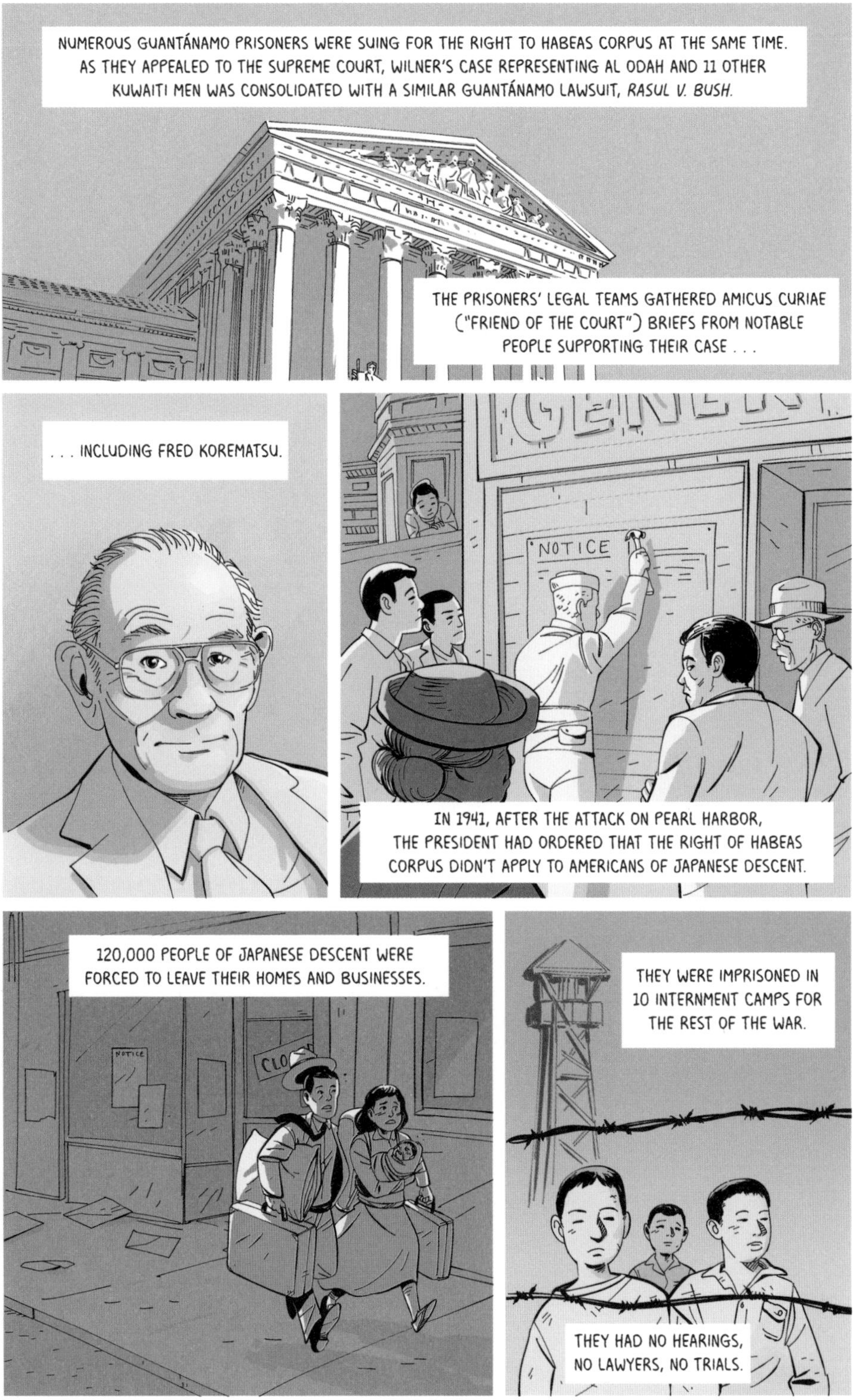
NUMEROUS GUANTÁNAMO PRISONERS WERE SUING FOR THE RIGHT TO HABEAS CORPUS AT THE SAME TIME. AS THEY APPEALED TO THE SUPREME COURT, WILNER'S CASE REPRESENTING AL ODAH AND 11 OTHER KUWAITI MEN WAS CONSOLIDATED WITH A SIMILAR GUANTÁNAMO LAWSUIT, *RASUL V. BUSH.*
THE PRISONERS' LEGAL TEAMS GATHERED AMICUS CURIAE ("FRIEND OF THE COURT") BRIEFS FROM NOTABLE PEOPLE SUPPORTING THEIR CASE . . .
. . . INCLUDING FRED KOREMATSU.
NOTICE
IN 1941, AFTER THE ATTACK ON PEARL HARBOR, THE PRESIDENT HAD ORDERED THAT THE RIGHT OF HABEAS CORPUS DIDN'T APPLY TO AMERICANS OF JAPANESE DESCENT.
120,000 PEOPLE OF JAPANESE DESCENT WERE FORCED TO LEAVE THEIR HOMES AND BUSINESSES.
NOTICE
THEY WERE IMPRISONED IN 10 INTERNMENT CAMPS FOR THE REST OF THE WAR.
THEY HAD NO HEARINGS, NO LAWYERS, NO TRIALS.

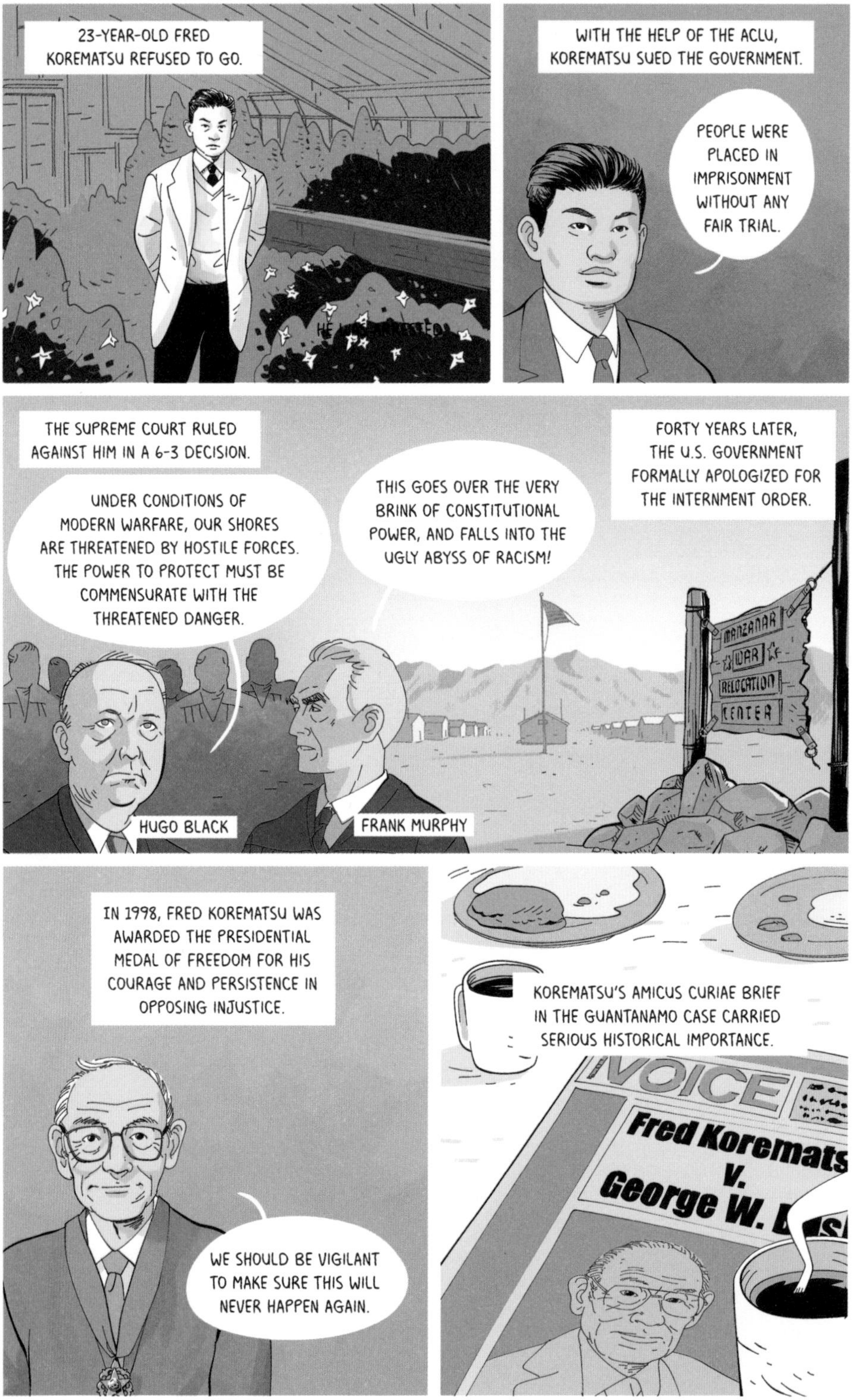
23-YEAR-OLD FRED KOREMATSU REFUSED TO GO.
WITH THE HELP OF THE ACLU, KOREMATSU SUED THE GOVERNMENT.
PEOPLE WERE PLACED IN IMPRISONMENT WITHOUT ANY FAIR TRIAL.
THE SUPREME COURT RULED AGAINST HIM IN A 6-3 DECISION.
UNDER CONDITIONS OF MODERN WARFARE, OUR SHORES ARE THREATENED BY HOSTILE FORCES. THE POWER TO PROTECT MUST BE COMMENSURATE WITH THE THREATENED DANGER.
HUGO BLACK
THIS GOES OVER THE VERY BRINK OF CONSTITUTIONAL POWER, AND FALLS INTO THE UGLY ABYSS OF RACISM!
FRANK MURPHY
FORTY YEARS LATER, THE U.S. GOVERNMENT FORMALLY APOLOGIZED FOR THE INTERNMENT ORDER.
MANZANAR WAR RELOCATION CENTER
IN 1998, FRED KOREMATSU WAS AWARDED THE PRESIDENTIAL MEDAL OF FREEDOM FOR HIS COURAGE AND PERSISTENCE IN OPPOSING INJUSTICE.
WE SHOULD BE VIGILANT TO MAKE SURE THIS WILL NEVER HAPPEN AGAIN.
KOREMATSU'S AMICUS CURIAE BRIEF IN THE GUANTANAMO CASE CARRIED SERIOUS HISTORICAL IMPORTANCE.
VOICE
v.

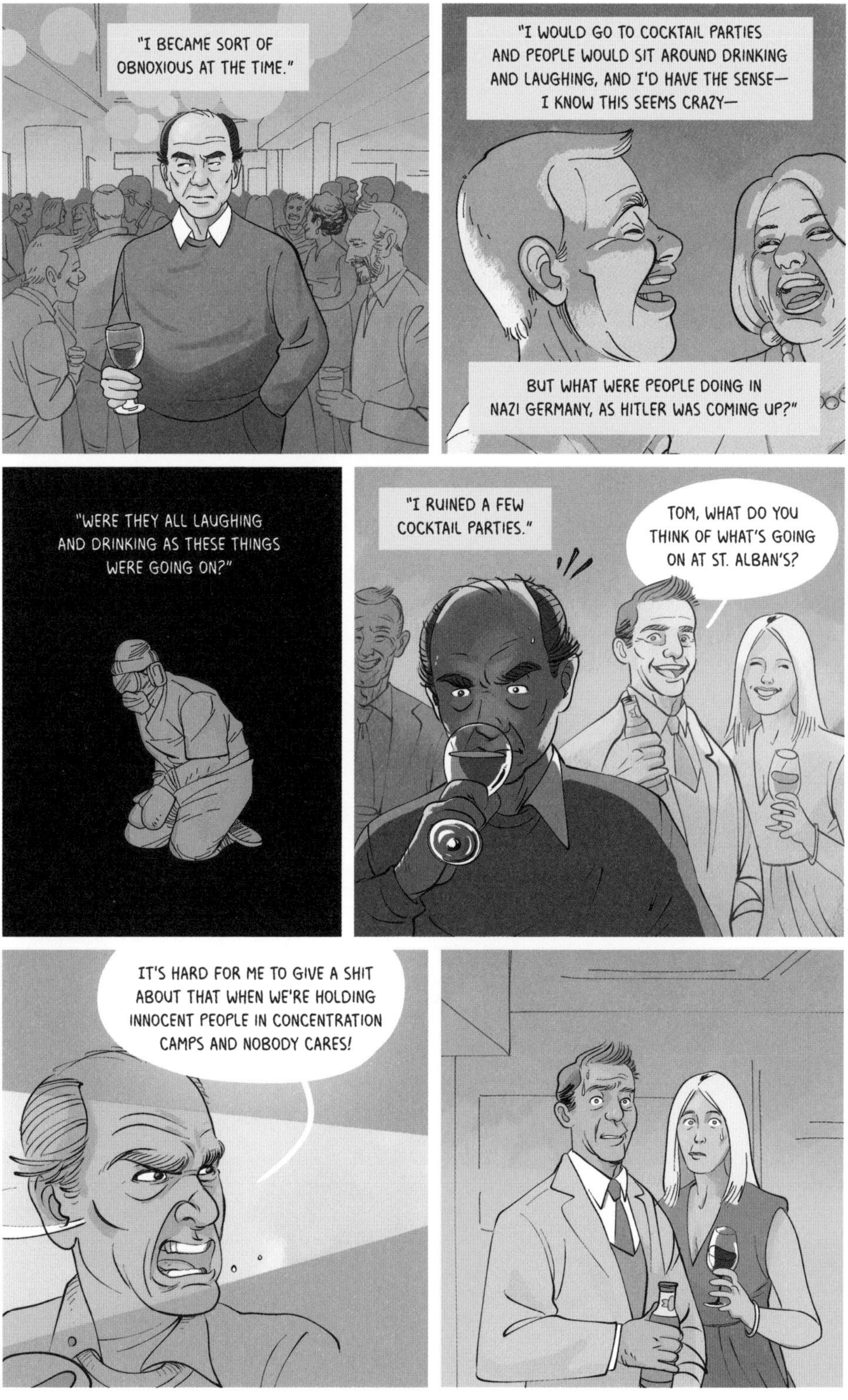
"I BECAME SORT OF OBNOXIOUS AT THE TIME."
"I WOULD GO TO COCKTAIL PARTIES AND PEOPLE WOULD SIT AROUND DRINKING AND LAUGHING, AND I'D HAVE THE SENSE— I KNOW THIS SEEMS CRAZY—
BUT WHAT WERE PEOPLE DOING IN NAZI GERMANY, AS HITLER WAS COMING UP?"
"WERE THEY ALL LAUGHING AND DRINKING AS THESE THINGS WERE GOING ON?"
"I RUINED A FEW COCKTAIL PARTIES."
TOM, WHAT DO YOU THINK OF WHAT'S GOING ON AT ST. ALBAN'S?
IT'S HARD FOR ME TO GIVE A SHIT ABOUT THAT WHEN WE'RE HOLDING INNOCENT PEOPLE IN CONCENTRATION CAMPS AND NOBODY CARES!

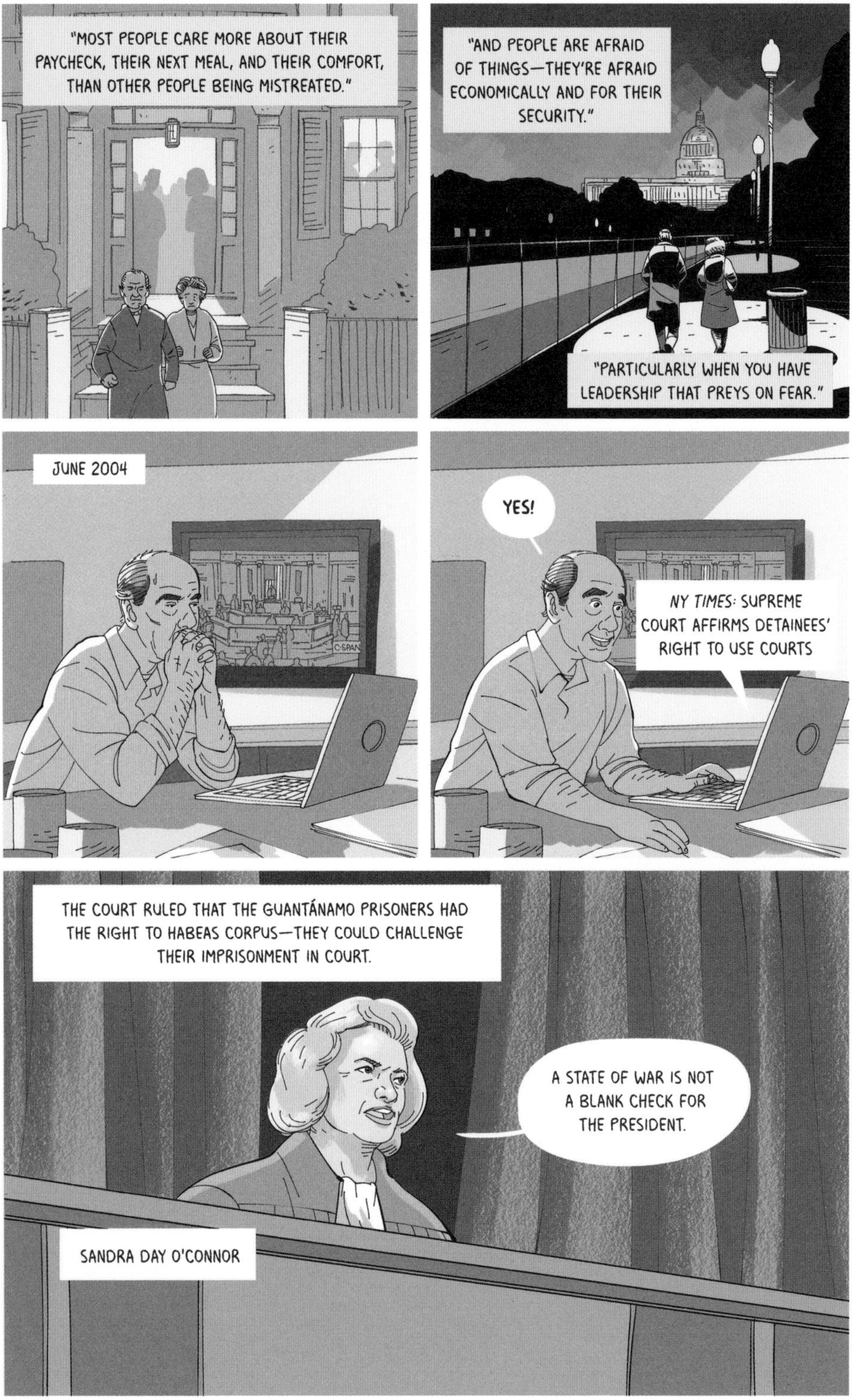
"MOST PEOPLE CARE MORE ABOUT THEIR PAYCHECK, THEIR NEXT MEAL, AND THEIR COMFORT, THAN OTHER PEOPLE BEING MISTREATED."
"AND PEOPLE ARE AFRAID OF THINGS—THEY'RE AFRAID ECONOMICALLY AND FOR THEIR SECURITY."
"PARTICULARLY WHEN YOU HAVE LEADERSHIP THAT PREYS ON FEAR."
JUNE 2004
C-SPAN
YES!
NY TIMES: SUPREME COURT AFFIRMS DETAINEES' RIGHT TO USE COURTS
THE COURT RULED THAT THE GUANTÁNAMO PRISONERS HAD THE RIGHT TO HABEAS CORPUS—THEY COULD CHALLENGE THEIR IMPRISONMENT IN COURT.
A STATE OF WAR IS NOT A BLANK CHECK FOR THE PRESIDENT.
SANDRA DAY O'CONNOR

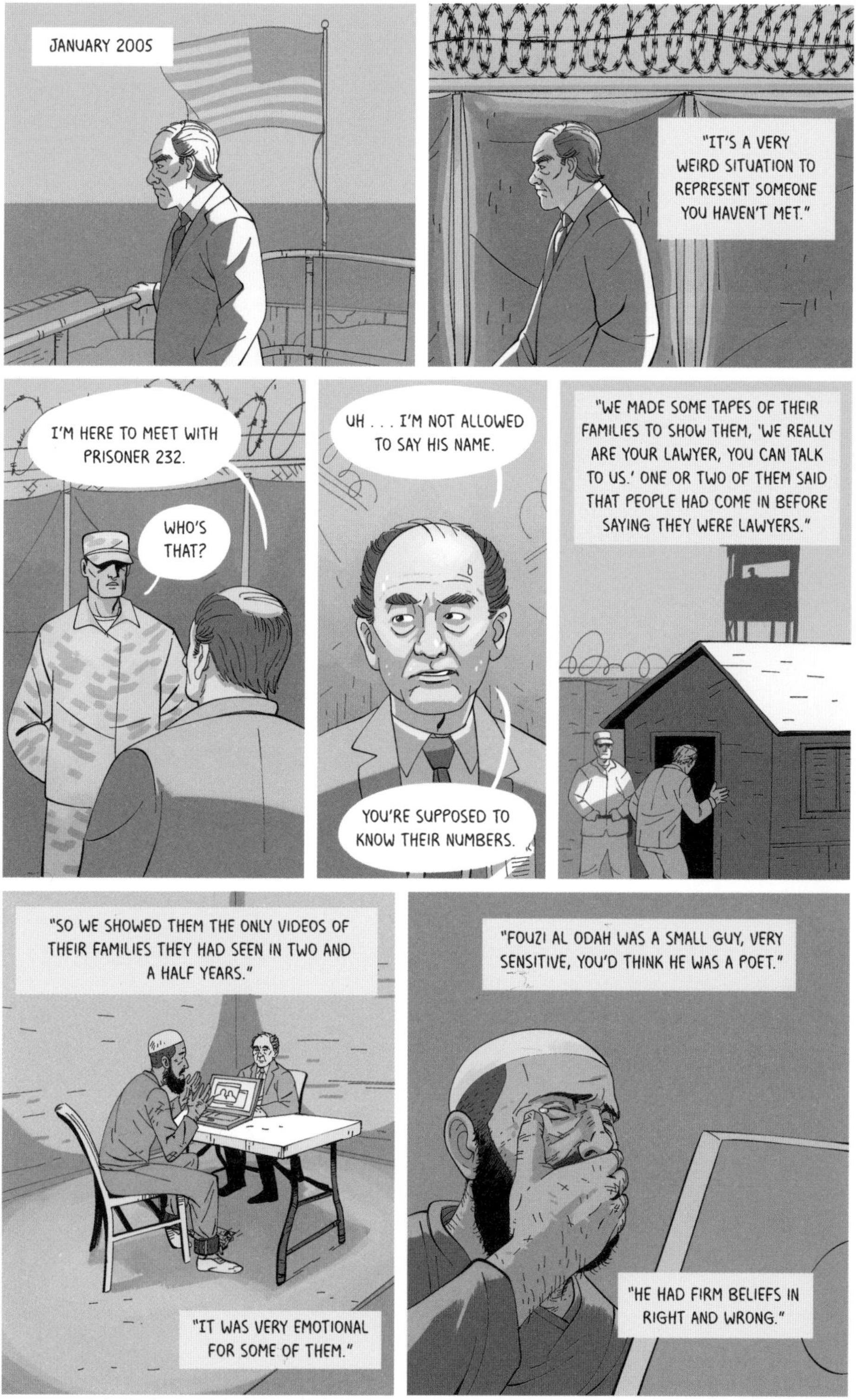
JANUARY 2005
"IT'S A VERY WEIRD SITUATION TO REPRESENT SOMEONE YOU HAVEN'T MET."
I'M HERE TO MEET WITH PRISONER 232.
WHO'S THAT?
UH . . . I'M NOT ALLOWED TO SAY HIS NAME.
YOU'RE SUPPOSED TO KNOW THEIR NUMBERS.
"WE MADE SOME TAPES OF THEIR FAMILIES TO SHOW THEM, 'WE REALLY ARE YOUR LAWYER, YOU CAN TALK TO US.' ONE OR TWO OF THEM SAID THAT PEOPLE HAD COME IN BEFORE SAYING THEY WERE LAWYERS."
"SO WE SHOWED THEM THE ONLY VIDEOS OF THEIR FAMILIES THEY HAD SEEN IN TWO AND A HALF YEARS."
"IT WAS VERY EMOTIONAL FOR SOME OF THEM."
"FOUZI AL ODAH WAS A SMALL GUY, VERY SENSITIVE, YOU'D THINK HE WAS A POET."
"HE HAD FIRM BELIEFS IN RIGHT AND WRONG."

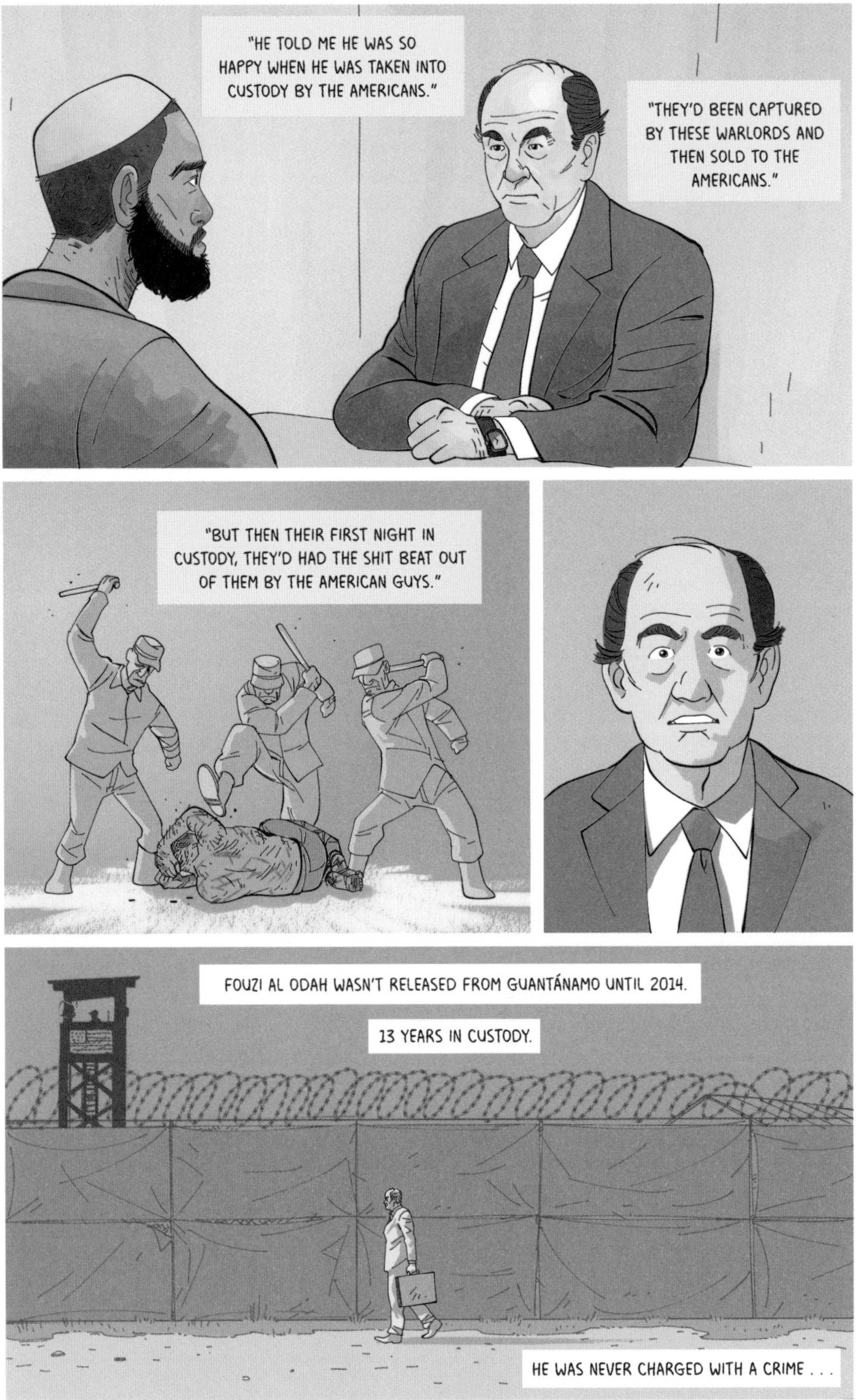
"HE TOLD ME HE WAS SO HAPPY WHEN HE WAS TAKEN INTO CUSTODY BY THE AMERICANS."
"THEY'D BEEN CAPTURED BY THESE WARLORDS AND THEN SOLD TO THE AMERICANS."
"BUT THEN THEIR FIRST NIGHT IN CUSTODY, THEY'D HAD THE SHIT BEAT OUT OF THEM BY THE AMERICAN GUYS."
FOUZI AL ODAH WASN'T RELEASED FROM GUANTÁNAMO UNTIL 2014.
13 YEARS IN CUSTODY.
HE WAS NEVER CHARGED WITH A CRIME . . .

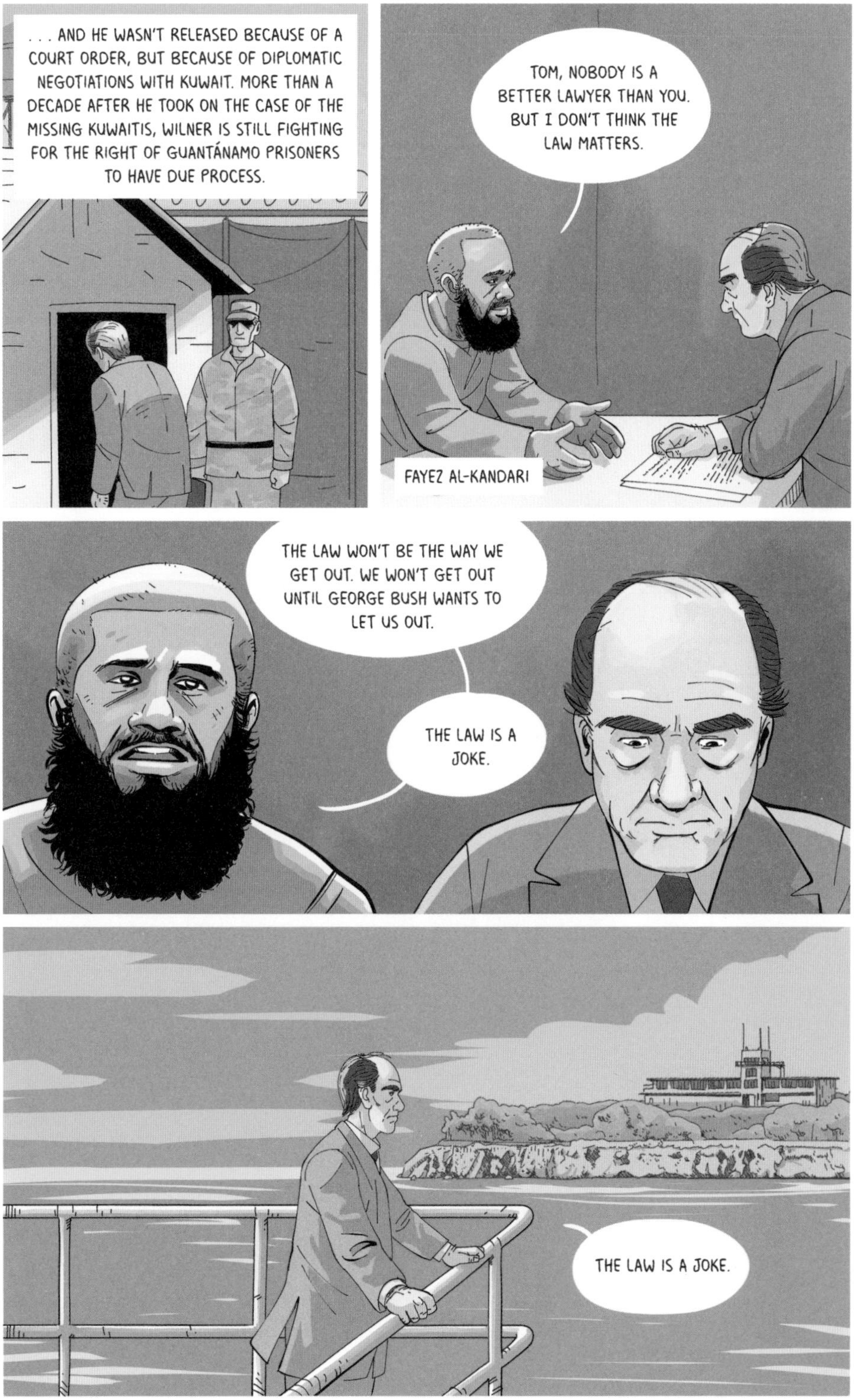
. . . AND HE WASN'T RELEASED BECAUSE OF A COURT ORDER, BUT BECAUSE OF DIPLOMATIC NEGOTIATIONS WITH KUWAIT. MORE THAN A DECADE AFTER HE TOOK ON THE CASE OF THE MISSING KUWAITIS, WILNER IS STILL FIGHTING FOR THE RIGHT OF GUANTÁNAMO PRISONERS TO HAVE DUE PROCESS.
TOM, NOBODY IS A BETTER LAWYER THAN YOU. BUT I DON'T THINK THE LAW MATTERS.
FAYEZ AL-KANDARI
THE LAW WON'T BE THE WAY WE GET OUT. WE WON'T GET OUT UNTIL GEORGE BUSH WANTS TO LET US OUT.
THE LAW IS A JOKE.
THE LAW IS A JOKE.

CHAPTER SIX

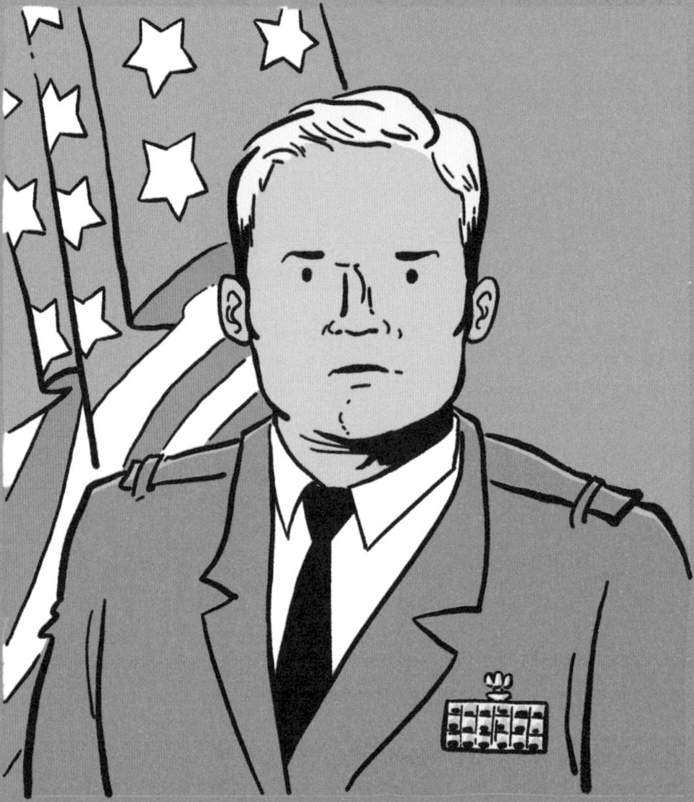

COLONEL MORRIS DAVIS

TWENTY-FIVE-YEAR AIR FORCE VETERAN AND CHIEF PROSECUTOR FOR THE GUANTÁNAMO BAY MILITARY COMMISSIONS, SEPTEMBER 2005 TO OCTOBER 2007

ILLUSTRATED BY JEREMY NGUYEN

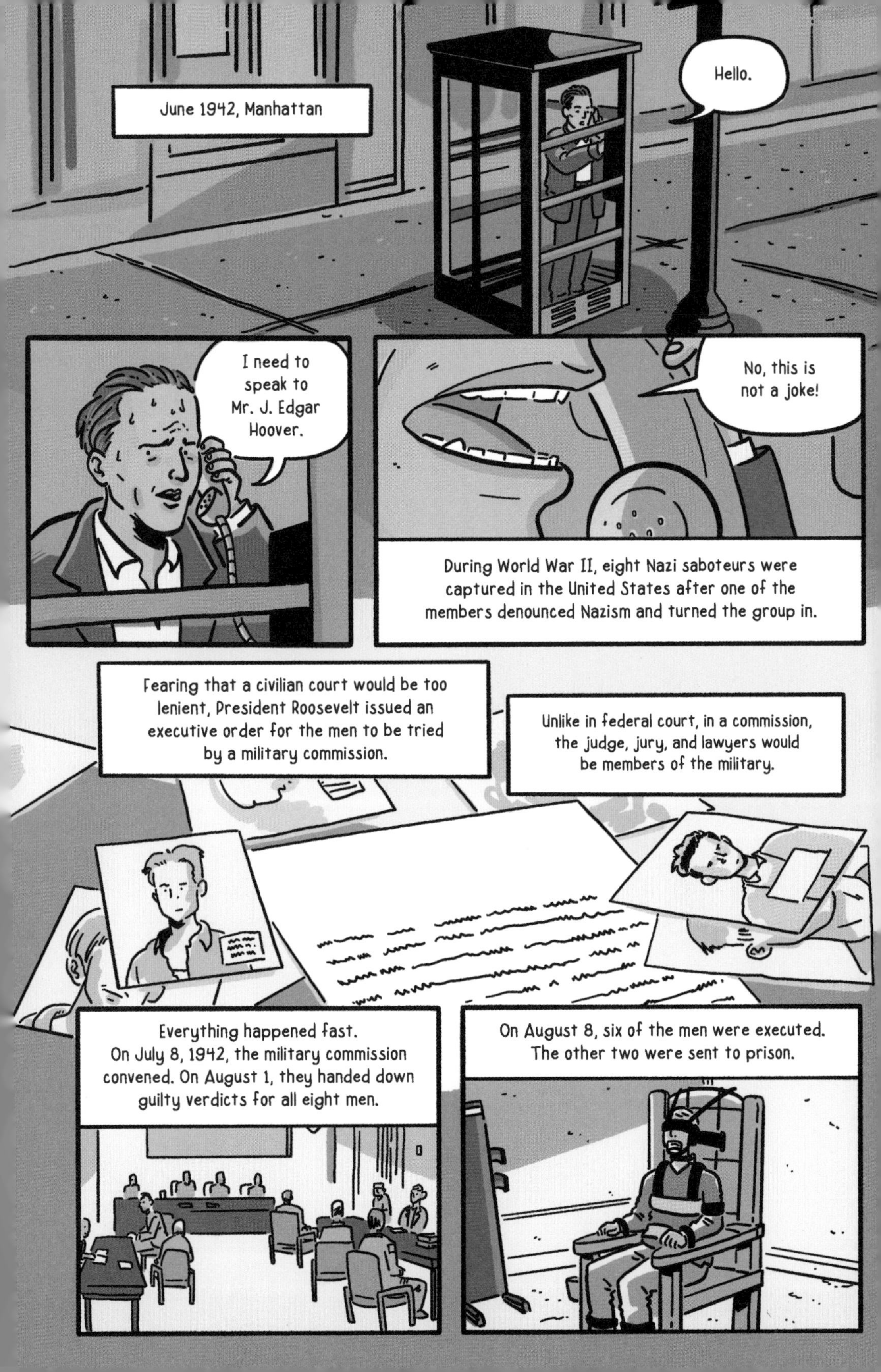
June 1942, Manhattan
Hello.
I need to speak to Mr. J. Edgar Hoover.
No, this is not a joke!
During World War II, eight Nazi saboteurs were captured in the United States after one of the members denounced Nazism and turned the group in.
Fearing that a civilian court would be too lenient, President Roosevelt issued an executive order for the men to be tried by a military commission.
Unlike in federal court, in a commission, the judge, jury, and lawyers would be members of the military.
Everything happened fast.
On July 8, 1942, the military commission convened. On August 1, they handed down guilty verdicts for all eight men.
On August 8, six of the men were executed.
The other two were sent to prison.

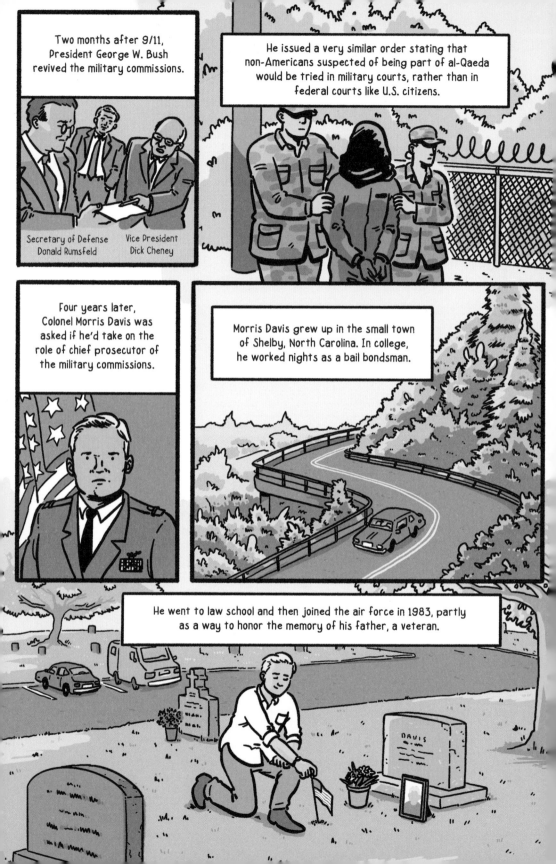

Two months after 9/11, President George W. Bush revived the military commissions.

Secretary of Defense
Donald Rumsfeld

Vice President
Dick Cheney

He issued a very similar order stating that non-Americans suspected of being part of al-Qaeda would be tried in military courts, rather than in federal courts like U.S. citizens.

Four years later, Colonel Morris Davis was asked if he'd take on the role of chief prosecutor of the military commissions.

Morris Davis grew up in the small town of Shelby, North Carolina. In college, he worked nights as a bail bondsman.

He went to law school and then joined the air force in 1983, partly as a way to honor the memory of his father, a veteran.

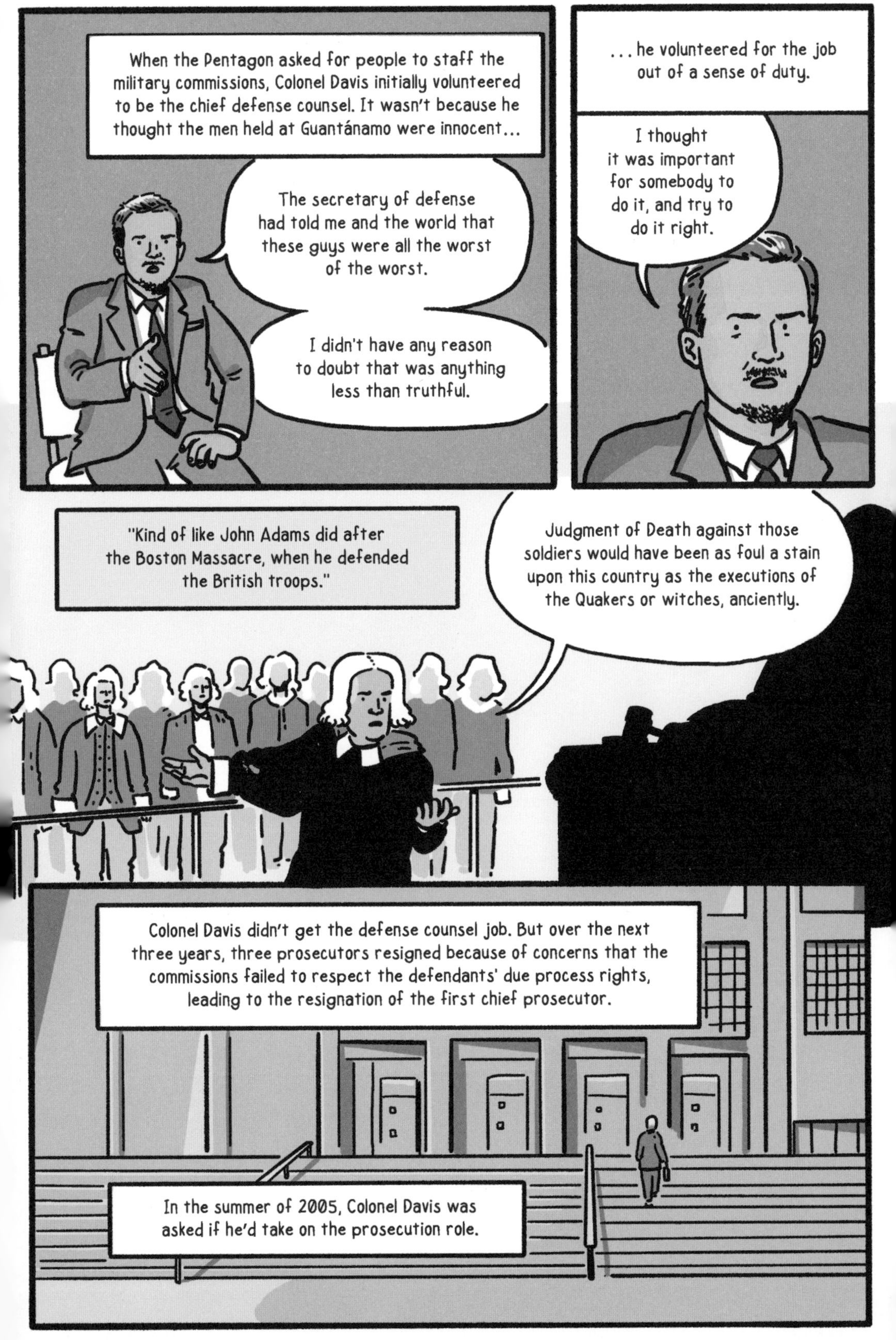
When the Pentagon asked for people to staff the military commissions, Colonel Davis initially volunteered to be the chief defense counsel. It wasn't because he thought the men held at Guantánamo were innocent...
The secretary of defense had told me and the world that these guys were all the worst of the worst.
I didn't have any reason to doubt that was anything less than truthful.
... he volunteered for the job out of a sense of duty.
I thought it was important for somebody to do it, and try to do it right.
"Kind of like John Adams did after the Boston Massacre, when he defended the British troops."
Judgment of Death against those soldiers would have been as foul a stain upon this country as the executions of the Quakers or witches, anciently.
Colonel Davis didn't get the defense counsel job. But over the next three years, three prosecutors resigned because of concerns that the commissions failed to respect the defendants' due process rights, leading to the resignation of the first chief prosecutor.
In the summer of 2005, Colonel Davis was asked if he'd take on the prosecution role.

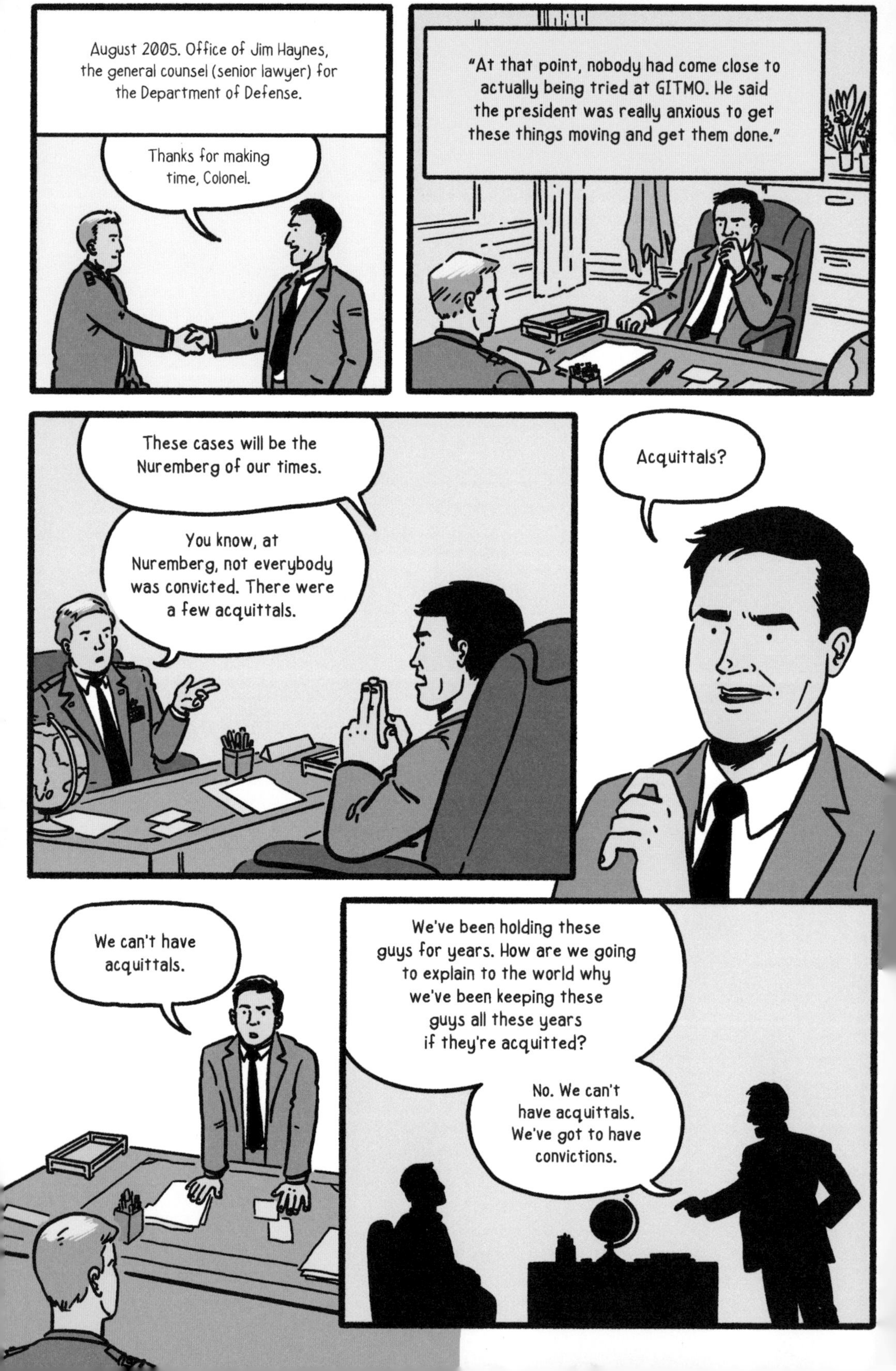

August 2005. Office of Jim Haynes, the general counsel (senior lawyer) for the Department of Defense.
Thanks for making time, Colonel.
"At that point, nobody had come close to actually being tried at GITMO. He said the president was really anxious to get these things moving and get them done."
These cases will be the Nuremberg of our times.
You know, at Nuremberg, not everybody was convicted. There were a few acquittals.
Acquittals?
We can't have acquittals.
We've been holding these guys for years. How are we going to explain to the world why we've been keeping these guys all these years if they're acquitted?
No. We can't have acquittals. We've got to have convictions.

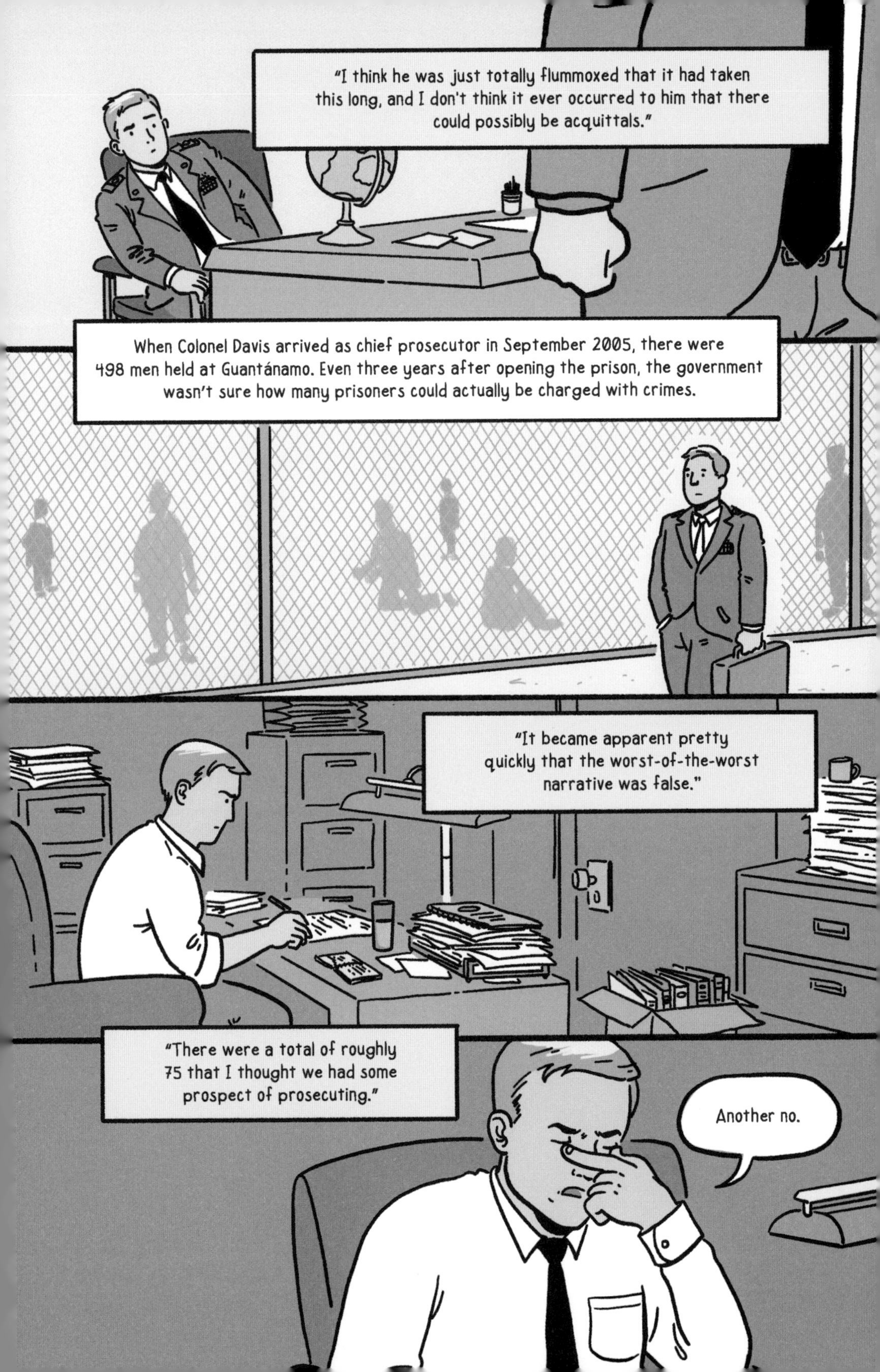
"I think he was just totally flummoxed that it had taken this long, and I don't think it ever occurred to him that there could possibly be acquittals."
When Colonel Davis arrived as chief prosecutor in September 2005, there were 498 men held at Guantánamo. Even three years after opening the prison, the government wasn't sure how many prisoners could actually be charged with crimes.
"It became apparent pretty quickly that the worst-of-the-worst narrative was false."
"There were a total of roughly 75 that I thought we had some prospect of prosecuting."
Another no.

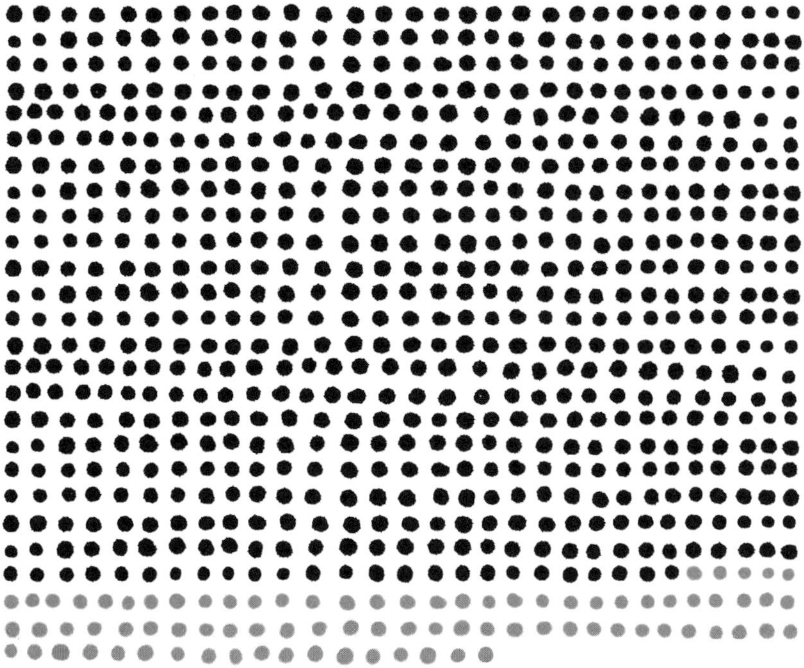

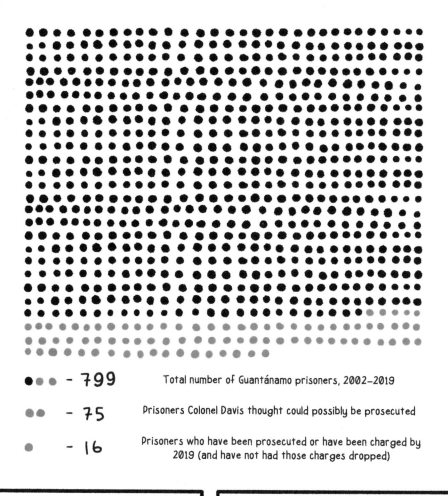

- 799 Total number of Guantánamo prisoners, 2002–2019

- 75 Prisoners Colonel Davis thought could possibly be prosecuted

- 16 Prisoners who have been prosecuted or have been charged by 2019 (and have not had those charges dropped)

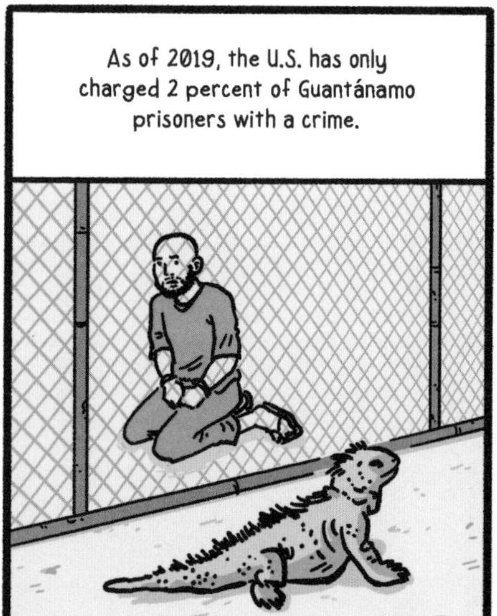
As of 2019, the U.S. has only charged 2 percent of Guantánamo prisoners with a crime.

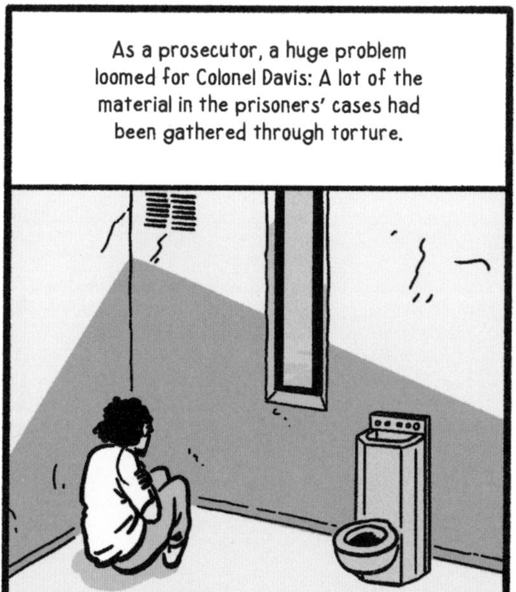
As a prosecutor, a huge problem loomed for Colonel Davis: A lot of the material in the prisoners' cases had been gathered through torture.

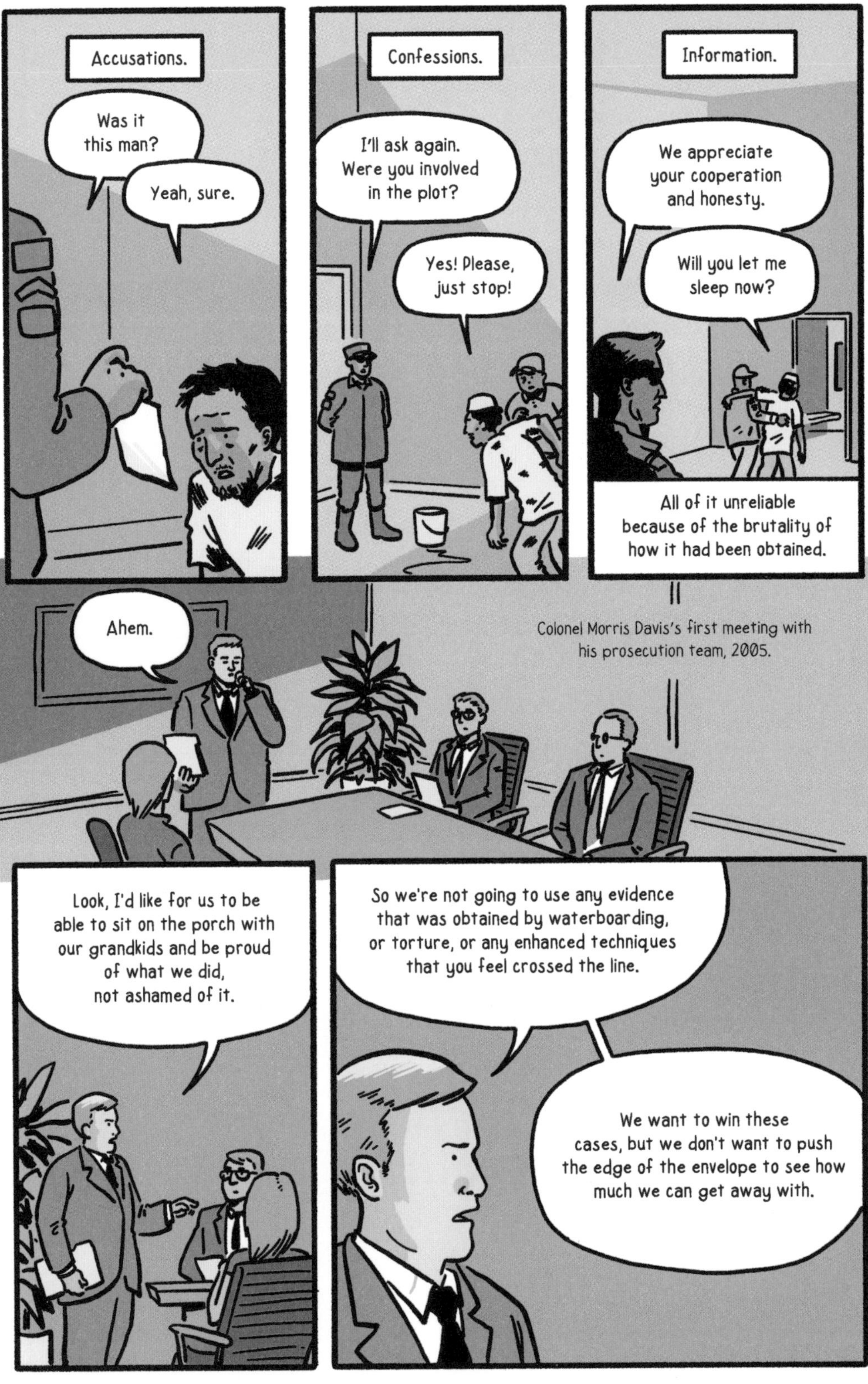
Accusations.
Was it this man?
Yeah, sure.
Confessions.
I'll ask again. Were you involved in the plot?
Yes! Please, just stop!
Information.
We appreciate your cooperation and honesty.
Will you let me sleep now?
All of it unreliable because of the brutality of how it had been obtained.
Ahem.
Colonel Morris Davis's first meeting with his prosecution team, 2005.
Look, I'd like for us to be able to sit on the porch with our grandkids and be proud of what we did, not ashamed of it.
So we're not going to use any evidence that was obtained by waterboarding, or torture, or any enhanced techniques that you feel crossed the line.
We want to win these cases, but we don't want to push the edge of the envelope to see how much we can get away with.

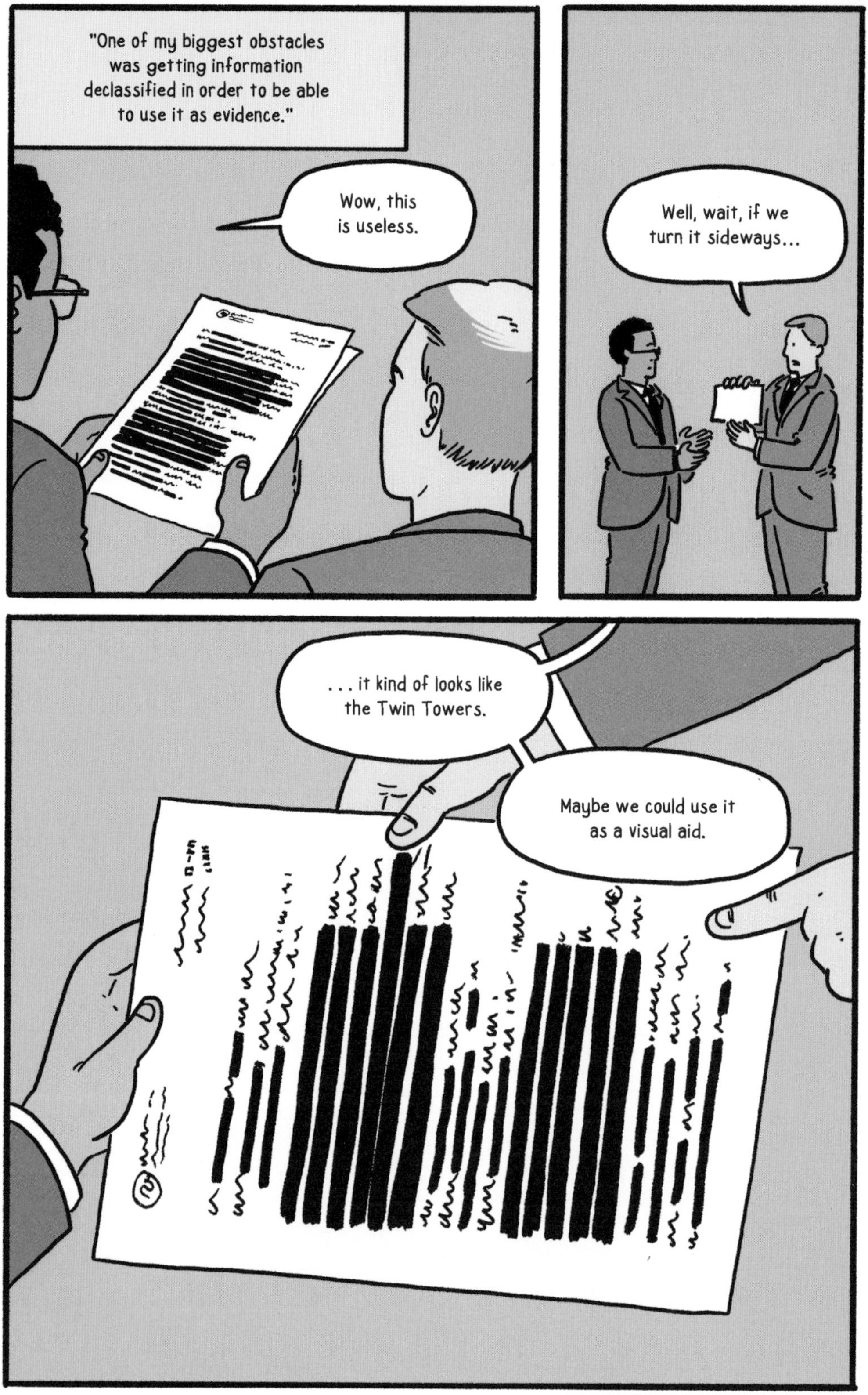
"One of my biggest obstacles was getting information declassified in order to be able to use it as evidence."
Wow, this is useless.
Well, wait, if we turn it sideways...
. . . it kind of looks like the Twin Towers.
Maybe we could use it as a visual aid.

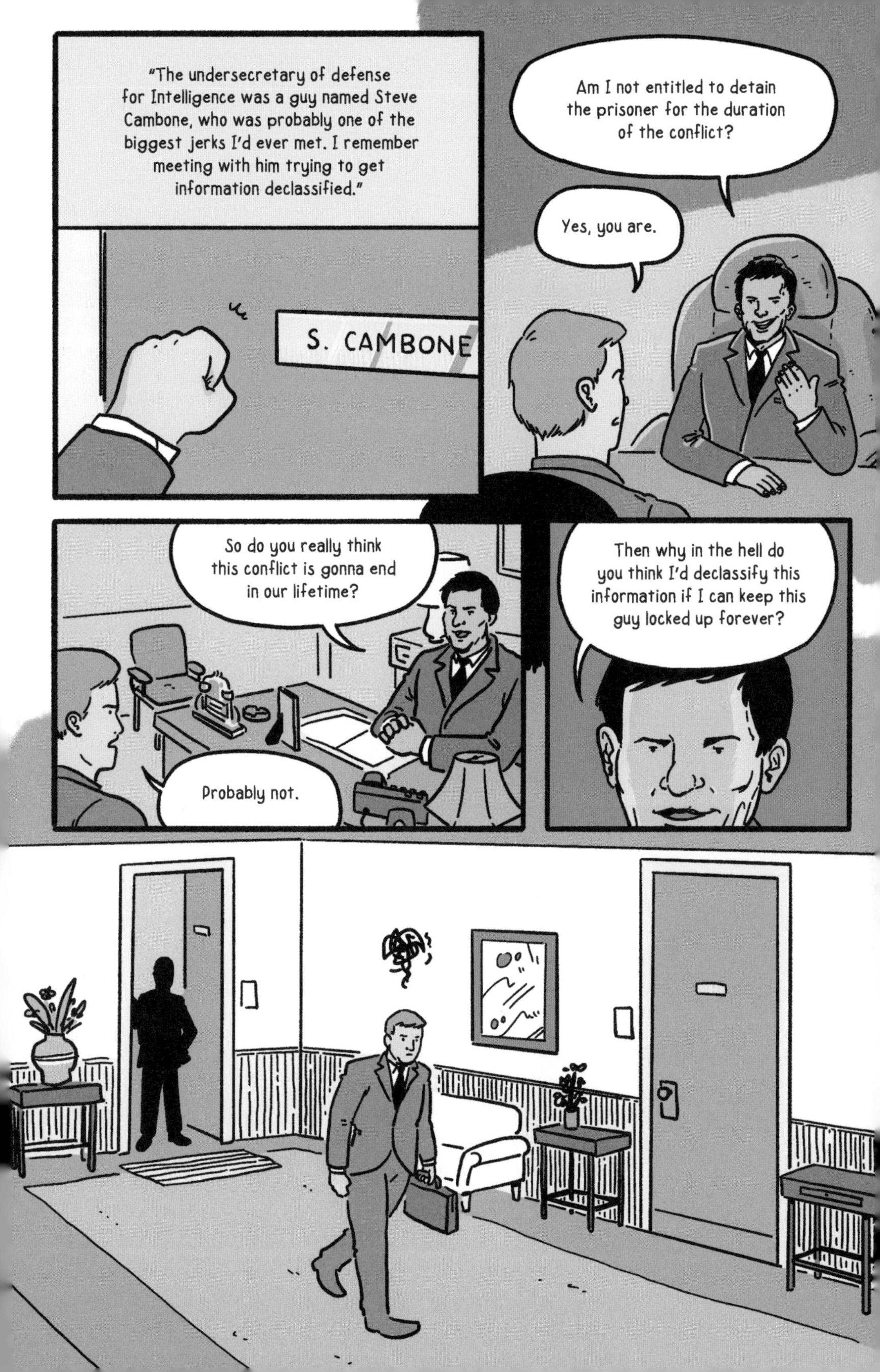
"The undersecretary of defense for Intelligence was a guy named Steve Cambone, who was probably one of the biggest jerks I'd ever met. I remember meeting with him trying to get information declassified."
S. CAMBONE
Am I not entitled to detain the prisoner for the duration of the conflict?
Yes, you are.
So do you really think this conflict is gonna end in our lifetime?
Probably not.
Then why in the hell do you think I'd declassify this information if I can keep this guy locked up forever?

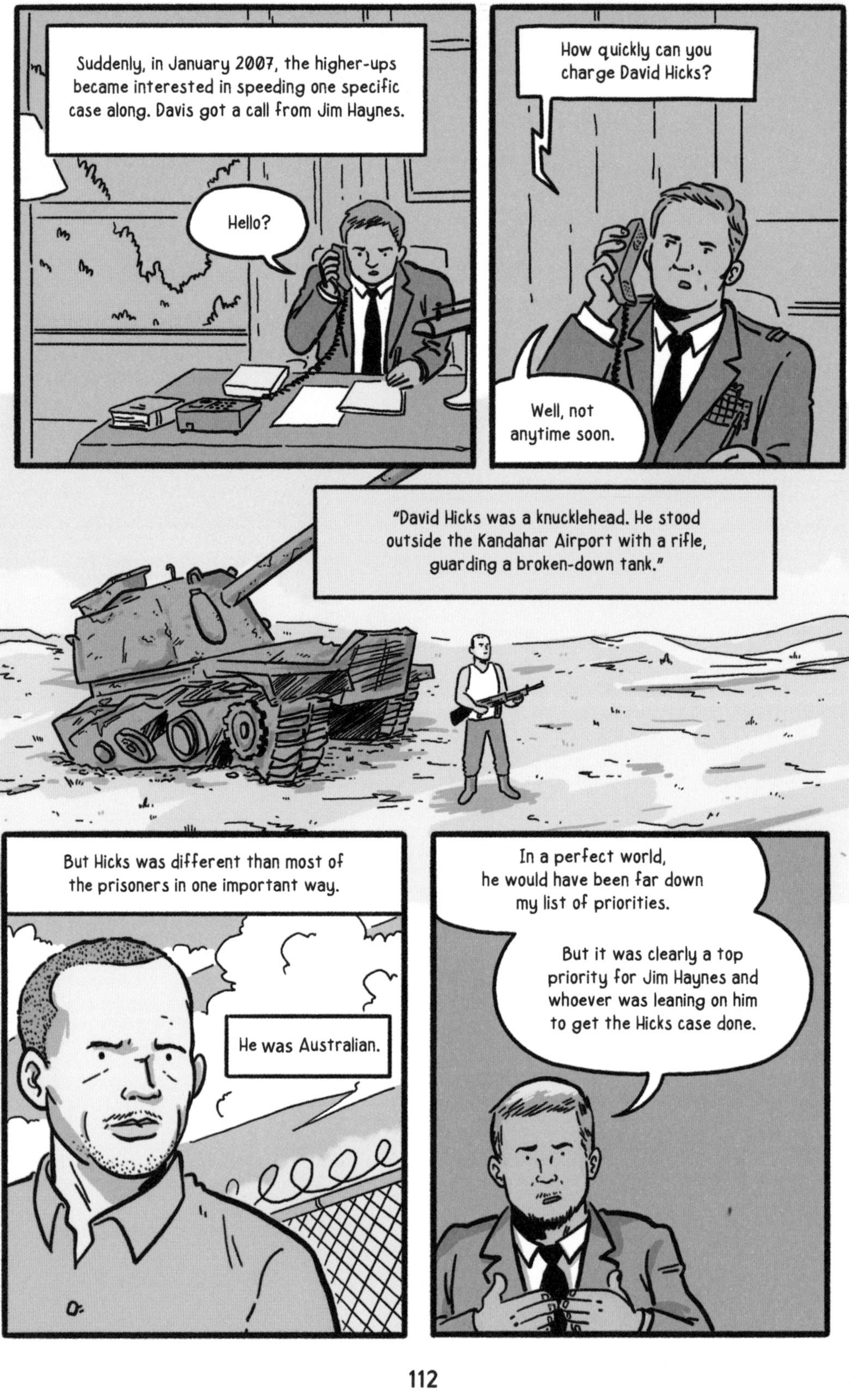

Suddenly, in January 2007, the higher-ups became interested in speeding one specific case along. Davis got a call from Jim Haynes.
Hello?
How quickly can you charge David Hicks?
Well, not anytime soon.
"David Hicks was a knucklehead. He stood outside the Kandahar Airport with a rifle, guarding a broken-down tank."
But Hicks was different than most of the prisoners in one important way.
He was Australian.
In a perfect world, he would have been far down my list of priorities.
But it was clearly a top priority for Jim Haynes and whoever was leaning on him to get the Hicks case done.

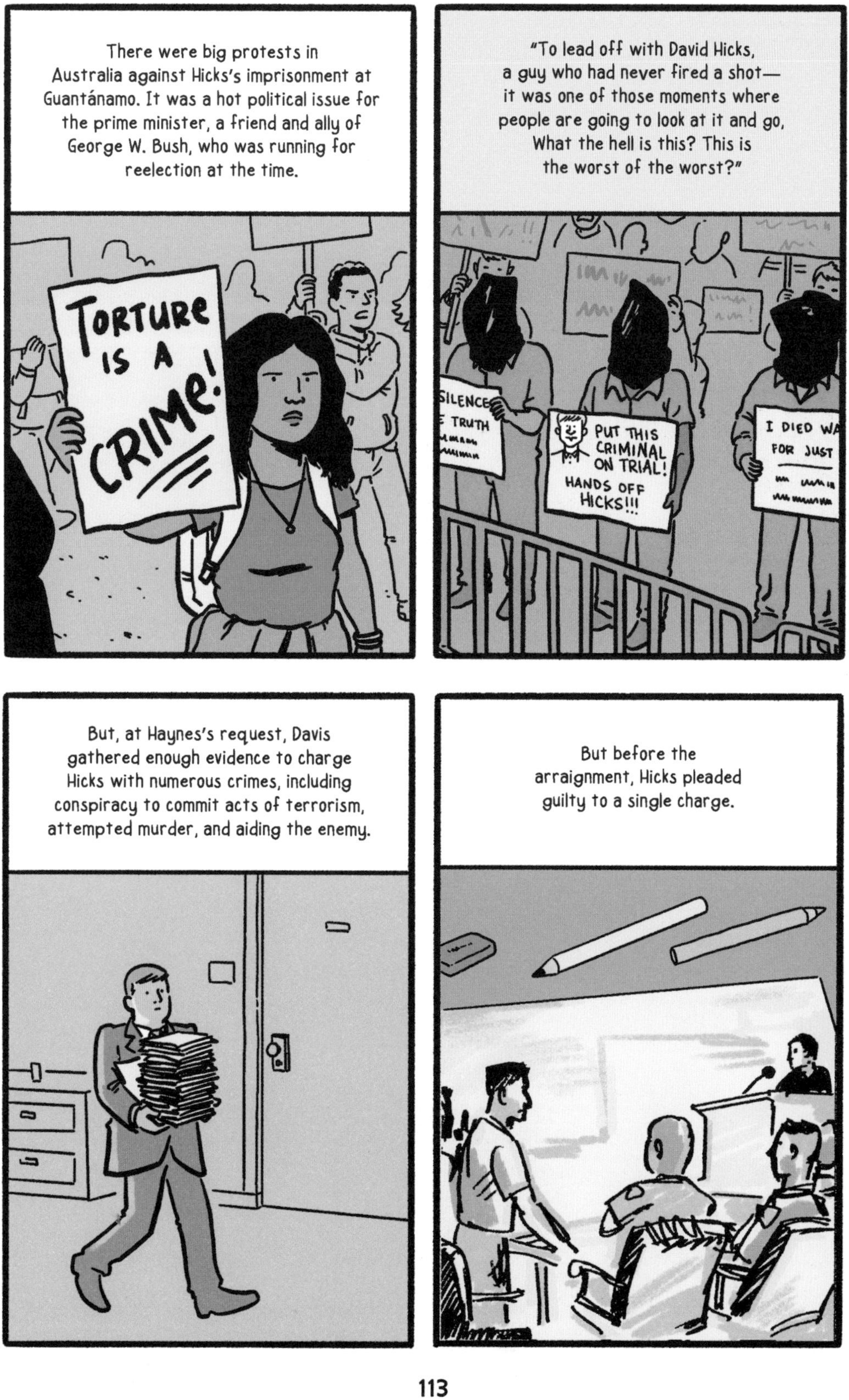

There were big protests in Australia against Hicks's imprisonment at Guantánamo. It was a hot political issue for the prime minister, a friend and ally of George W. Bush, who was running for reelection at the time.
TORTURE IS A CRIME!
"To lead off with David Hicks, a guy who had never fired a shot—it was one of those moments where people are going to look at it and go, What the hell is this? This is the worst of the worst?"
PUT THIS CRIMINAL ON TRIAL!
HANDS OFF HICKS!!!
FOR JUST
But, at Haynes's request, Davis gathered enough evidence to charge Hicks with numerous crimes, including conspiracy to commit acts of terrorism, attempted murder, and aiding the enemy.
But before the arraignment, Hicks pleaded guilty to a single charge.

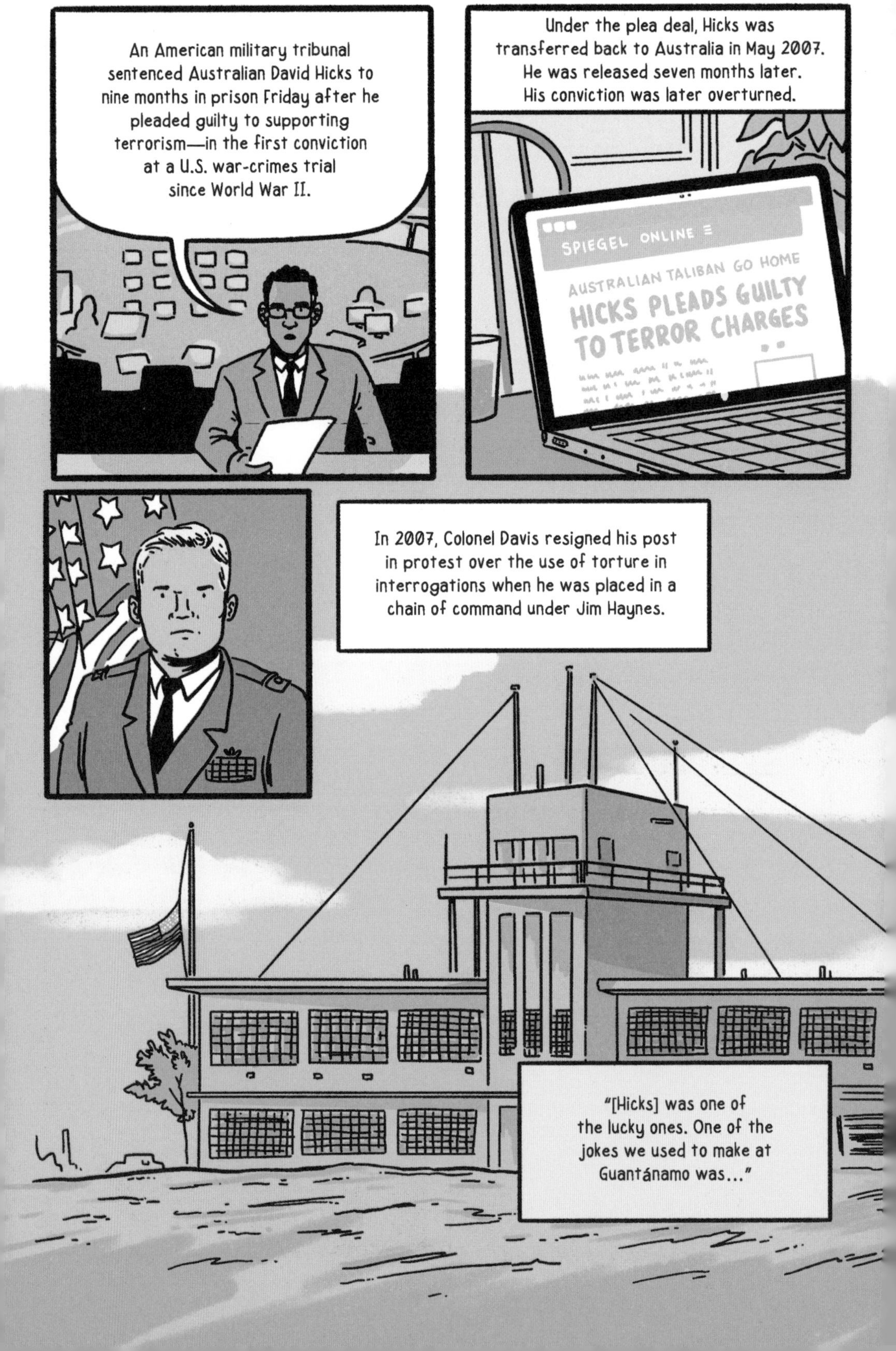

An American military tribunal sentenced Australian David Hicks to nine months in prison Friday after he pleaded guilty to supporting terrorism—in the first conviction at a U.S. war-crimes trial since World War II.
Under the plea deal, Hicks was transferred back to Australia in May 2007. He was released seven months later. His conviction was later overturned.
SPIEGEL ONLINE
AUSTRALIAN TALIBAN GO HOME
HICKS PLEADS GUILTY TO TERROR CHARGES
In 2007, Colonel Davis resigned his post in protest over the use of torture in interrogations when he was placed in a chain of command under Jim Haynes.
"[Hicks] was one of the lucky ones. One of the jokes we used to make at Guantánamo was..."

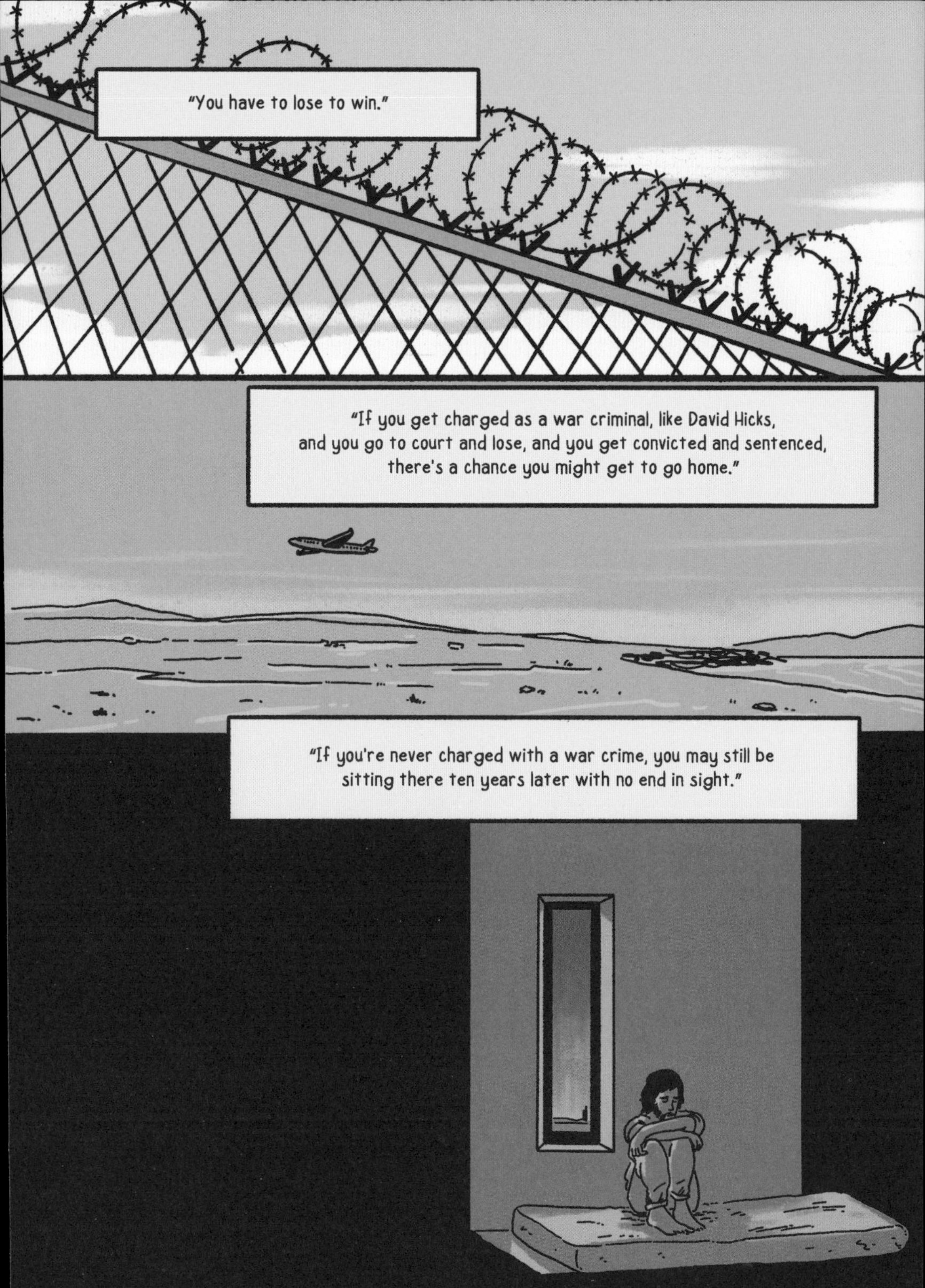
"You have to lose to win."
"If you get charged as a war criminal, like David Hicks, and you go to court and lose, and you get convicted and sentenced, there's a chance you might get to go home."
"If you're never charged with a war crime, you may still be sitting there ten years later with no end in sight."

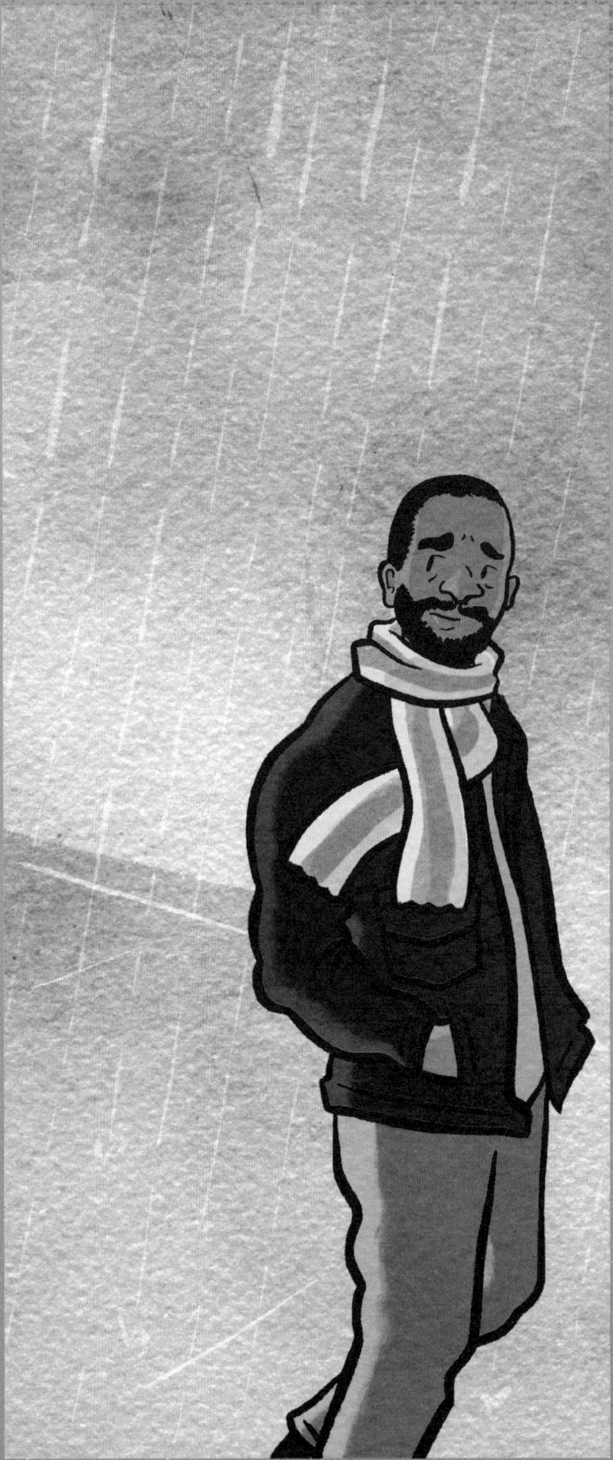

ILLUSTRATED BY KANE LYNCH

CHAPTER SEVEN

MANSOOR ADAYFI

GUANTÁNAMO PRISONER 441

FEBRUARY 2002 TO JULY 2016

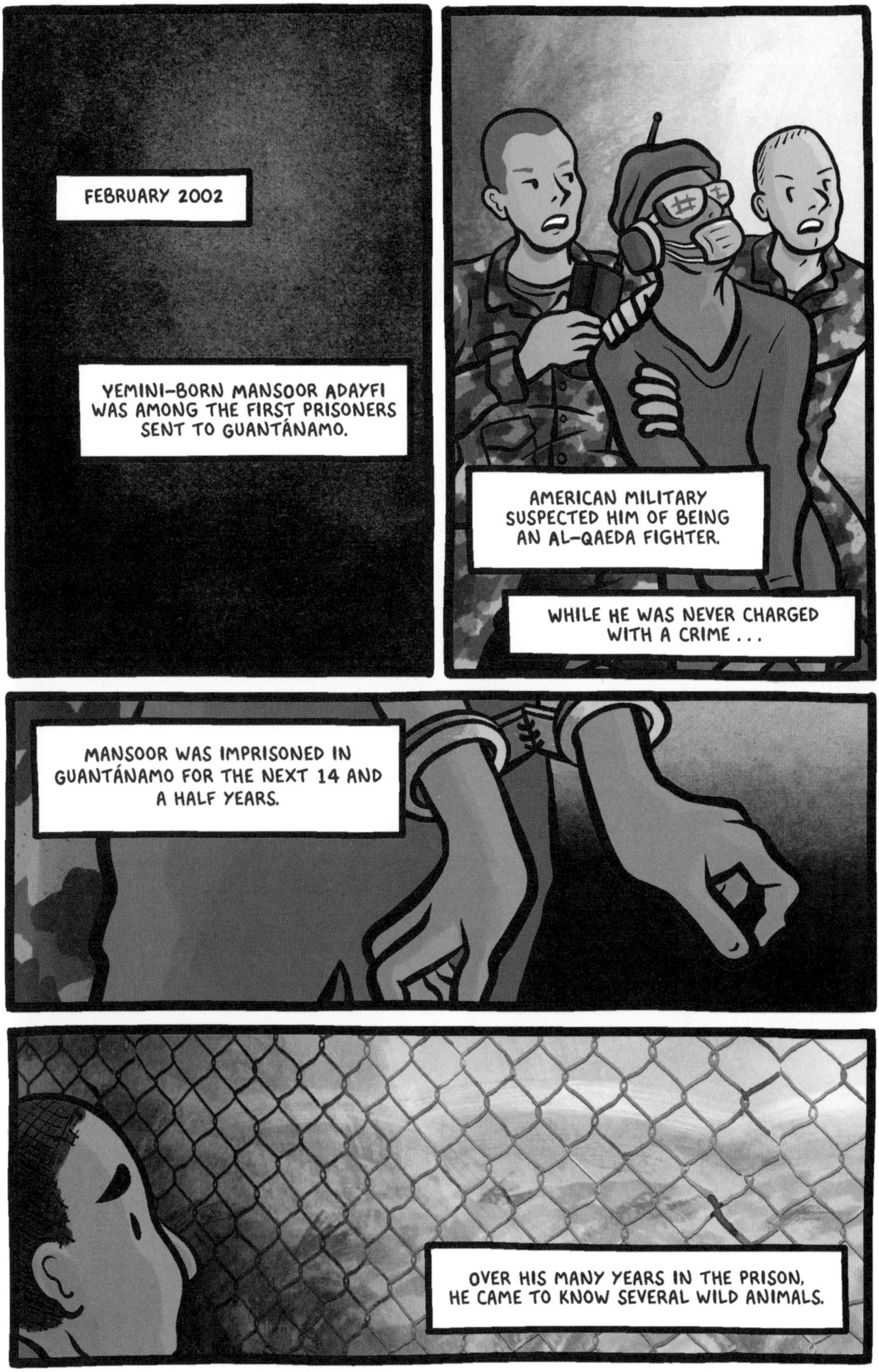
FEBRUARY 2002
YEMINI-BORN MANSOOR ADAYFI WAS AMONG THE FIRST PRISONERS SENT TO GUANTÁNAMO.
AMERICAN MILITARY SUSPECTED HIM OF BEING AN AL-QAEDA FIGHTER.
WHILE HE WAS NEVER CHARGED WITH A CRIME . . .
MANSOOR WAS IMPRISONED IN GUANTÁNAMO FOR THE NEXT 14 AND A HALF YEARS.
OVER HIS MANY YEARS IN THE PRISON, HE CAME TO KNOW SEVERAL WILD ANIMALS.

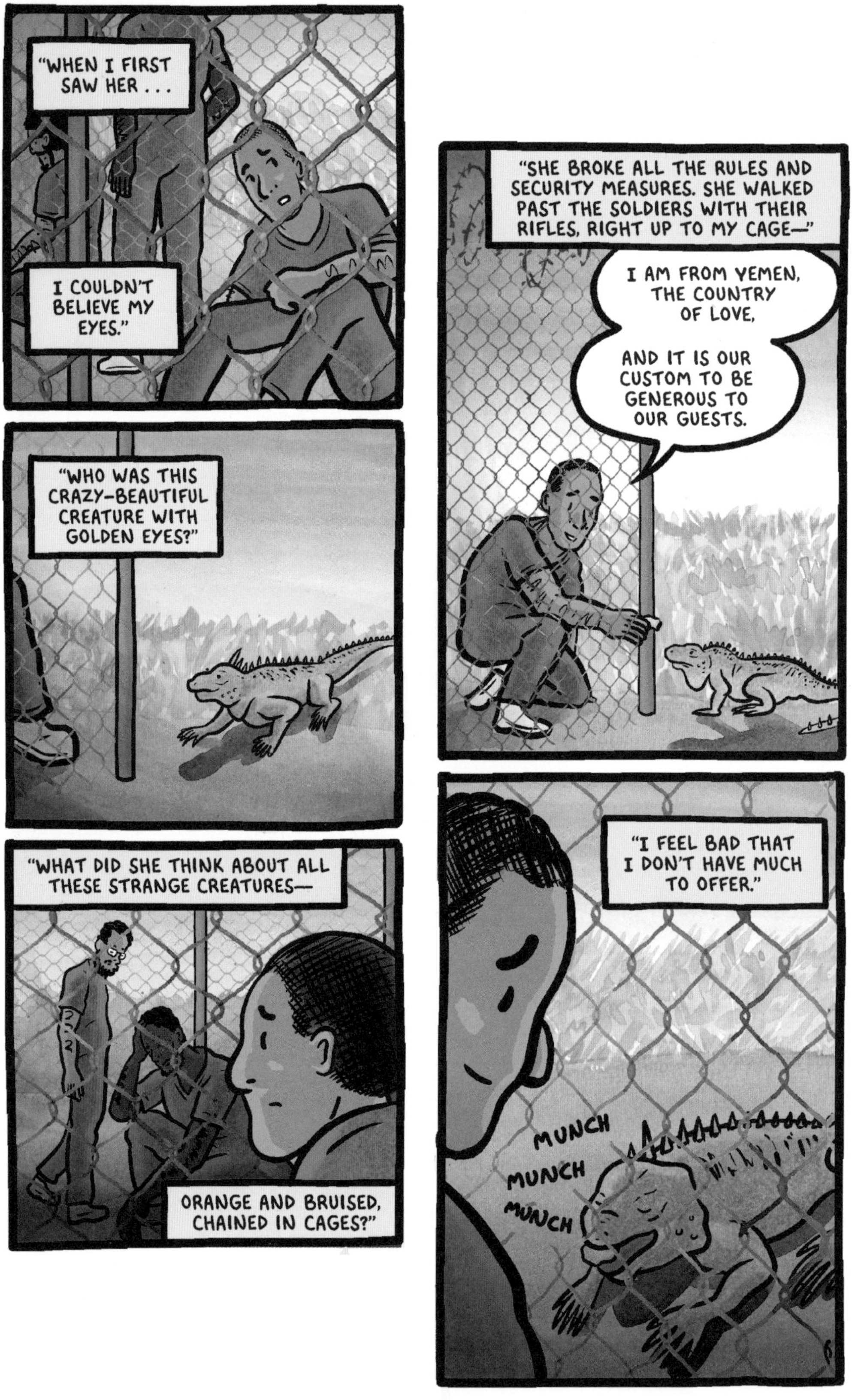
"WHEN I FIRST SAW HER . . .
I COULDN'T BELIEVE MY EYES."
"WHO WAS THIS CRAZY-BEAUTIFUL CREATURE WITH GOLDEN EYES?"
"WHAT DID SHE THINK ABOUT ALL THESE STRANGE CREATURES—
ORANGE AND BRUISED, CHAINED IN CAGES?"
"SHE BROKE ALL THE RULES AND SECURITY MEASURES. SHE WALKED PAST THE SOLDIERS WITH THEIR RIFLES, RIGHT UP TO MY CAGE—"
I AM FROM YEMEN, THE COUNTRY OF LOVE,
AND IT IS OUR CUSTOM TO BE GENEROUS TO OUR GUESTS.
"I FEEL BAD THAT I DON'T HAVE MUCH TO OFFER."
MUNCH
MUNCH
MUNCH

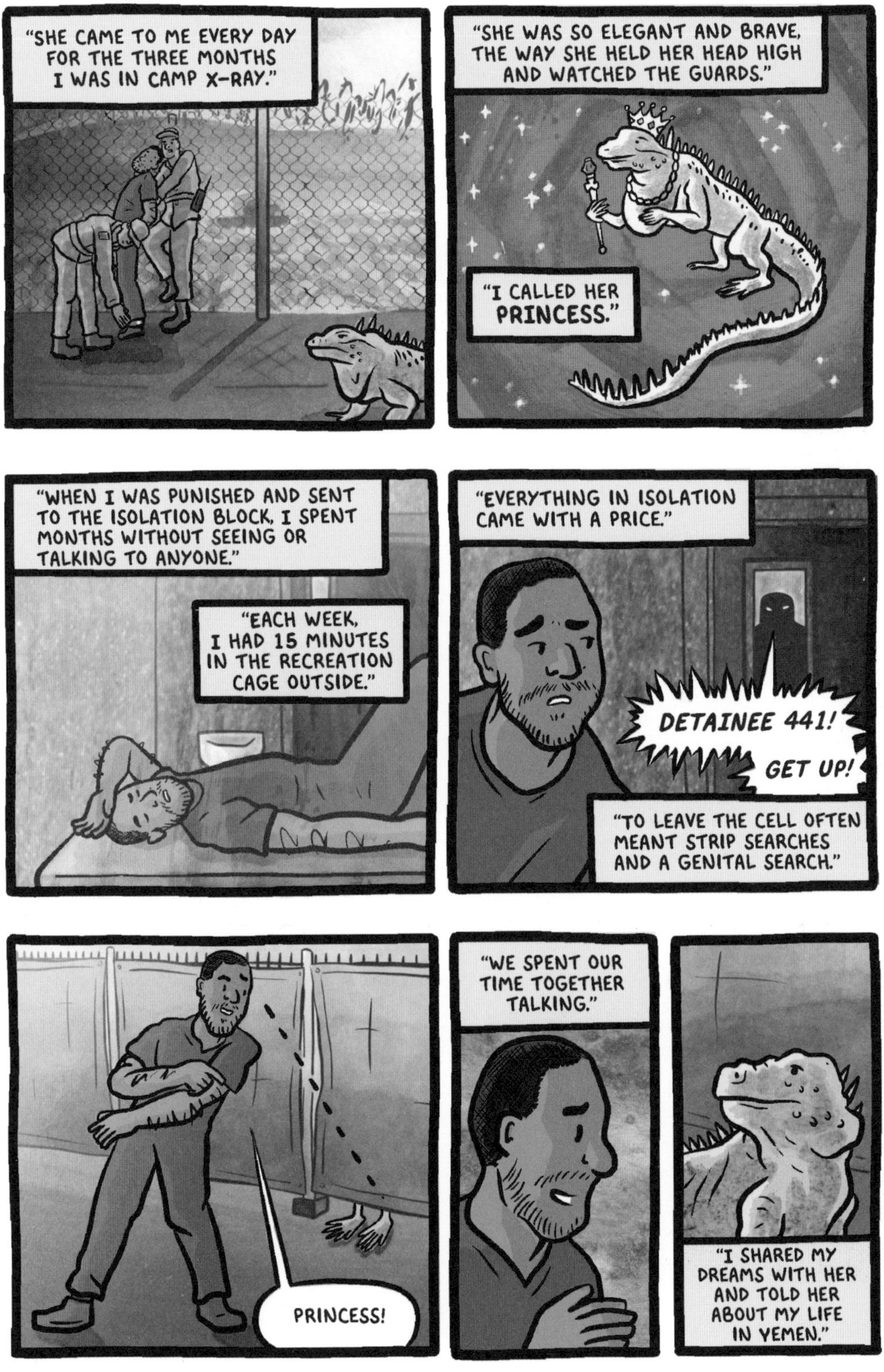
"SHE CAME TO ME EVERY DAY FOR THE THREE MONTHS I WAS IN CAMP X-RAY."
"SHE WAS SO ELEGANT AND BRAVE, THE WAY SHE HELD HER HEAD HIGH AND WATCHED THE GUARDS."
"I CALLED HER PRINCESS."
"WHEN I WAS PUNISHED AND SENT TO THE ISOLATION BLOCK, I SPENT MONTHS WITHOUT SEEING OR TALKING TO ANYONE."
"EACH WEEK, I HAD 15 MINUTES IN THE RECREATION CAGE OUTSIDE."
"EVERYTHING IN ISOLATION CAME WITH A PRICE."
DETAINEE 441!
GET UP!
"TO LEAVE THE CELL OFTEN MEANT STRIP SEARCHES AND A GENITAL SEARCH."
PRINCESS!
"WE SPENT OUR TIME TOGETHER TALKING."
"I SHARED MY DREAMS WITH HER AND TOLD HER ABOUT MY LIFE IN YEMEN."

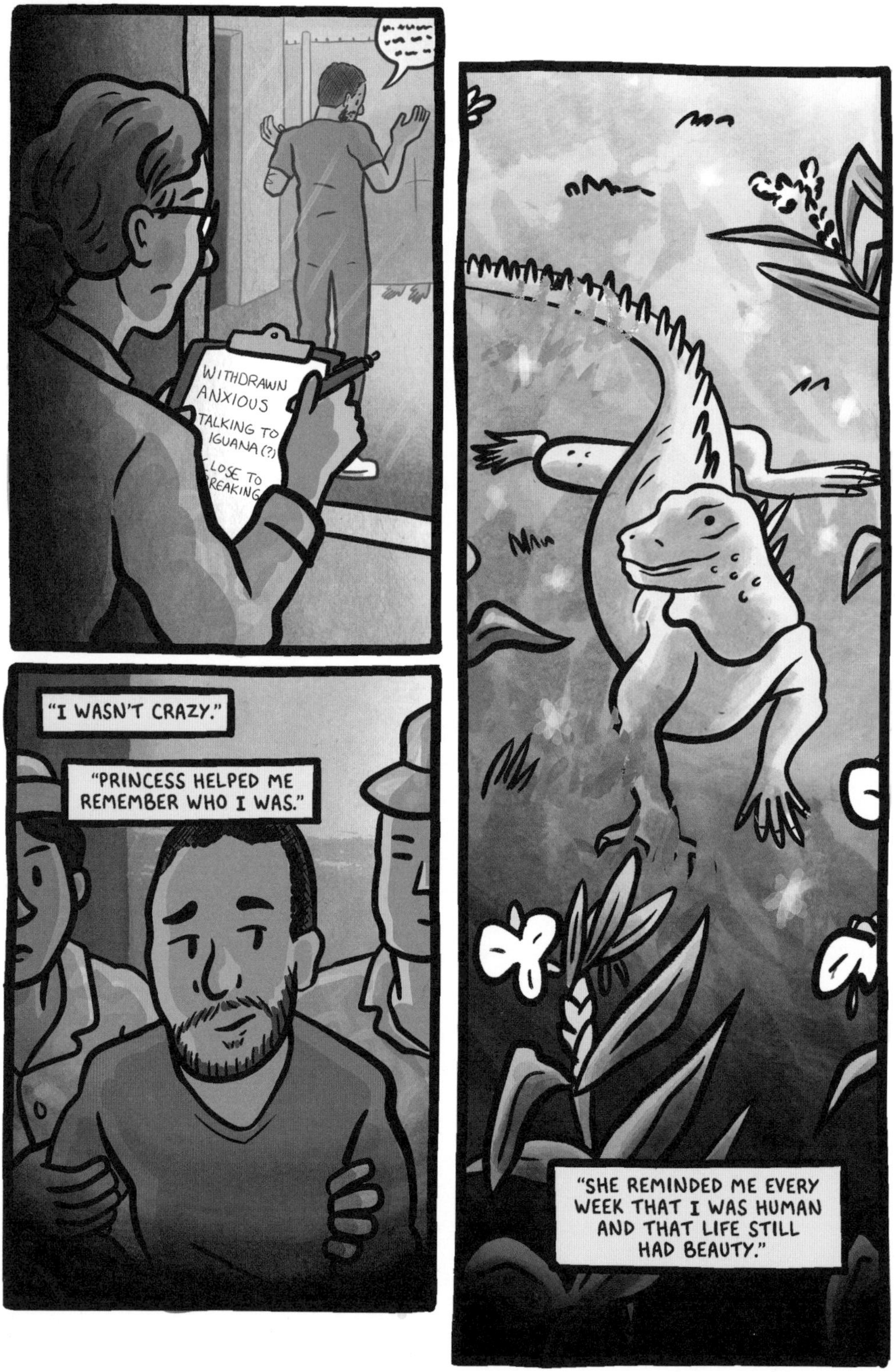
WITHDRAWN
ANXIOUS
TALKING TO IGUANA (?)
CLOSE TO BREAKING
"I WASN'T CRAZY."
"PRINCESS HELPED ME REMEMBER WHO I WAS."
"SHE REMINDED ME EVERY WEEK THAT I WAS HUMAN AND THAT LIFE STILL HAD BEAUTY."

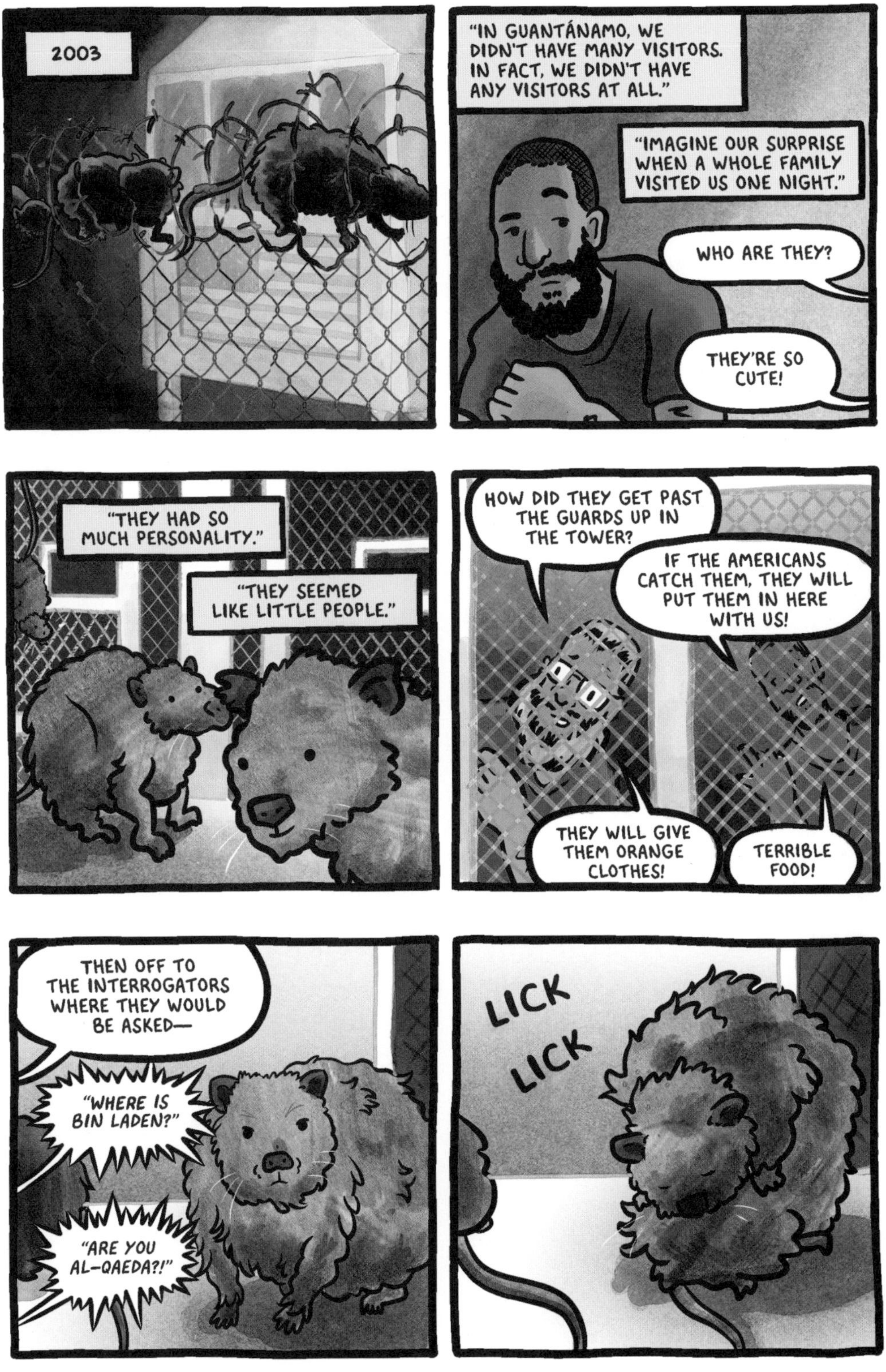
2003
"IN GUANTÁNAMO, WE DIDN'T HAVE MANY VISITORS. IN FACT, WE DIDN'T HAVE ANY VISITORS AT ALL."
"IMAGINE OUR SURPRISE WHEN A WHOLE FAMILY VISITED US ONE NIGHT."
WHO ARE THEY?
THEY'RE SO CUTE!
"THEY HAD SO MUCH PERSONALITY."
"THEY SEEMED LIKE LITTLE PEOPLE."
HOW DID THEY GET PAST THE GUARDS UP IN THE TOWER?
IF THE AMERICANS CATCH THEM, THEY WILL PUT THEM IN HERE WITH US!
THEY WILL GIVE THEM ORANGE CLOTHES!
TERRIBLE FOOD!
THEN OFF TO THE INTERROGATORS WHERE THEY WOULD BE ASKED—
"WHERE IS BIN LADEN?"
"ARE YOU AL-QAEDA?!"
LICK
LICK

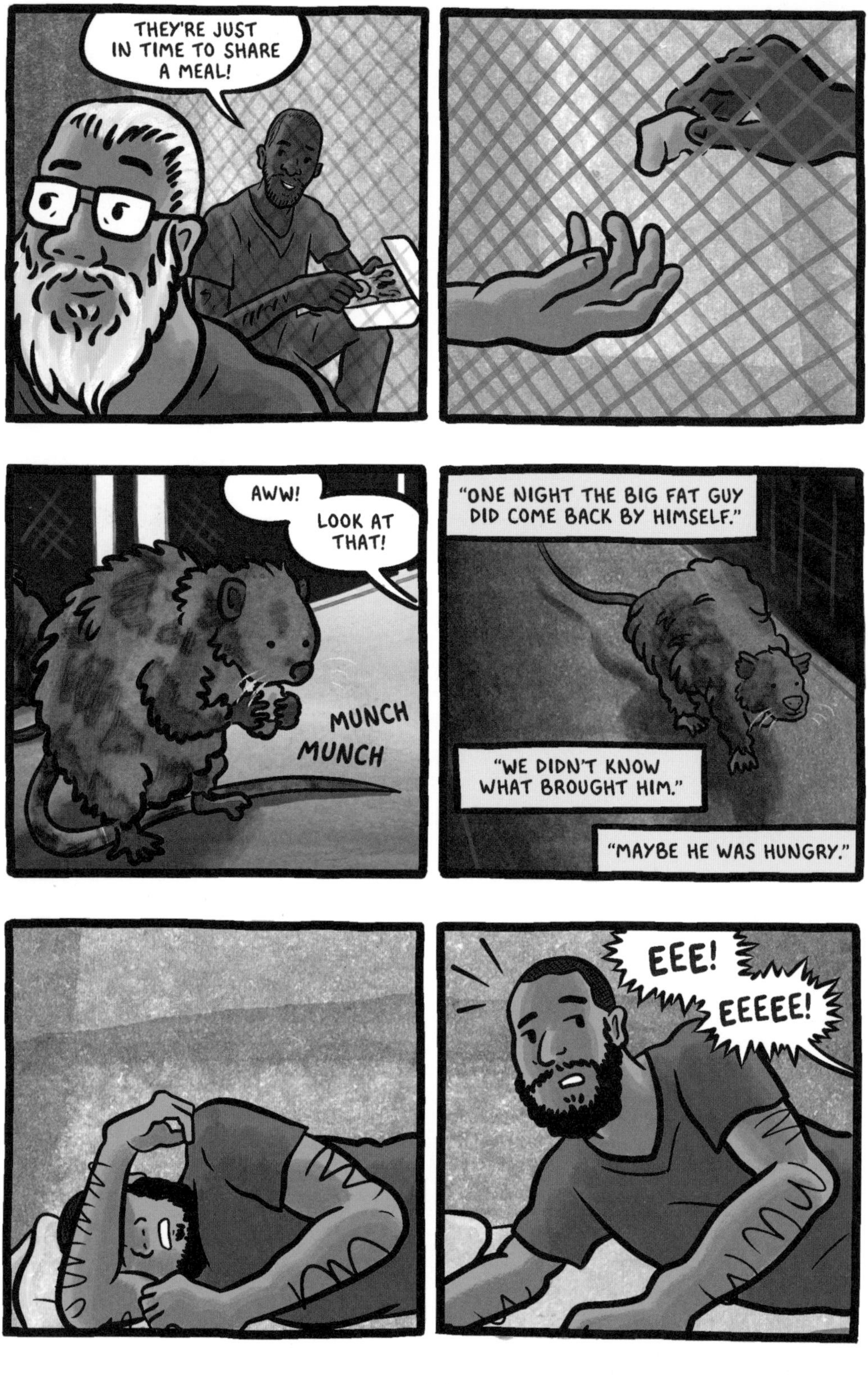
THEY'RE JUST IN TIME TO SHARE A MEAL!
AWW!
LOOK AT THAT!
MUNCH
MUNCH
"ONE NIGHT THE BIG FAT GUY DID COME BACK BY HIMSELF."
"WE DIDN'T KNOW WHAT BROUGHT HIM."
"MAYBE HE WAS HUNGRY."
EEE!
EEEEE!

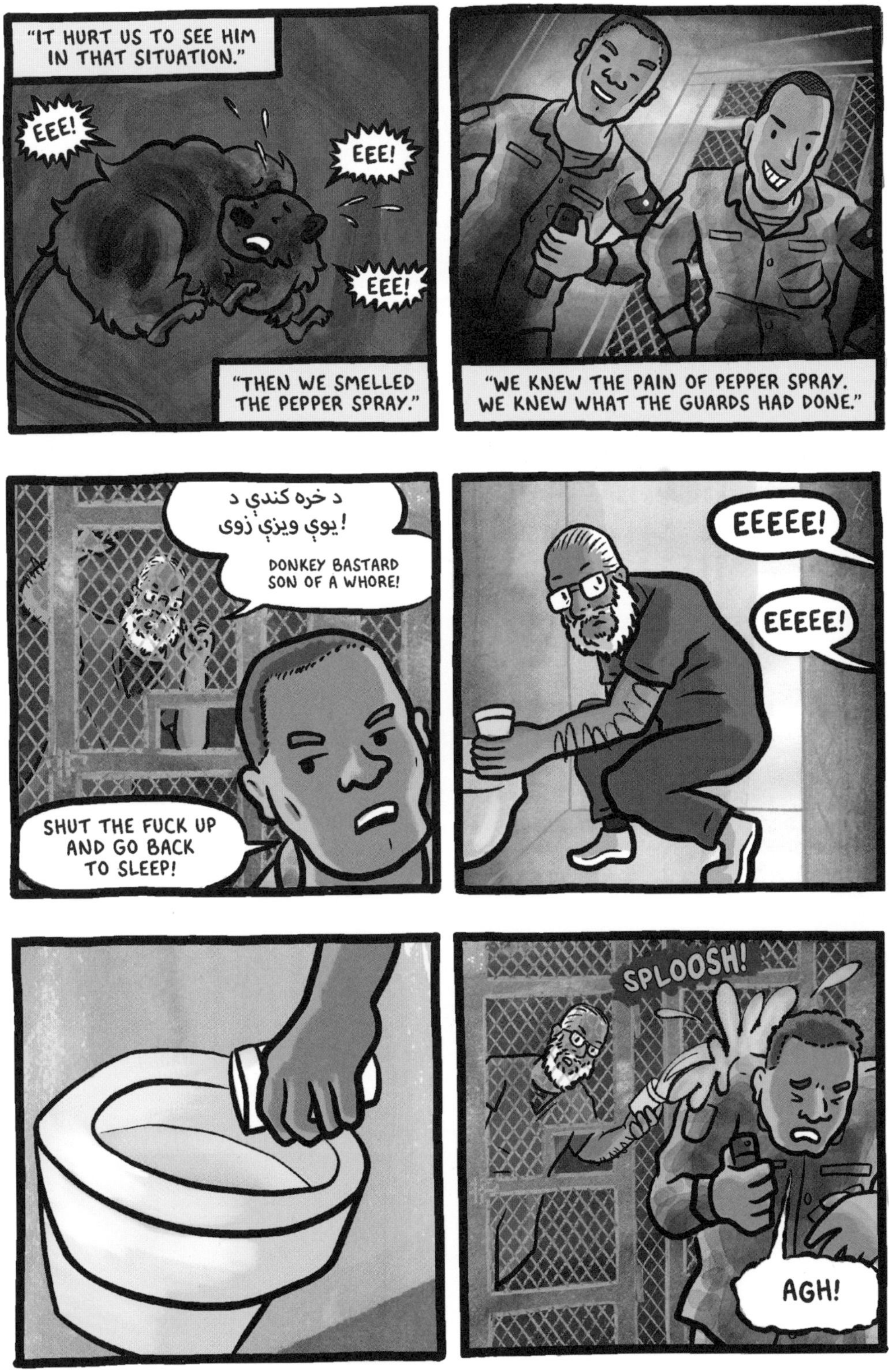
"IT HURT US TO SEE HIM IN THAT SITUATION."
EEE!
EEE!
EEE!
"THEN WE SMELLED THE PEPPER SPRAY."
"WE KNEW THE PAIN OF PEPPER SPRAY. WE KNEW WHAT THE GUARDS HAD DONE."
د خره کنډي د
يوې ويزې زوی !
DONKEY BASTARD SON OF A WHORE!
SHUT THE FUCK UP AND GO BACK TO SLEEP!
EEEEE!
EEEEE!
SPLOOSH!
AGH!

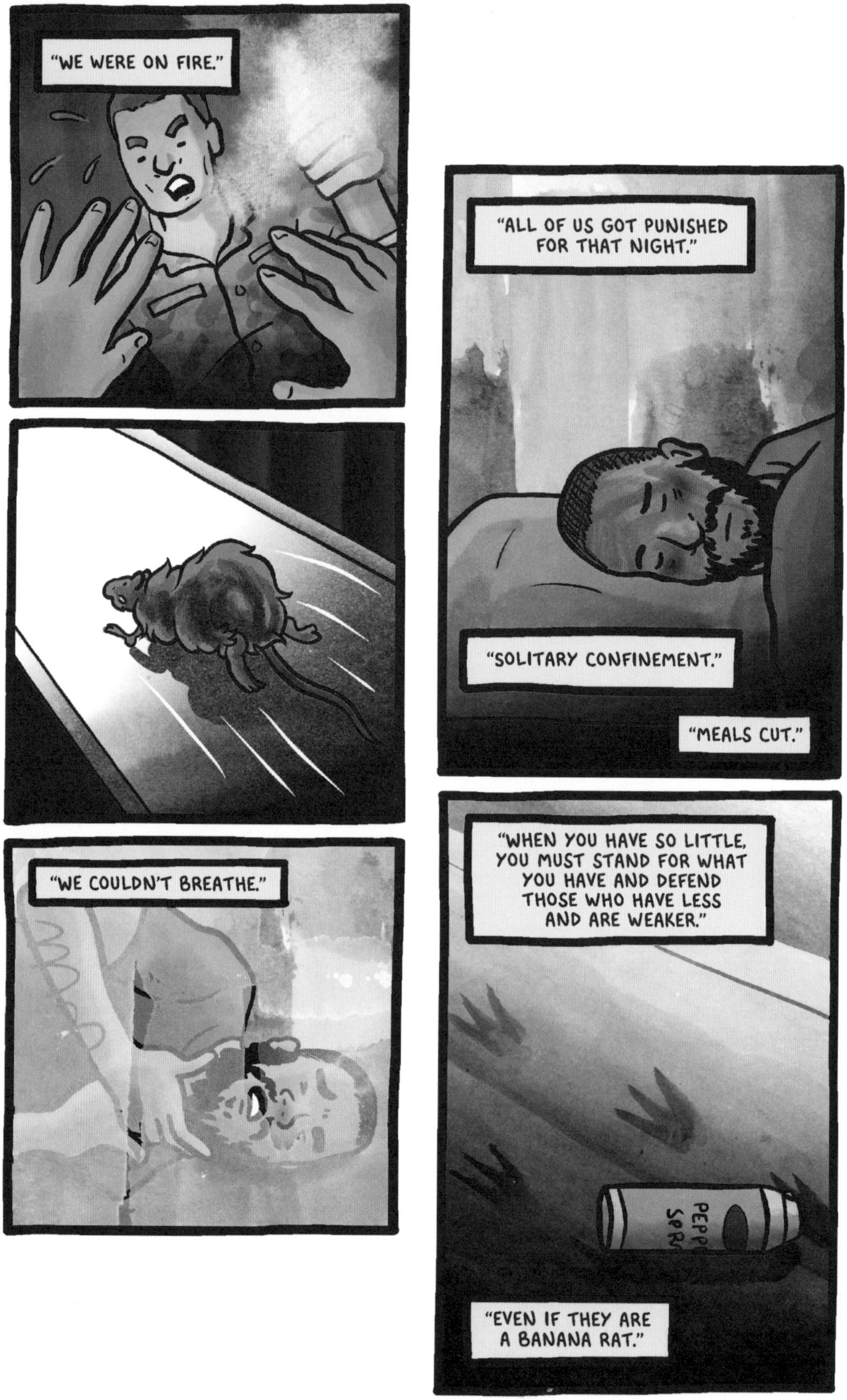
"WE WERE ON FIRE."
"WE COULDN'T BREATHE."
"ALL OF US GOT PUNISHED FOR THAT NIGHT."
"SOLITARY CONFINEMENT."
"MEALS CUT."
"WHEN YOU HAVE SO LITTLE, YOU MUST STAND FOR WHAT YOU HAVE AND DEFEND THOSE WHO HAVE LESS AND ARE WEAKER."
"EVEN IF THEY ARE A BANANA RAT."

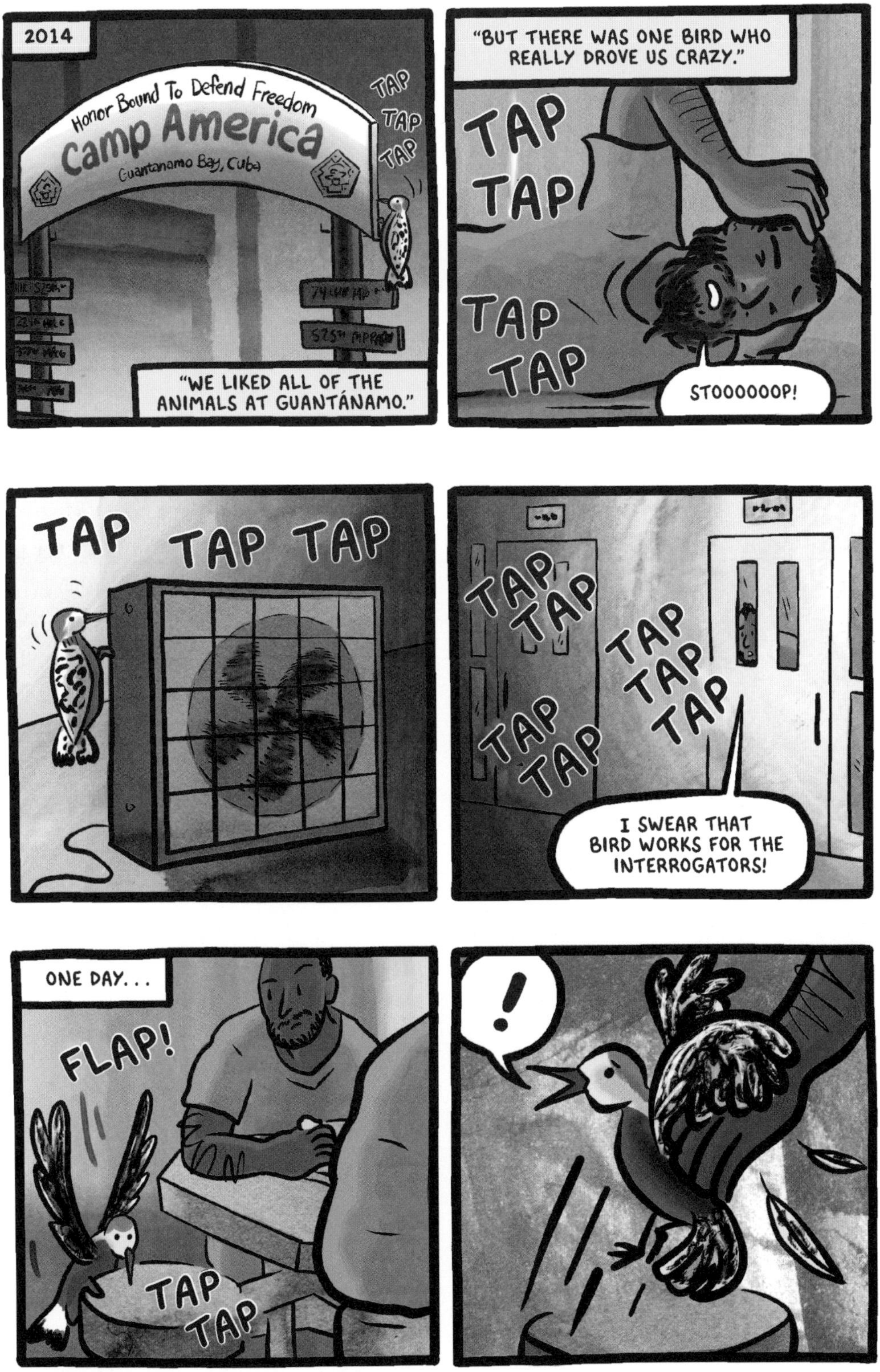
2014
Honor Bound To Defend Freedom
Camp America
Guantanamo Bay, Cuba
TAP
TAP
TAP
"WE LIKED ALL OF THE ANIMALS AT GUANTÁNAMO."
"BUT THERE WAS ONE BIRD WHO REALLY DROVE US CRAZY."
TAP
TAP
TAP
TAP
STOOOOOOP!
TAP
TAP TAP
TAP
TAP
TAP
TAP
TAP
TAP
TAP
I SWEAR THAT BIRD WORKS FOR THE INTERROGATORS!
ONE DAY. . .
FLAP!
TAP
TAP
!

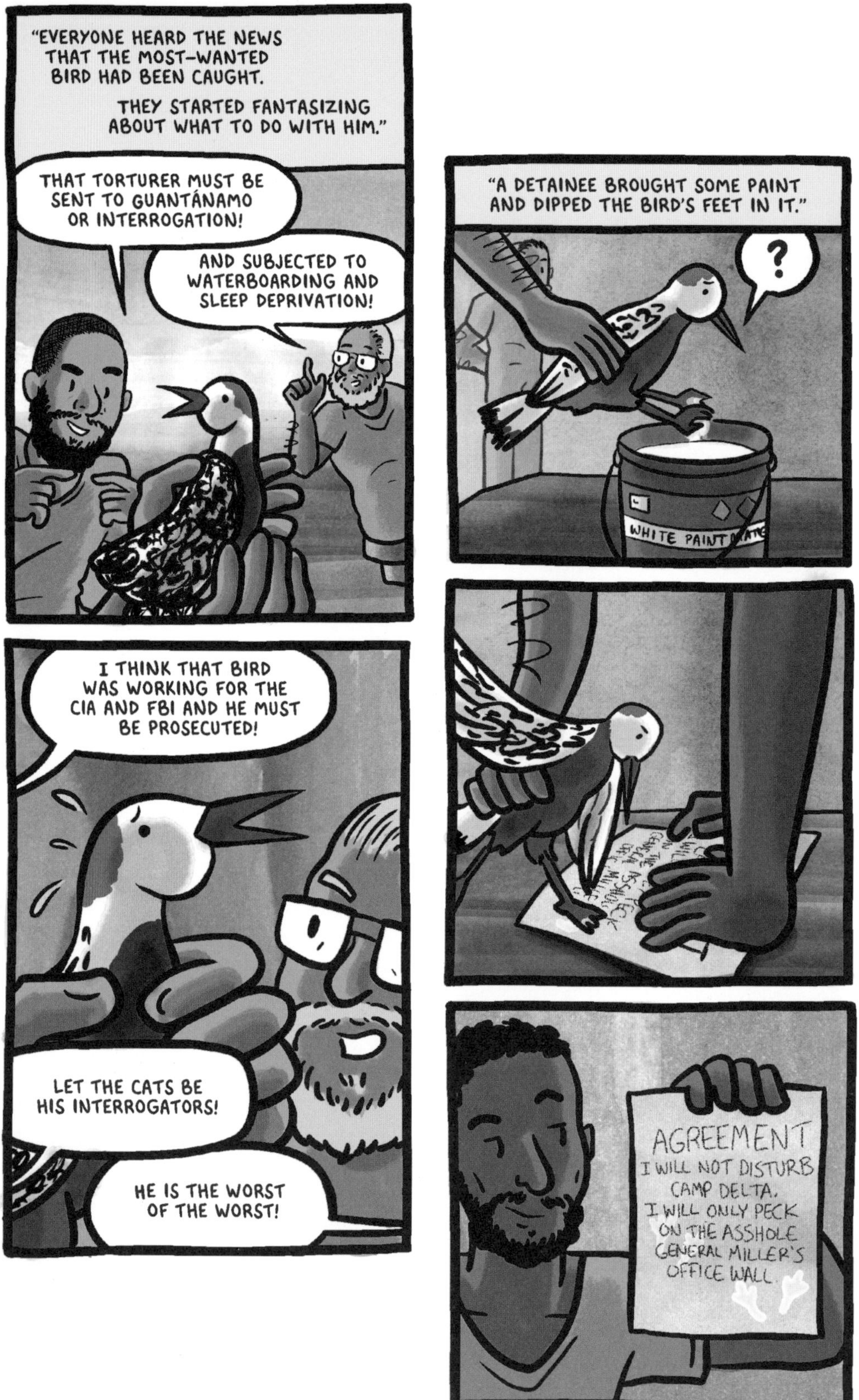
"EVERYONE HEARD THE NEWS THAT THE MOST-WANTED BIRD HAD BEEN CAUGHT.
THEY STARTED FANTASIZING ABOUT WHAT TO DO WITH HIM."
THAT TORTURER MUST BE SENT TO GUANTÁNAMO OR INTERROGATION!
AND SUBJECTED TO WATERBOARDING AND SLEEP DEPRIVATION!
I THINK THAT BIRD WAS WORKING FOR THE CIA AND FBI AND HE MUST BE PROSECUTED!
LET THE CATS BE HIS INTERROGATORS!
HE IS THE WORST OF THE WORST!
"A DETAINEE BROUGHT SOME PAINT AND DIPPED THE BIRD'S FEET IN IT."
?
WHITE PAINT
AGREEMENT
I WILL NOT DISTURB CAMP DELTA.
I WILL ONLY PECK ON THE ASSHOLE GENERAL MILLER'S OFFICE WALL.

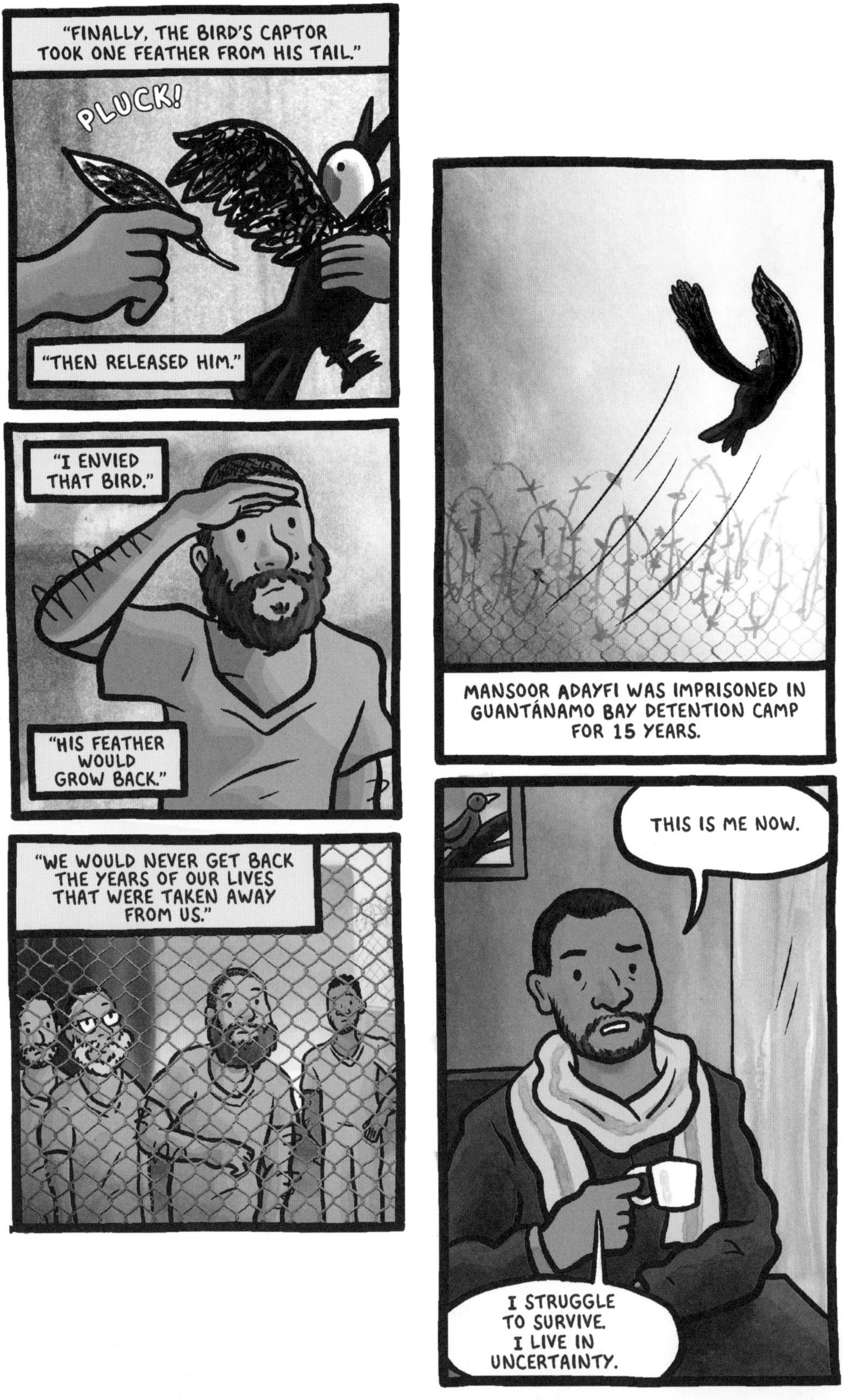
"FINALLY, THE BIRD'S CAPTOR TOOK ONE FEATHER FROM HIS TAIL."
PLUCK!
"THEN RELEASED HIM."
"I ENVIED THAT BIRD."
"HIS FEATHER WOULD GROW BACK."
"WE WOULD NEVER GET BACK THE YEARS OF OUR LIVES THAT WERE TAKEN AWAY FROM US."
MANSOOR ADAYFI WAS IMPRISONED IN GUANTÁNAMO BAY DETENTION CAMP FOR 15 YEARS.
THIS IS ME NOW.
I STRUGGLE TO SURVIVE. I LIVE IN UNCERTAINTY.

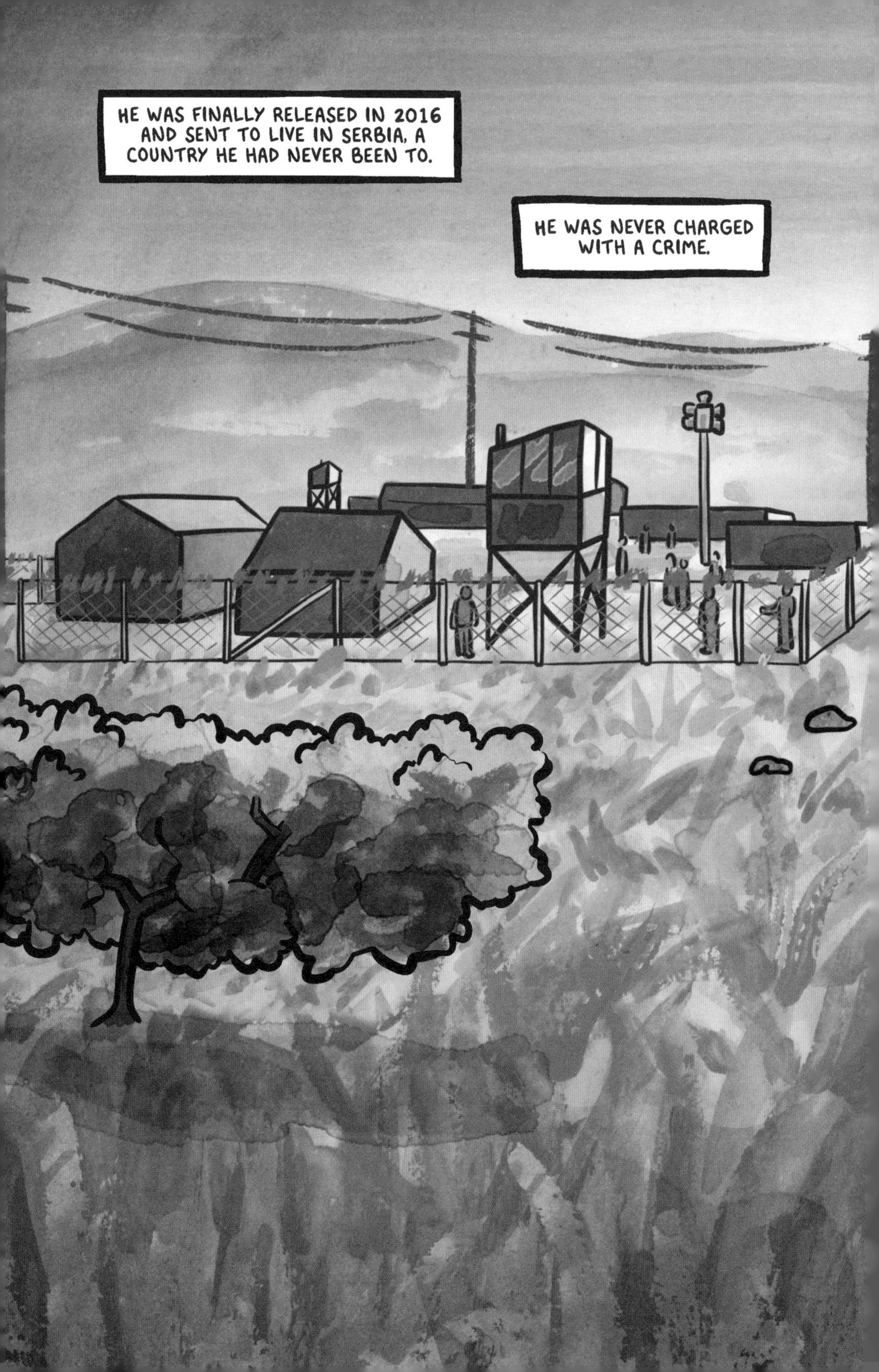
HE WAS FINALLY RELEASED IN 2016 AND SENT TO LIVE IN SERBIA, A COUNTRY HE HAD NEVER BEEN TO.
HE WAS NEVER CHARGED WITH A CRIME.

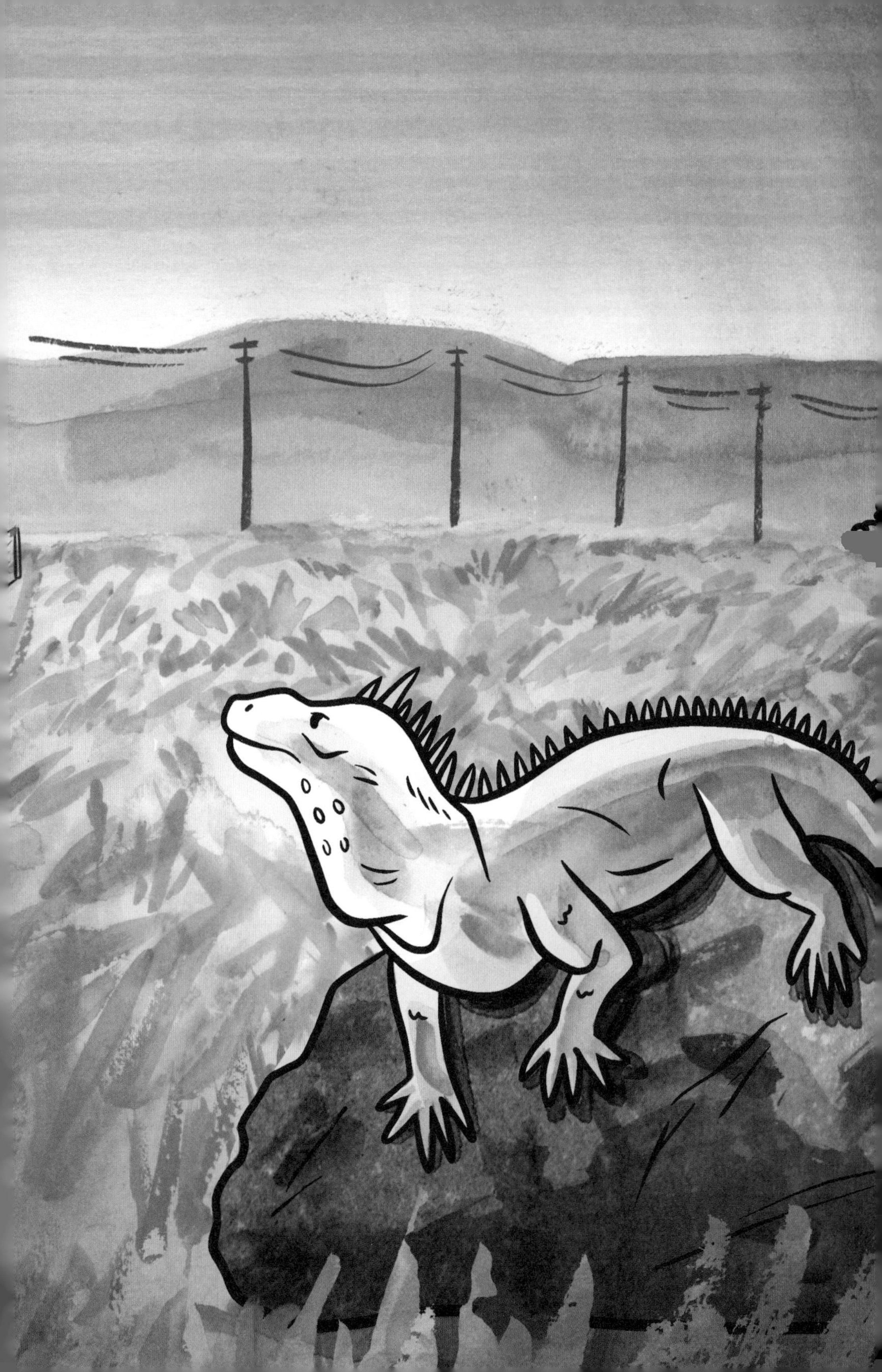

CHAPTER EIGHT

ALKA PRADHAN

HUMAN RIGHTS LAWYER
AND ATTORNEY FOR
GUANTÁNAMO PRISONERS

ILLUSTRATED BY TRACY CHAHWAN

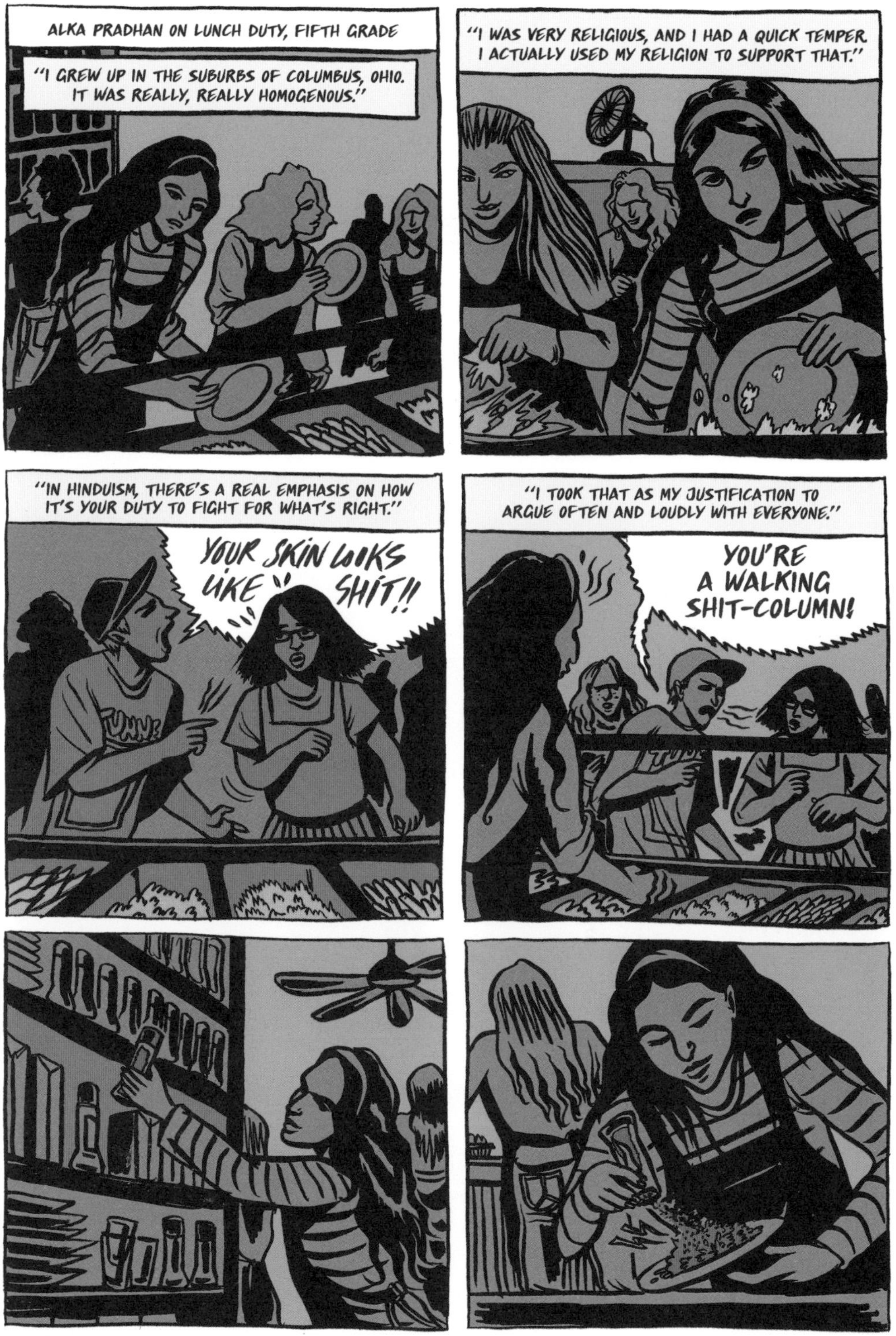
ALKA PRADHAN ON LUNCH DUTY, FIFTH GRADE
"I GREW UP IN THE SUBURBS OF COLUMBUS, OHIO. IT WAS REALLY, REALLY HOMOGENOUS."
"I WAS VERY RELIGIOUS, AND I HAD A QUICK TEMPER. I ACTUALLY USED MY RELIGION TO SUPPORT THAT."
"IN HINDUISM, THERE'S A REAL EMPHASIS ON HOW IT'S YOUR DUTY TO FIGHT FOR WHAT'S RIGHT."
YOUR SKIN LOOKS LIKE SHIT!!
"I TOOK THAT AS MY JUSTIFICATION TO ARGUE OFTEN AND LOUDLY WITH EVERYONE."
YOU'RE A WALKING SHIT-COLUMN!

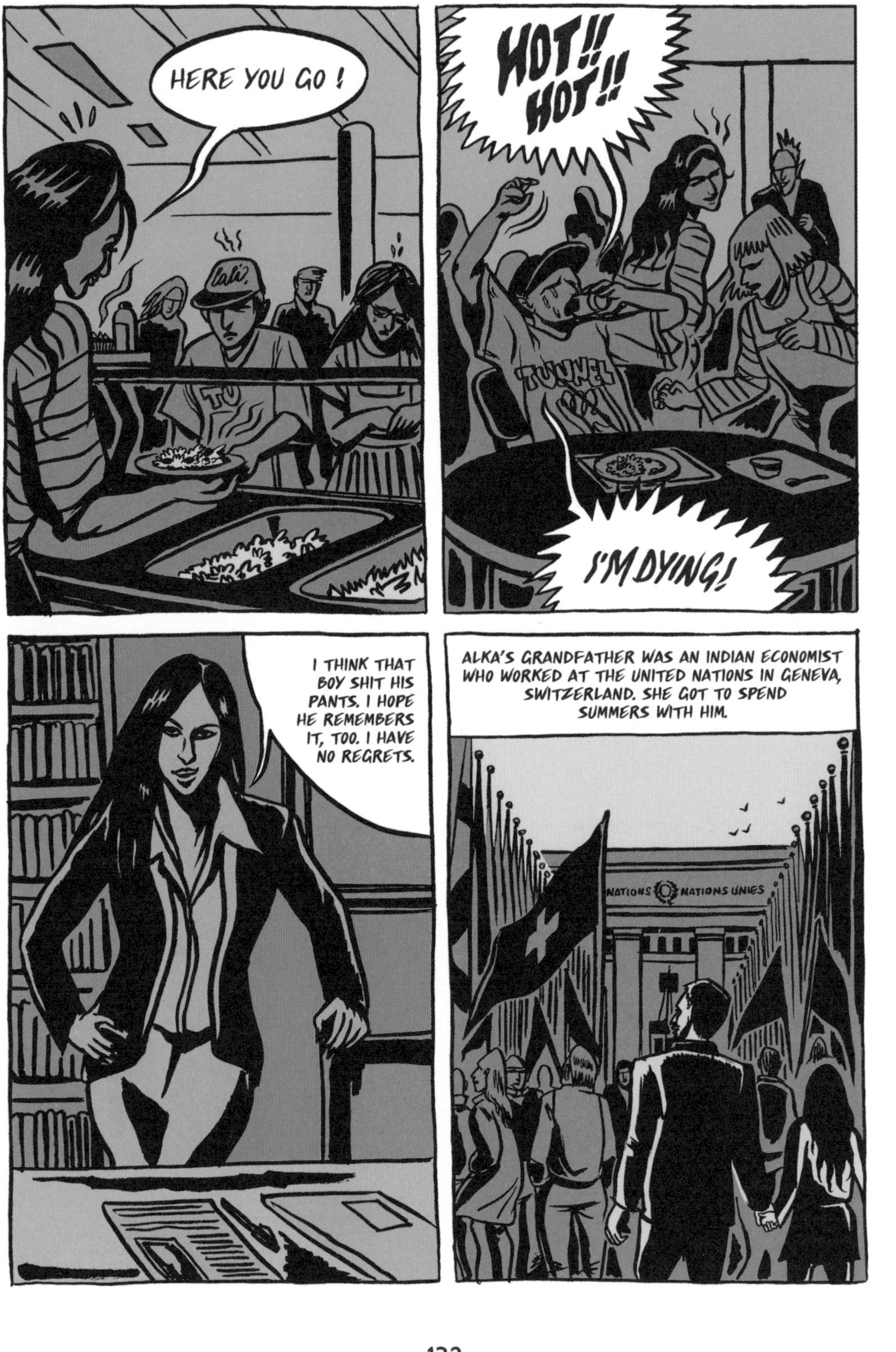
HERE YOU GO !
HOT!! HOT!!
I'M DYING!
I THINK THAT BOY SHIT HIS PANTS. I HOPE HE REMEMBERS IT, TOO. I HAVE NO REGRETS.
ALKA'S GRANDFATHER WAS AN INDIAN ECONOMIST WHO WORKED AT THE UNITED NATIONS IN GENEVA, SWITZERLAND. SHE GOT TO SPEND SUMMERS WITH HIM.
NATIONS NATIONS UNIES

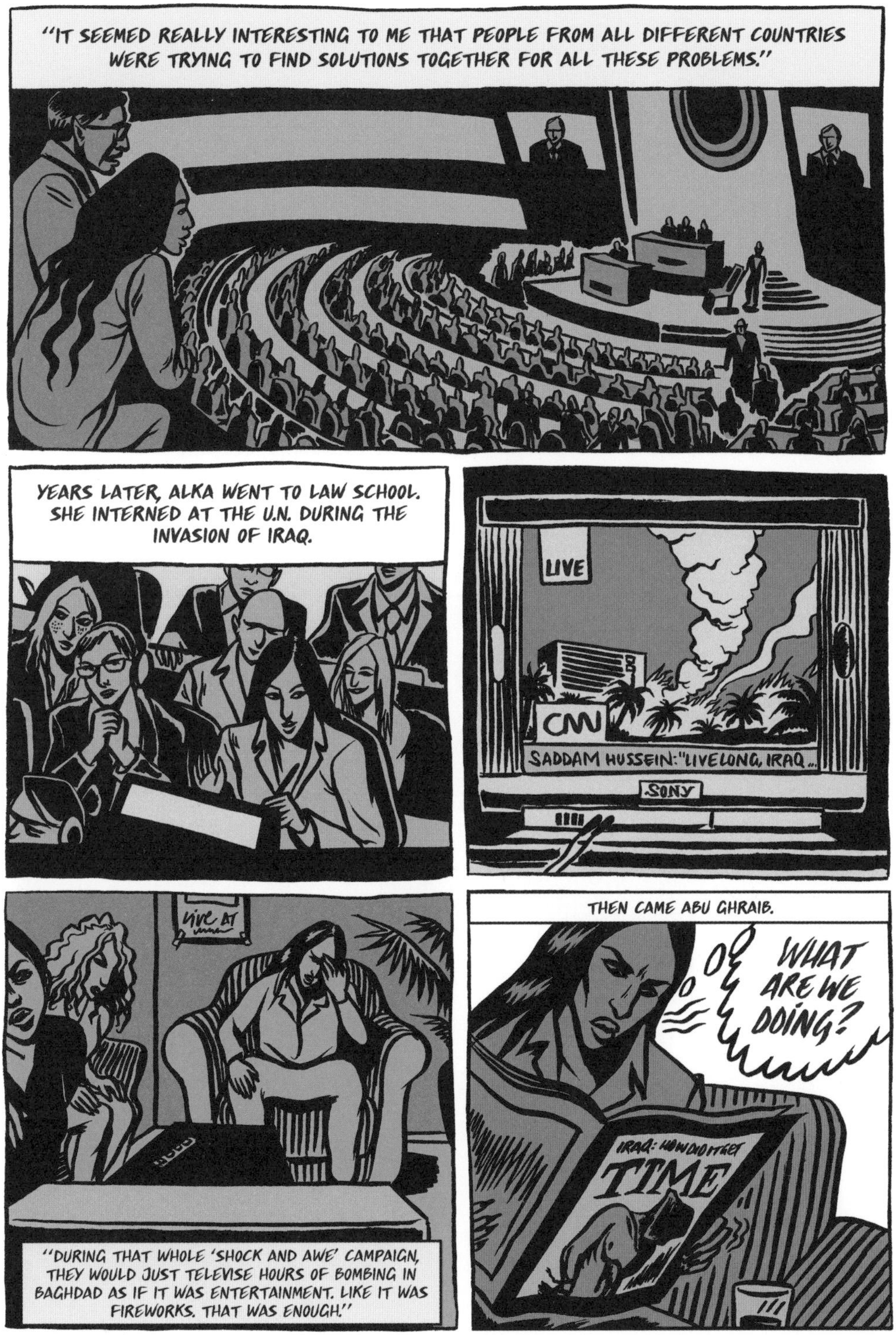

"IT SEEMED REALLY INTERESTING TO ME THAT PEOPLE FROM ALL DIFFERENT COUNTRIES WERE TRYING TO FIND SOLUTIONS TOGETHER FOR ALL THESE PROBLEMS."
YEARS LATER, ALKA WENT TO LAW SCHOOL. SHE INTERNED AT THE U.N. DURING THE INVASION OF IRAQ.
LIVE
CNN
SADDAM HUSSEIN: "LIVE LONG, IRAQ...
SONY
"DURING THAT WHOLE 'SHOCK AND AWE' CAMPAIGN, THEY WOULD JUST TELEVISE HOURS OF BOMBING IN BAGHDAD AS IF IT WAS ENTERTAINMENT. LIKE IT WAS FIREWORKS. THAT WAS ENOUGH."
THEN CAME ABU GHRAIB.
WHAT ARE WE DOING?
TIME

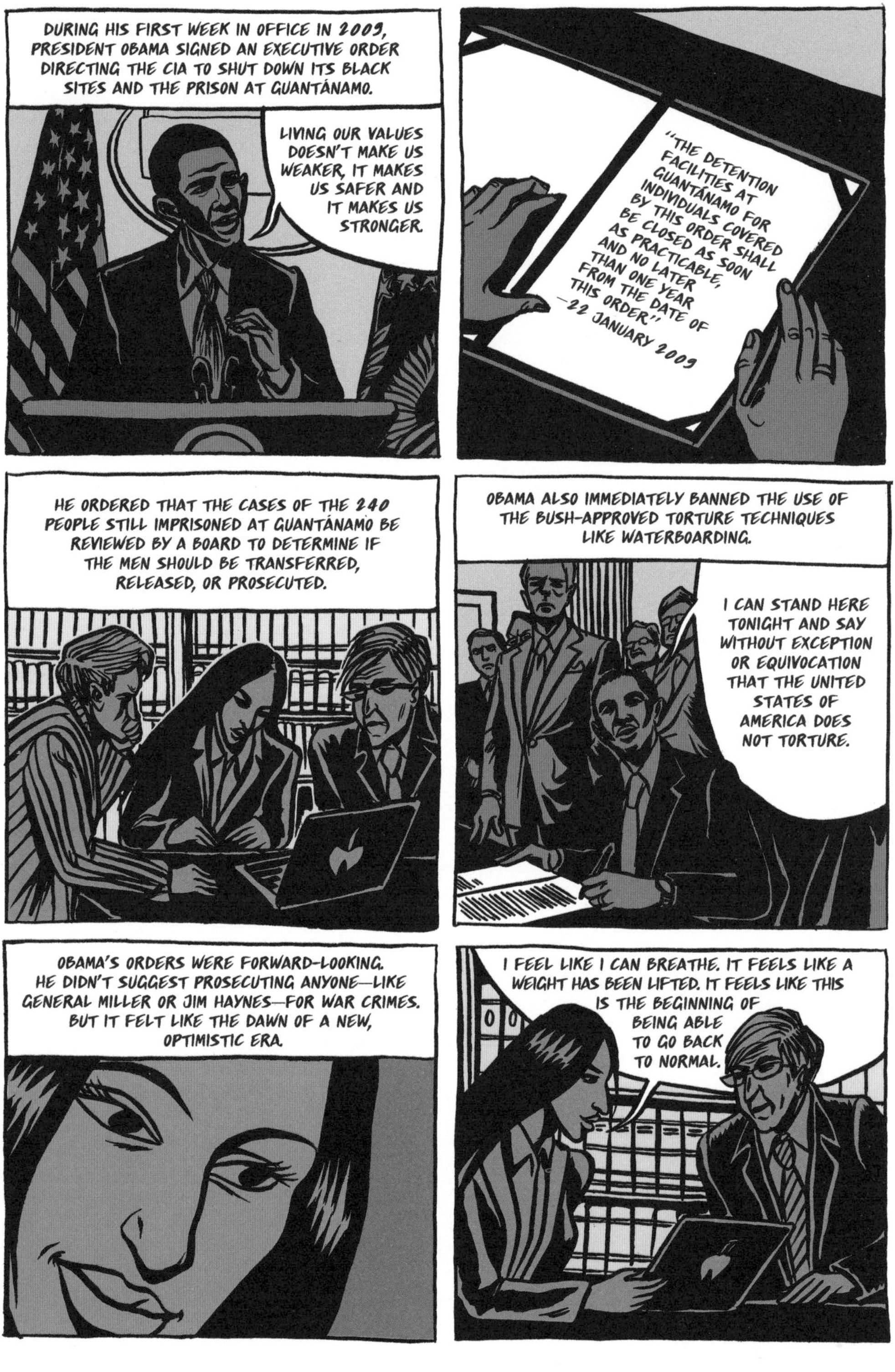
DURING HIS FIRST WEEK IN OFFICE IN 2009, PRESIDENT OBAMA SIGNED AN EXECUTIVE ORDER DIRECTING THE CIA TO SHUT DOWN ITS BLACK SITES AND THE PRISON AT GUANTÁNAMO.
LIVING OUR VALUES DOESN'T MAKE US WEAKER, IT MAKES US SAFER AND IT MAKES US STRONGER.
"THE DETENTION FACILITIES AT GUANTÁNAMO FOR INDIVIDUALS COVERED BY THIS ORDER SHALL BE CLOSED AS SOON AS PRACTICABLE, AND NO LATER THAN ONE YEAR FROM THE DATE OF THIS ORDER." —22 JANUARY 2009
HE ORDERED THAT THE CASES OF THE 240 PEOPLE STILL IMPRISONED AT GUANTÁNAMO BE REVIEWED BY A BOARD TO DETERMINE IF THE MEN SHOULD BE TRANSFERRED, RELEASED, OR PROSECUTED.
OBAMA ALSO IMMEDIATELY BANNED THE USE OF THE BUSH-APPROVED TORTURE TECHNIQUES LIKE WATERBOARDING.
I CAN STAND HERE TONIGHT AND SAY WITHOUT EXCEPTION OR EQUIVOCATION THAT THE UNITED STATES OF AMERICA DOES NOT TORTURE.
OBAMA'S ORDERS WERE FORWARD-LOOKING. HE DIDN'T SUGGEST PROSECUTING ANYONE—LIKE GENERAL MILLER OR JIM HAYNES—FOR WAR CRIMES. BUT IT FELT LIKE THE DAWN OF A NEW, OPTIMISTIC ERA.
I FEEL LIKE I CAN BREATHE. IT FEELS LIKE A WEIGHT HAS BEEN LIFTED. IT FEELS LIKE THIS IS THE BEGINNING OF BEING ABLE TO GO BACK TO NORMAL.

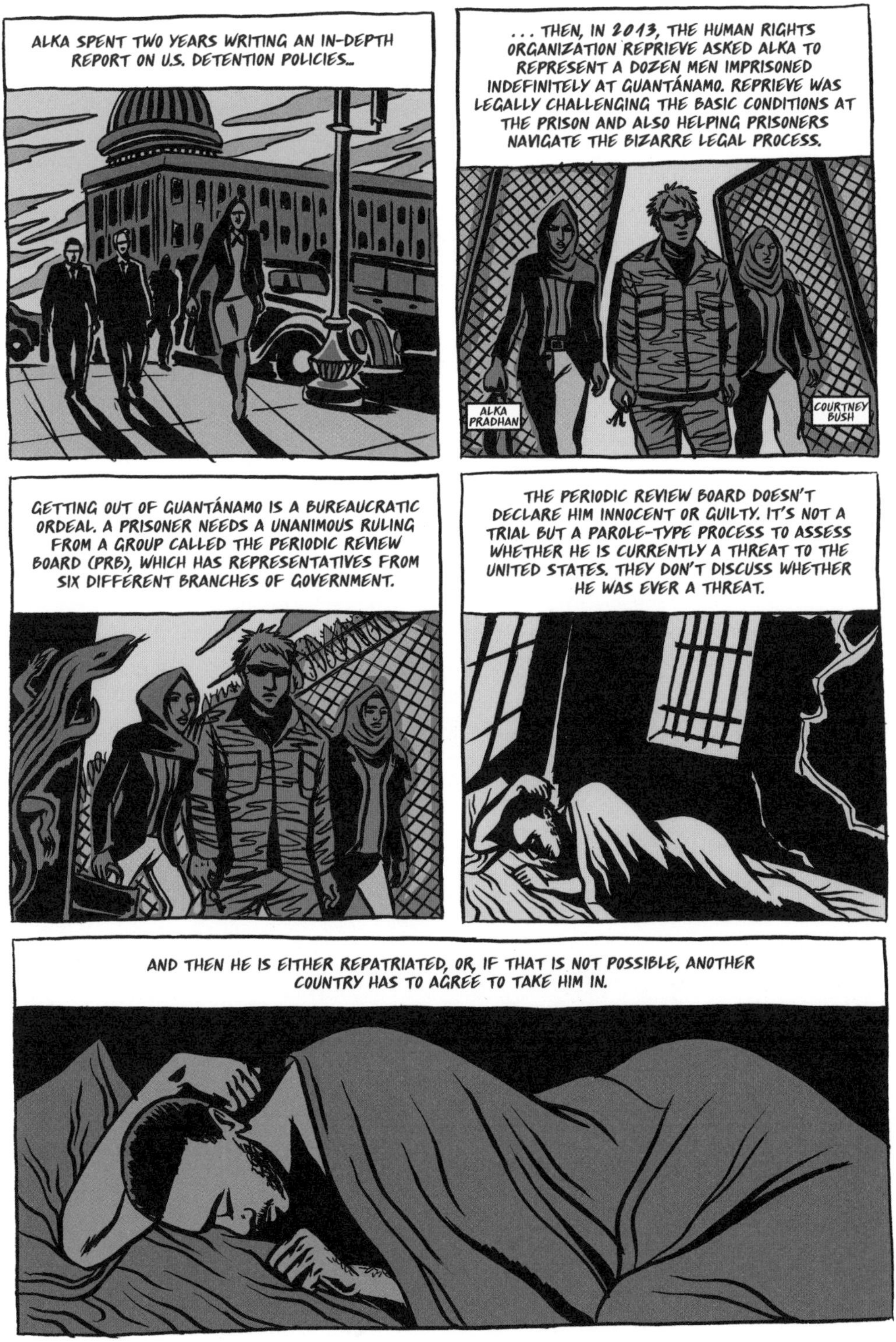
ALKA SPENT TWO YEARS WRITING AN IN-DEPTH REPORT ON U.S. DETENTION POLICIES...
. . . THEN, IN 2013, THE HUMAN RIGHTS ORGANIZATION REPRIEVE ASKED ALKA TO REPRESENT A DOZEN MEN IMPRISONED INDEFINITELY AT GUANTÁNAMO. REPRIEVE WAS LEGALLY CHALLENGING THE BASIC CONDITIONS AT THE PRISON AND ALSO HELPING PRISONERS NAVIGATE THE BIZARRE LEGAL PROCESS.
ALKA PRADHAN
COURTNEY BUSH
GETTING OUT OF GUANTÁNAMO IS A BUREAUCRATIC ORDEAL. A PRISONER NEEDS A UNANIMOUS RULING FROM A GROUP CALLED THE PERIODIC REVIEW BOARD (PRB), WHICH HAS REPRESENTATIVES FROM SIX DIFFERENT BRANCHES OF GOVERNMENT.
THE PERIODIC REVIEW BOARD DOESN'T DECLARE HIM INNOCENT OR GUILTY. IT'S NOT A TRIAL BUT A PAROLE-TYPE PROCESS TO ASSESS WHETHER HE IS CURRENTLY A THREAT TO THE UNITED STATES. THEY DON'T DISCUSS WHETHER HE WAS EVER A THREAT.
AND THEN HE IS EITHER REPATRIATED, OR, IF THAT IS NOT POSSIBLE, ANOTHER COUNTRY HAS TO AGREE TO TAKE HIM IN.

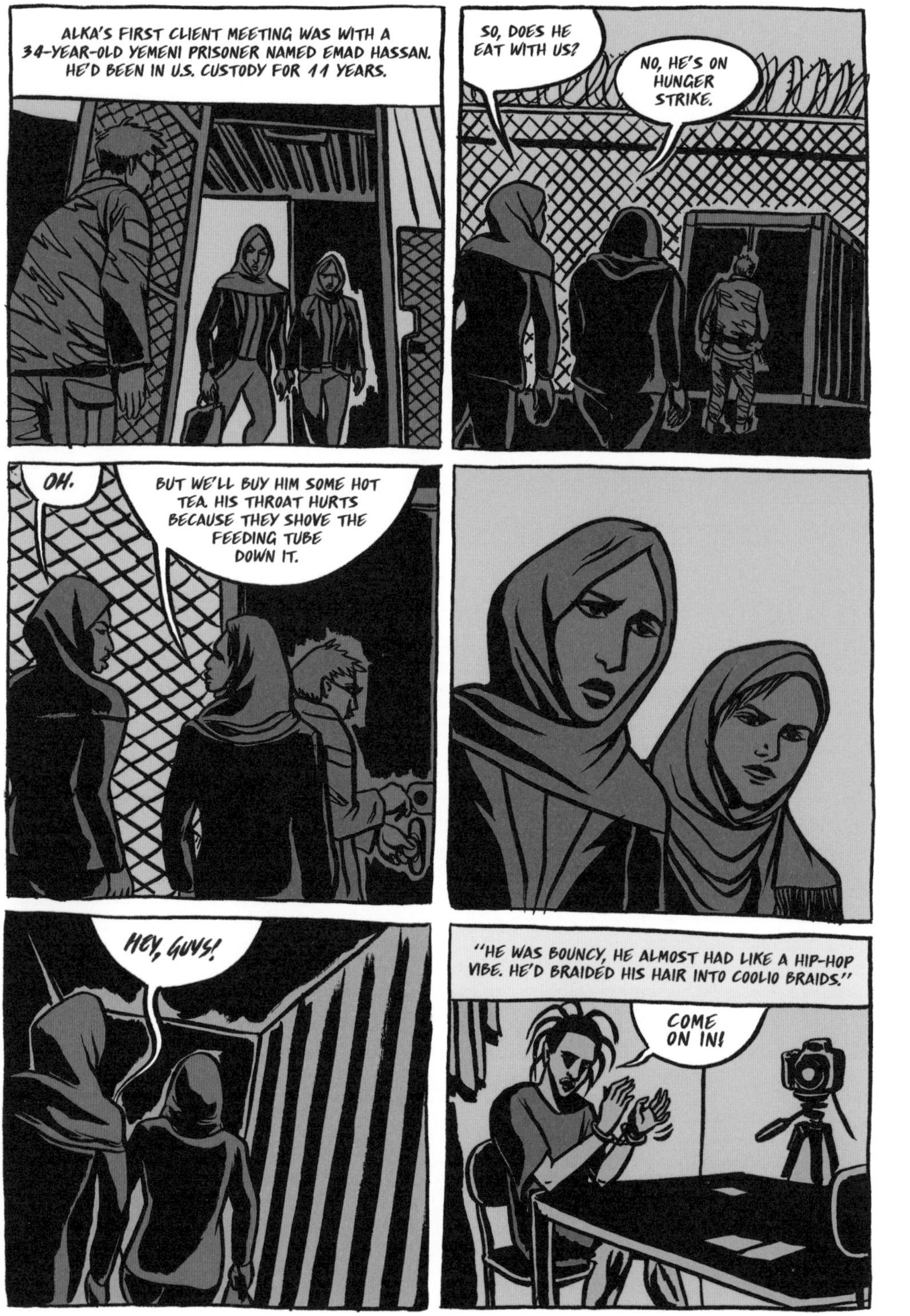
ALKA'S FIRST CLIENT MEETING WAS WITH A 34-YEAR-OLD YEMENI PRISONER NAMED EMAD HASSAN. HE'D BEEN IN U.S. CUSTODY FOR 11 YEARS.
SO, DOES HE EAT WITH US?
NO, HE'S ON HUNGER STRIKE.
OH.
BUT WE'LL BUY HIM SOME HOT TEA. HIS THROAT HURTS BECAUSE THEY SHOVE THE FEEDING TUBE DOWN IT.
HEY, GUYS!
"HE WAS BOUNCY, HE ALMOST HAD LIKE A HIP-HOP VIBE. HE'D BRAIDED HIS HAIR INTO COOLIO BRAIDS."
COME ON IN!

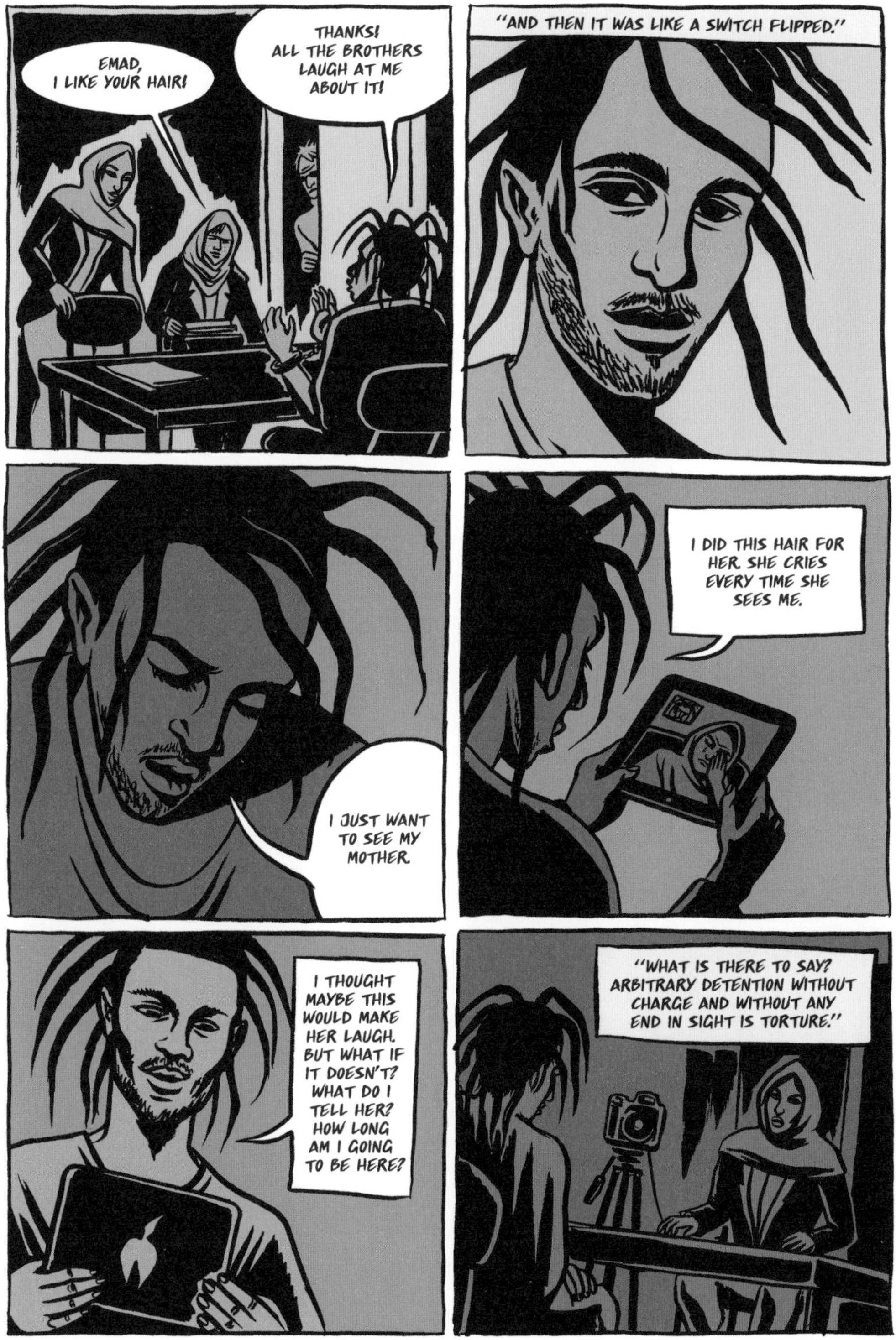
EMAD, I LIKE YOUR HAIR!
THANKS! ALL THE BROTHERS LAUGH AT ME ABOUT IT!
"AND THEN IT WAS LIKE A SWITCH FLIPPED."
I JUST WANT TO SEE MY MOTHER.
I DID THIS HAIR FOR HER. SHE CRIES EVERY TIME SHE SEES ME.
I THOUGHT MAYBE THIS WOULD MAKE HER LAUGH. BUT WHAT IF IT DOESN'T? WHAT DO I TELL HER? HOW LONG AM I GOING TO BE HERE?
"WHAT IS THERE TO SAY? ARBITRARY DETENTION WITHOUT CHARGE AND WITHOUT ANY END IN SIGHT IS TORTURE."

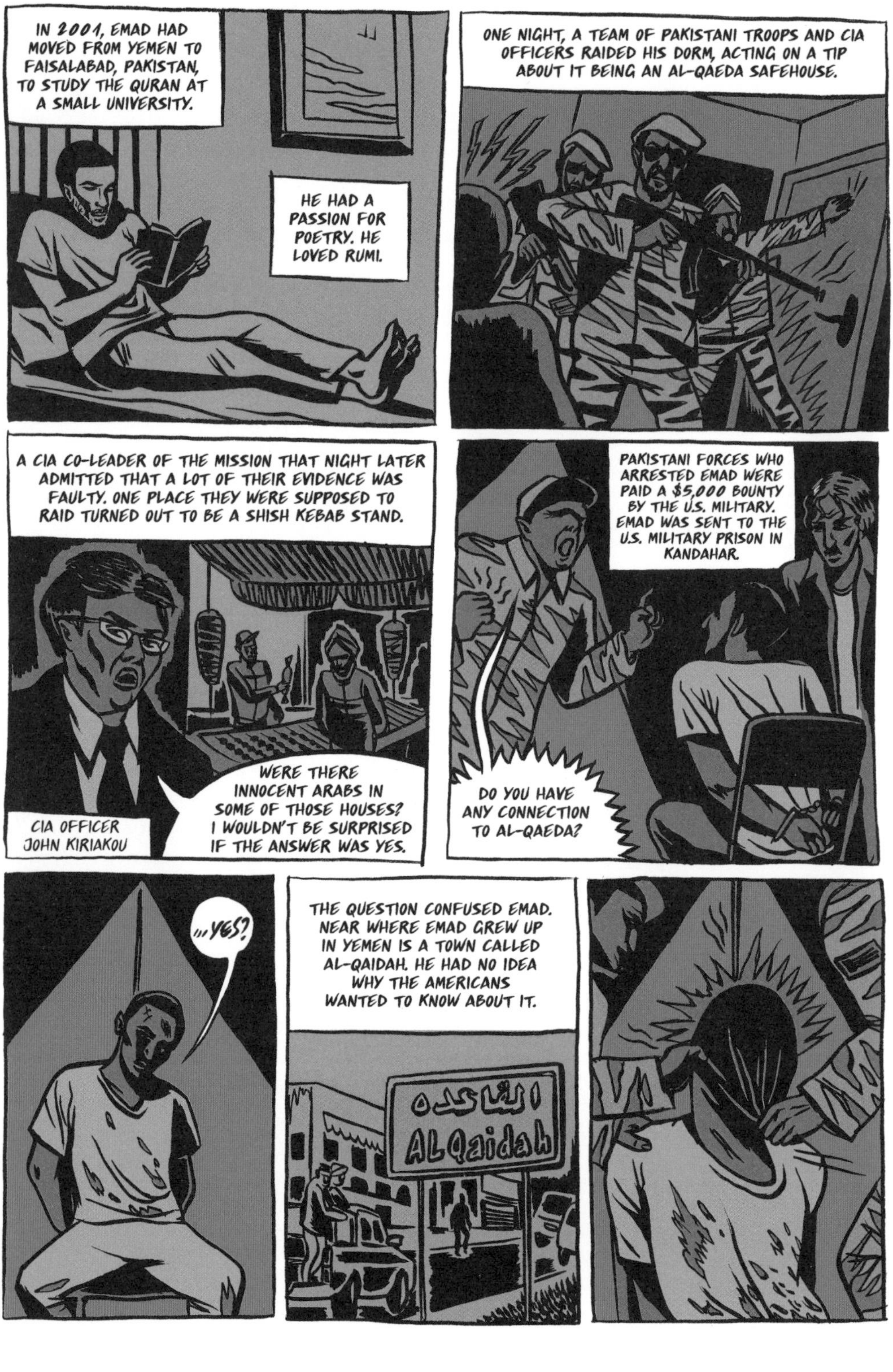
IN 2001, EMAD HAD MOVED FROM YEMEN TO FAISALABAD, PAKISTAN, TO STUDY THE QURAN AT A SMALL UNIVERSITY.
HE HAD A PASSION FOR POETRY. HE LOVED RUMI.
ONE NIGHT, A TEAM OF PAKISTANI TROOPS AND CIA OFFICERS RAIDED HIS DORM, ACTING ON A TIP ABOUT IT BEING AN AL-QAEDA SAFEHOUSE.
A CIA CO-LEADER OF THE MISSION THAT NIGHT LATER ADMITTED THAT A LOT OF THEIR EVIDENCE WAS FAULTY. ONE PLACE THEY WERE SUPPOSED TO RAID TURNED OUT TO BE A SHISH KEBAB STAND.
CIA OFFICER JOHN KIRIAKOU
WERE THERE INNOCENT ARABS IN SOME OF THOSE HOUSES? I WOULDN'T BE SURPRISED IF THE ANSWER WAS YES.
PAKISTANI FORCES WHO ARRESTED EMAD WERE PAID A $5,000 BOUNTY BY THE U.S. MILITARY. EMAD WAS SENT TO THE U.S. MILITARY PRISON IN KANDAHAR.
DO YOU HAVE ANY CONNECTION TO AL-QAEDA?
...YES?
THE QUESTION CONFUSED EMAD. NEAR WHERE EMAD GREW UP IN YEMEN IS A TOWN CALLED AL-QAIDAH. HE HAD NO IDEA WHY THE AMERICANS WANTED TO KNOW ABOUT IT.
AL Qaidah

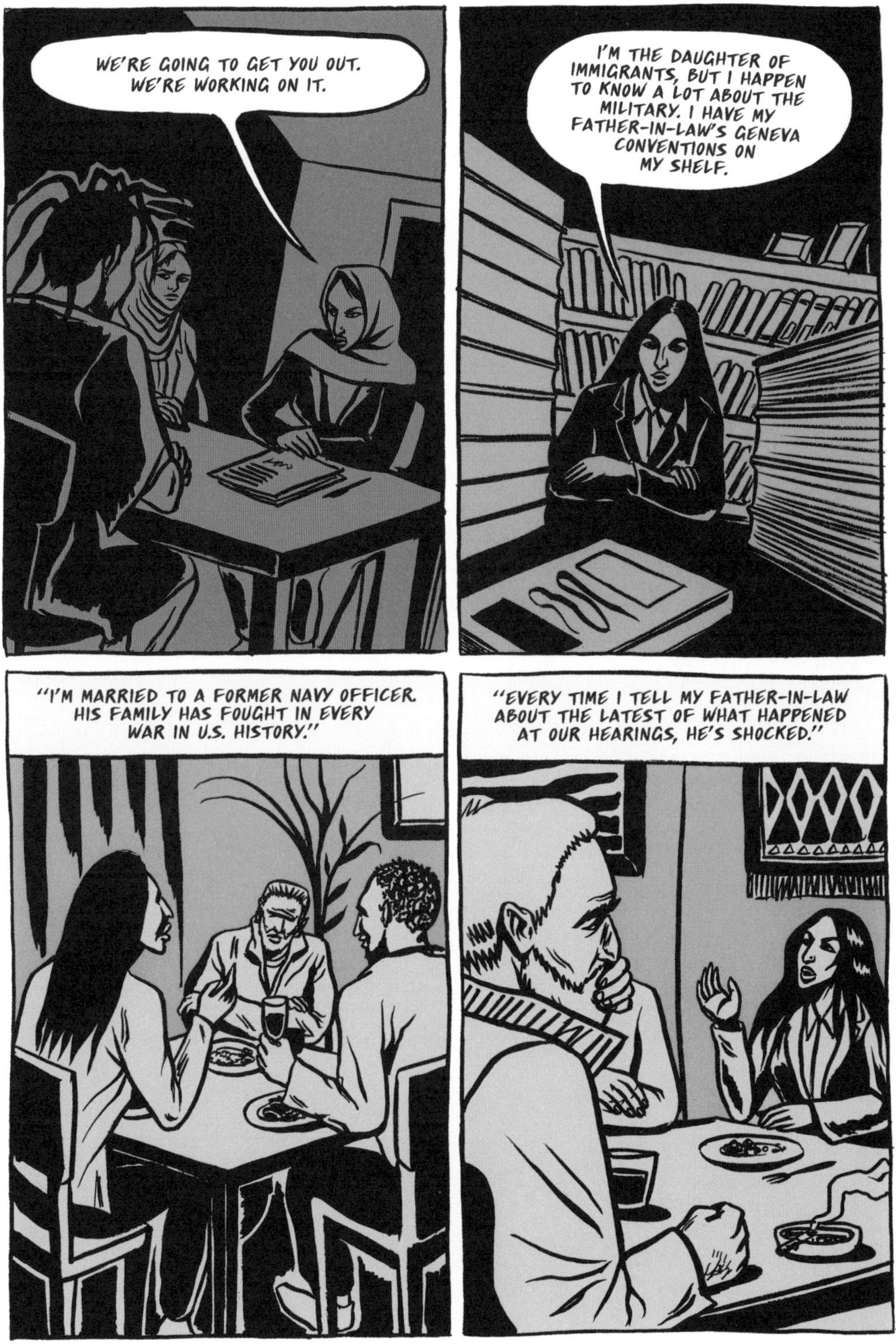
WE'RE GOING TO GET YOU OUT. WE'RE WORKING ON IT.
I'M THE DAUGHTER OF IMMIGRANTS, BUT I HAPPEN TO KNOW A LOT ABOUT THE MILITARY. I HAVE MY FATHER-IN-LAW'S GENEVA CONVENTIONS ON MY SHELF.
"I'M MARRIED TO A FORMER NAVY OFFICER. HIS FAMILY HAS FOUGHT IN EVERY WAR IN U.S. HISTORY."
"EVERY TIME I TELL MY FATHER-IN-LAW ABOUT THE LATEST OF WHAT HAPPENED AT OUR HEARINGS, HE'S SHOCKED."

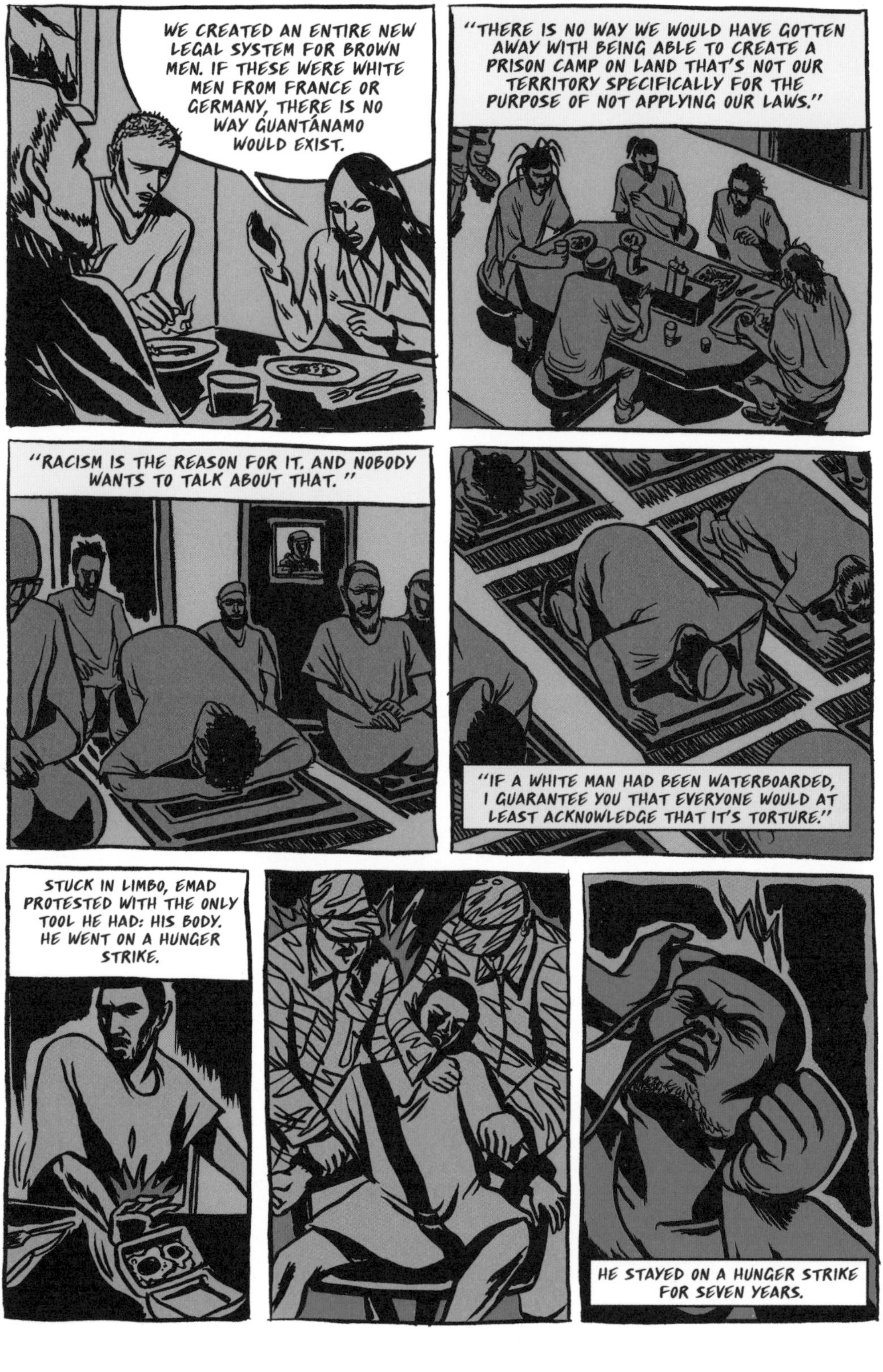
WE CREATED AN ENTIRE NEW LEGAL SYSTEM FOR BROWN MEN. IF THESE WERE WHITE MEN FROM FRANCE OR GERMANY, THERE IS NO WAY GUANTÁNAMO WOULD EXIST.
"THERE IS NO WAY WE WOULD HAVE GOTTEN AWAY WITH BEING ABLE TO CREATE A PRISON CAMP ON LAND THAT'S NOT OUR TERRITORY SPECIFICALLY FOR THE PURPOSE OF NOT APPLYING OUR LAWS."
"RACISM IS THE REASON FOR IT. AND NOBODY WANTS TO TALK ABOUT THAT."
"IF A WHITE MAN HAD BEEN WATERBOARDED, I GUARANTEE YOU THAT EVERYONE WOULD AT LEAST ACKNOWLEDGE THAT IT'S TORTURE."
STUCK IN LIMBO, EMAD PROTESTED WITH THE ONLY TOOL HE HAD: HIS BODY. HE WENT ON A HUNGER STRIKE.
HE STAYED ON A HUNGER STRIKE FOR SEVEN YEARS.

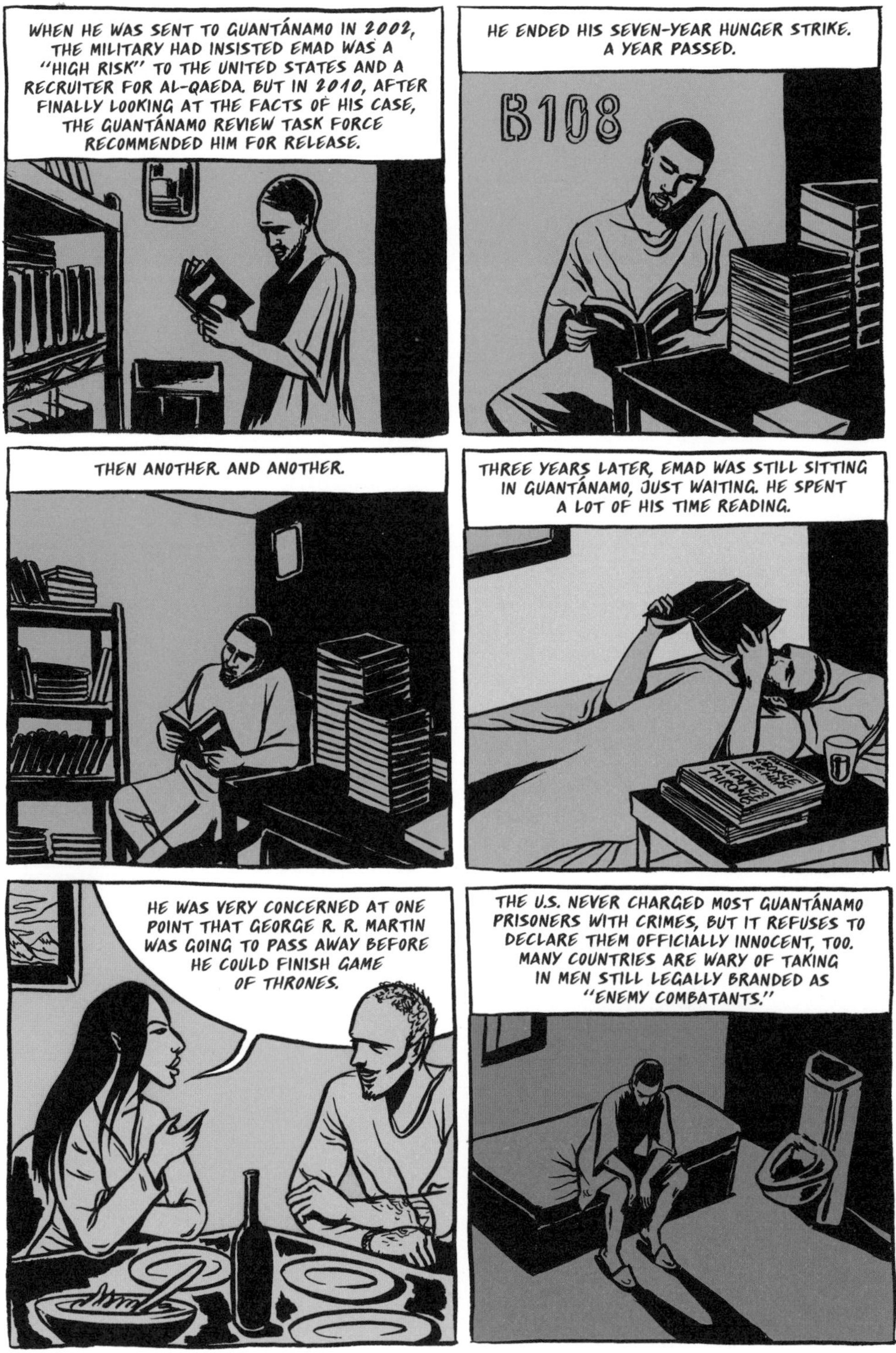
WHEN HE WAS SENT TO GUANTÁNAMO IN 2002, THE MILITARY HAD INSISTED EMAD WAS A "HIGH RISK" TO THE UNITED STATES AND A RECRUITER FOR AL-QAEDA. BUT IN 2010, AFTER FINALLY LOOKING AT THE FACTS OF HIS CASE, THE GUANTÁNAMO REVIEW TASK FORCE RECOMMENDED HIM FOR RELEASE.
HE ENDED HIS SEVEN-YEAR HUNGER STRIKE. A YEAR PASSED.
B108
THEN ANOTHER AND ANOTHER.
THREE YEARS LATER, EMAD WAS STILL SITTING IN GUANTÁNAMO, JUST WAITING. HE SPENT A LOT OF HIS TIME READING.
HE WAS VERY CONCERNED AT ONE POINT THAT GEORGE R. R. MARTIN WAS GOING TO PASS AWAY BEFORE HE COULD FINISH GAME OF THRONES.
THE U.S. NEVER CHARGED MOST GUANTÁNAMO PRISONERS WITH CRIMES, BUT IT REFUSES TO DECLARE THEM OFFICIALLY INNOCENT, TOO. MANY COUNTRIES ARE WARY OF TAKING IN MEN STILL LEGALLY BRANDED AS "ENEMY COMBATANTS."

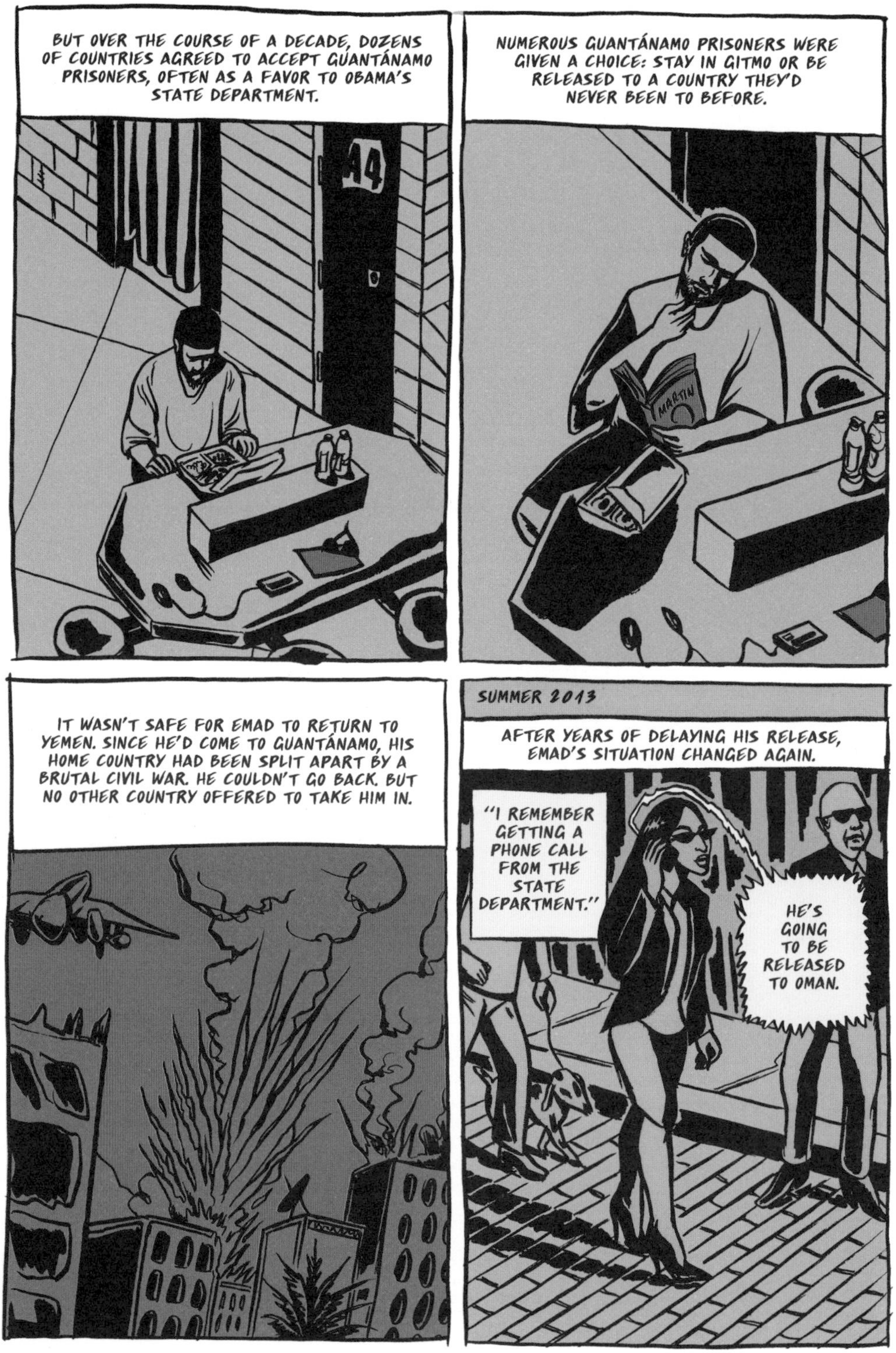
BUT OVER THE COURSE OF A DECADE, DOZENS OF COUNTRIES AGREED TO ACCEPT GUANTÁNAMO PRISONERS, OFTEN AS A FAVOR TO OBAMA'S STATE DEPARTMENT.
A4
NUMEROUS GUANTÁNAMO PRISONERS WERE GIVEN A CHOICE: STAY IN GITMO OR BE RELEASED TO A COUNTRY THEY'D NEVER BEEN TO BEFORE.
MARTIN
IT WASN'T SAFE FOR EMAD TO RETURN TO YEMEN. SINCE HE'D COME TO GUANTÁNAMO, HIS HOME COUNTRY HAD BEEN SPLIT APART BY A BRUTAL CIVIL WAR. HE COULDN'T GO BACK. BUT NO OTHER COUNTRY OFFERED TO TAKE HIM IN.
SUMMER 2013
AFTER YEARS OF DELAYING HIS RELEASE, EMAD'S SITUATION CHANGED AGAIN.
"I REMEMBER GETTING A PHONE CALL FROM THE STATE DEPARTMENT."
HE'S GOING TO BE RELEASED TO OMAN.

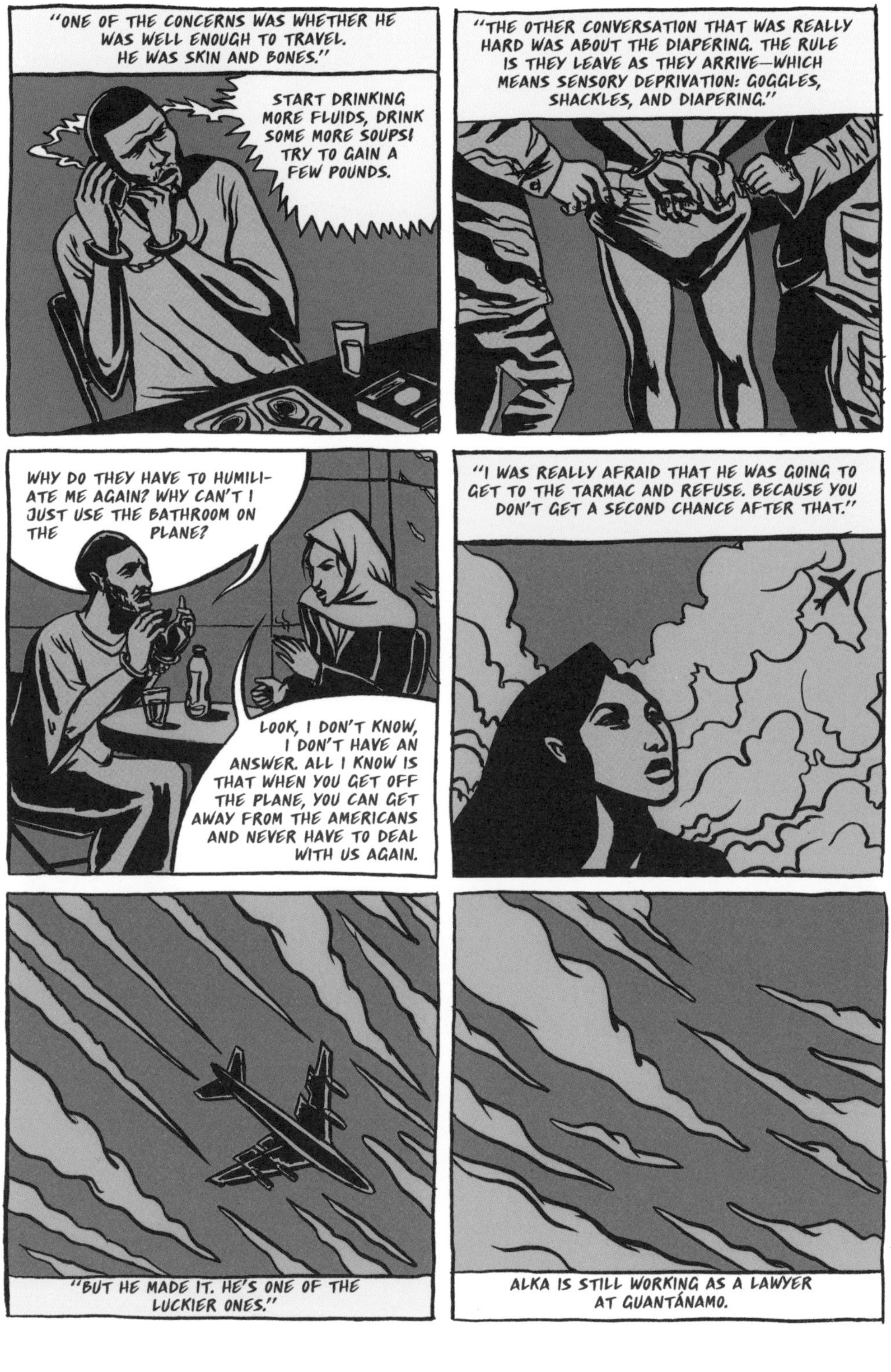
"ONE OF THE CONCERNS WAS WHETHER HE WAS WELL ENOUGH TO TRAVEL. HE WAS SKIN AND BONES."
START DRINKING MORE FLUIDS, DRINK SOME MORE SOUPS! TRY TO GAIN A FEW POUNDS.
"THE OTHER CONVERSATION THAT WAS REALLY HARD WAS ABOUT THE DIAPERING. THE RULE IS THEY LEAVE AS THEY ARRIVE—WHICH MEANS SENSORY DEPRIVATION: GOGGLES, SHACKLES, AND DIAPERING."
WHY DO THEY HAVE TO HUMILIATE ME AGAIN? WHY CAN'T I JUST USE THE BATHROOM ON THE PLANE?
LOOK, I DON'T KNOW, I DON'T HAVE AN ANSWER. ALL I KNOW IS THAT WHEN YOU GET OFF THE PLANE, YOU CAN GET AWAY FROM THE AMERICANS AND NEVER HAVE TO DEAL WITH US AGAIN.
"I WAS REALLY AFRAID THAT HE WAS GOING TO GET TO THE TARMAC AND REFUSE. BECAUSE YOU DON'T GET A SECOND CHANCE AFTER THAT."
"BUT HE MADE IT. HE'S ONE OF THE LUCKIER ONES."
ALKA IS STILL WORKING AS A LAWYER AT GUANTÁNAMO.

CHAPTER NINE

SHELBY SULLIVAN-BENNIS
ATTORNEY FOR GUANTÁNAMO PRISONERS

ILLUSTRATED BY KASIA BABIS

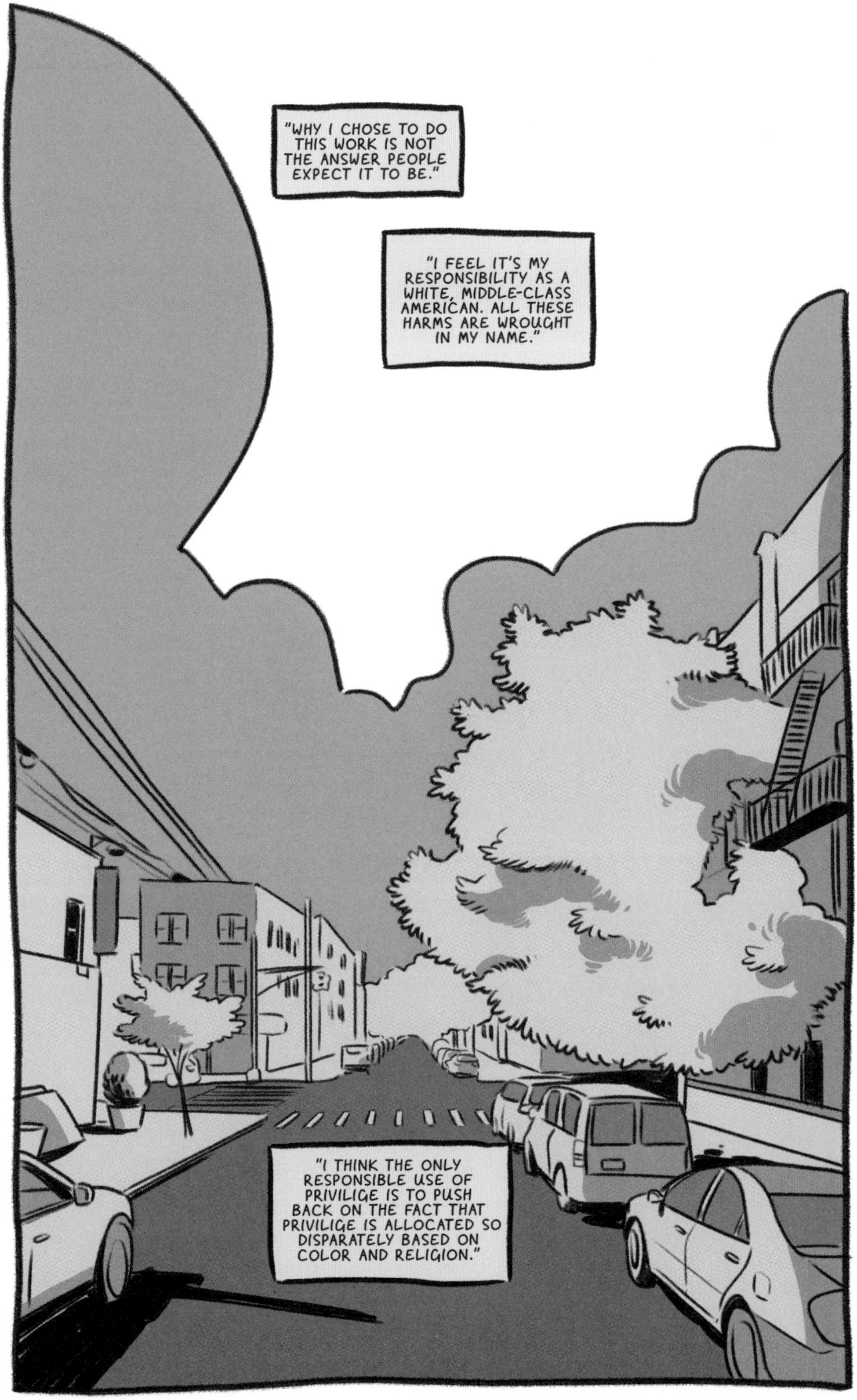
"WHY I CHOSE TO DO THIS WORK IS NOT THE ANSWER PEOPLE EXPECT IT TO BE."
"I FEEL IT'S MY RESPONSIBILITY AS A WHITE, MIDDLE-CLASS AMERICAN. ALL THESE HARMS ARE WROUGHT IN MY NAME."
"I THINK THE ONLY RESPONSIBLE USE OF PRIVILIGE IS TO PUSH BACK ON THE FACT THAT PRIVILIGE IS ALLOCATED SO DISPARATELY BASED ON COLOR AND RELIGION."

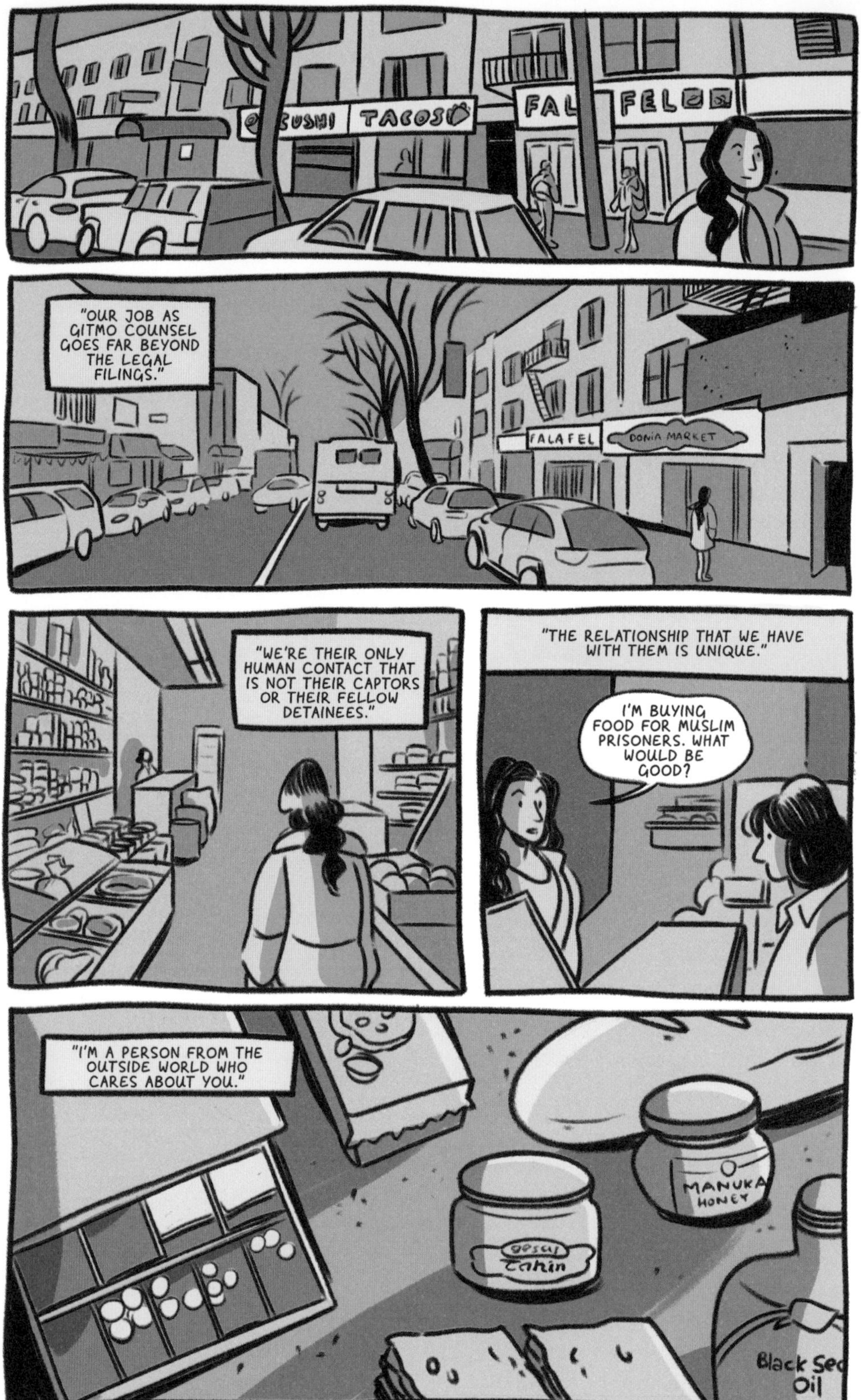

SUSHI
TACOS
FAL FEL
"OUR JOB AS GITMO COUNSEL GOES FAR BEYOND THE LEGAL FILINGS."
FALAFEL
DONIA MARKET
"WE'RE THEIR ONLY HUMAN CONTACT THAT IS NOT THEIR CAPTORS OR THEIR FELLOW DETAINEES."
"THE RELATIONSHIP THAT WE HAVE WITH THEM IS UNIQUE."
I'M BUYING FOOD FOR MUSLIM PRISONERS. WHAT WOULD BE GOOD?
"I'M A PERSON FROM THE OUTSIDE WORLD WHO CARES ABOUT YOU."
MANUKA HONEY
Tahin
Black Sed Oil

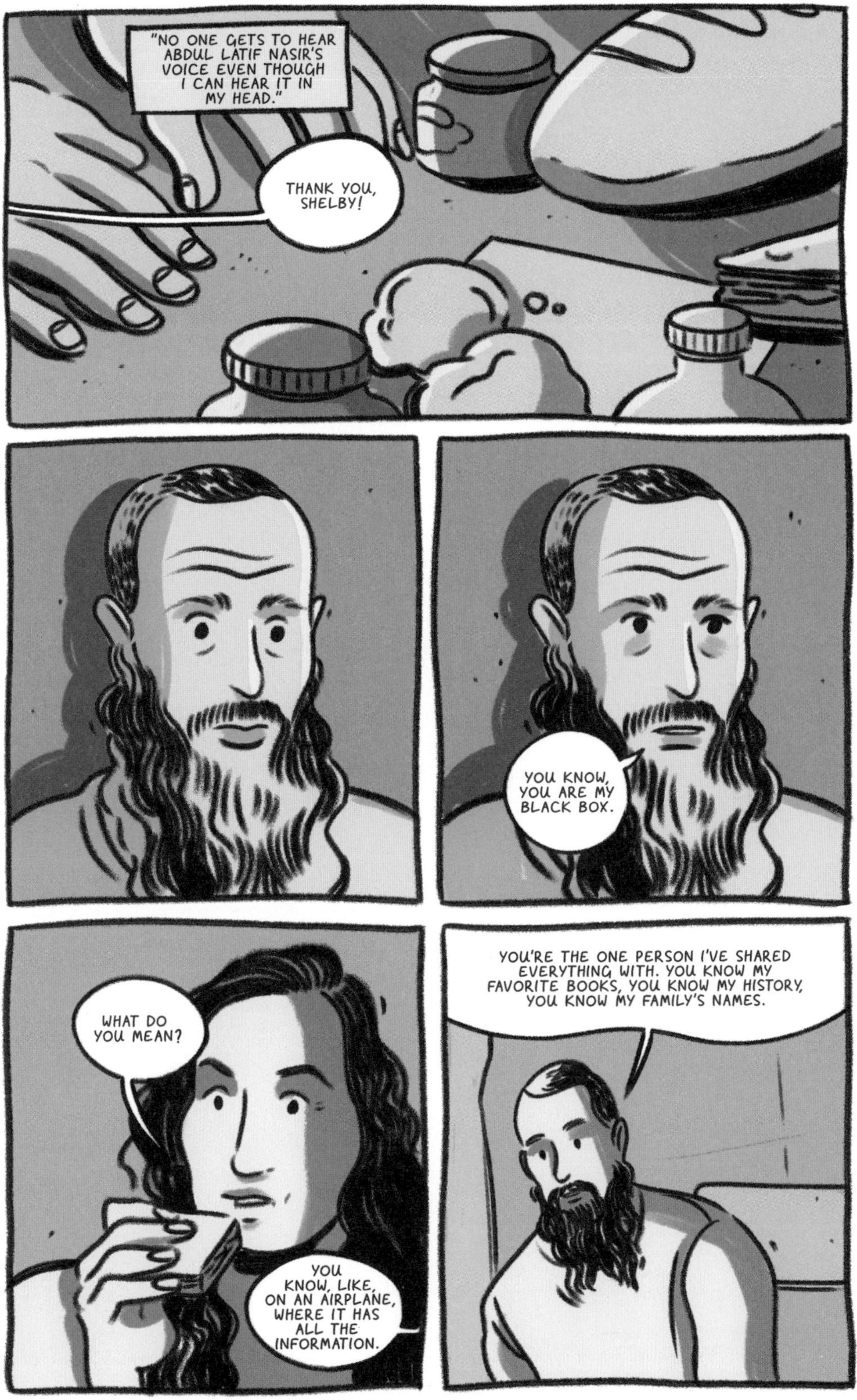
"NO ONE GETS TO HEAR ABDUL LATIF NASIR'S VOICE EVEN THOUGH I CAN HEAR IT IN MY HEAD."
THANK YOU, SHELBY!
YOU KNOW, YOU ARE MY BLACK BOX.
WHAT DO YOU MEAN?
YOU KNOW, LIKE, ON AN AIRPLANE, WHERE IT HAS ALL THE INFORMATION.
YOU'RE THE ONE PERSON I'VE SHARED EVERYTHING WITH. YOU KNOW MY FAVORITE BOOKS, YOU KNOW MY HISTORY, YOU KNOW MY FAMILY'S NAMES.

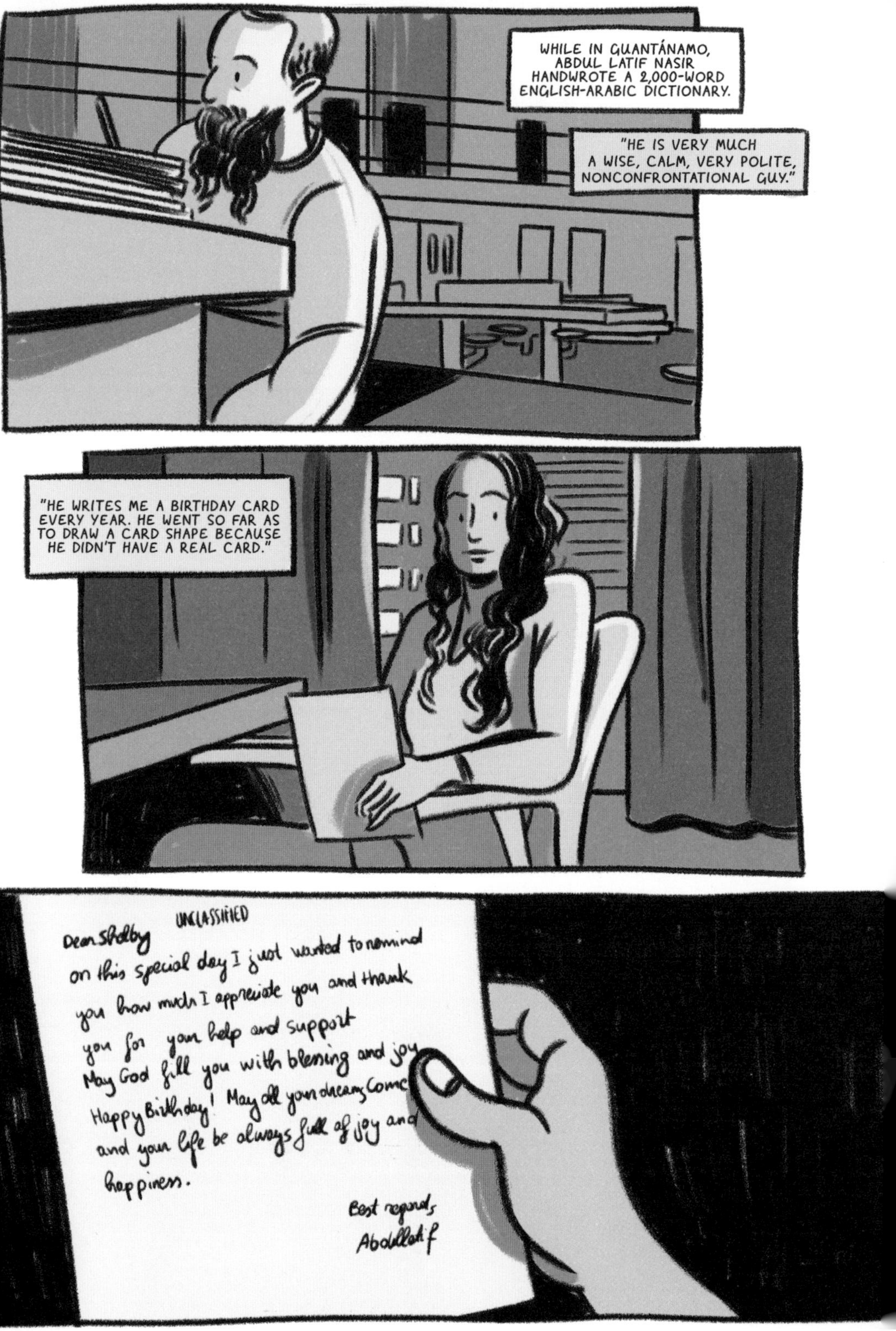
WHILE IN GUANTÁNAMO, ABDUL LATIF NASIR HANDWROTE A 2,000-WORD ENGLISH-ARABIC DICTIONARY.
"HE IS VERY MUCH A WISE, CALM, VERY POLITE, NONCONFRONTATIONAL GUY."
"HE WRITES ME A BIRTHDAY CARD EVERY YEAR. HE WENT SO FAR AS TO DRAW A CARD SHAPE BECAUSE HE DIDN'T HAVE A REAL CARD."
UNCLASSIFIED
Dear Shelby
on this special day I just wanted to remind
you how much I appreciate you and thank
you for your help and support
May God fill you with blesing and joy
Happy Birthday! May all your dreams come
and your life be always full of joy and
happiness.
Best regards
Abdullatif

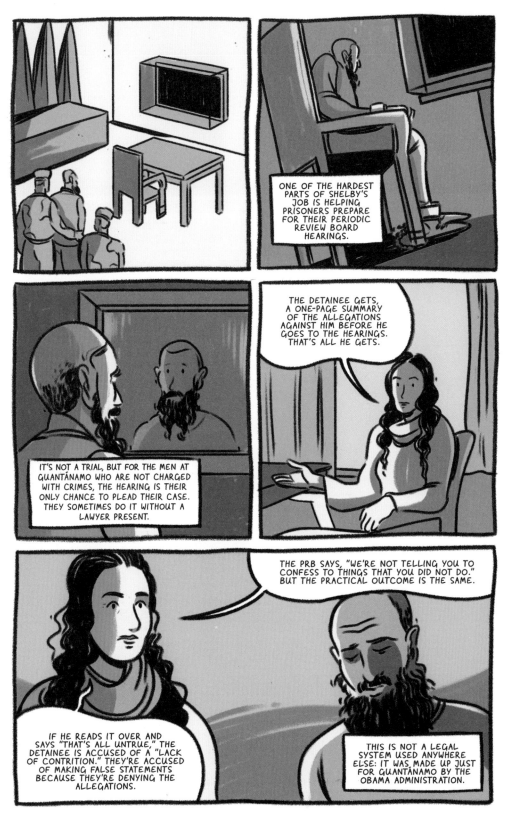

ONE OF THE HARDEST PARTS OF SHELBY'S JOB IS HELPING PRISONERS PREPARE FOR THEIR PERIODIC REVIEW BOARD HEARINGS.

IT'S NOT A TRIAL, BUT FOR THE MEN AT GUANTÁNAMO WHO ARE NOT CHARGED WITH CRIMES, THE HEARING IS THEIR ONLY CHANCE TO PLEAD THEIR CASE. THEY SOMETIMES DO IT WITHOUT A LAWYER PRESENT.

THE DETAINEE GETS, A ONE-PAGE SUMMARY OF THE ALLEGATIONS AGAINST HIM BEFORE HE GOES TO THE HEARINGS. THAT'S ALL HE GETS.

THE PRB SAYS, "WE'RE NOT TELLING YOU TO CONFESS TO THINGS THAT YOU DID NOT DO." BUT THE PRACTICAL OUTCOME IS THE SAME.

IF HE READS IT OVER AND SAYS "THAT'S ALL UNTRUE," THE DETAINEE IS ACCUSED OF A "LACK OF CONTRITION." THEY'RE ACCUSED OF MAKING FALSE STATEMENTS BECAUSE THEY'RE DENYING THE ALLEGATIONS.

THIS IS NOT A LEGAL SYSTEM USED ANYWHERE ELSE: IT WAS MADE UP JUST FOR GUANTÁNAMO BY THE OBAMA ADMINISTRATION.

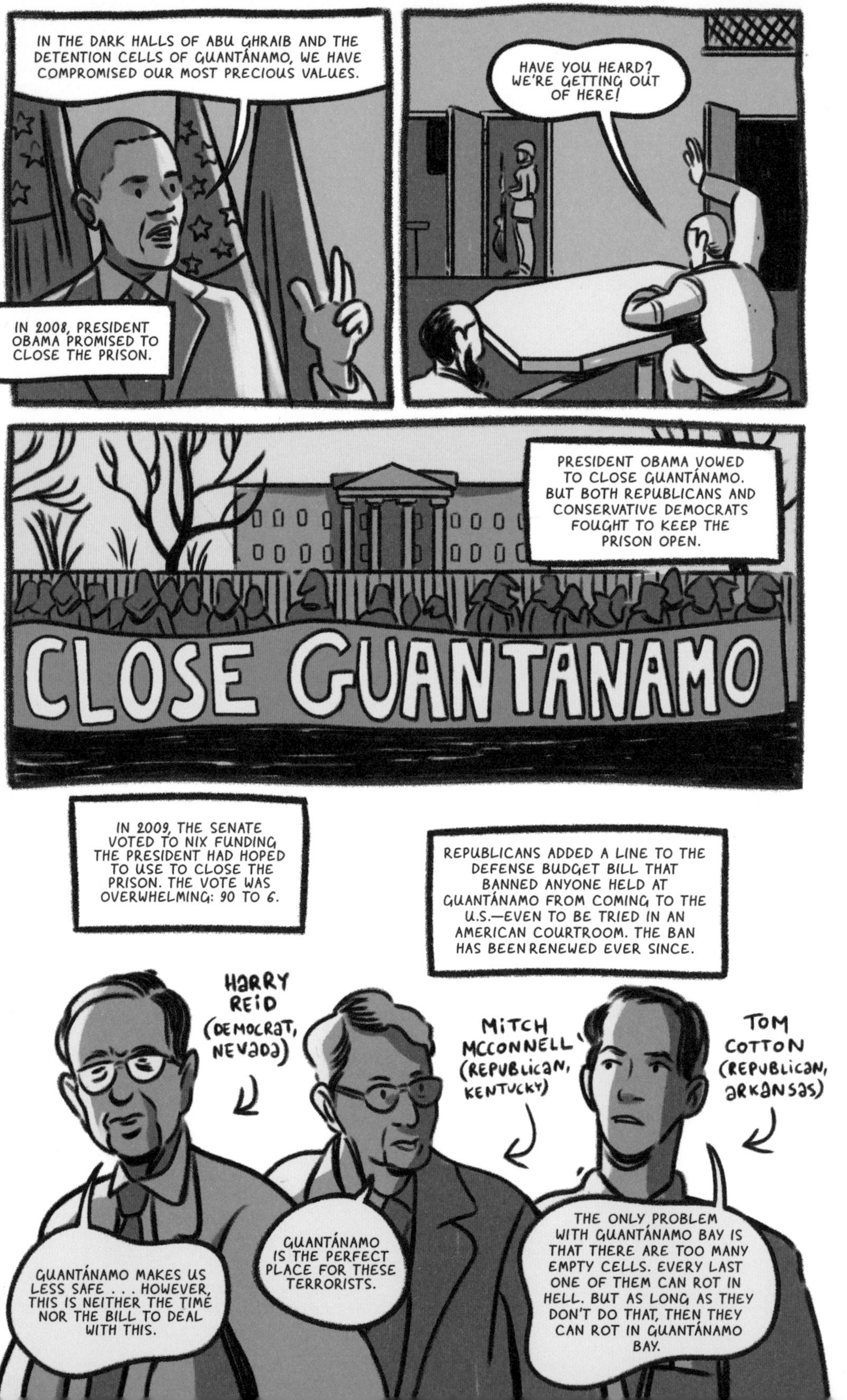
IN THE DARK HALLS OF ABU GHRAIB AND THE DETENTION CELLS OF GUANTÁNAMO, WE HAVE COMPROMISED OUR MOST PRECIOUS VALUES.
IN 2008, PRESIDENT OBAMA PROMISED TO CLOSE THE PRISON.
HAVE YOU HEARD? WE'RE GETTING OUT OF HERE!
PRESIDENT OBAMA VOWED TO CLOSE GUANTÁNAMO. BUT BOTH REPUBLICANS AND CONSERVATIVE DEMOCRATS FOUGHT TO KEEP THE PRISON OPEN.
CLOSE GUANTANAMO
IN 2009, THE SENATE VOTED TO NIX FUNDING THE PRESIDENT HAD HOPED TO USE TO CLOSE THE PRISON. THE VOTE WAS OVERWHELMING: 90 TO 6.
REPUBLICANS ADDED A LINE TO THE DEFENSE BUDGET BILL THAT BANNED ANYONE HELD AT GUANTÁNAMO FROM COMING TO THE U.S.—EVEN TO BE TRIED IN AN AMERICAN COURTROOM. THE BAN HAS BEEN RENEWED EVER SINCE.
HARRY REID (DEMOCRAT, NEVADA)
MITCH MCCONNELL (REPUBLICAN, KENTUCKY)
TOM COTTON (REPUBLICAN, ARKANSAS)
GUANTÁNAMO MAKES US LESS SAFE . . . HOWEVER, THIS IS NEITHER THE TIME NOR THE BILL TO DEAL WITH THIS.
GUANTÁNAMO IS THE PERFECT PLACE FOR THESE TERRORISTS.
THE ONLY PROBLEM WITH GUANTÁNAMO BAY IS THAT THERE ARE TOO MANY EMPTY CELLS. EVERY LAST ONE OF THEM CAN ROT IN HELL. BUT AS LONG AS THEY DON'T DO THAT, THEN THEY CAN ROT IN GUANTÁNAMO BAY.

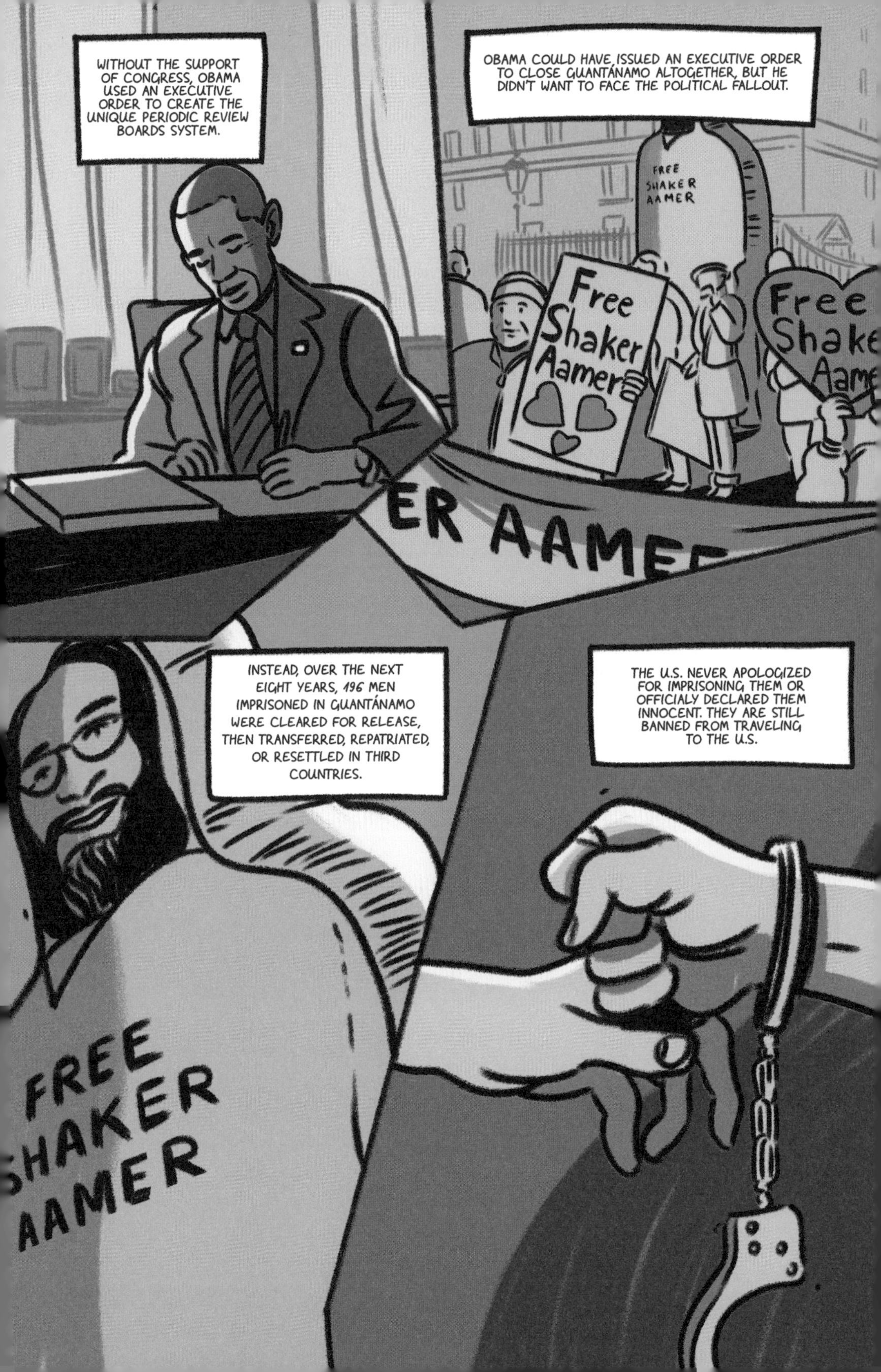
WITHOUT THE SUPPORT OF CONGRESS, OBAMA USED AN EXECUTIVE ORDER TO CREATE THE UNIQUE PERIODIC REVIEW BOARDS SYSTEM.
OBAMA COULD HAVE ISSUED AN EXECUTIVE ORDER TO CLOSE GUANTÁNAMO ALTOGETHER, BUT HE DIDN'T WANT TO FACE THE POLITICAL FALLOUT.
FREE SHAKER AAMER
Free Shaker Aamer
Free Shake Aame
ER AAMER
INSTEAD, OVER THE NEXT EIGHT YEARS, 196 MEN IMPRISONED IN GUANTÁNAMO WERE CLEARED FOR RELEASE, THEN TRANSFERRED, REPATRIATED, OR RESETTLED IN THIRD COUNTRIES.
THE U.S. NEVER APOLOGIZED FOR IMPRISONING THEM OR OFFICIALY DECLARED THEM INNOCENT. THEY ARE STILL BANNED FROM TRAVELING TO THE U.S.
FREE SHAKER AAMER

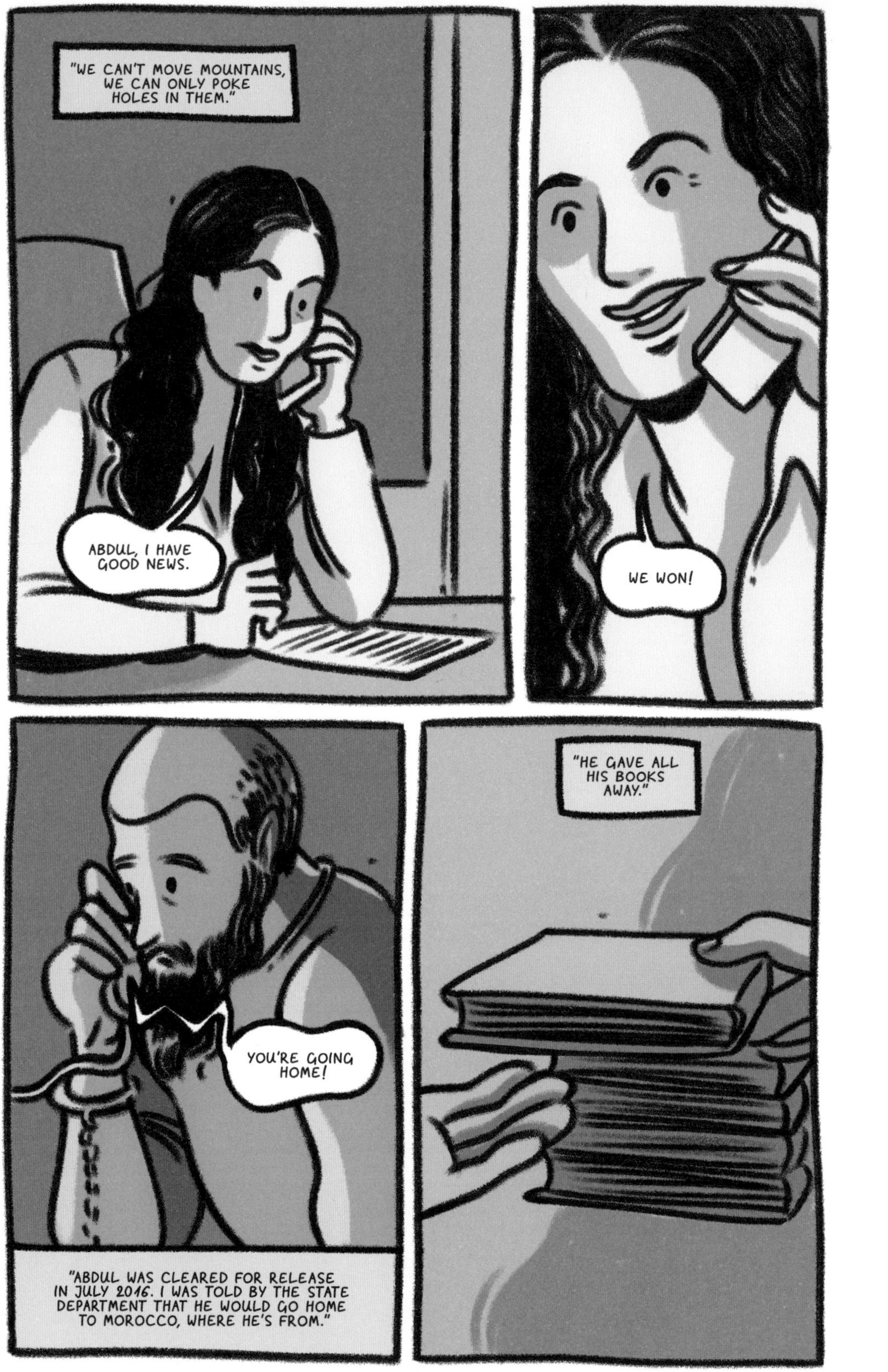
"WE CAN'T MOVE MOUNTAINS, WE CAN ONLY POKE HOLES IN THEM."
ABDUL, I HAVE GOOD NEWS.
WE WON!
YOU'RE GOING HOME!
"ABDUL WAS CLEARED FOR RELEASE IN JULY 2016. I WAS TOLD BY THE STATE DEPARTMENT THAT HE WOULD GO HOME TO MOROCCO, WHERE HE'S FROM."
"HE GAVE ALL HIS BOOKS AWAY."

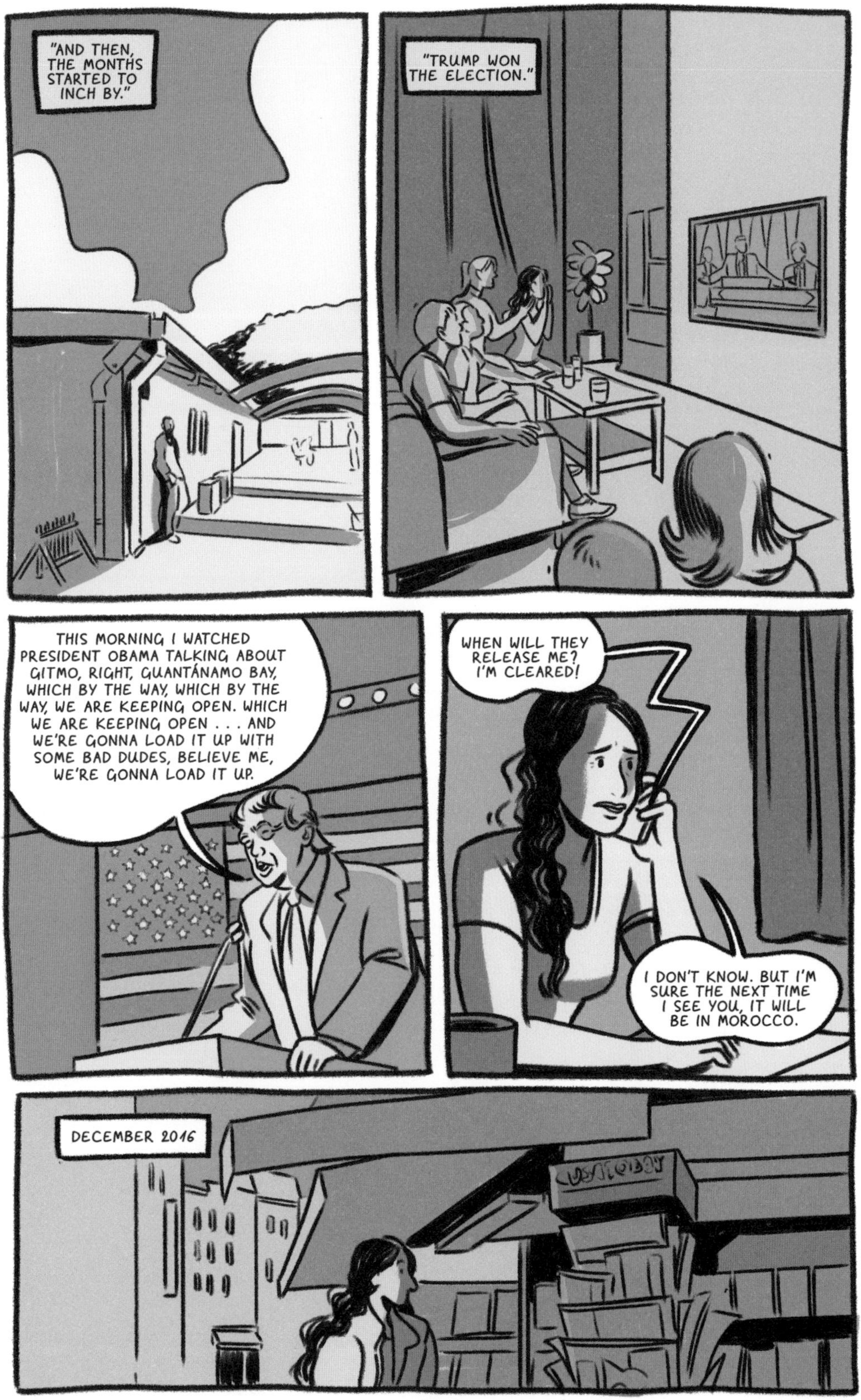
"AND THEN, THE MONTHS STARTED TO INCH BY."
"TRUMP WON THE ELECTION."
THIS MORNING I WATCHED PRESIDENT OBAMA TALKING ABOUT GITMO, RIGHT, GUANTÁNAMO BAY, WHICH BY THE WAY, WHICH BY THE WAY, WE ARE KEEPING OPEN. WHICH WE ARE KEEPING OPEN . . . AND WE'RE GONNA LOAD IT UP WITH SOME BAD DUDES, BELIEVE ME, WE'RE GONNA LOAD IT UP.
WHEN WILL THEY RELEASE ME? I'M CLEARED!
I DON'T KNOW. BUT I'M SURE THE NEXT TIME I SEE YOU, IT WILL BE IN MOROCCO.
DECEMBER 2016

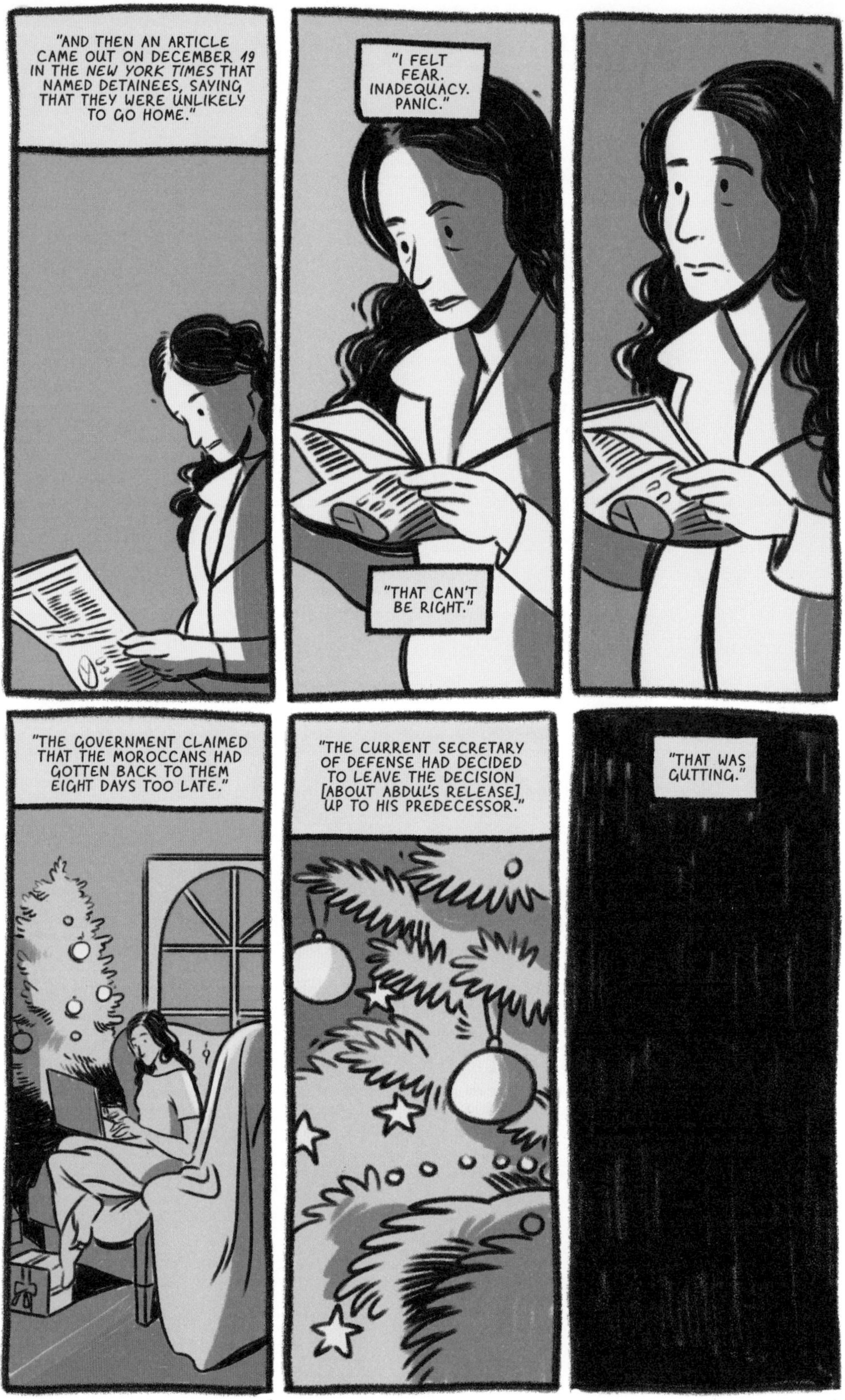
"AND THEN AN ARTICLE CAME OUT ON DECEMBER 19 IN THE *NEW YORK TIMES* THAT NAMED DETAINEES, SAYING THAT THEY WERE UNLIKELY TO GO HOME."
"I FELT FEAR. INADEQUACY. PANIC."
"THAT CAN'T BE RIGHT."
"THE GOVERNMENT CLAIMED THAT THE MOROCCANS HAD GOTTEN BACK TO THEM EIGHT DAYS TOO LATE."
"THE CURRENT SECRETARY OF DEFENSE HAD DECIDED TO LEAVE THE DECISION [ABOUT ABDUL'S RELEASE] UP TO HIS PREDECESSOR."
"THAT WAS GUTTING."

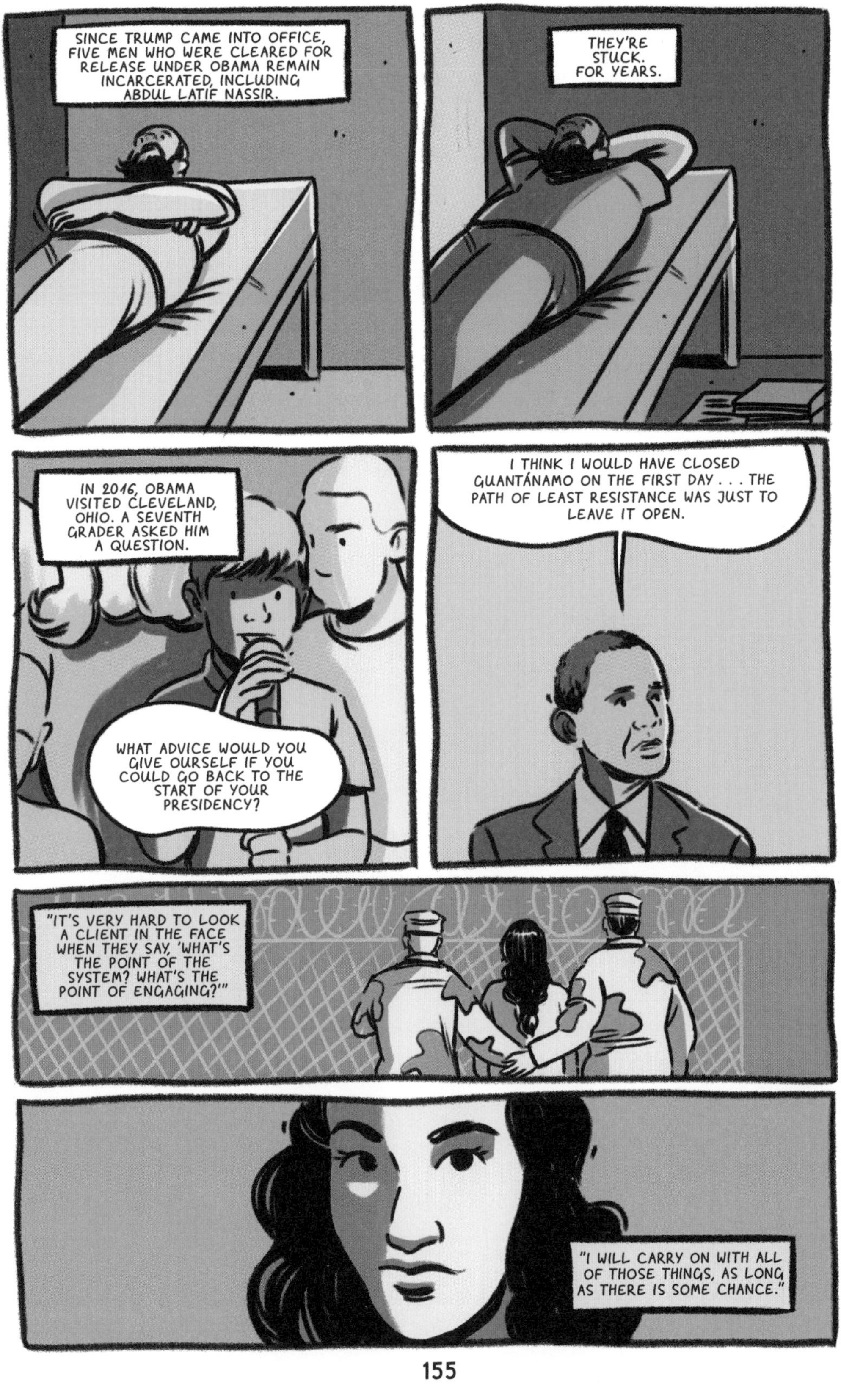
SINCE TRUMP CAME INTO OFFICE, FIVE MEN WHO WERE CLEARED FOR RELEASE UNDER OBAMA REMAIN INCARCERATED, INCLUDING ABDUL LATIF NASSIR.
THEY'RE STUCK. FOR YEARS.
IN 2016, OBAMA VISITED CLEVELAND, OHIO. A SEVENTH GRADER ASKED HIM A QUESTION.
WHAT ADVICE WOULD YOU GIVE OURSELF IF YOU COULD GO BACK TO THE START OF YOUR PRESIDENCY?
I THINK I WOULD HAVE CLOSED GUANTÁNAMO ON THE FIRST DAY . . . THE PATH OF LEAST RESISTANCE WAS JUST TO LEAVE IT OPEN.
"IT'S VERY HARD TO LOOK A CLIENT IN THE FACE WHEN THEY SAY, 'WHAT'S THE POINT OF THE SYSTEM? WHAT'S THE POINT OF ENGAGING?'"
"I WILL CARRY ON WITH ALL OF THOSE THINGS, AS LONG AS THERE IS SOME CHANCE."

CHAPTER TEN

KATIE TAYLOR

DEPUTY DIRECTOR AT REPRIEVE
AND COORDINATOR OF THE LIFE
AFTER GUANTÁNAMO PROJECT

ILLUSTRATED BY CHELSEA SAUNDERS

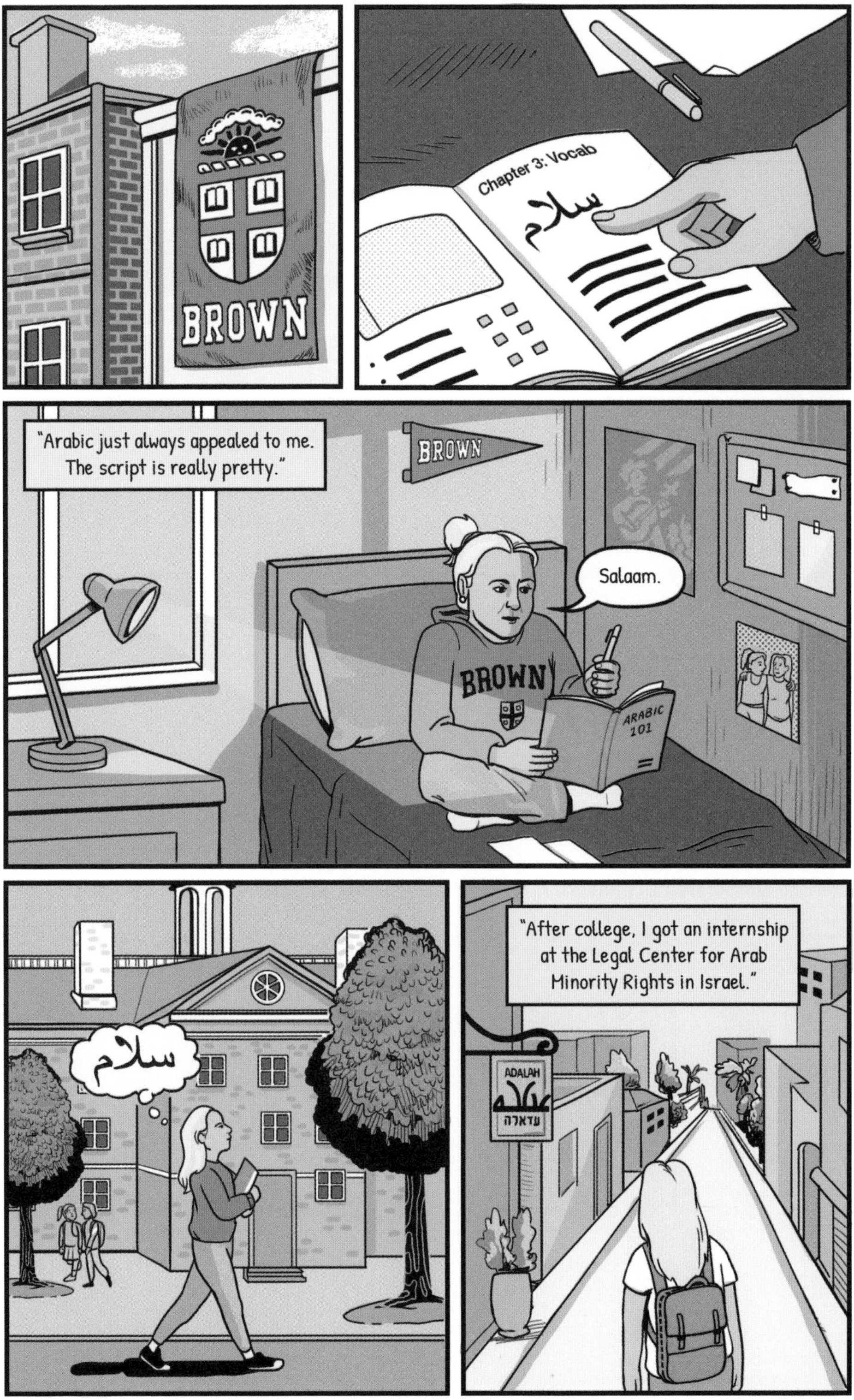
BROWN
Chapter 3: Vocab
سلام
"Arabic just always appealed to me. The script is really pretty."
BROWN
Salaam.
BROWN
ARABIC 101
سلام
"After college, I got an internship at the Legal Center for Arab Minority Rights in Israel."
ADALAH
עדאלה

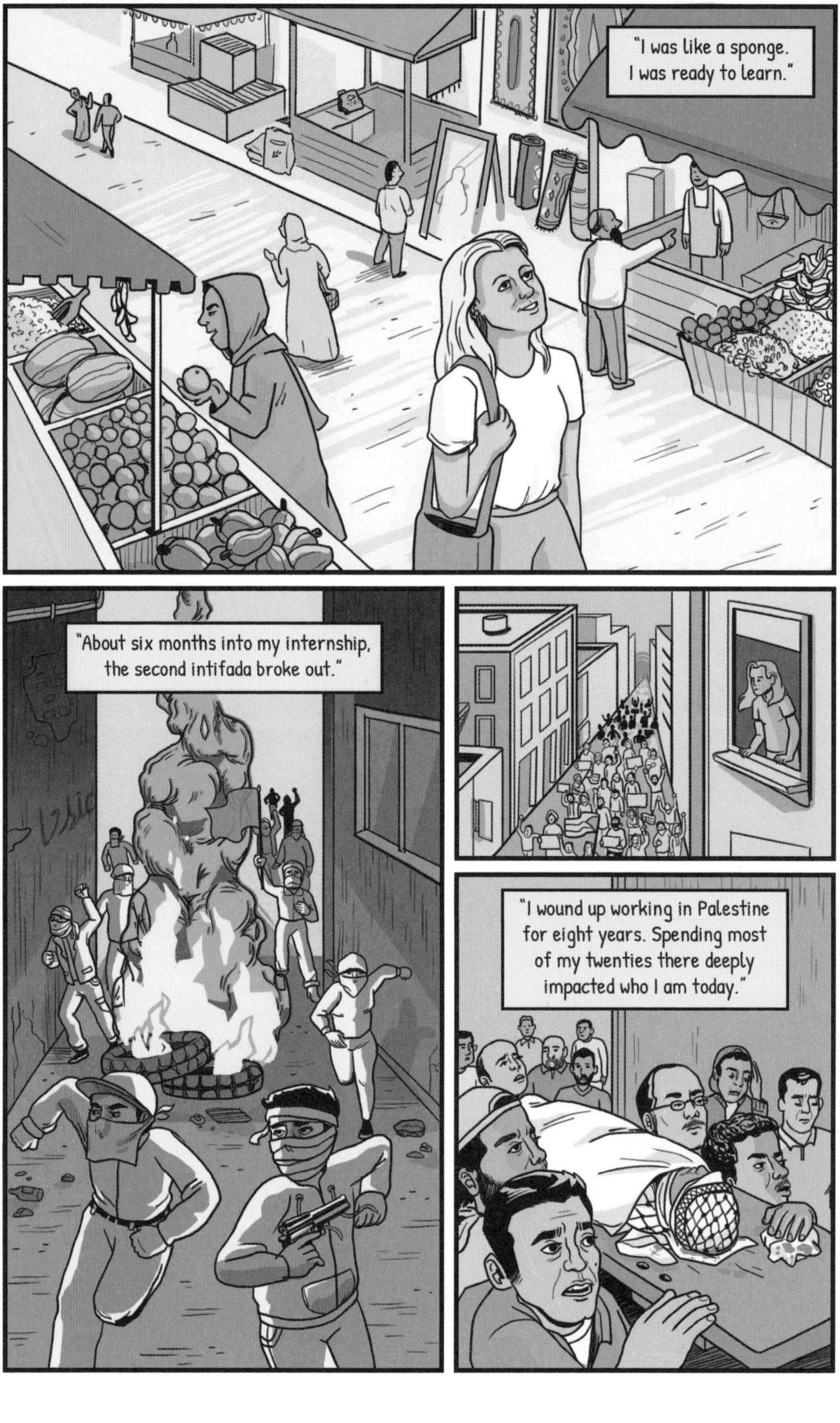
"I was like a sponge. I was ready to learn."
"About six months into my internship, the second intifada broke out."
"I wound up working in Palestine for eight years. Spending most of my twenties there deeply impacted who I am today."

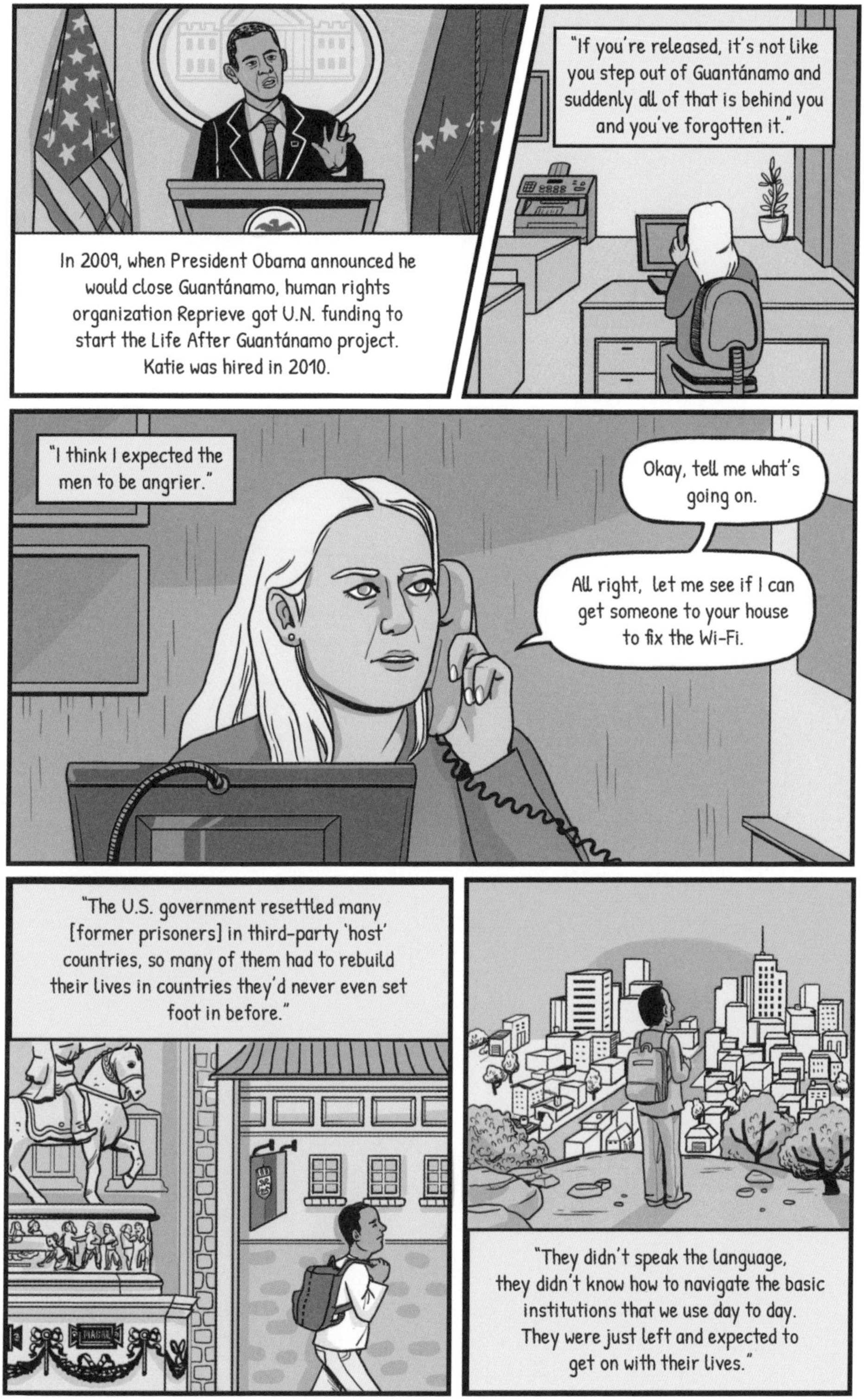
In 2009, when President Obama announced he would close Guantánamo, human rights organization Reprieve got U.N. funding to start the Life After Guantánamo project. Katie was hired in 2010.
"If you're released, it's not like you step out of Guantánamo and suddenly all of that is behind you and you've forgotten it."
"I think I expected the men to be angrier."
Okay, tell me what's going on.
All right, let me see if I can get someone to your house to fix the Wi-Fi.
"The U.S. government resettled many [former prisoners] in third-party 'host' countries, so many of them had to rebuild their lives in countries they'd never even set foot in before."
"They didn't speak the language, they didn't know how to navigate the basic institutions that we use day to day. They were just left and expected to get on with their lives."

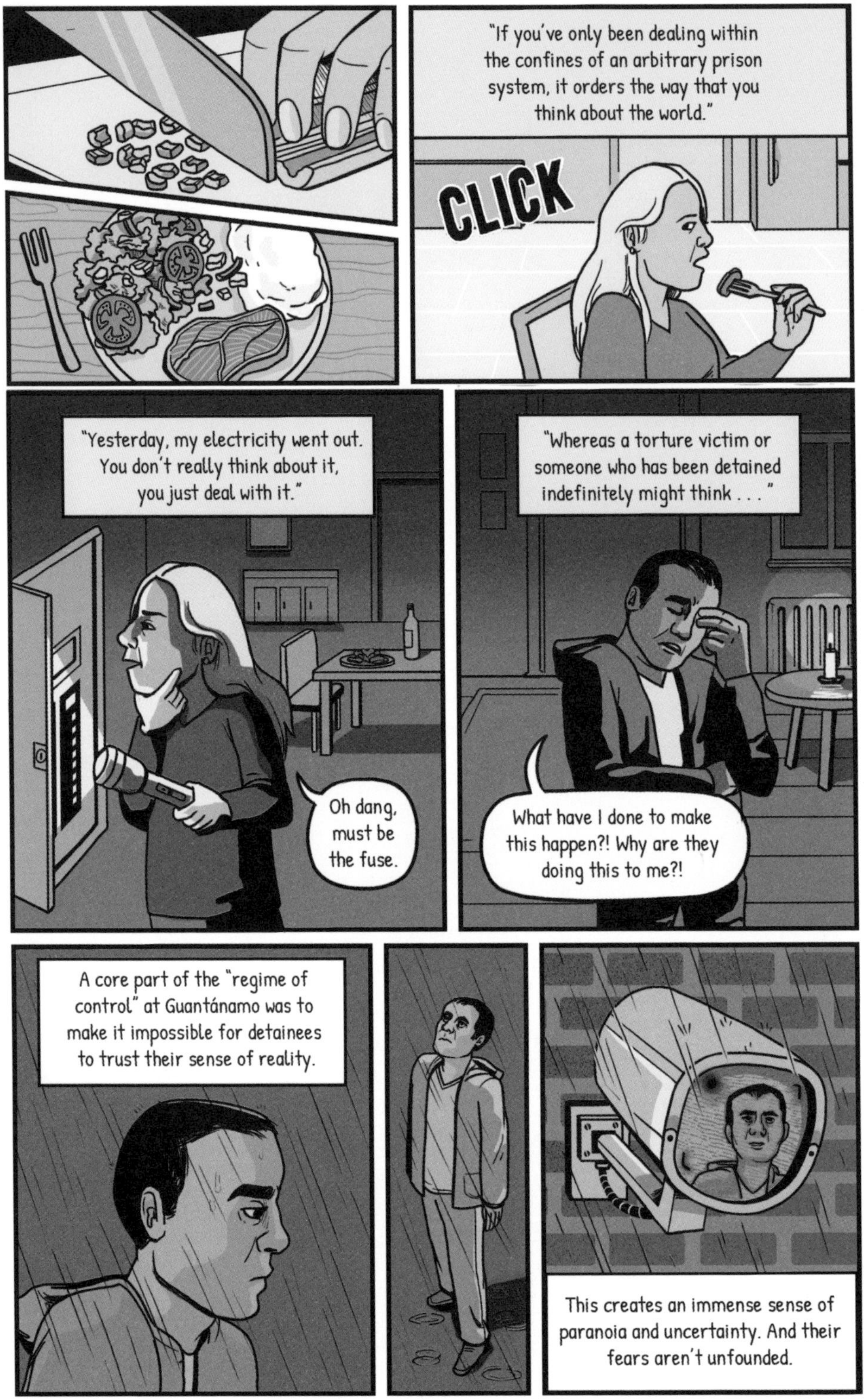
"If you've only been dealing within the confines of an arbitrary prison system, it orders the way that you think about the world."
CLICK
"Yesterday, my electricity went out. You don't really think about it, you just deal with it."
Oh dang, must be the fuse.
"Whereas a torture victim or someone who has been detained indefinitely might think . . ."
What have I done to make this happen?! Why are they doing this to me?!
A core part of the "regime of control" at Guantánamo was to make it impossible for detainees to trust their sense of reality.
This creates an immense sense of paranoia and uncertainty. And their fears aren't unfounded.

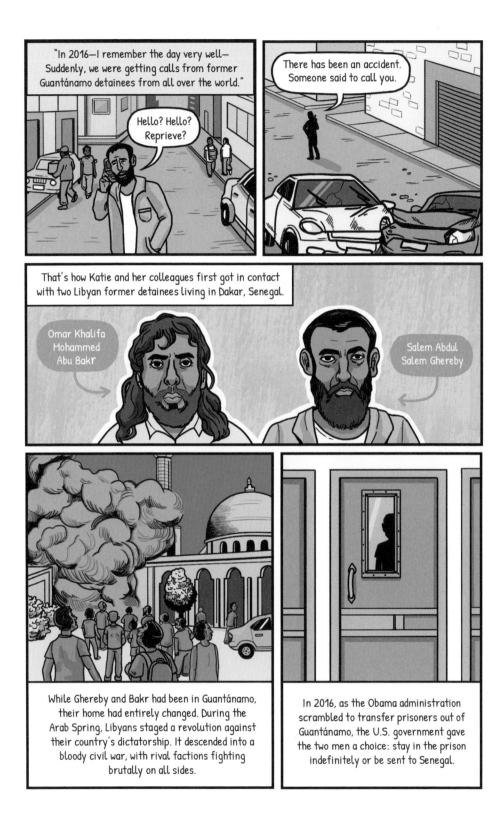

"In 2016—I remember the day very well— Suddenly, we were getting calls from former Guantánamo detainees from all over the world."

Hello? Hello? Reprieve?

There has been an accident. Someone said to call you.

That's how Katie and her colleagues first got in contact with two Libyan former detainees living in Dakar, Senegal.

Omar Khalifa Mohammed Abu Bakr

Salem Abdul Salem Ghereby

While Ghereby and Bakr had been in Guantánamo, their home had entirely changed. During the Arab Spring, Libyans staged a revolution against their country's dictatorship. It descended into a bloody civil war, with rival factions fighting brutally on all sides.

In 2016, as the Obama administration scrambled to transfer prisoners out of Guantánamo, the U.S. government gave the two men a choice: stay in the prison indefinitely or be sent to Senegal.

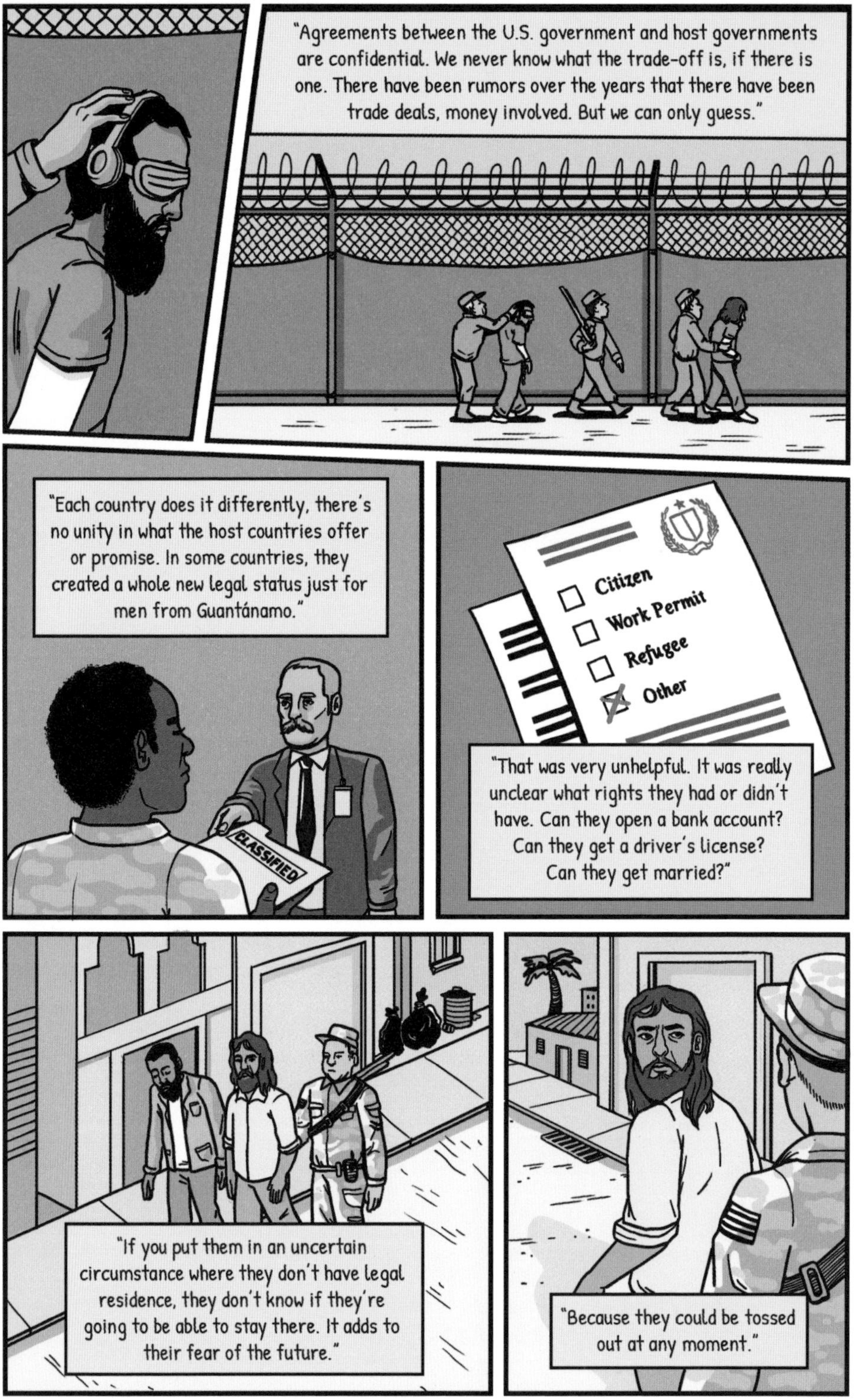
"Agreements between the U.S. government and host governments are confidential. We never know what the trade-off is, if there is one. There have been rumors over the years that there have been trade deals, money involved. But we can only guess."
"Each country does it differently, there's no unity in what the host countries offer or promise. In some countries, they created a whole new legal status just for men from Guantánamo."
CLASSIFIED
Citizen
Work Permit
Refugee
Other
"That was very unhelpful. It was really unclear what rights they had or didn't have. Can they open a bank account? Can they get a driver's license? Can they get married?"
"If you put them in an uncertain circumstance where they don't have legal residence, they don't know if they're going to be able to stay there. It adds to their fear of the future."
"Because they could be tossed out at any moment."

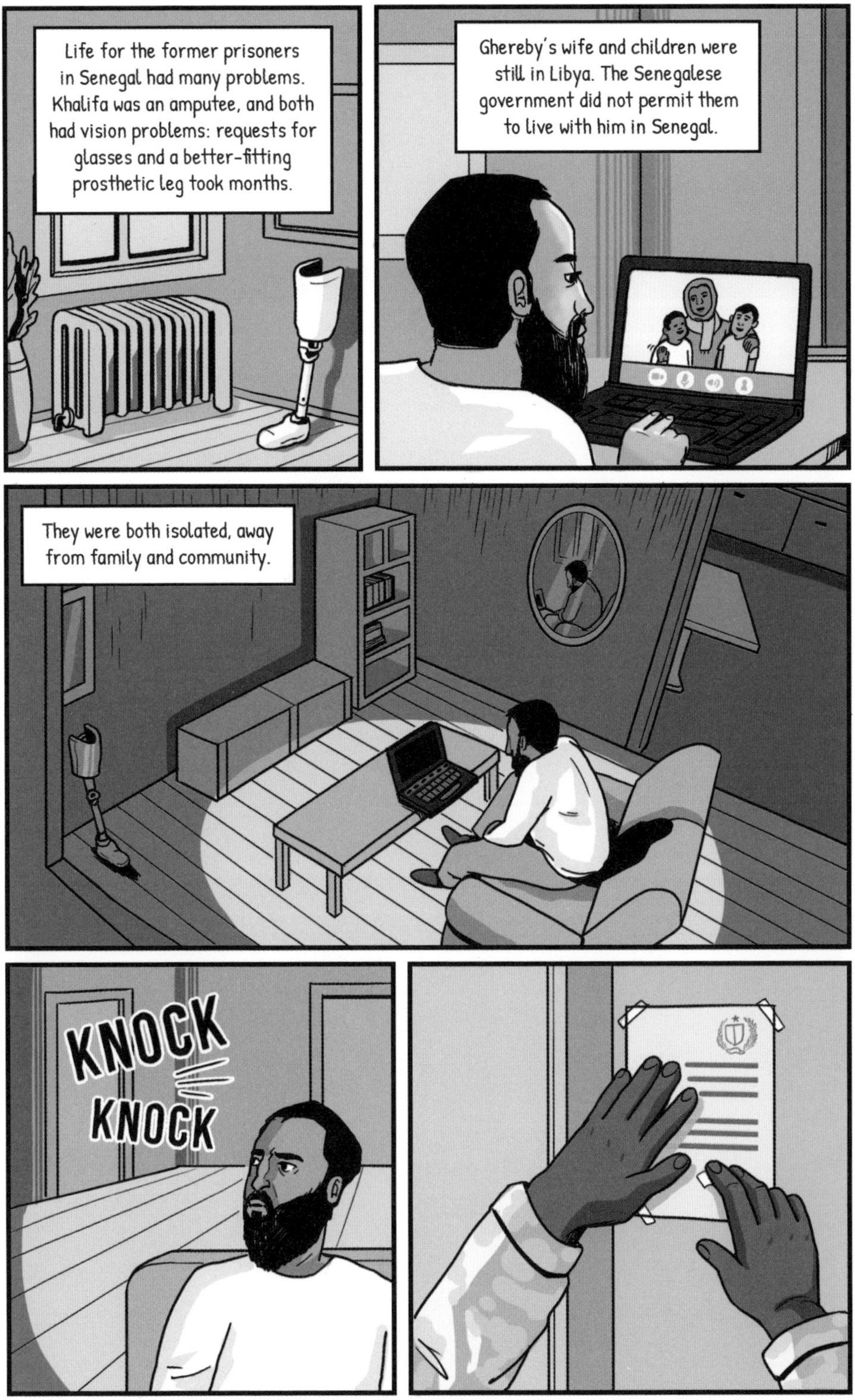

Life for the former prisoners in Senegal had many problems. Khalifa was an amputee, and both had vision problems: requests for glasses and a better-fitting prosthetic leg took months.
Ghereby's wife and children were still in Libya. The Senegalese government did not permit them to live with him in Senegal.
They were both isolated, away from family and community.
KNOCK
KNOCK

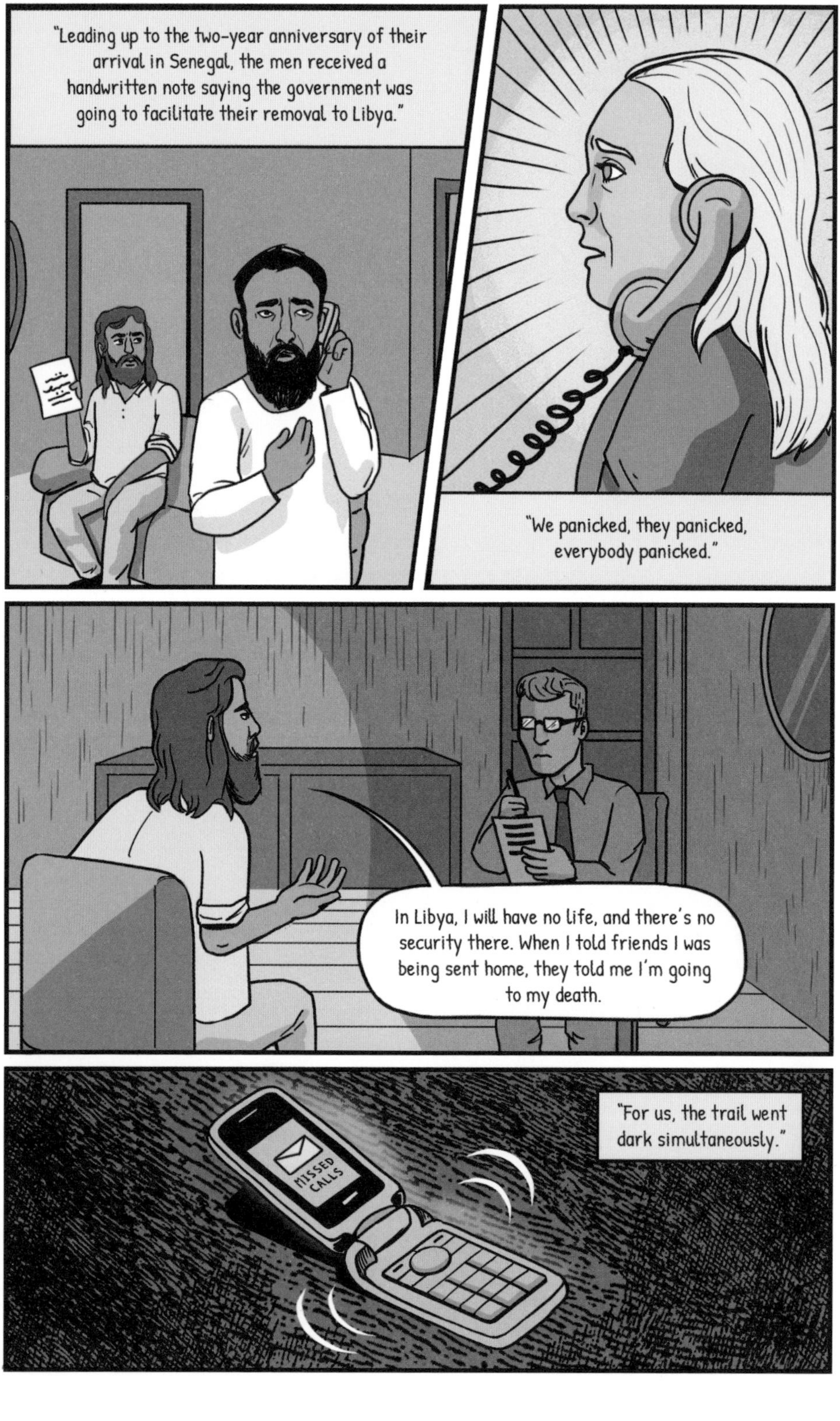
"Leading up to the two-year anniversary of their arrival in Senegal, the men received a handwritten note saying the government was going to facilitate their removal to Libya."
"We panicked, they panicked, everybody panicked."
In Libya, I will have no life, and there's no security there. When I told friends I was being sent home, they told me I'm going to my death.
MISSED CALLS
"For us, the trail went dark simultaneously."

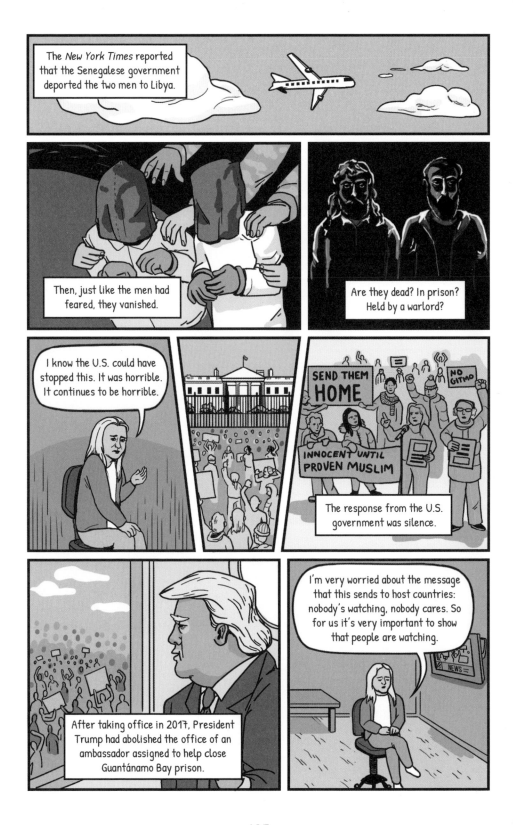

The *New York Times* reported that the Senegalese government deported the two men to Libya.

Then, just like the men had feared, they vanished.

Are they dead? In prison? Held by a warlord?

I know the U.S. could have stopped this. It was horrible. It continues to be horrible.

SEND THEM HOME

NO GITMO

INNOCENT UNTIL PROVEN MUSLIM

The response from the U.S. government was silence.

After taking office in 2017, President Trump had abolished the office of an ambassador assigned to help close Guantánamo Bay prison.

I'm very worried about the message that this sends to host countries: nobody's watching, nobody cares. So for us it's very important to show that people are watching.

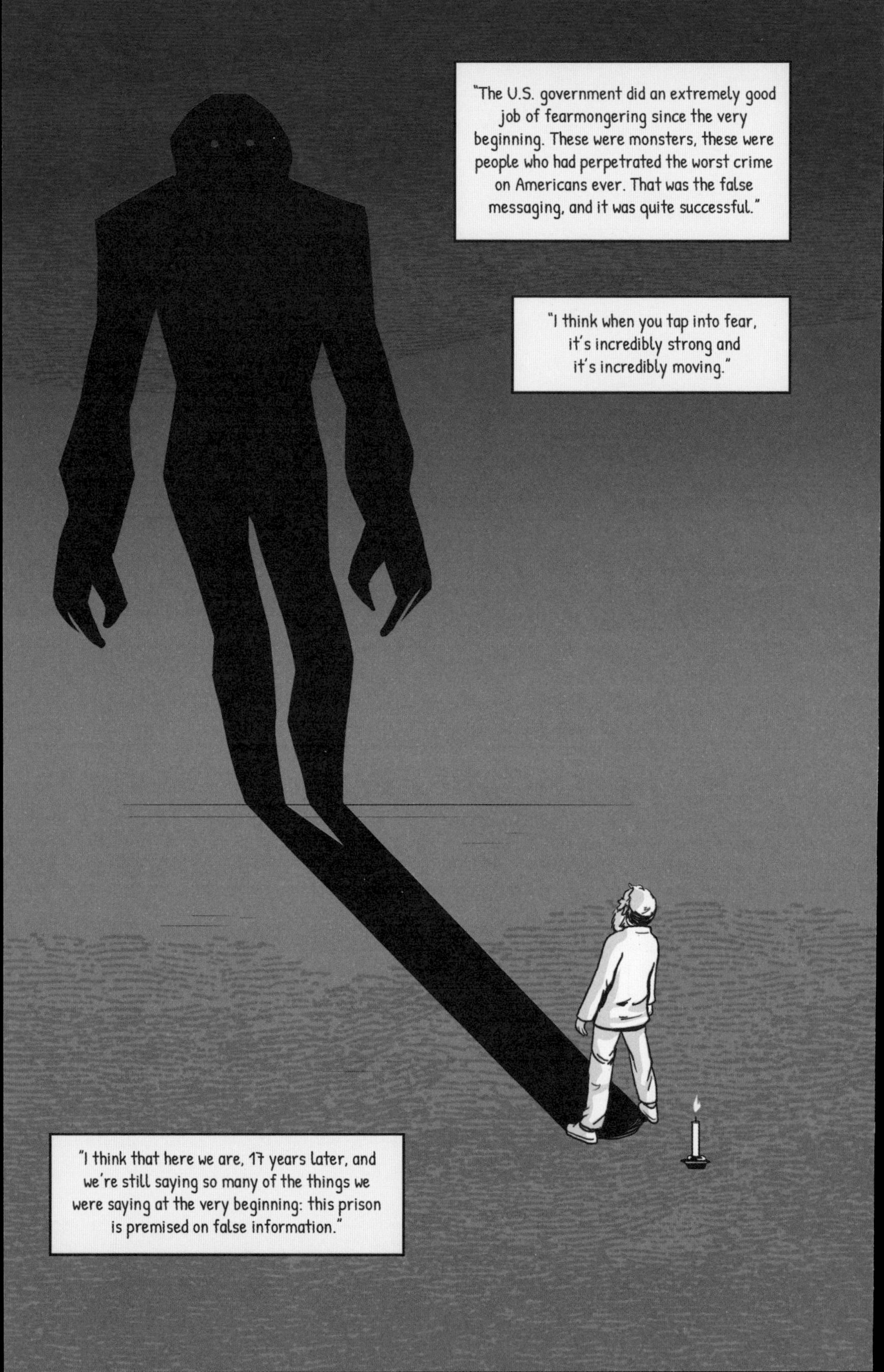
"The U.S. government did an extremely good job of fearmongering since the very beginning. These were monsters, these were people who had perpetrated the worst crime on Americans ever. That was the false messaging, and it was quite successful."
"I think when you tap into fear, it's incredibly strong and it's incredibly moving."
"I think that here we are, 17 years later, and we're still saying so many of the things we were saying at the very beginning: this prison is premised on false information."

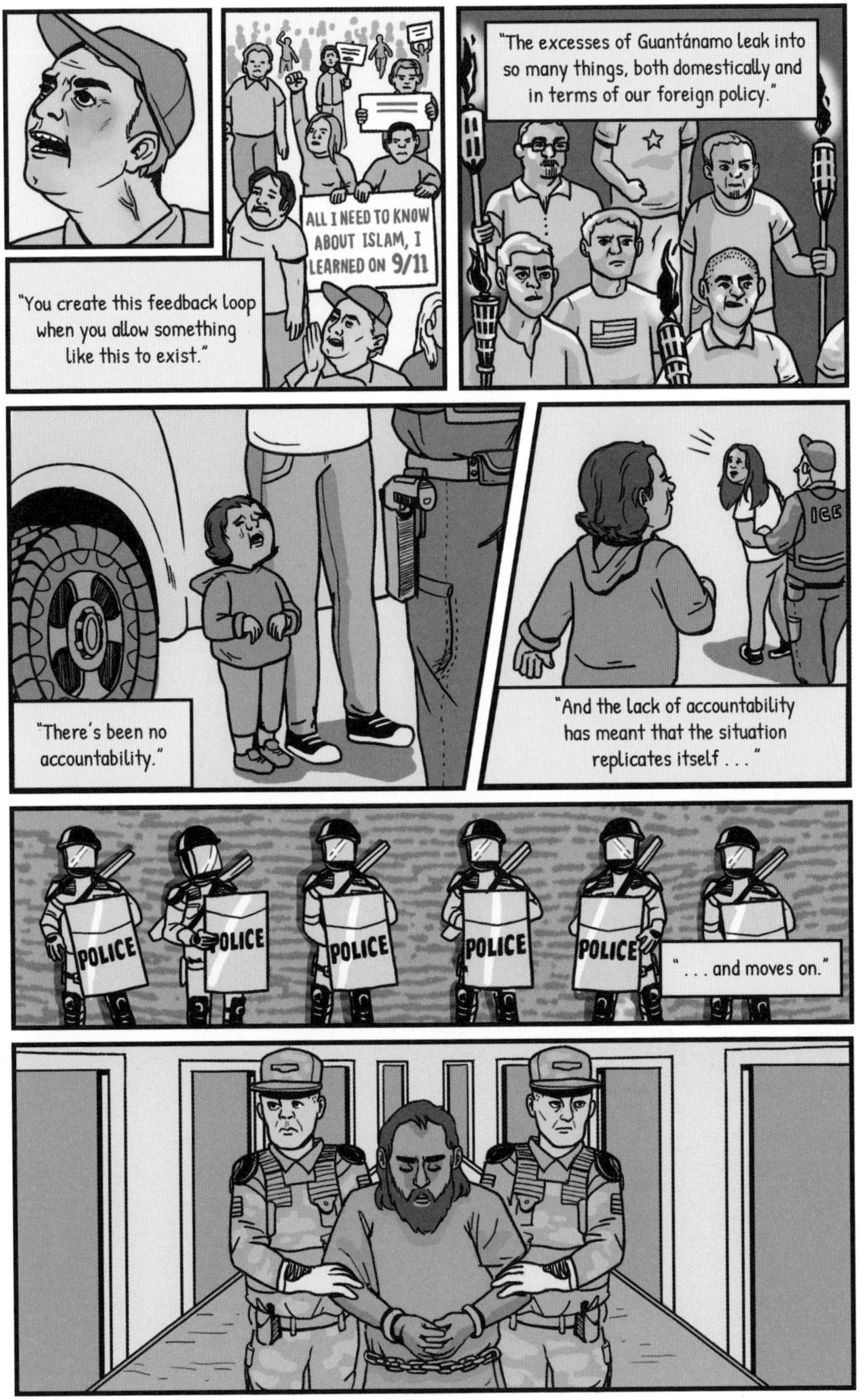
ALL I NEED TO KNOW ABOUT ISLAM, I LEARNED ON 9/11
"You create this feedback loop when you allow something like this to exist."
"The excesses of Guantánamo leak into so many things, both domestically and in terms of our foreign policy."
"There's been no accountability."
ICE
"And the lack of accountability has meant that the situation replicates itself . . ."
POLICE
POLICE
POLICE
POLICE
POLICE
" . . . and moves on."

CHAPTER ELEVEN

RETURN TO GUANTÁNAMO

ILLUSTRATED BY HAZEL NEWLEVANT

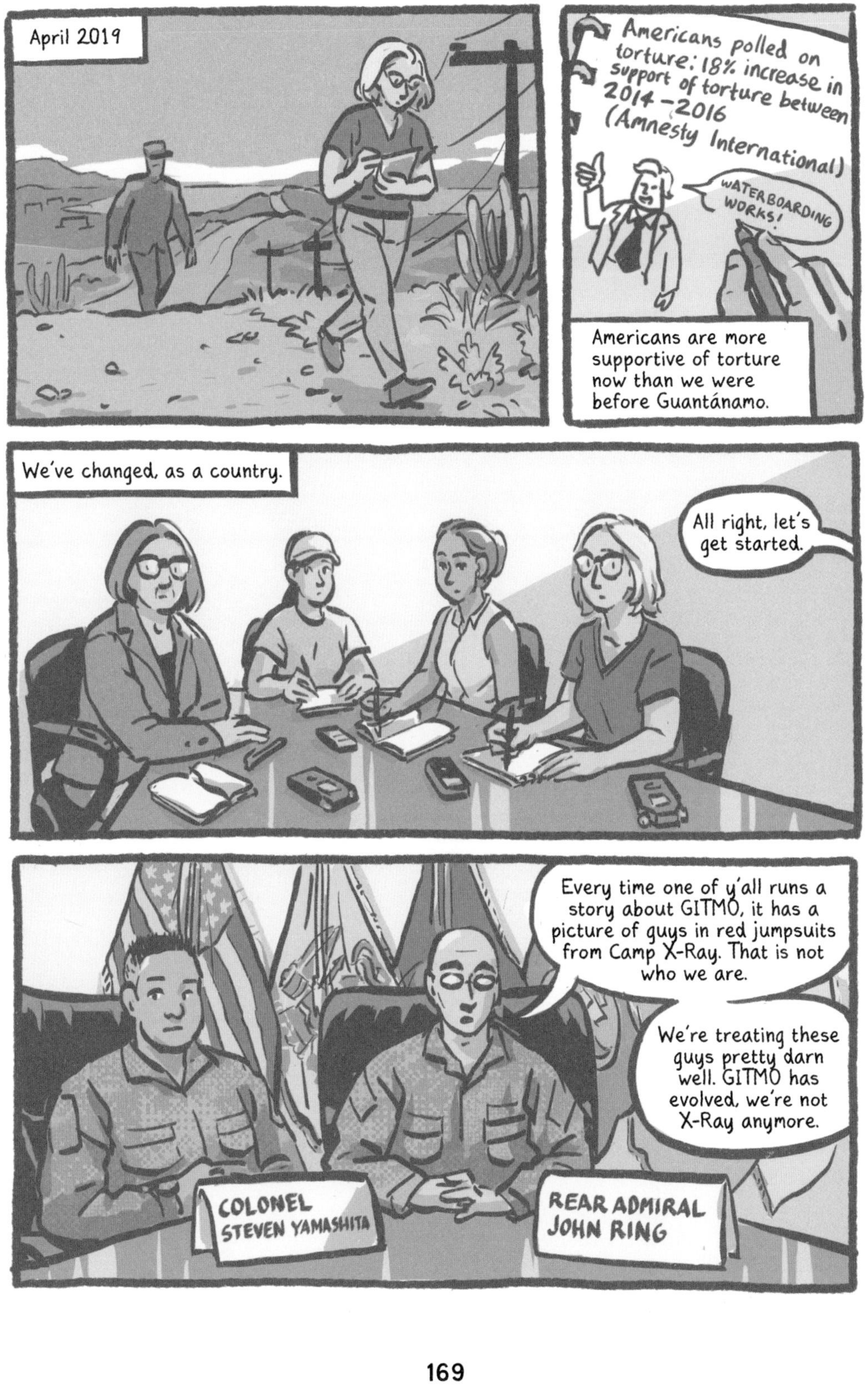
April 2019
Americans polled on torture: 18% increase in support of torture between 2014 - 2016 (Amnesty International)
WATERBOARDING WORKS!
Americans are more supportive of torture now than we were before Guantánamo.
We've changed, as a country.
All right, let's get started.
Every time one of y'all runs a story about GITMO, it has a picture of guys in red jumpsuits from Camp X-Ray. That is not who we are.
We're treating these guys pretty darn well. GITMO has evolved, we're not X-Ray anymore.
COLONEL STEVEN YAMASHITA
REAR ADMIRAL JOHN RING

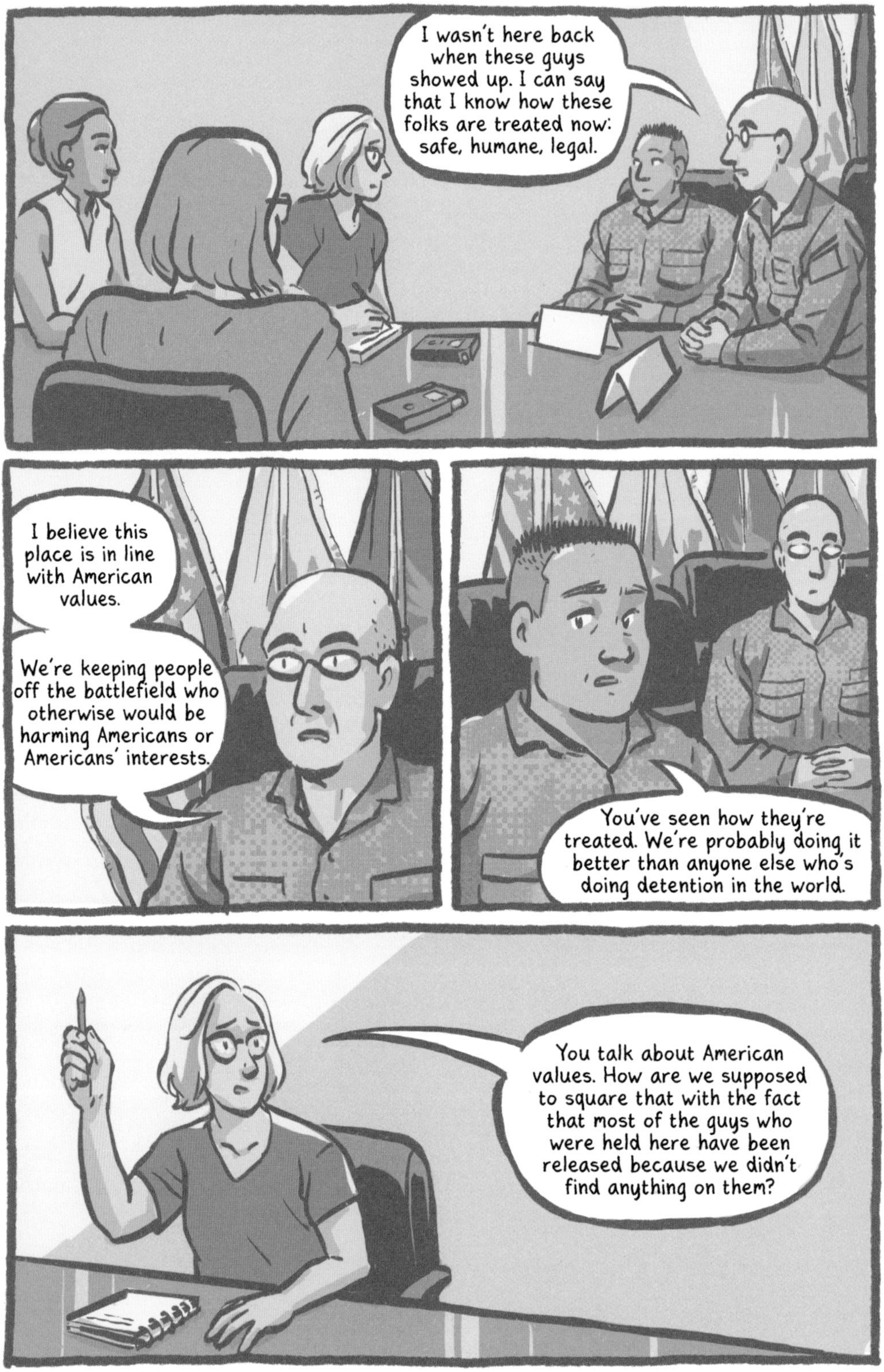
I wasn't here back when these guys showed up. I can say that I know how these folks are treated now: safe, humane, legal.
I believe this place is in line with American values.
We're keeping people off the battlefield who otherwise would be harming Americans or Americans' interests.
You've seen how they're treated. We're probably doing it better than anyone else who's doing detention in the world.
You talk about American values. How are we supposed to square that with the fact that most of the guys who were held here have been released because we didn't find anything on them?

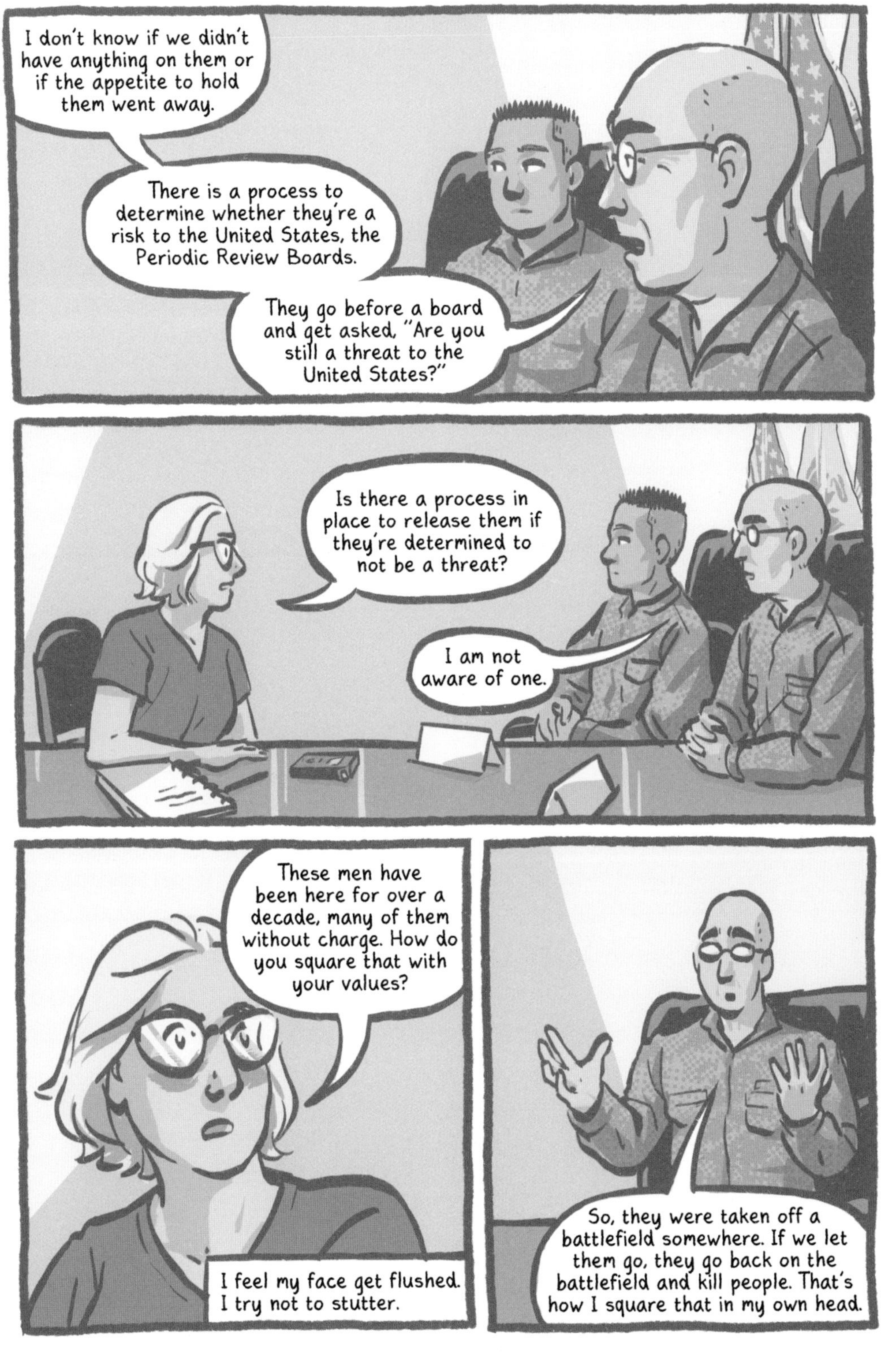
I don't know if we didn't have anything on them or if the appetite to hold them went away.
There is a process to determine whether they're a risk to the United States, the Periodic Review Boards.
They go before a board and get asked, "Are you still a threat to the United States?"
Is there a process in place to release them if they're determined to not be a threat?
I am not aware of one.
These men have been here for over a decade, many of them without charge. How do you square that with your values?
I feel my face get flushed. I try not to stutter.
So, they were taken off a battlefield somewhere. If we let them go, they go back on the battlefield and kill people. That's how I square that in my own head.

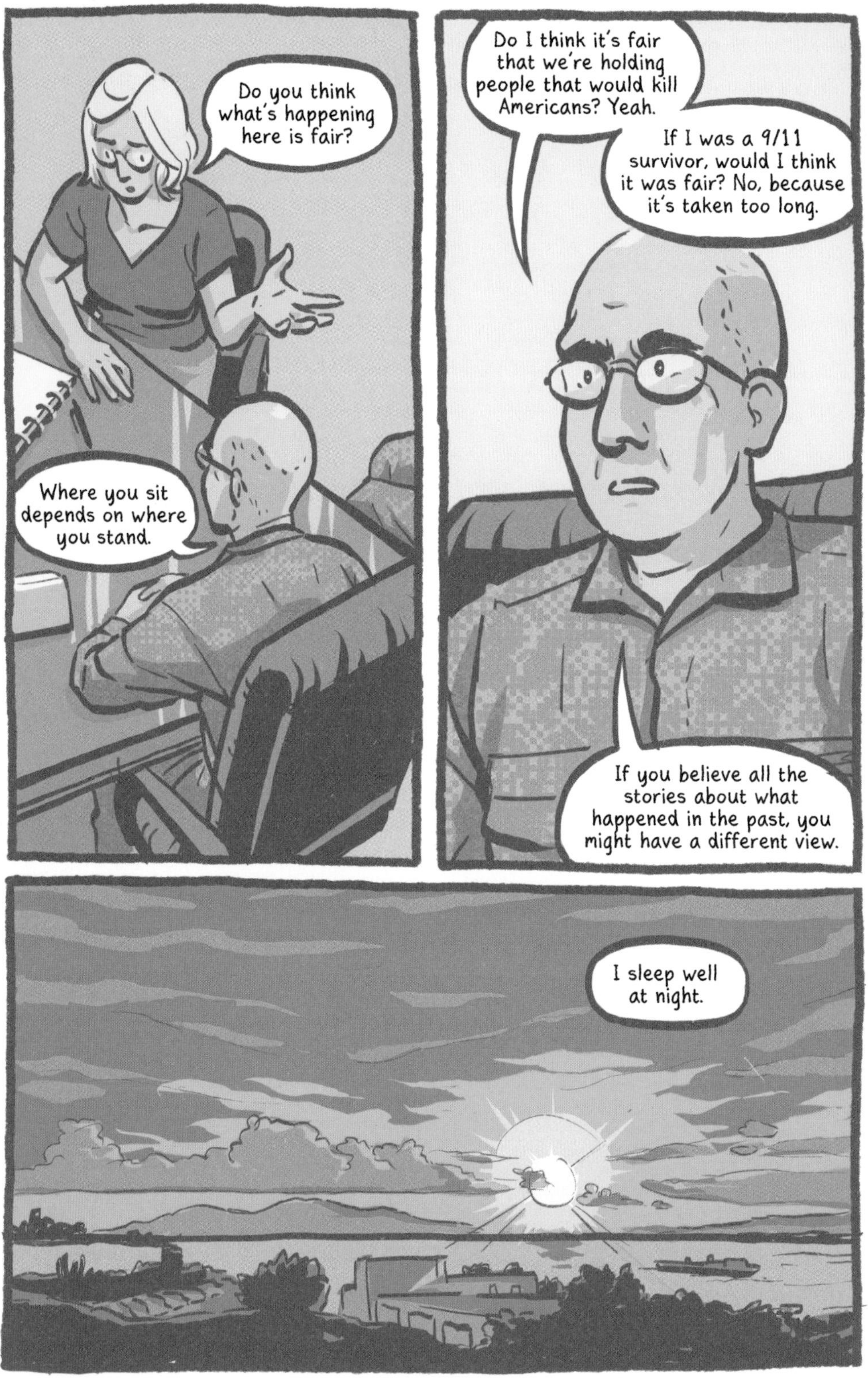
Do you think what's happening here is fair?
Where you sit depends on where you stand.
Do I think it's fair that we're holding people that would kill Americans? Yeah.
If I was a 9/11 survivor, would I think it was fair? No, because it's taken too long.
If you believe all the stories about what happened in the past, you might have a different view.
I sleep well at night.

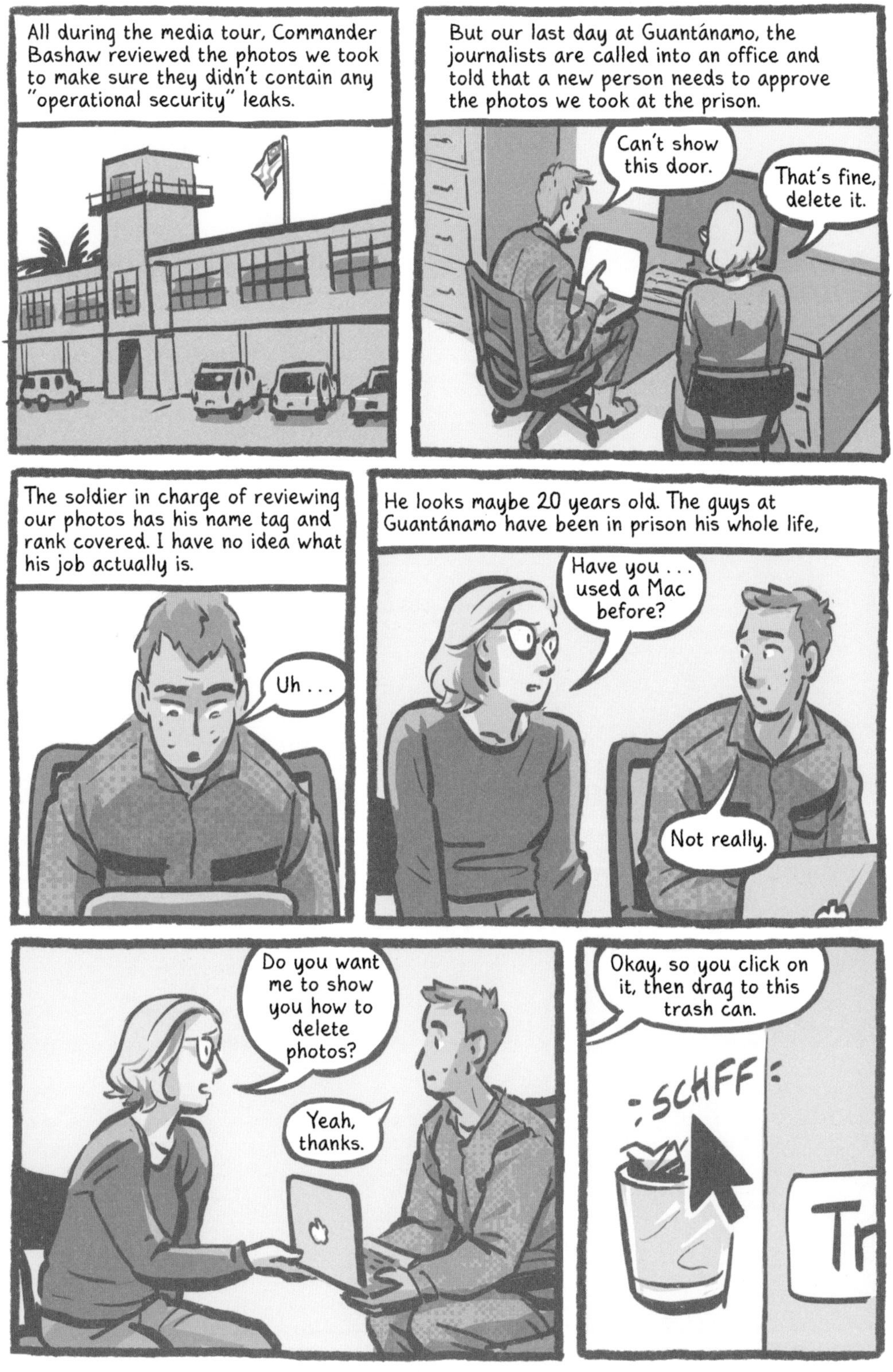
All during the media tour, Commander Bashaw reviewed the photos we took to make sure they didn't contain any "operational security" leaks.
But our last day at Guantánamo, the journalists are called into an office and told that a new person needs to approve the photos we took at the prison.
Can't show this door.
That's fine, delete it.
The soldier in charge of reviewing our photos has his name tag and rank covered. I have no idea what his job actually is.
Uh . . .
He looks maybe 20 years old. The guys at Guantánamo have been in prison his whole life.
Have you . . . used a Mac before?
Not really.
Do you want me to show you how to delete photos?
Yeah, thanks.
Okay, so you click on it, then drag to this trash can.
SCHFF

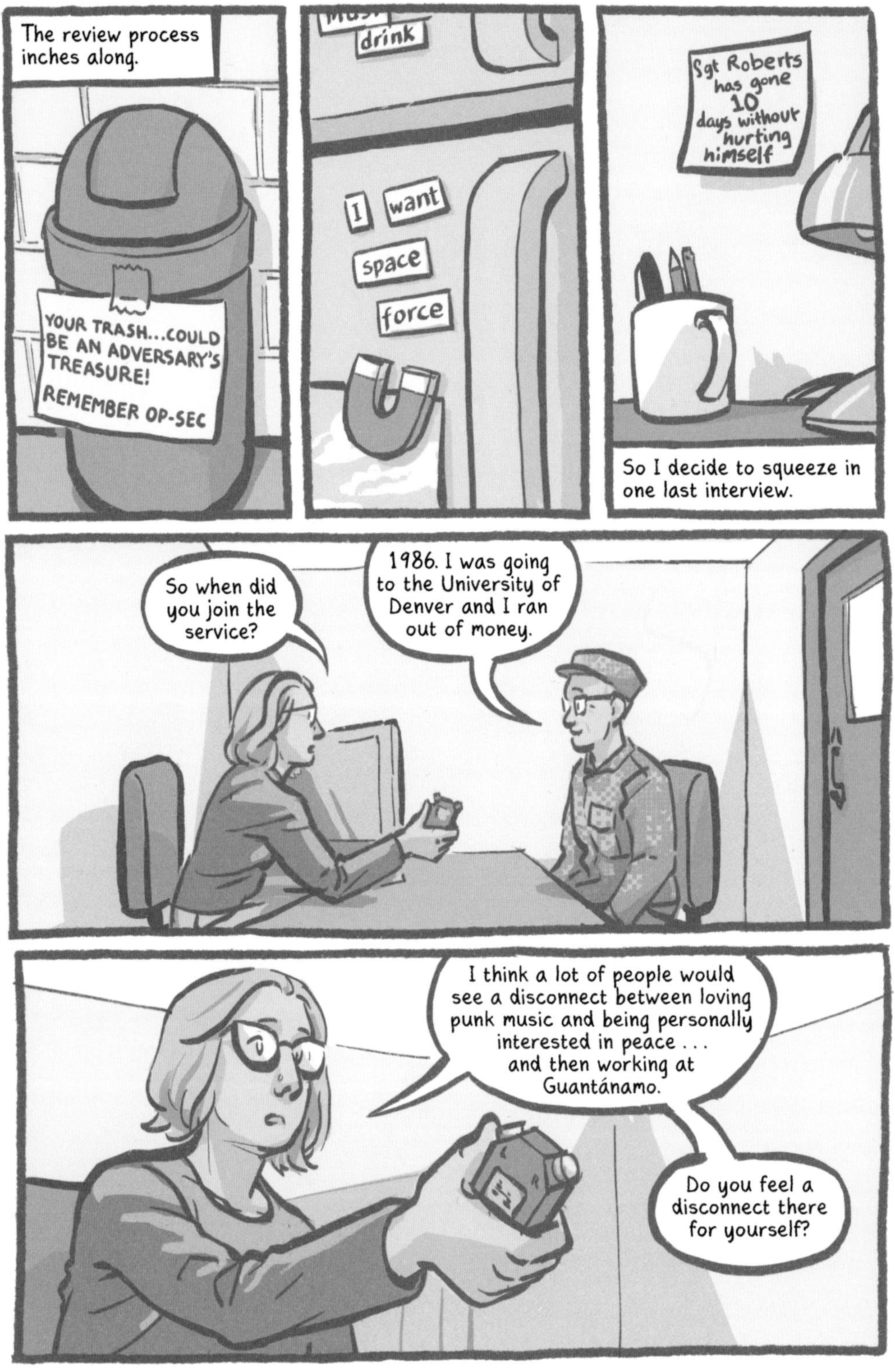
The review process inches along.
YOUR TRASH...COULD BE AN ADVERSARY'S TREASURE!
REMEMBER OP-SEC
drink
I want space force
Sgt Roberts has gone 10 days without hurting himself
So I decide to squeeze in one last interview.
So when did you join the service?
1986. I was going to the University of Denver and I ran out of money.
I think a lot of people would see a disconnect between loving punk music and being personally interested in peace . . . and then working at Guantánamo.
Do you feel a disconnect there for yourself?

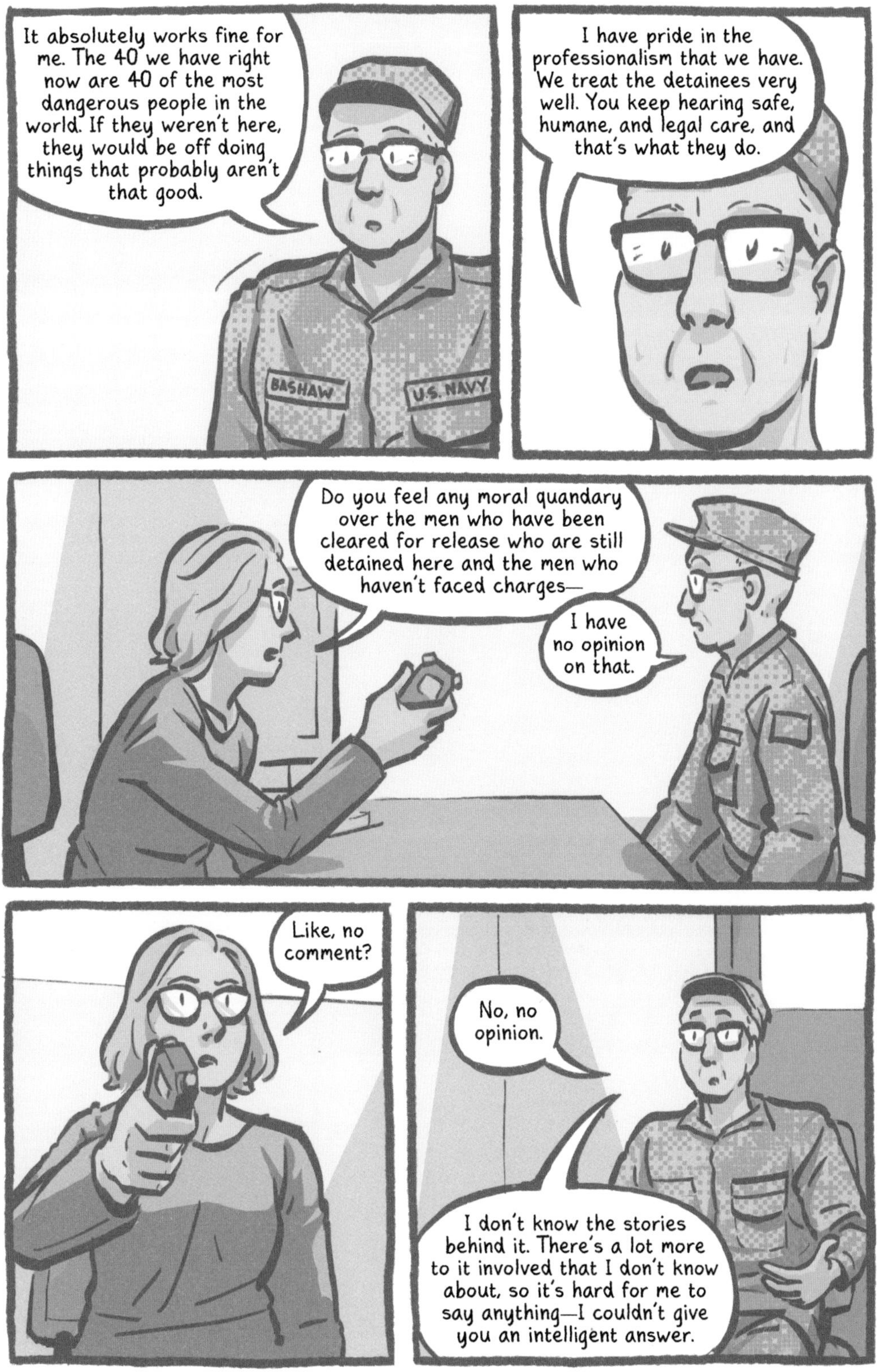
It absolutely works fine for me. The 40 we have right now are 40 of the most dangerous people in the world. If they weren't here, they would be off doing things that probably aren't that good.
BASHAW
U.S. NAVY
I have pride in the professionalism that we have. We treat the detainees very well. You keep hearing safe, humane, and legal care, and that's what they do.
Do you feel any moral quandary over the men who have been cleared for release who are still detained here and the men who haven't faced charges—
I have no opinion on that.
Like, no comment?
No, no opinion.
I don't know the stories behind it. There's a lot more to it involved that I don't know about, so it's hard for me to say anything—I couldn't give you an intelligent answer.

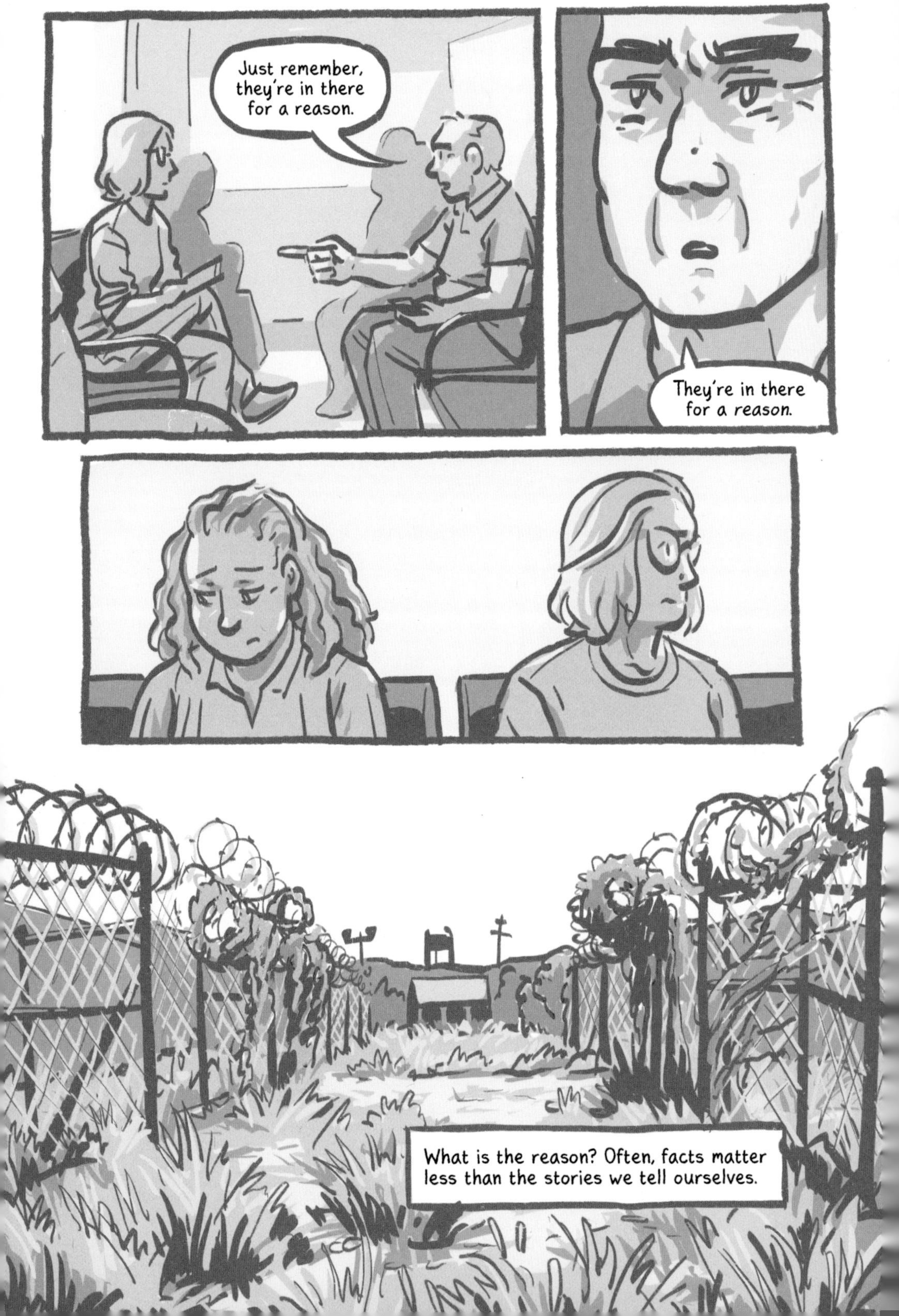

Just remember, they're in there for a reason.
They're in there for a *reason*.
What is the reason? Often, facts matter less than the stories we tell ourselves.

"ONE PERSON CAN MAKE A DIFFERENCE,
EVEN IF IT TAKES FORTY YEARS."
—FRED KOREMATSU

ART FROM ABU ZUBAYDAH

Originally published in "How America Tortures," 2019

The drawings on these pages are by Abu Zubaydah, a man who has been in U.S. custody since 2002. His torture at Guantánamo is described in Chapter Two of this book. In 2019, a group of Seton Hall University School of Law professors asked Zubaydah to illustrate the torture techniques American interrogators subjected him to for a report called "How America Tortures." His drawings on these pages show how he was shackled in stress positions, waterboarded, and forced into tiny confinement boxes for hours at a time. Of the last experience, Zubaydah writes, "The very strong pain made me scream unconsciously."

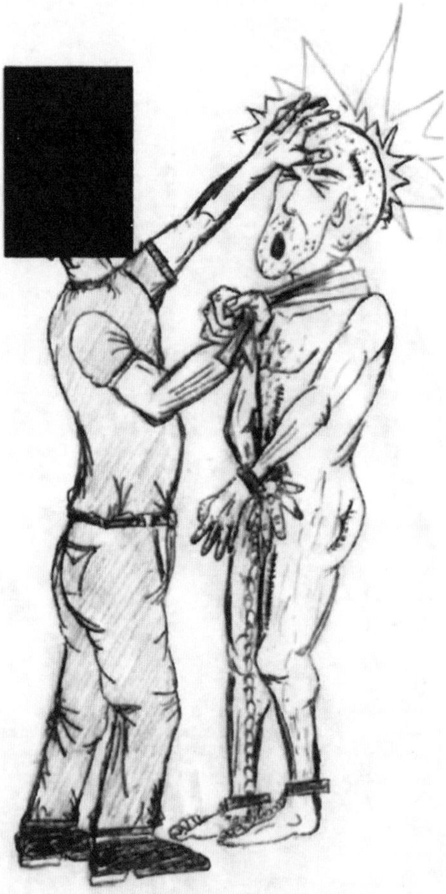

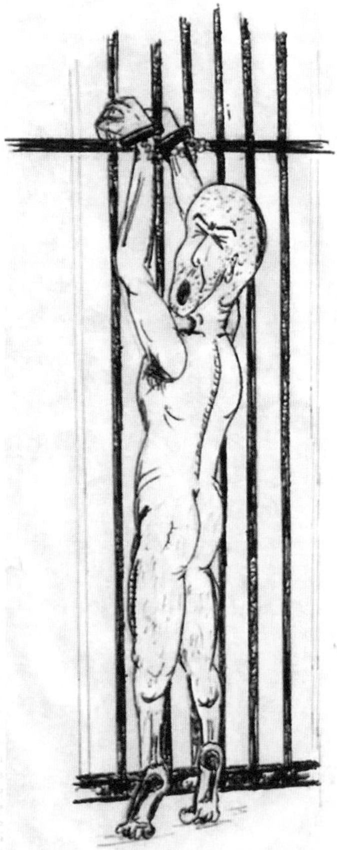

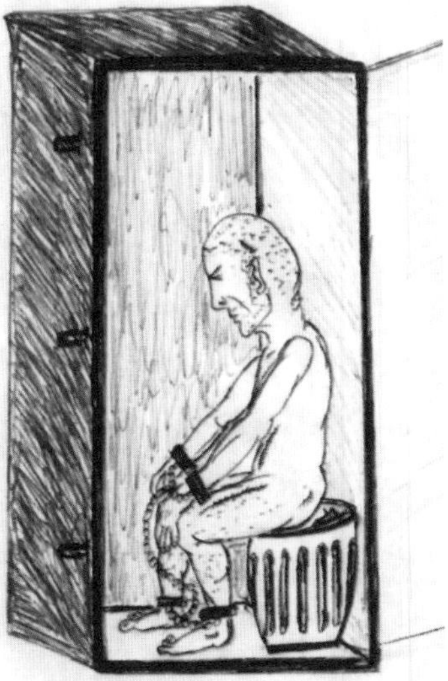

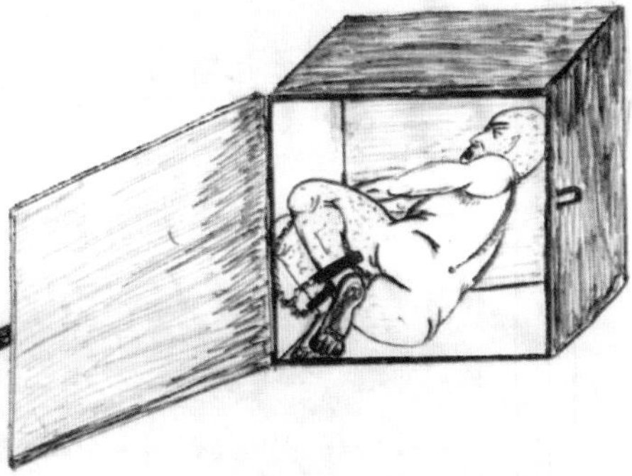

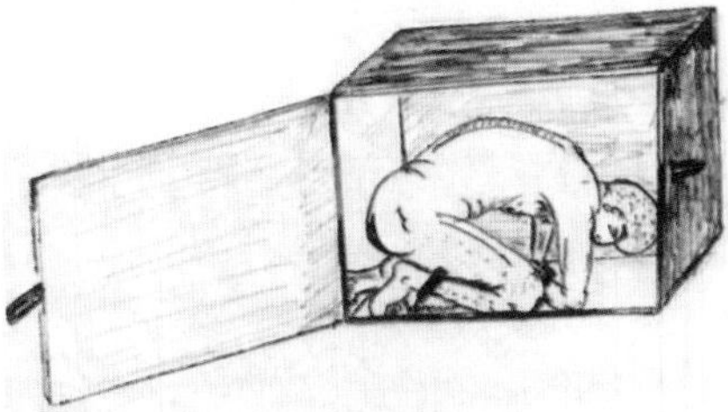

#10016

10016

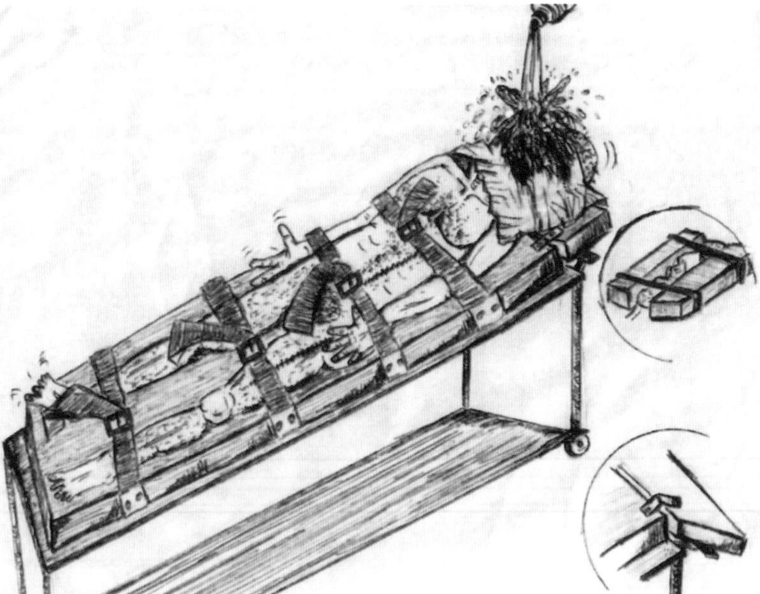

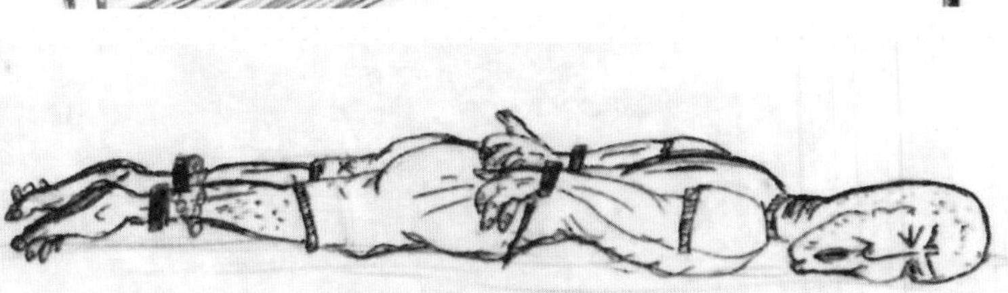

HOW THIS BOOK WAS MADE

For each chapter of this book, I interviewed someone about their experiences at Guantánamo. Then I transcribed the interview and edited their quotes into a comic script. When writing a comic, I think about how to tell each story in a visual way. The script winds up looking a lot like a screenplay, with dialogue, narration, and images for each panel, plus footnotes for facts and quotes.

Here's an example of a page from Chapter One, which is based on my visit to Guantánamo.

Panel one
An iconic image of Camp X-Ray from 2002.
    a.   Narration: In January 2002, the old makeshift refugee jail was turned into Camp X-Ray. It became the most infamous prison in the world.

Panel two
Camp X-Ray, overgrown with weeds and grasses.
    a.   Narration: Now it's an overgrown ruin.

Panel three
Commander Bashaw, other reporters, and me hiking through knee-high grass down a hill. The minivan is on the road at the top of the hill, in the background.
    a.   Bashaw: One good thing to know about Guantánamo Bay is there are no venomous snakes or spiders here.[1]

Panel four
Another image of Camp X-Ray, totally overgrown. A wooden guard tower is framed against the landscape. I'm standing next to a young-looking Alabama National Guardsman who's happily talking to me (Sgt Hearn).
    a.   Sergeant Hearn: At nighttime, this is a really nice place to look at the stars. It's pretty dark out here.[2]
    b.   Narration: Already, what happened here feels like ancient history.

Before I sent the script to the artists, I scoured public domain archives and put together a folder of visual references that would help them draw each scene. Clearly, each comic is not a photo-realistic representation of the world, but we tried to draw details accurately whenever possible. Here are two photos I took at Guantánamo that artist Hazel Newlevant used for this page.

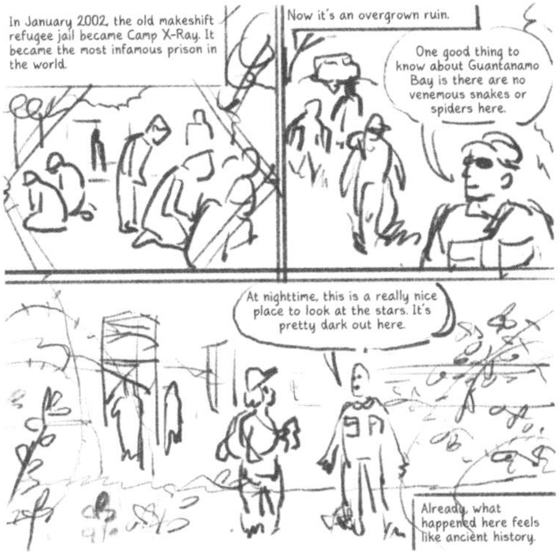
In January 2002, the old makeshift refugee jail became Camp X-Ray. It became the most infamous prison in the world.
Now it's an overgrown ruin.
One good thing to know about Guantanamo Bay is there are no venemous snakes or spiders here.
At nighttime, this is a really nice place to look at the stars. It's pretty dark out here.
Already, what happened here feels like ancient history.

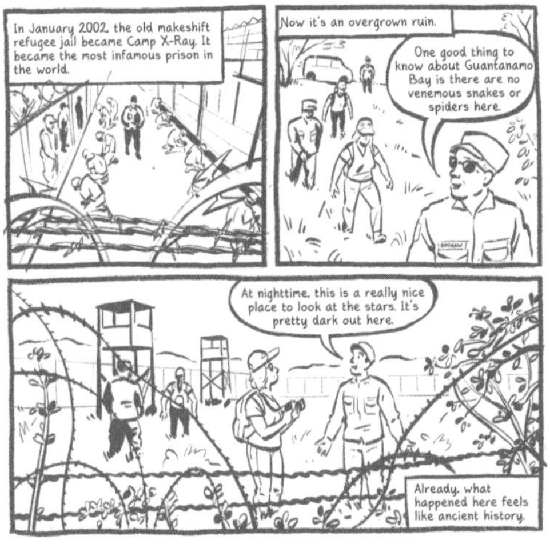
In January 2002, the old makeshift refugee jail became Camp X-Ray. It became the most infamous prison in the world.
Now it's an overgrown ruin.
One good thing to know about Guantanamo Bay is there are no venemous snakes or spiders here.
At nighttime, this is a really nice place to look at the stars. It's pretty dark out here.
Already, what happened here feels like ancient history.

Once the script was fact-checked and copyedited, the artists spent five months drawing the book. The first step is drawing thumbnails (which look like a storyboard), then pencils, inks, and finally colors. You can see how Hazel's art evolved from pencils to inks on the left.

I encourage the artists I work with to make whatever creative decisions they think are right. For example, Hazel combined two of the panels in the script into one to allow for a wider scene in the middle of the page. I find comics always turn out better when each collaborator has the ability to bring their own vision to the story. The final step of the art process is coloring. I wanted the colors to help create a somewhat cohesive visual feel for the book, since each of the twelve artists has a very different drawing style.

Because the content of the history is so dark, I envisioned a "sunset tones" color palette that would help draw readers into each story and evoke the surreal contrast between the beauty of Guantánamo Bay as a place and the horror of what has happened there. Artist Kazimir Lee developed this color palette, which the artists used as the dominant colors in their chapters.

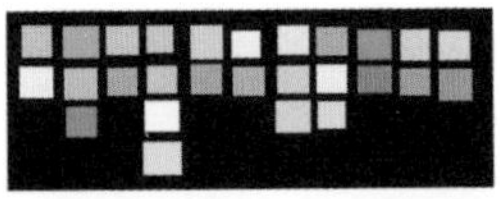

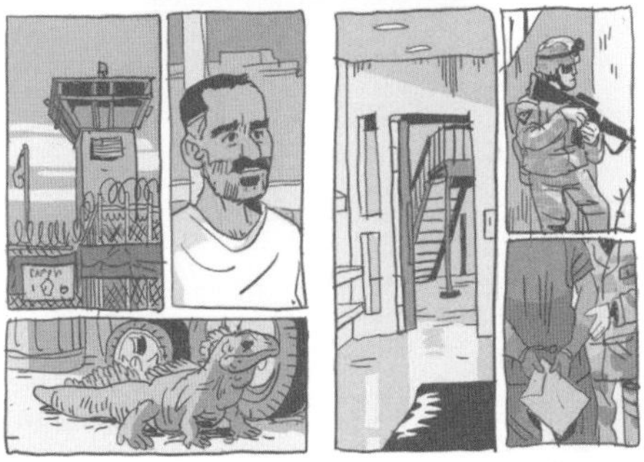

ABOUT THE ARTISTS

Gerardo Alba is a cartoonist from Mexico City whose work ranges from journalism to slice-of-life and fantasy. He's the art director of Little Red Bird Press, a small-press comics publisher. He currently lives with his wife and two cats in New Jersey, where they all constantly indulge in bagels and watching hockey.

Kasia Babis is a Polish cartoonist and political activist with an online following of more than 100,000 fans. Her viral comics succinctly skewer social issues ranging from racism to street harassment from a distinctly feminist perspective. She lives in Warsaw, Poland.

Alexandra Beguez is a Cuban American illustrator and cartoonist based in New Jersey. Her comics and illustrations have appeared in *Little Nemo: Dream Another Dream*, the *Nib*, the *Believer*, Longreads, and Buzzfeed, among others.

Tracy Chahwan is a comic book artist and illustrator. Her first graphic novel *Beirut Bloody Beirut* is published by Hachette in France. She has also worked on multiple short comics including *Stray Girls*, *Don't You Know Who My Mother Is?*, and *The Suicide*. She lives in Beirut, Lebanon.

Nomi Kane is an alumna of the Center for Cartoon Studies a contributor to the *New Yorker,* the *Nib*, CollegeHumor, and *Mad* magazine. By day she designs toys at Super7 HQ and teaches cartooning at California College of the Arts. She lives in Oakland, California, with her dog, Dino. Nomi's infographic illustrations appear on pages ix–xv.

Omar Khouri is a cofounder of *Samandal Comics*, the first experimental comics periodical in the Arab world. In 2010, his sociopolitical comic strip *Utopia* won Best Arabic Comic at the International Festival of Comics (FIBDA) in Algeria. He currently lives and works in north Lebanon.

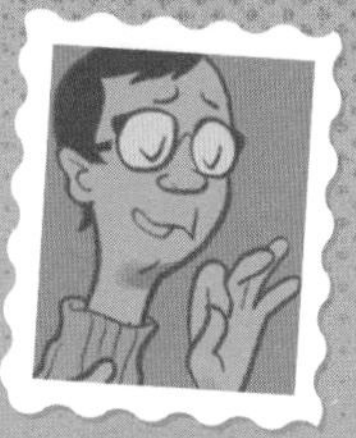

Kazimir Lee developed the color palette for this book. They are a Lambda Literary Award–winning cartoonist and illustrator based in Brooklyn, New York. They are a queer parent, pornographer, and journalist, and have contributed to *Oh Joy Sex Toy* and *Slate*.

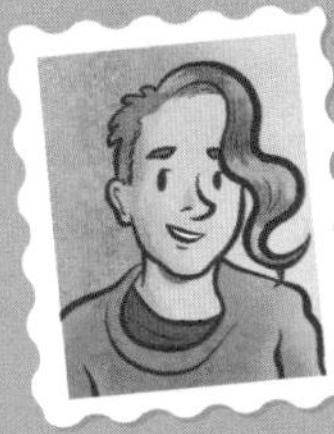

Kane Lynch is a cartoonist based in Portland, Oregon, whose comics and illustrations have appeared in publications including *Slate*, the *Nib*, and *Psychology Today*.

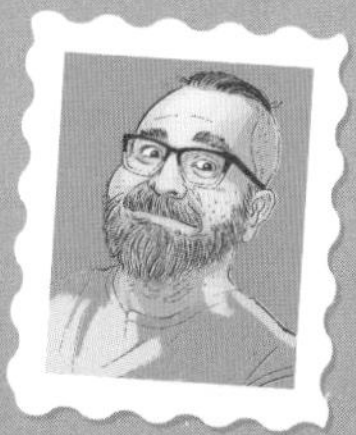

Maki Naro is an award-winning cartoonist, illustrator, and science communicator. Since 2010, he has been producing a body of work that can be best classified as "fan art for science." He is the author of seven self-published comic books spanning multiple topics from historical comedies to the importance of vaccination. Maki lives in Upstate New York with his loving partner and two dogs.

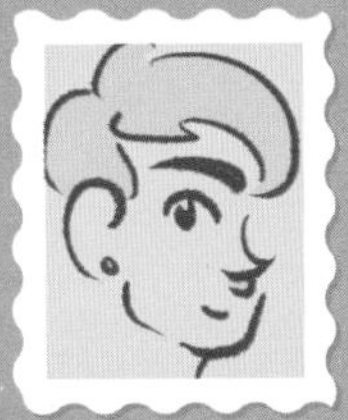

Hazel Newlevant is a Portland-raised, Queens-residing cartoonist whose comics include *No Ivy League, Sugar Town, If This Be Sin*, and *Tender-Hearted*. They have edited and published the anthologies *Chainmail Bikini* and *Comics for Choice*. Their work as a cartoonist and editor has been honored with the Ignatz Award, the Eisner Award, and the Prism Comics Queer Press Grant.

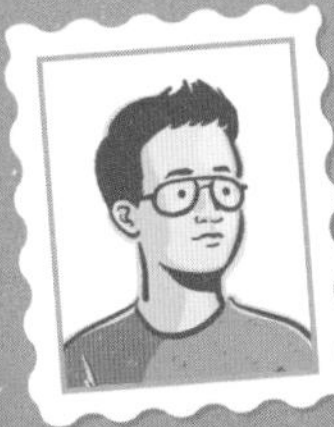

Jeremy Nguyen is an illustrator living in New York whose art and comics have been featured in the *New Yorker*, *Wired*, the *Guardian*, the *Nib*, *Time Out New York*, and *Brooklyn Magazine*.

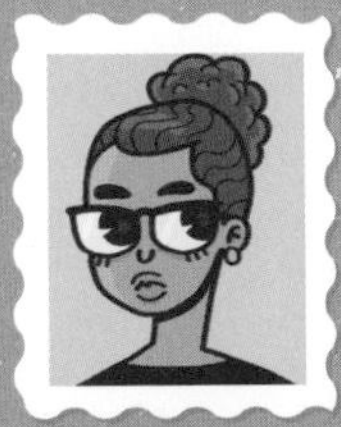

Chelsea Saunders is a freelance illustrator residing in New York. Since graduating from Boston University, she has drawn editorial illustrations and political comics for publications such as *Current Affairs*, *Holler*, and the *Nib*. She was the winner of the 2019 John Locher Memorial Award for cartoonists under twenty-six whose work demonstrates both clear opinions and strong artistry on political and social topics.

SOURCES

Many of the basic facts about Guantánamo are hotly debated. This book was fact-checked by historian and investigative journalist Andy Worthington. He is the author of *The Guantánamo Files* (Pluto Press, 2007), among other books, and fact-checked this book in September 2019.

GUANTÁNAMO FACTS

Number of prisoners in Guantánamo: "The Guantánamo Docket," *New York Times*. (last accessed Jan 13, 2020) https://www.nytimes.com/interactive/projects/guantanamo. This simple number is actually more difficult to pin down than one might imagine. From September 2003 to March 2004, the CIA operated a "black site" within the base, and researchers have established that five prisoners were held there. They were subsequently moved to other "black sites," and four of them were returned to Guantánamo in September 2006, but the other prisoner, Ibn Shaykh al-Libi, never made it back. He was transferred to Libyan custody, and died, reportedly by committing suicide, in May 2009. See: *CIA Torture Unredacted*. The Rendition Project and the Bureau of Investigative Journalism. July 2019. https://www.therenditionproject.org.uk/unredacted/index.html

Age of juvenile prisoners: "Youngest Guantanamo inmates freed," BBC, Jan 29, 2004, http://news.bbc.co.uk/2/hi/americas/3442781.stm.

Age of elderly prisoners: *Guantánamo by the Numbers*, ACLU, (last updated May 2018) https://www.aclu.org/issues/national-security/detention/guantanamo-numbers.

Number of juvenile prisoners: Andy Worthington, "WikiLeaks and the 22 Children of Guantánamo," Andyworthington.co.uk, Nov 6, 2011, http://www.andyworthington.co.uk/2011/06/11/wikileaks-and-the-22-children-of-guantanamo/.

Number of prisoners currently in Guantánamo: "The Guantánamo Docket: Current Detainees," *New York Times*.

Longest-held prisoners at Guantánamo: Carol Rosenberg, "Guantánamo by the Numbers," *Miami Herald*, Oct 25, 2016, https://www.miamiherald.com/news/nation-world/world/americas/guantanamo/article2163210.html.

Citizenship of prisoners: "The Guantánamo Docket: Overview," *New York Times*.

Rates of former Guantánamo prisoners who engaged in violence: "Recidivism" in *Report of the Constitution Project's Task Force on Detainee Treatment* (Washington, D.C.: The Constitution Project, Apr 16, 2013), 300, https://detaineetaskforce.org/pdf/Chapter-9_Recidivism.pdf.

Cost of bounties and number of prisoners sold for bounties: "A Brief History of Guantanamo Post 9-11," San Francisco: Witness to Guantanamo, (accessed Jan 13, 2010) http://witnesstoguantanamo.com/story-of-gtmo/.

Cost of operating Guantánamo: *Guantánamo by the Numbers*, ACLU.

Average cost of federal prisoner: U.S. Prisons Bureau, *Annual Determination of Average Cost of Incarceration*, Washington, D.C.: Federal Bureau of Prisons, Apr 2018.

CHAPTER ONE

7 "$4,085 a year": Miriam Pensack, "An American Century of Brutal Overseas Conquest Began at Guantánamo Bay," *Intercept*, Jul 4, 2018, https://theintercept.com/2018/07/04/guantanamo-bay-cuba/.

8 "They're assigned to GITMO for anywhere from four months to a year": Kathleen T. Rhem, "Deploying to Guantanamo Bay," American Forces Press Services, Apr 15, 2019.

9 "one former internment camp to start holding migrant children": Molly Hennessy-Fiske, "Japanese internment camp survivors protest Ft. Still migrant detention center," *Los Angeles Times*, Jun 22, 2019, https://www.latimes.com/nation/la-na-japanese-internment-fort-sill-2019-story.html

10 "only charged nine with crimes": "The Guantánamo Docket: Current Detainees," *New York Times*.

CHAPTER TWO

General references

Senate Select Committee on Intelligence, *Committee Study of the Central Intelligence Agency's Detention and Interrogation Program*, Chairman Dianne Feinstein, Dec 9, 2014, https://www.intelligence.senate.gov/sites/default/files/publications/CRPT-113srpt288.pdf.

Many of the scenes and quotes in this chapter are drawn from Mark Fallon's memoir: Mark Fallon, *Unjustifiable Means: The Inside Story of How the CIA, Pentagon, and US Government Conspired to Torture* (New York: Regan Arts, 2017).

19 "17 Americans were killed": CNN Staff, "USS Cole Bombing Fast Facts," CNN, Oct 5, 2019, https://www.cnn.com/2013/09/18/world/meast/uss-cole-bombing-fast-facts/index.html.

20 scenes from the TV show *24*: Jon Cassar, "Day 4: 7:00 a.m.–8:00 a.m.," *24*, Fox, Jan 9, 2005. (This episode had an initial viewership of 15.3 million Americans.)

21 "Yemeni courts sentenced him to 10 years": CNN Staff, "USS Cole Bombing Fast Facts," CNN, Oct 5, 2019, https://www.cnn.com/2013/09/18/world/meast/uss-cole-bombing-fast-facts/index.html.

22 "America was targeted": George W. Bush, "9/11 Address to the Nation," Sep 11, 2001, The White House, http://edition.cnn.com/2001/US/09/11/bush.speech.text/.

23 "extraordinary emergency exists": The White House, *Military Order of November 13, 2001*, by George W. Bush, Nov 13, 2001, https://fas.org/irp/offdocs/eo/mo-111301.htm.

24 "the least worst place we could have selected": Donald H. Rumsfeld, "DoD News Briefing - Secretary Rumsfeld and Gen. Myers," Dec 27, 2001, http://avalon.law.yale.edu/sept11/dod_brief137.asp.

24 "These are people that would gnaw through hydraulic lines": "Shackled detainees arrive in Guantanamo," CNN, Jan 11, 2002, http://edition.cnn.com/2002/WORLD/asiapcf/central/01/11/ret.detainee.transfer/index.html.

28 "What the fuck? Who *are* these guys?": Fallon, *Unjustifiable Means*, 48.

29 This CIA flyer is available online at https://commons.wikimedia.org/wiki/File:Taliban_bounty_flyer.jpg.

29 "$3 million in cash": "Guantanamo inmates say they were 'sold'," Associated Press, May 31, 2005, http://www.nbcnews.com/id/8049868/ns/world_news/t/guantanamo-inmates-say-they-were-sold/.

31 "Many Held at Guantanamo Not Likely Terrorists": Greg Miller, "Many Held at Guantanamo Not Likely Terrorists," *Los Angeles Times*, Dec 22, 2002, https://www.latimes.com/archives/la-xpm-2002-dec-22-la-na-gitmo22dec22-story.html.

31 "I was in 'Nam! I know how to do interrogations!": Fallon, *Unjustifiable Means*, 53.

32 "He was captured while trying to cross the Pakistani border": U.S. Department of Defense, *JTF-GTMO Detainee Assessment: Mohammed al Qahtani*, Oct 30, 2008, accessed: https://www.nytimes.com/interactive/projects/guantanamo/detainees/63-mohammed-al-qahtani.

34 "We've got to show them that we have more teeth than they have ass, hoo-ah": Fallon, *Unjustifiable Means*, 95.

35 All text is from the interrogator's official logs: U.S. Department of Defense, *Interrogation Log: Detainee 063*, Department of Defense, 2002–2003, accessed: http://content.time.com/time/2006/log/log.pdf.

36 "President Bush signed a secret order": *Committee Study of the Central Intelligence Agency's Detention and Interrogation Program*, 19.

36 "covertly arresting and interrogating people at 'black sites'": Ryan Tate, "Nine CIA 'Black Sites' Where Detainees Were Tortured," *Intercept*, Dec 9, 2014, https://theintercept.com/2014/12/09/map-of-cia-black-sites/.

36 "partly to avoid having to declare the prisoners' existence to the International Red Cross": *Committee Study of the Central Intelligence Agency's Detention and Interrogation Program*, iii.

37 "ghost detainees": Douglas Jehl, "The Struggle for Iraq: Prisoners; Some Iraqis Held Outside Control of Top General," *New York Times*, May 17, 2004, https://www.nytimes.com/2004/05/17/world/the-struggle-for-iraq-prisoners-some-iraqis-held-outside-control-of-top-general.html.

37 "wrote up another secret order.": U.S. Department of Justice, Office of Legal Counsel, *Application of Treaties and Laws to al Qaeda and Taliban Detainees*, by John Yoo, Jan 9, 2002, accessed: https://en.wikipedia.org/wiki/File:Yoo_memo.pdf.

37 "It said that international laws about how to treat prisoners of war, the Geneva Conventions, didn't apply": The White House, *Humane Treatment of Taliban and al Qaeda Detainees*, by George W. Bush, Feb 7, 2002, accessed: http://www.pegc.us/archive/White_House/bush_memo_20020207_ed.pdf.

38 "The agency secretly paid two psychologists millions of dollars": Robert Windrem, "CIA Paid Torture Teachers More than $80 Million," NBC, Dec 9, 2014, https://www.nbcnews.com/storyline/cia-torture-report/cia-paid-torture-teachers-more-80-million-n264756.

38 "Neither psychologist had experience": *Committee Study of the Central Intelligence Agency's Detention and Interrogation Program*, 21.

39 Descriptions of torture: *Committee Study of the Central Intelligence Agency's Detention and Interrogation Program*, 12–13 of the torture report, and Denbeaux et al, "How America Tortures" (Nov 27, 2019), https://ssrn.com/abstract=3494533.

41 "agents destroyed videotapes": *Committee Study of the Central Intelligence Agency's Detention and Interrogation Program*, vii.

41 "the men would be there forever": David Johnston and Mark Mazzetti, "A Window Into C.I.A.'s Embrace of Secret Jails," *New York Times*, Aug 12, 2009, https://www.nytimes.com/2009/08/13/world/13foggo.html.

41 "inaccurate in every single case": *Committee Study of the Central Intelligence Agency's Detention and Interrogation* Program, xi.

41 "the CIA eventually concluded that Abu Zubaydah was not actually a member of Al-Qaeda": ibid, 410.

CHAPTER THREE

45 "angel of death": Richard K. De Atley, "'Angel of Death' Dies in Prison," *Press-Enterprise*, Aug 12, 2010.

48 *Time* magazine cover: Matt Mahurin, *Time*, May 17, 2004.

49 "Instead of coming to give us support . . .": Samira Simone, "Abu Ghraib head finds vindication in newly released memos," CNN, Apr 22, 2009, http://www.cnn.com/2009/US/04/22/us.torture.karpinski.index.html.

50 "Indefinite detention for the purpose..." and "History and common sense...": Justice Sandra Day O'Connor, *Hamdi et al v. Rumsfeld*, Jun 28, 2004, 13 and 23, https://www.supremecourt.gov/opinions/03pdf/03-6696.pdf.

50 "The Bush administration refused to reveal who was imprisoned in Guantanamo.": "U.S. Reveals Identities of Detainees," Associated Press, Mar 4, 2006, https://www.nytimes.com/2006/03/04/politics/us-reveals-identities-of-detainees.html.

58 "This current list came . . .": Renee Montagne and Scott Silliman, "Pentagon Releases Names of Guantanamo Prisoners," NPR, *Morning Edition*, Apr 20, 2006, https://www.npr.org/templates/story/story.php?storyId=5352799.

60 "she thought it might be a joke.": Tim Golden, "Naming Names at GITMO," *New York Times Magazine*, Oct 21, 2007, https://www.nytimes.com/2007/10/21/magazine/21Diaz-t.html.

61 "he received the Distinguished Service Medal": Thom Shanker, "General in Abu Ghraib Case Retires After Forced Delay," *New York Times*, Aug 1, 2006, https://www.nytimes.com/2006/08/01/washington/01military.html.

CHAPTER FOUR

General reference

Many of the scenes and quotes in this chapter are drawn from Moazzam Begg's memoir: Moazzam Begg and Victoria Brittain, *Enemy Combatant* (New York: New Press, 2006).

75 "Moazzam traveled whenever he could.": Tim Golden, "Jihadish or Victim? Ex-Detainee Makes a Case," *New York Times*, Jun 15, 2006, https://www.nytimes.com/2006/06/15/world/15begg.html.

77 This page depicts the beating and murder of 22-year-old Afghan taxi driver Dilawar, who was held in the cell next to Begg. See: Tim Golden, "In U.S. Report, Brutal Details of 2 Afghan Inmates' Deaths," *New York Times*, May 20, 2005, https://www.nytimes.com/2005/05/20/world/asia/in-us-report-brutal-details-of-2-afghan-inmates-deaths.html and *Taxi to the Dark Side*, directed by Alex Gibney (New York: ThinkFilm, 2007).

79 "The Joint Task Force said . . .": U.S. Department of Defense. *Recommendation to Retain Under DoD Control for Guantanamo Detainee Moazzam Begg*, Nov 11, 2003, accessed: https://www.nytimes.com/interactive/projects/guantanamo/detainees/558-moazzam-begg/documents/11.

CHAPTER FIVE

General references

Many of Thomas Wilner's quotes in this chapter are drawn from an interview conducted by the Rule of Law Oral History Project at Columbia University. The quotes are used with permission.

Thomas Wilner, "The Reminiscences of Thomas B. Wilner," interview by Ronald J. Grele, Rule of Law Oral History Project, Oral History Archives at Columbia, Rare Book & Manuscript Library, Columbia University in the City of New York, 2010, http://www.columbia.edu/cu/libraries/inside/ccoh_assets/ccoh_8626509_transcript.pdf.

87 "Shackled Detainees Arrive . . .": "Shackled detainees arrive in Guantanamo," CNN, Jan 11, 2002, http://edition.cnn.com/2002/WORLD/asiapcf/central/01/11/ret.detainee.transfer/index.html.

91 "74% of the people were released after the hearings": Marc Falkoff, "What I would have said about Gitmo," *Northwest Herald*, Dec 3, 2009, https://www.nwherald.com/2009/12/03/guest-column-what-i-would-have-said-about-gitmo/ag486f1/.

94 "High Approval Ratings for President Bush Continue": "Presidential Approval Ratings -- George W. Bush," *Gallup*, https://news.gallup.com/poll/116500/presidential-approval-ratings-george-bush.aspx.

96 Quotes from justices: Hugo Black and Frank Murphy, *Korematsu v. United States*, https://www.law.cornell.edu/supremecourt/text/323/214#writing-USSC_CR_0323_0214_ZD.

96 "We should be vigilant to make sure this will never happen again.": *Khaled A. F. Al Odah et al v. United States. Brief of Amicus Curiae Fred Korematsu*, http://www.pegc.us/archive/Supreme_Court/Al-Odah_Rasul_cert/cert_amicus_Koramatsu.htm.

96 *"Fred Korematsu v. George W. Bush"*: Nat Hentoff, "Fred Korematsu v. George W. Bush," *Village Voice*, Feb 17, 2004, https://www.villagevoice.com/2004/02/17/fred-koramatsu-v-george-w-bush/.

98 "A state of war is not a blank check for the President": O'Connor, *Hamdi v. Rumsfeld*, 29.

CHAPTER SIX

General references

Many of Morris Davis's quotes in this chapter are drawn from an interview conducted by the Rule of Law Oral History Project at Columbia University. The quotes are used with permission.

Morris D. Davis, "The Reminiscences of Morris D. Davis," interview by Myron A. Farber, Rule of Law Oral History Project, Oral History Archives at Columbia, Rare Book & Manuscript Library, Columbia University in the City of New York, 2012, http://www.columbia.edu/cu/libraries/inside/ccoh_assets/ccoh_10110362_transcript.pdf.

103 "President Roosevelt issued an executive order": "Nazi Saboteurs Trial," Library of Congress, Military Legal Resources, Aug 15, 2014, https://www.loc.gov/rr/frd/Military_Law/nazi-saboteurs-trial.html.

103 "they handed down guilty verdicts for all eight men.": ibid.

104 "He issued a very similar order": The White House, *Military Order of November 13, 2001*.

105 "Judgment of Death against those soldiers": "The Boston Massacre Trials," John Adams Historical Society, http://www.john-adams-heritage.com/boston-massacre-trials/.

106 "These cases will be the Nuremberg of our times.": This exchange is recorded from Col. Davis's perspective in his Rule of Law interview, 36–39.

108 infographic numbers: Carol Rosenberg, "Guantánamo by the Numbers" and "The Guantánamo Docket: Overview," *New York Times*.

108 "As of 2019, the U.S. has only charged 2 percent of Guantánamo prisoners with a crime": Others have been charged, but have had those charges dropped. Even of those convicted, three have had their convictions overturned, and one had his conviction partially overturned. See: "Dropped Charges, Overturned Convictions, and Delayed Trials in Guantanamo Military Commissions," Human Rights First, Feb 16, 2018, https://www.humanrightsfirst.org/resource/dropped-charges-overturned-convictions-and-delayed-trials-guantanamo-military-commissions.

111 "Am I not entitled to detain the prisoner for the duration of the conflict?": This exchange is recorded from Col. Davis's perspective in his Rule of Law interview, 140.

112 "How quickly can you charge David Hicks?" This exchange is recorded from Col. Davis's perspective in his Rule of Law interview, 74, 80–81. He has shared this anecdote widely with media for many years. See: Jason Leopold, "My Tortured Journey With Former Guantanamo Detainee David Hicks," *Truthout*, Feb 16, 2011, https://truthout.org/articles/my-tortured-journey-with-former-guantanamo-detainee-david-hicks/.

113 "at Haynes's request, Davis gathered enough evidence . . .": "U.S. Acknowledges Conviction of David Hicks, Guantanamo Detainee, Should Not Stand," *ProPublica*, Jan 28, 2015, https://www.propublica.org/article/u.s.-acknowledges-conviction-of-david-hicks-guantanamo-detainee-not-valid.

114 "An American military tribunal": "Australian Hicks must serve 9 Months," NBC, Mar 30, 2007, http://www.nbcnews.com/id/17870312/ns/world_news-terrorism/t/australian-hicks-must-serve-months/#.XQq3SNNKjyU.

114 "Australian Taliban to Go Home.": "Australian Taliban to Go Home: Hicks Pleads Guilty to Terror Charges," *der Spiegel*, Mar 27, 2007, https://www.spiegel.de/international/world/australian-taliban-to-go-home-hicks-pleads-guilty-to-terror-charges-a-474140.html.

114 "His conviction was later overturned": "Australian David Hicks overturns US terrorism conviction," BBC, Feb 19, 2015, https://www.bbc.com/news/world-australia-31528159.

114 "Colonel Davis resigned his post in protest": Amanda Terkel, "Chief Guantanamo Prosecutor Resigned When Placed Under Command of Torture Advocate," ThinkProgress, Dec 11, 2007, https://thinkprogress.org/chief-guantanamo-prosecutor-resigned-when-placed-under-command-of-torture-advocate-c682a18b85b3/.

CHAPTER SEVEN

This chapter was adapted from a work-in-progress memoir by Mansoor Adayfi, with editing assistance from Antonio Aiello. This comic was originally published by the *Nib* and is adapted and reprinted here with permission.

CHAPTER EIGHT

134 "President Obama signed an executive order directing the CIA": Mark Mazzetti and William Glaberson, "Obama Issues Directive to Shut Down Guantánamo Bay," *New York Times*, Jan 21, 2009, https://www.nytimes.com/2009/01/22/us/politics/22gitmo.html.

134 "Living our values doesn't make us weaker": "'America does not torture,' Obama tells Congress, Reuters, Feb 24, 2009, https://www.reuters.com/article/us-obama-torture-sb/america-does-not-torture-obama-tells-congress-idUSTRE51O0RY20090225.

134 "He ordered that the cases of the 240 people . . .": Department of Justice et al. *Final Report*, Guantanamo Review Task Force, Jan 22, 2010, https://www.justice.gov/sites/default/files/ag/legacy/2010/06/02/guantanamo-review-final-report.pdf.

138 "He had a passion for poetry. He loved Rumi": "Emad Hassan," Reprieve. http://reprieve.org/cases/emad-hassan/.

138 "a team of Pakistani troops and CIA officers raided his dorm, acting on a tip about it being an al-Qaeda safehouse": Lauren Walker, "How a Botched Translation Landed Emad Hassan in Gitmo," *Newsweek*, Sept 10, 2015, https://www.newsweek.com/2015/09/18/emad-hassan-guantanamo-bay-hunger-strike-al-qaeda-370475.html.

138 "Were there innocent Arabs in some of those houses?": ibid.

138 "$5,000 bounty": ibid.

141 "the military had insisted Emad was a 'high risk' to the United States and a recruiter for al-Qaeda": U.S. Department of Defense, *JTF-GTMO Detainee Assessment: Emad Hassan*, Oct 31, 2008, accessed: https://www.nytimes.com/interactive/projects/guantanamo/detainees/680-emad-abdalla-hassan.

CHAPTER NINE

148 "Abdul Latif Nasir handwrote a 2,000-word English-Arabic dictionary": "Cleared Guantánamo Prisoner Files Last-Ditch Lawsuit Seeking Immediate Release," Reprieve, Jan 19, 2017, https://www.commondreams.org/newswire/2017/01/19/cleared-guantanamo-prisoner-files-last-ditch-lawsuit-seeking-immediate-release.

150 "In the dark halls of Abu Ghraib": Barack Obama, "The War We Need to Win," Aug 1, 2007, Washington, D.C., https://www.americanrhetoric.com/speeches/barackobamawilsoncenter.htm.

150 "Have you heard? We're getting out of here!" Connie Bruck, "Why Obama Has Failed to Close Guantánamo," *New Yorker*, Jul 25, 2016, anamohttps://www.newyorker.com/magazine/2016/08/01/why-obama-has-failed-to-close-guantanamo.

150 "Guantánamo makes us less safe . . ." and "Guantánamo is the perfect place for these terrorists.": David M. Herszenhorn, "Funds to Close Guantánamo Denied," *New York Times*, May 20, 2009. https://www.nytimes.com/2009/05/21/us/politics/21detain.html.

150 "The only problem with Guantánamo Bay is that there are too many empty cells . . .": Max Brantley, "Tom Cotton's 'bizarre speech' on Guantanamo," *Arkansas Times*, Feb 6, 2015, https://arktimes.com/arkansas-blog/2015/02/06/tom-cottons-bizarre-speech-on-guantanamo.

151 "Obama used an executive order . . ." The White House, Office of the Press Secretary, *Executive Order 13567*, by Barack Obama, March 7, 2011, https://obamawhitehouse.archives.gov/the-press-office/2011/03/07/executive-order-13567-periodic-review-individuals-detained-guant-namo-ba.

151 "196 men imprisoned in Guantánamo were cleared for release": "Facts About the Transfer of Guantanamo Detainees," Human Rights First, Oct 10, 2018, https://www.humanrightsfirst.org/resource/facts-about-transfer-guantanamo-detainees

153 "This morning, I watched President Obama talking about GITMO . . .": David Welna, "Trump Has Vowed to Fill Guantanamo with 'Some Bad Dudes'—But Who?" *All Things Considered*, NPR, Nov 14, 2016, https://www.npr.org/sections/parallels/2016/11/14/502007304/trump-has-vowed-to-fill-guantanamo-with-some-bad-dudes-but-who.

154 "an article came out on the December 19 in the *New York Times* that named detainees . . .": Charlie Savage, "Obama Administration Intends to Transfer 17 or 18 Guantánamo Detainees," *New York Times*, Dec 19, 2016, https://www.nytimes.com/2016/12/19/us/politics/guantanamo-bay-obama.html.

154 "The government claimed that the Moroccans had gotten back to them eight days too late.": ibid. Under legislation passed by Congress, the secretary of defense had to provide 30 days' notification to lawmakers before releasing a Guantánamo prisoner; the Moroccan government got back to the U.S. government just 22 days before Obama left office.

155 "A seventh grader asked him a question": Bruck, "Why Obama Has Failed to Close Guantanamo."

CHAPTER TEN

161 "the U.S. government gave the two men a choice": Charlie Savage, "2 Libyan Guantánamo Inmates Are Transferred to Senegal," *New York Times*, Apr 4, 2016, https://www.nytimes.com/2016/04/05/us/politics/guantanamo-transfers.html?module=inline.

164 "In Libya, I will have no life . . .": Dionne Searcey and Charlie Savage, "Senegal Eyes Deporting Ex-Detainee as Critics Accuse U.S. of Neglect," *New York Times*, Apr 5, 2018, https://www.nytimes.com/2018/04/05/us/politics/guantanamo-detainees-senegal-libya.html?module=inline.

167 "All I need to know about Islam" sign is based on an actual poster: Nicholas Brooklier, "Islamophobia: The Stereotyping and Prejudice Towards Muslims Since 9/11," *Law and Justice in Real Time*, Washington State University, Dec 17, 2015, https://hub.wsu.edu/law-justice-realtime/2015/12/17/islamophobia-the-stereotyping-and-prejudice-towards-muslims-since-911/.

CHAPTER ELEVEN

169 "Americans are more supportive of torture now": Horace Payne, "Surprising Changes in Public Views on Torture, Immigration," *Harvard Political Review*, Jan 10, 2017, https://harvardpolitics.com/united-states/surprising-changes-public-views-torture-immigration/.

176 "You are loaded into a machine, a very organized system . . .": Elaine Ganley, "Ex-Guantanamo prisoner now steering Europe's youths away from jihad," CTV News, Jun 7, 2015, https://www.ctvnews.ca/world/ex-guantamamo-prisoner-now-steering-europe-s-youths-away-from-jihad-1.2410449.

ABOUT THE COVER

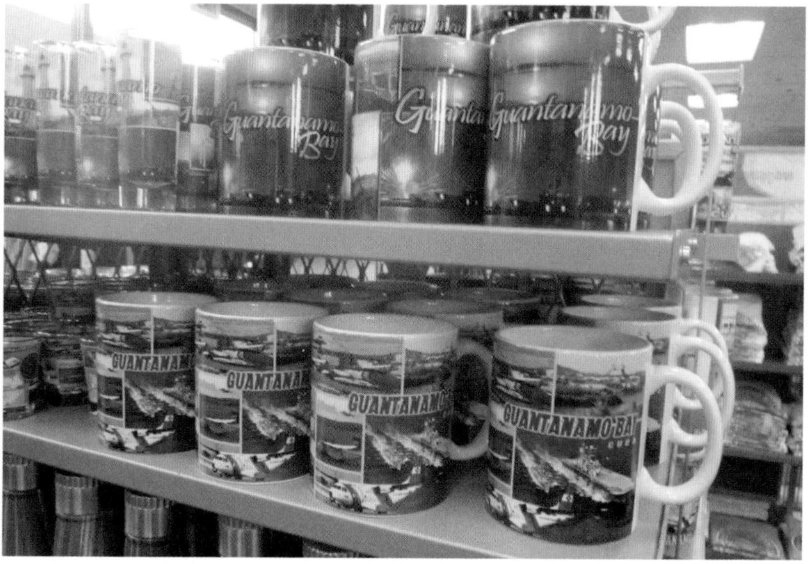
Guantanamo Bay
GUANTANAMO BAY

Did you know there is a gift shop at Guantánamo Bay? The gift shop at the Navy Exchange on the base sells everything from "Straight Outta GITMO" T-shirts to stuffed animal iguanas. Many of the 7,800 service members and civilians who work on base want to take home souvenirs from their time at Guantánamo. The design for this cover, by artist Maria Nguyen, is inspired by a postcard sold in the Guantánamo Bay gift shop. The postcard highlights the way the government portrays Guantánamo: that the prison is "safe, humane, and legal" and prisoners aren't having such a bad time on a tropical island.

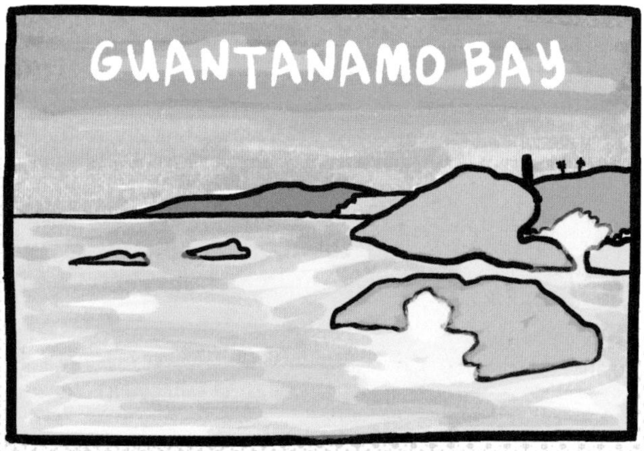
GUANTANAMO BAY

ACKNOWLEDGMENTS

For ten years, this book was impossible to write. It took me that long to find the skills, the sources, and the support I needed. I owe an immense debt to the people featured in these pages—thank you for trusting me to share your stories. And I'm overwhelmed with gratitude for the artists who spent months penciling, inking, and coloring this book. Thanks to each of you for taking a chance on this complicated project. A specific and heartfelt thanks to Kazimir Lee, who developed the innovative color palette and is somehow the speediest artist on planet Earth.

It's weird that my name is on the cover because this book was a team effort. Editor Charlotte Greenbaum's name should be in a big, bold font. May she will receive a mountain of credit for guiding this book calmly from beginning to end. Omar El Akkad's words stayed in my head for months and guided my writing. Antonio Aiello is a true gem of an editor/human who helped Mansoor's chapter come together. Fiona Kenshole heard my idea for this book and showed me how to make it possible. There's nothing more powerful than that.

Throughout the process of writing this book, several people offered crucial emotional and logistical labor when I was in despair: Juan Carlos Chavez, Matt Henriksen, Kat York, Erik Thurman, Joe Martinez, Rogan Motis, and Zuzanna Brezezinksa. I received translation help from Genvieve Metson, Andrew Hutchinson, and Mustafa Salem. Havi Brooks let me stay at her house. Suzi Steffen sent me $100 right when I ran out of money. Carl Larson sent me a book by Jenny Holzer.

My colleagues at the *Nib* (Eleri Harris, Matt Bors, Matt Lubchansky, and Andy Warner) taught me how to write nonfiction comics. They are also stellar individuals who I can't believe I get to be friends with. This project started years ago with artist Lucy Bellwood and only grew because she was such an astoundingly talented collaborator.

This book builds on the detailed reporting and documentation of others. The Rule of Law oral history project at Columbia University generously let me use quotes from their detailed interviews with Guantánamo prisoners and staff. Everything I needed to know about Guantánamo was already in the essential works of journalists like Jane Mayer, Carol Rosenberg, and Andy Worthington, and the memoirs of Mohammed Ould Slahi, Moazzam Begg, and Mahvish Khan. Thanks to superstar attorneys Steve Wax and Laila Nazarali Fedida, whose work inspired me years ago in ways they don't even know. Thanks to the groups that created and maintain archives that are crucial to understanding Guantánamo, including the *New York*

Times' Guantánamo Docket and the massive oral history project Witness to Guantánamo. This sounds corny, but thanks to the volunteers who add government reports and images to Wikipedia. Their collective work has kept Guantánamo photos and documents from slipping into obscurity and made accountability possible for future generations.

Thanks to my partner Ben for sitting with me on the floor that one time when I was too overwhelmed to stand up. Sorry for not taking your advice on going to therapy while writing this book—you were right, that would have helped.

Just as the first draft of this manuscript was due, I crashed on my bike and was unable to use my right hand. I promised myself that I would get this book done even if I had to finish typing it left-handed. Which I did. So thanks to my past self for getting through that.

In closing, thanks to each and every person who faces the hard stuff of our history and works to make a more just future, even when it's impossible to see what that path forward will look like.